A VOID IN ETHIOPIAN HISTORY

1865-1941

A VOID IN ETHIOPIAN HISTORY

1865-1941

UNTOLD HISTORY OF THE SOUTHERN ETHIOPIAN PEOPLES

FANTAYE A. KESHEBO

Cover Design by Chelsea Jewell

A Void in Ethiopian History 1865-1941.
Untold History of the Southern Ethiopian Peoples.
By Fantaye A. Keshebo. fantakb1@outlook.com

Contents

List of Tables

Preface

I was born in a peasant family household in southern Ethiopia and was raised as a typical rural boy helping my parents with farming, grazing cattle, and doing chores of the countryside. As far as I could remember, there was no event or situation either in my early childhood or in my high school years which accounts for my interest in Ethiopian history. The seed of this book - my initial interest in Ethiopian history - was conceived in my mind when I was a student at Addis Ababa University in the 1980s. Then I heard several conflicting stories related to the modern Ethiopian state formation era. The stories were brand new to me and, hence, they sparked great curiosity in me. Over the next several years, I started developing interest in Ethiopian history, which gradually narrowed down to the Emperor Menelik's reign, expansions, and incorporation of various Ethiopian peoples.

In the late 1990s I found several interesting books at the University of Nairobi Library: Ernesta Cerulli's *Peoples of South-West Ethiopia and its Borderland* (1956), Frederick J. Simon's *North-West Ethiopia: Peoples and Economy* (1960), G.W.B. Huntingford's *The Galla of Ethiopia, The Kingdoms of Kafa and Janjero* (1956), and Richard Greenfield's *Ethiopia: A New Political History* (1965). This was my first time to read books written about socio-cultural and historical conditions of various Ethiopian peoples. I took several notes from these books. Not only they enriched the notes I already had, but also, they influenced my thought process to transition from reading for the sake of curiosity to the notion of writing a book. And after that time, I envisioned what I ought to write.

Coming to the United States offered more opportunity to access valuable archival resources and to carry out research independently. In particular, the great collection of books on Ethiopian studies at the Iowa State University Parks Library was invaluable to my research. I also benefited from the Des Moines Public Libraries, the Simpson College Library in Indianola, as well as from influential online research publications. More importantly, I established a home library and stocked it with an Ethiopian and African studies books, which enabled me to spend more time on the project and to utilize my spare time more effectively. I also benefited from the Institute of Ethiopian Studies library and museum visits in Addis Ababa in June 2018.

There are no shortages of scholarly and biographical works about Emperor Menelik's life, reign, and his spectacular victory over Italy at the Battle of Adwa. However, one of the greatest historical phenomena which shaped and reshaped the Ethiopian society and region at large – the *agar maqnat* process and incorporation of various Southern Ethiopian territories and peoples – was not studied or investigated. What we have so far is only a fragmented patch work of half-hearted historians and sensational writers. Likewise, historical, and cultural heritages of the southern Ethiopian peoples was largely ignored and sidelined for many years by historians. It goes without saying that the Southern Ethiopian peoples' history and cultures are intertwined with and inextricable from the history and culture of the rest of the Ethiopian peoples. Yet, little or no attention was given to it. Lack of comprehensive works on *agar maqnat* process and the southern peoples' history had, undoubtedly, left an apparent void in Ethiopian history for so long.

Inclusive historiography, I believe, is crucial for nation-building process. It ought to include all and embraces all that had happened during our national state formation process – successes and failures, the bad and the good, the glorious and ignominious.

The purpose of this book is to shed some light on untold history of the southern Ethiopian peoples – ignored, silenced, sidelined, or forgotten history. I firmly believe that a balanced and inclusive history enriches national understanding and enhances nation-building efforts by fostering common understanding among various peoples, leaders, and citizens alike. I hope this book will provide a preliminary contribution in this regard.

Written accounts of southern kingdoms and territories of the pre-Menelik's era; and accounts of conquests are scant and almost non-existent. I invested a lot of time and energy in gathering bits and pieces of information from various works of historians, writers, early travelers, ethnographers, and anthropologists. Accounts of 19th century and early 20th century European travelers such as William Cornwallis Harris (1843), Walter Chichele Plowden (1868), Alexander Ksaverievich Bulatovich (1897) & (1900), Sir Montague Sinclair Wellby (1901), Oscar Neumann (1902), Robert Peet Skinner (1906), and dispatches sent from an American Consulate General in Addis Ababa and Aden during the first decade of 1900s provided relevant background information about the condition of the country and the on-going modern Ethiopian state formation process. For the Gibe states, I mainly relied on the works of Mohammed Hassen (1994) and Herbert S. Lewis's (1965). For Hadiya and some of the southern societies Ulrich Braukamper's works (1983, 2004, 2012) provided me great insight. As someone who was born and grew up in southern Ethiopia, my own exposure to the region, its people, and cultures; and the Ethiopian society in general had added an important perspective to my work.

From the time an idea was conceived several decades ago until it was completed in the form of this book, I have been working on it in one way or the other. At times, it was shelved away for a long time. Even in those occasions, a day or a week barely passes by without me thinking and pondering about it. Sometimes just picking up one of my notebooks and looking at it for few minutes was enough to keep the thing in me alive. In addition to investing my spare times during weekdays, I spent countless sleepless nights and weekends working on all aspect of this book. As they say, it became a passion and mission at the same time. One thing I never did was rushing to complete it.

No. I took as many months or even years as it needed to get it right. Patience, persistence, and undying desire to fill the void in Ethiopian history eventually produced this uniquely original book.

The book aspires to shed a light on one of the major Ethiopian historical experience, on the personalities who played prominent roles during the last major encounter between the north led by the Shewa king and kingdom on the one hand, and various southern peoples on the other hand. It uniquely highlights how that encounter set in motion new dynamics and enduring legacies which permanently shaped the directions of our national discourse; and influenced, for better or worse, the unfolding historical process of the modern Ethiopian state formation.

I do not pretend, however, to comprehend the history of southern Ethiopian peoples' or the complexity of the historical period under discussion. Likewise, I do not pretend to present a comprehensive work in this book. Although the book covered several original previously untouched areas and topics, some of them are discussed broadly and they merit further research. My aim is to pave the way for further investigation and research. I painstakingly researched to back up the work with authoritative references and invested a lot of time to ensure accuracy and objectivity. If you notice any error, including typographical error, please forgive me for any error and understand that it is unintentional.

This book is divided into 5 main parts, 17 chapters, 39 sub-chapters, and 43 sub-sub chapters, and 2 appendixes. Part I comprises chapters 1-3. Chapter one skims over an Ethiopian historiography and its shortcomings and mirrors the author's perspective for inclusive historiography which fosters nation-building efforts in Ethiopia. Chapter two attempts to specify or define two words often used by historians and writers carelessly and sometimes in ambiguous and misleading ways – the 'South' and 'Shewa.' Chapter 3 highlights socio-cultural and historical status of *some* of the southern peoples prior to their incorporation into the Ethiopian state. Part II included chapters 4-6 which discussed Menelik's wars of conquests, tactics of the armies used during *zemechas*, and the main factors which contributed to Menelik's victories. For the sake of convenience, I divided periods of conquests into four major phases: the Initial Phase of Conquests (1866-1881), the Second Phase of Conquest, 1882-1888), the Third Phase of Conquest (1889-1895), and the Final Phase (1896-1906). Part III consisted chapters 7-11 which discussed historical and administrative injustices prevailed in post-conquest South. Part IV highlights a 'mixed system' of governance which existed in the country. Gojjam is cited as a prime example of the mixed system. Part V comprised chapters 13-17 which examined the rise of the Shewa-Amhara ruling class which dominated the Ethiopian socio-cultural and political arena for several decades. Appendix I and II listed the most powerful men -the movers and shakers- of the Menelik era.

Fantaye A. Keshebo
June 2020

Part I

The South and Southern Peoples before Conquest

"...there were people who thought we didn't have a past. What I was doing was to say politely that we did - here it is."
- Chinua Achebe, *There Was A Country: A Personal History of Biafra* 2012:58

Chapter 1

Introduction

1.1. The New Reality

Menelik's reign which span nearly fifty years, first as a *negus,* king, of Shewa (1865-1889) and then as a *neguse negest,* king of kings, of Ethiopia (1889-1913), was crucial epoch in Ethiopian history. One of the major accomplishments of Menelik II, besides his monumental victory over Italy at the Battle of Adwa, was his expansionary conquests and incorporation of the southern territories and kingdoms. Menelik's successful marches of conquests and incorporations ushered, undoubtedly, an era of a new reality and dynamics at all levels: local, regional, and national framework of the nation.

First, it was during Menelik's reign that the formation of modern Ethiopian state, as we know it today, came into existence. Menelik II was arguably the main, if not the only, architect of the present-day Ethiopian state formation. Kassa Hailu of Quara (Tewodros II), 1855-1868, ended the turbulent period of *Zemene-Mesafint* (Era of Princes) and established centralized and consolidated government. But his domains were confined to the Northern provinces of the historical Amhara-Tigre regions. His successor was Wagshum Gobaze of Lasta and Semein (Tekle Giorgis), 1868-1871. His short years of reign was largely limited to Begemder, Gojjam, and initially to Tigray. Kassa Mercha of Tigre defeated Tekle Giorgis (who was his brother-in-law[1]) and crowned himself as Emperor Yohannes IV (1872-1889). He emerged as a powerful ruler who was able to assert his authority over all northern provinces, and, after 1878 on the kingdom of Shewa. From the time he seized power until he died in Metemma in March 1889, Emperor Yohannes was kept busy fighting foreign adversaries (Egyptians, Italians, & Mahdists), engaging dip-lomatically the powers with colonial ambitions (Anglo-Egyptian & Italian), dealing with powerful but reluctant vassals (Menelik & Tekle Haymanot), pacifying revolts caused by his fanatic decrees (Wollo Moslem), and handling warlords. It was only in 1878 Yohannes se-cured Menelik's vassalage. The latter, however, continued defaulting on his tribute payments and dealing with foreigners independently of the former. Yohannes's southward physical march was limited to the northern parts of the Shewa kingdom to secure his lordship over Menelik. Some argued that Menelik's vassalage would mean Yohannes reigning all parts of the country. It erroneous to interpret that either Yohannes or Menelik reigned the South because large parts of the South were not even under Menelik's rule at the time of the emperor's death in Metemma.[2]

Thus, it was Menelik who succeeded in subduing and incorporat-ing various kingdoms and territories in the south-central, south-east, and south-western regions at the end of the nineteenth century. He was able to coerce the traditional rulers of the Northern provinces into submission immediately after Yohannes's death. Also, he de-marcated international borders and concluded treaties with colonial powers of the day – Italy in Eritrea & Italian Somaliland; British in Kenya, British Somaliland, and Sudan; and France in Djibouti. Hence the formation of modern Ethiopian State.

Second, the process of state formation, which was carried out through *zemecha*[3], had resulted in permanent occupation of con-quered lands and peoples; unlike past times when the purpose of *zemecha* was plunder and coercion for tribute payment. Permanent occupation introduced permanent structural changes. This was true both for peacefully submitted areas and for those which put up armed resistance. The difference between peacefully submitted and those which put up resistance was the style and severity of governance. The former areas kept limited local authority while the latter areas came under direct and immediate military administration and control.

Some writers and historians, misled by the notion of 'local autonomy', stated incorrectly that peacefully submitted areas such as Wollega and Jimma had autonomous administration and were immune from interference of imperial government. Although both Wollega and Jimma were designated as *maed bet* and pay their tributes directly to the emperor; they were hardly autonomous in literal sense. Moroda Bakare and his son, Kumsa Moroda, who was christened as *Gabre Egeziabeher* (slave of God), and Jote Tullu were, at one time or another, under direct command of central government representatives in Wollega.[4] Some parts of Wollega was controlled and ruled by *ras* Gobana and his vast army.[5] Religious and church affairs in Wollega were directly controlled by the Patriarch in Addis Ababa and local priests in Nekemete. Kumsa had little or no say on this matter.[6] Beside mandatory annual tributes, Kumsa had to pay huge amount of taxes for maintenance and provision of government army stationed in Wollega. By 1917, almost 35 years after Wollega's submission, Kumsa was "lamenting" about "too much" tribute which turned his domain "into a desert."[7] Likewise, Jimma Abba Jifar II was under oversight jurisdiction of the governors of southwestern regions, *ras* Wolde Giorgis and his successors. He was often called to fight against other indigenous peoples who resisted or rebelled against occupation [Greenfield (1965), Lewis (1965), Bahru (2001 1991)]. Although Abba Jifar II managed to stay in power and spared his domain from church building, his subjects had to pay a heavy price for their limited autonomy, which was later rescinded by Haile Selassie I.

> In exchange for local autonomy Abba Jiffar II was required
> to pay annually 300,000 Maria Theresa thalers in cash or
> in kind, which was the single largest tribute paid by any
> regional leader in Ethiopia.[8]

Thirdly, permanent occupation of conquered regions was followed by settlements of soldiers and armed peasants, commonly referred to as *neftegna,* from the north. Mass immigration and re-settlement of those who accompanied conquests (soldiers, peasants, priests, administrators, their servants, and families) and other new arrivals had brought immediate, fundamental, and lasting demographic, socio-economic and cultural changes. As Shack (1966) and Kaufeler (1988) argued, however, the officials and soldiers were "less permanently settled" in some parts of the South than other areas. Likewise, permanent settlements had resulted in "severe exploitation" in some areas than others depending mainly on types of crops and staple foods "favored" or "disliked" by the "highland peoples." Hence areas where *ensete* was a staple diet were "fortunate" because it was "less attractive" to draw settler communities. Regardless, in all regions "human resources were exploited."[9]

Fourthly, after permanent settlements, an imposition of *gabbar*[10] system reduced southerners at large to tenant-serfs, in the words of Ulrich Braukamper, "serfs of the state,"[11] who were required to pay tributes and provide free labor for the households and farms of settler communities. Shack wrote: "In Gurage and the Sidamo provinces, the position of the *gabbar* was hardly distinguishable from slavery."[12] Establishing themselves in "settler colonies"[13] or *ketemas*[14] the new administrators and settlers exerted their influence outwards. Orthodox churches were built first in the outposts and then gradually expanded to other areas, primarily to cater spiritual and cultural needs of those associated with administrative and military apparatus.[15] Conversions and enculturation became a litmus test for *balabats*[16] who, in the words of Dr. Messay Kebede (1999) "were wholly Amharized."[17] Thus, demographic and cultural landscape of the South was altered for good (detail discussion in Part II).

Fifthly, the northern regions - Tigray, Begemeder and Semein (now Gondar), Gojjam, and Wollo - were brought under Menelik reign after the death of Yohannes IV in Metemma (Gallabat) in March 1889, several years after most of the southern regions were conquered by Menelik., They, unlike southern regions, retained their culture, local administration and their native rulers: *negus* Tekle Haymanot Tessema in Gojjam, Mangesha Yohannes in Tigray, Wole Bitul and Gugsa Wole in parts of Begemeder, & Wollo, Mikael Ali in Wollo, Meshesha Tewodros in Lasta and parts of Semein. Their descendants likewise continued holding higher offices and exerting their influence at local and national level throughout Haile Selassie's reign. Gojjam, for instance, was fixated on regionalism and opposed 'outsiders' - Shewa-Amhara governors (see chapter12.2). Northern provinces were also allowed to continue practicing the *rist* or communal land ownership system and, with it, the right of inheritance. Except for their allegiance to the emperor, the status quo was maintained. In other words, socio-cultural and political systems were kept intact.

In contrast, southern regions - from provincial, district, sub-district and, in some cases, at village level - were administered by military and civilian rulers of northern descent (see a chapter in 'Dual Society). The rulers were assisted by *balabats* at local level. An ethnographer, Data De'a's (2000) description sums up the recruitment methods of *balabat* and their duties:

> Mostly people from former royal lineages and locally dominant clans were put in charge of lower sections of the administrative machinery and thus served as intermediaries between their own people and the northern governors, who claimed ownership of the new Ethiopian state.[18]

As Donham (2002) noted the *balabat* system was itself one of those ruling mechanisms "brought from north to the south."[19] Although not identical, the system has similarities with the British Indirect Rule. Beideman, in *The Culture of Colonialism: The Cultural Subjection of Ukanguru,* wrote: "Co-opting local natives to help foreigners' rule was a practice common in empires for centuries...Indirect Rule was a seemingly practical, commonsensical policy wherever a handful of Europeans tried to rule masses of natives in Africa."[20]

The six, and the last but not the least, new dynamics and reality was regarding land ownership. In conquered regions communal land ownership system, *rist,* was replaced by *gult* land tenure system which required peasants to pay tributes and to provide corvee labor for *gult* holders under the ignominious *gabbar* system. Mixed system of governance between north and south emerged which continued to be practiced during Haile Selassie era. Messay (1999) hesitatingly defended the "mixed system" of land tenure, which he said was meant to control southerners until their "Ethiopianization" was ensured.

> The…land policy of Menelik..was designed to introduce such gult rights, the only difference being that people who were ethnically different from the southern peoples were placed on top of the social hierarchy, whereas in the north no such ethnic disparity existed. The well-founded nature of this mixed system cannot be seriously disputed. It ensured control until deeper forms of integration and Ethiopianization became effective.[21]

Messay's point of view (further discussed below) was not uncommon among Ethiopian scholars. Regardless, the validity of 'mixed system' espoused by Messay has obvious shortcomings. First, it justifies "mixed system" of land ownership – allowing *rist system* in the north and its abolition and the imposition *gabbar* systems in the south. Secondly, it also justifies another "mixed system" of governance. Northern provinces, by and large, were governed by native administrators whereas southerners were ruled by "people who were ethnically different" than them. The third shortcoming which arises from contention in the "mixed system" was the indefinite nature of the "control" imposed upon southern societies. There was no way of measuring when the "deeper forms of integration and Ethiopianization became effective" among southerners or not. Fourthly, Messay's view also implies that the southerners were not Ethiopians until they were deeply integrated and Ethiopianized. The "deeper forms of integration" process, among other things, required conversions, speaking Amharic, and learning the customs and manners of the ruling class.[22] See chapter 12 for more discussion on 'mixed system.'

1.2. Of Ethiopian History and Historians

It should be noted that history, for much of human existence, was written from the vintage point of victors and conquerors, i.e. from the perspective of the powerful groups and nations. The conquered and vanquished were often left out and portrayed as bad enemies and primitives who deserved what they got. They were often regarded as backward and uncivilized people with nothing to tell or write about them. Writing about American history and the selective nature of history and historians, Michael Parenti, in his book, *History as Mystery,* wrote: "If people know little about standard history, they know even less about the silenced, hidden part of history."[23] Often the 'silenced' and 'hidden part of history' was that of the vanquished and the minorities.

An Ethiopian history, for generations, had been a crossbreed of ecclesiastical narratives and palace chronicles. Tesfaye Habisso noted the drawbacks in Ethiopian historiography and the need to adopt inclusive and comprehensive methods and approaches.

> Most of the hitherto written history of Ethiopia which begins in the later Middle Ages from the pens of monks and court historians and whose main purpose is the laudation of Abyssinian kings does not deal with the comprehensive history of Ethiopia and the Ethiopians at large. It does not particularly touch upon the history of the regions and peoples incorporated by Emperor Menelik II to the Ethiopian Empire-state towards the end of the 19th century…though they had their own independent kingdoms and sultanates as well as loosely confederated traditional polities….Hence it will be the duty of historians, particularly those from these regions, to write the history of their peoples so that the history of modern Ethiopia will be complete.[24]

As Teshale in *The Making of Modern Ethiopia 1896-1974* noted it was "a story of a succession of rulers and dynasties, *taameres* (miracles), *gadles* (struggle of saints), and *wudasies* (praises of the powers that be, heavenly or otherwise), wars and expansions, etc."[25] Not only it revolved around the narrative, but also it became synonymous to it. In doing so, it entirely left out majority of Ethiopians. Despite incorporation of various ethno-cultural groups and subsequent formation of modern Ethiopian state; "the Ethiopian history from Aksum to Haile Selassie was seen as being basically the same."[26]

Our historiography, besides being chronicles of rulers, was built around what Teshale (1995) called "Geez Civilization;" and Bahru (1991) and others called "the core." Those who found themselves at the periphery of "Geez civilization" and "the core" had to accept and follow a clearly defined prescription to be part of it,, which Messay (1999) stated as a "deeper forms of integration and Ethiopianization."

Attributing the nation's history merely to 'Geez civilization' or 'the core' created what I called stakeholders and subjects among Ethiopians. It accorded the former with ownership of the nation's history and culture; and, in Keller's (1988) words, it presented for the latter the "primary informal requirement for full incorporation into Abyssinian society."[27] As Teshale succinctly put it, "...the Aksumite paradigm articulated a consciousness of having a History, which "Others" lack."[28] The 'ownership of history' perspective placed the former in the position of givers and the latter in that of the receivers; and defined Ethiopian history and culture as monolithic and monophyte. Hence, it presented a one-direction flow of history, ideas, and civilization from north to south only – the "Geez Civilization." Such thesis did not give a room for historical interactions of ideas and civilizations from various corners or directions.

One place where this approach had been institutionalized was in the Ethiopian academia, particularly in the field of history, where a highly sensitive culture developed and drove scholarly works to revolve only around familiar topics of 'mainstream' story lines. In depth discussions and researches, particularly on topics related to *agar maqnat* process, were often overlooked, and sidelined by design.

When such topics were discussed, they were aligned along 'accepted' point of view and presented as such. Whenever other peoples of 'The Ethiopian Borderlands," to use Pankhurst's phrase, were included it was in way of substantiating the bigger 'Geez Civilization' thesis – when and if those peoples were ruled or paid tributes in one time or another, if any.

Because of one-dimensional and institutionalized approach to Ethiopian history; a void was created, sustained, and existed in Ethiopian historiography regarding conquests and the southern peoples' history before and after their incorporation. Among several shortcomings of such historiographical approach, I briefly discussed five of them.

The *first* shortcoming was its adoption of above the surface method of conducting the nation's history. Save some scanty but important works of recent years, there was no comprehensive historical work devoted to Menelik's monumental legacy: his southern conquests and subsequent incorporation of the southern Ethiopian peoples. General muteness prevailed regarding the methods and tactics of *zemechas*. Military expeditions and wars of conquests were often described merely in such general and ambiguous words as 'ዘመቱ,' waged military campaign, 'አስገበሩ,' subdued/forced them pay tribute, አመጸኞችን ቀጥተው ተመለሱ, punished the rebel (s) and returned, 'አመጹን አጥፍተው ተመለሱ, put down the rebellion & pacified. Such descriptions did not discriminate between the areas and peoples which met Menelik's armies for the first time, and those which rebelled. Regions often mentioned by most historians as being conquered were mainly those which put up fierce resistance and those which submitted peacefully. Several other conquered regions and peoples, including those which also suffered the consequences of resistance, were not mentioned at all, which leaves wrong impression that those areas were already under Menelik's domain. Years of conquests[29] were often varied from one author's work to another. Most historians described them in such generalized terms as "toward the end of nineteenth century,' 'early nineteenth century,' 'in 1890s', 'at the beginning of twentieth century,' 'in 1800s,' at the end of the century,' 'toward the end of the last century and beginning of twentieth century,' and so on. Even established and reputable Ethiopian historians did not distinguish themselves from amateurs in this regard. In short, general muteness appeared to have prevailed for a long time. Due to such muteness, one would barely find in Ethiopian history books complete or even near complete historical accounts of conquests. Hence, incomplete, partial, and, sometimes, contradictory accounts of Menelik's conquests recycled.

Secondly, when it comes to Menelik's conquests, Ethiopian history books were devoid of well-organized resistances, rebellions, and fighting put up by southern peoples' which, in some instances, took years. In Arsi, Wolayta, Kaffa, Chaha-Gurage, Borana, Konso, Qebena-Hadiya, Kambaata, and others, initial attempts of conquests were met with resistance by autochthonous inhabitants. For instance, the initial venture of conquest against Gurage in 1876 was met with heavy defeat of Shewa's army.[30] In the ensuing years even the army of "Ras Gobana had failed in several previous attempts" to subdue them until "Fitaurari Habte Giorgis, under order from Menelik, finally put down the rebellious Gurage" in late 1880s.[31] Guragelands and Qabeena areas were brought into the empire more than a decade after initial incursion "after fierce engagement"[32] *Woma*[33] Dilbato Degoye of Kambata and his cabinet rejected peaceful submission and resorted to defend their kingdom. As a result, as Pankhurst (1968) noted, the occupation of Kambaata which began in 1890 was completed three years later in 1893. The Kamabaata king and his cabinets were killed in 1892 but the people continued resistance until the kingdom was pacified a year later. The Badaawacho Hadiya joined the Wolayta until they were subdued when Wolayta was conquered. Arsi put up one of the fiercest resistances which Harold Marcus described that the "Shoans sustained some bloody defeats before Darge was able to break the back of the organized forces pitted against him."[34] *Tato* Gaki Sherecho of Kaffa and *Kawo* Tona (Tsona) Gaga of Wolayta rallied their people and successfully resisted and overcame attempted incursions for years. They were finally succumbed due to possession of superior forces and firepower of the Menelik. Kaffa was finally defeated by "combined forces" of *ras* Wolde Giorgis, d*ejazmatch* Tessema, *dejazmtach* Demisse, armies of Abba Jifar II of Jimma, and armies of Kullo after *Tato* Gaki was captured in September 1897. All these armies had to endure more than eight months resistances of the Kaffa people. To end Wolayta's resistance, in addition to his personal army, Menelik ordered and mobilized all major armies of the country (See chapter 4 and 10).

Thirdly, one-sided historical approach often described that military expeditions were deployed because a certain rebel, ሽፍታ, had 'rebelled' (አምጿ), or 'refused to pay tribute' (አልገብርም ብሎ); when, in fact, it was the first time ever for both Menelik's armies and some of those native peoples to encounter each other. Although some of the southern territories were subjected to sporadic tribute payments in the 14th and 15th centuries; some of southern peoples had no contact with the north at all. Menelik's "warriors...were encountering these people for the first time, to whom they were just as foreign and incomprehensible as they were"[35] to other strangers.

Fourthly, the narratives related to the rationale of conquests are misleading. Menelik's southern 'marches' were presented as campaigns to reclaim his forefather's territories which existed since the 'Axumite Empire' *(ከአክሱም ዘመን አንሥቶ የነበረውን የአባታቸውን ግዛት ለማስመለስ)*. As a matter of fact, until Aksum collapsed because of blockage of sea trade and invasion by indigenous Beja people, its rule prevailed merely in the Northern provinces and across the Red Sea. It never ruled southern territories, as Tekle Tsadik and others would like to claim. Aksum's "territorial extent at its largest was confined to what is now Eritrea, Tigray, Northern Wallo, and at times parts of Arabia."[36] The *UNESCO General History of Africa: Volume II Ancient History of Africa,* based on archaeological findings concluded that territory of Axum kingdom is only 300 kilometers wide and 160 kilometers long (see chapter 3:1).

Fifthly, one of the major topics which most Ethiopian academia often avoided and/or skirted around was the status of southern peoples before Menelik's incorporation, and the post-conquests legacies of subjugation and pillage. Some historians generally avoided or focused on retelling the narratives of 'reclaiming lost territories.' Some mentioned it in few reproduced lines and paragraphs. Yet, others such as Dr. Messay (1999) tried to discuss it half-heartedly, that is, acknowledging conquest but misconstruing its rationale, outcome, and policy implementation.

Messay's views about southern conquest, which he widely discussed in his book, *Survival and Modernization: Ethiopia's Enigmatic Present: A Philosophical Discourse* (1999), not only lacked historical accuracy but also, they were at times self-contradictory. I presented some of his views here because they represent an *ambivalence and incoherence* existed among Ethiopian historians and intelligentsia at large. He wrote,

> Conquerors were not separated from the conquered by exclusive rights, and what the former had was not refused to the latter. That is why southern conquest has little in common with European colonialism and its indirect rule. Local chiefs were not maintained or raised as intermediaries; rather, they were wholly Amharized.[37]

It is true that "conquerors were not separated from the conquered," which, as I mentioned below, was worse off to the latter. It is unclear, however, what Messay meant when he said, "what the former ('conquerors') had was not refused to the latter ('conquered')." He did not specify what the conquerors had and what they shared with the conquered. Contrary to his assertion they exercised their "exclusive rights" of a conqueror. Obviously, they never shared their material wealth. Exercising its "exclusive rights" the government "imposed that infamous order, the *naftagnya* system" which "formed the dual society: conqueror and conquered."[38] His assertions about 'local chiefs' (*balabats*) was also questionable. First, the primary, if not the only, duties of *balabats* was being intermediaries and not the other way around. They were used as agents of indirect rule (see above 1.1). Secondly, obliging locals to be "wholly Amharized" or as he described elsewhere: "Rapid Ethiopianization and Christianization of the southern populations"[39] was not giving what you had. On the other hand, as Keller (1988) noted, it was taking away what they had – their language, beliefs, customs, and traditions.[40] Messay wrote:

> ...not all regions of the south were conquered by violent means, nor were they all disrupted ...True, just because force was not used and local leaders were not displaced, *it does not automatically mean that the conquest was not colonial.*[41] Italics by me.

Messay regarded that conquest was colonial (see italicized above) and then he wrote that the southern conquest was "the model of de-colonization."[42] This is not true unless he misunderstood the mean-ing of decolonization. He even argued that Menelik himself was used as an instrument by Oromo leaders as a "way of circumventing the difficulty" posed by *Gada* system to bring about Oromo unity;[43] and therefore "the southern conquest ...was a way of resolving the anomaly of the Oromo."[44] He was not alone on this. Dr. Kassahun Woldemariam (2006) even went further and described Menelik's ex-pansionary conquest as "the Oromo expansion that was spearheaded by one of their leaders, Emperor Menelik II."[45] This is undoubtedly absurd argument. For all practical reasons, Menelik's conquest was never set out to unite Oromos. On the contrary, Oromo leaders, led by *ras* Gobana Dache, were used as instruments to subdue the Oromos and other southern peoples (See chapter 4 and 17). Messay also stated that Menelik's "southern expansion" was carried out as a means of national "survival" because it "ensured access to exportable resources to buy the much-needed firearms and counter the threat of colonization. It also reinforced the defense capacity with the support of new peoples."[46]

He appeared to have missed two interrelated but significant historical events of Menelik's reign. First the genesis of Menelik's conquest goes back to the early years of his rule as a Shewa *negus*. At that time, he had *no* "threat of colonization" from any corner be-cause the Shewa kingdom was smaller and nestled in the hinterland.

The regions which faced imminent threats from Ethiopia's adversaries such as Italians, Egyptians, and Mahdists were the present-day Eritrea or the Tigre-Merab-Melash region, the western and northern frontiers of Tigre, Begemeder, and Gojjam. Likewise, the leaders which confronted and fought foreign invaders and paid enormous sacrifices while resisting and repelling foreign incursions were Emperor Tewodros II, Alula Aba Nega, Emperor Yohannes IV, and King Tekle Haymanot of Gojjam, but never Menelik. The latter's primary concern then was how to counter the threat of his northern master, Emperor Yohannes. For this end, he was engaged in consolidation of power and equipping Shewa army with modern weapons. He used resources from conquered lands to buy firearms mainly from Italy and European arms dealers. Secondly, by the time Menelik became emperor in 1889 he had already conquered most of south-west, west and eastern regions without having "the threat of colonization."

Menelik did not seem to have been concerned about looming foreign threat when he signed the Wuchale Treaty in May 2, 1889, ceding Merab Melash region to Italy; the very country where Alula defeated Italians in Dogali barely two years earlier in January 1887, and Yohannes fought with them barely a year earlier in 1888. He faced foreign threat (Italy's colonial ambitions) only after his favorite ally and signatory attempted to use Article XVII of Wuchale Treaty and declared Ethiopia as its protectorate; moved south from Asmara and started occupying Tigre lands few years after Wuchale Treaty was signed. Therefore, the "survival" argument is an apologetic sophistry.

In post-Adwa, however, Menelik emerged as a more confident and powerful statesman. Hence, he was enlisted as a partner by regional colonial powers who had already established themselves in the Ethiopian region for a long time (France, Britain, and Italy). He even competed with them for territories and they agreed to "share out" and demarcate international boundaries. Hence the formation of modern Ethiopian state.

1.3. *Agar Maqnat*

There is an obvious but seemingly unwritten law among Ethiopian academicians on using certain words and phrases pertaining to Menelik's conquest differently in Amharic and English. Anyone who read the works of Ethiopian historians and writers (with exception to Teshale, 1995) will easily notice that their most preferred words are መስፋፋት, (expansion), ዉህደት, (reunification), አንድ አደረጉ (incorporated), የጠፉ ግዛቶችን አስመለሱ (reclaimed lost territories), and አገር ማቅናት. The latter *(agar maqnat)* is one of the most frequently used Amharic phrase by 'mainstream' historians. While they use *ager maqnat* in Amharic writings, they barely use its English equivalent /definition. The dictionary definition of *agar maqnat* is colonizing a territory or a country (see Teshale's definition below). For reasons I discussed below, *aqar maqnat* is widely used in Amharic and is acceptable, whereas its English definition is shunned and avoided. Likewise, *zemecha* (military campaign/expedition) is most preferred but *worera* (invasion/conquest) is avoided.

Oxford Advanced Learner's Dictionary defines expansion as "an act of increasing or making something increase in size, amount, or importance." The same dictionary defines conquest, as "the act of taking control of a country, city, etc. by force;" "an area of land taken by force." In this case, conquest precedes territorial expansion; and the latter is the outcome of the former. Conquest is an act (military action) which produced expansion (conquering and controlling lands). So, conquest is the cause, and expansion is an outcome/effect. In this book I used 'conquest' it conveys the actions of parties involved (military raids/invasions by one party and resistance by the other), and the outcome (winners/conquerors vs. losers/conquered). That was exactly what happened when Menelik extended his rule and power beyond the frontiers of Shewa kingdom. He led series of *zemechas* (expeditions of conquest or plunder) from his ancestral home base in northern Shewa. He brought into submission the neighboring peoples and regions which was followed by several successful expeditions of conquests against the peoples and lands in the south, south-east, south-central and south-west.

As mentioned above, most Ethiopian historians and writers tend to prefer the word 'expansion' and avoid such words as 'invasion' and 'conquest.' Ethiopian intelligentsia are aware of denotations and connotations of such words as expansion, invasion, and conquest. They clearly understand that Menelik's *zemechas were* military expeditions designed to conquer, punish, or plunder targeted communities. Nevertheless, the word 'conquest' remained to be a very delicate and sensitive word rarely used. Preferred words are still 'expansion,' 'reunification,' 'reclaiming' and so on.

The Amharic equivalent for conquest/colonization is *agar maqnat*. Ironically, *agar maqnat* is often used with ease by all Ethiopians. But its English synonymous 'conquest' and 'colonization' are avoided, discouraged, and dissuaded; and using them will put one at the fringe. Perhaps, the best description of *agar maqnat* was given by an Ethiopian political scientist, Dr. Teshale Tibebu. In his book, *The Making of Modern Ethiopia, 1896 – 1974*, he described himself as a "Christian Amhara" born and raised in Gojjam, Debre Markos. He was a young lecturer at Addis Ababa University during my student years.[47] He wrote:

> Two key concepts epitomize the Menelikan Christian-Amharic conquest: *Agar maqnat,* and *dar agar. Agar maqnat* refers to colonization, cultivation, (and Christianization) of the land defined as "empty," waiting to be made used of. *Dar agar* (frontier) pertains to the end horizon of the expansion, the boundary of colonization.[48]

It is not uncommon to hear in Ethiopian media and to read in the literature such phrases as: ምንልክ አገር አቀኑ (Menelik colonized the country), ምንልክ ያቀኑት አገር (the country Menelik colonized/conquered). One would then pose a question: Why are Ethiopian academicians so sensitive to the extent of shying away from using the word 'conquest' or 'colony' all together? To my knowledge, there was no research conducted regarding this topic. However, I would like to suggest *six probable reasons* for Ethiopian academicians' avoidance and reluctance to use such words.

The *first* reason is associated with their desire or intention to neutralize or mitigate the strong, often negative, connotation associated with 'colony' or 'conquest.' Obviously, the word 'expansion' sounds mild, harmless, and seemingly positive; when compared to domineering, violent, and harmful tone of the word 'conquest' or 'colony.' *Secondly*, the words 'colony' and 'colonization' denote the presence of a conqueror and conquered, which are exclusively associated with white Europeans subjugation of other (non-white) peoples. Both denotative and connotative meanings of these words would spark instant feelings of domination of conquerors over the conquered. *Thirdly*, Ethiopians are rightly proud of their history of beating down Italy, a white colonizer, at the Battle of Adwa, under the leadership of Menelik II in March 1896. Hence, an independent and non-colonized people, except for five years of occupation during fascist Italy's second attempt of colonization. So, any suggestions which portrays Menelik as colonizer of the southern peoples would send a 'wrong' message of associating him with white European colonizers he fought back. *Fourthly*, for many Ethiopians' the notion of colonizing is associated with foreign power against other nation, one race (white) against the other (black), although, as Teshale rightly noted, people of same race and skin color had historically been colonizing each other.

> True, colonialism, both old and new, does not have to be racial. There can be black-on-black colonialism, just as there was white-on-white colonialism (England-Ireland), or yellow-on-yellow colonialism (Japan-Korea). Black colonialism can't be ruled out a priori on racial grounds, as if blacks can't colonize other blacks. Colonialism is based on unequal *relationship* of power between the colonizer and colonized. And it is no divine mandate that the two sides of the power divide be of different races.[49]

The *fifth* reason for Ethiopian historians' and writers' reluctance and hypersensitivity may be ascribed to the prevailing culture of political correctness and self-censorship. The *sixth* reason may be linked to the background and composition of Ethiopian intelligentsia. Most well-known Ethiopian writers and historians, just like the ruling-class which dominated the nation until the Ethiopian Revolution, originated from Shewa-Amhara and few from other Amhara regions (see chapter 14); and very few from other regions. Due to their affiliation, orientation, or enculturation, such historians[50] and writers would undoubtedly find it uncomfortable to use the words 'conquest' or 'colonists.'

Because of the above reasons it appears that an unwritten law which opposes, chastise, and discredits anyone who goes beyond prescribed narratives of history, has prevailed in the country. Ethiopian adherents of such unwritten law would automatically paint and label anyone who tries to provide a new perspective in Ethiopian history as 'unpatriotic,' 'traitors,' 'leftists,' ideologues of the 1960s', and 'clueless' who are bent on 'twisting history.'[51]

It should also be noted here that some observers of Ethiopian history regarded Menelik's conquest and permanent occupation as an "internal colonization" which is defined as "the way that heartlands of a country exploitatively treat peripheral regions of the same state."[52] Ethnologist Braukamper Ulrich, who specialized in south-central Ethiopian peoples, described it "as a particularly harsh type of heteronomy which may also be labelled 'endo-colonialism.' "[53] Regardless of whether there is consensus or not; and whether the conquest resulted in colonization or 're-unification,' or 'internal colonization' or heteronomy;' the presence of several markers of conquest and colonization was, however, apparent. Some of the markers included waging organized warfare and invasion using military force, and subsequent permanent occupation of conquered lands and peoples (see chapter 4 &5); administrative monopoly in the conquered regions by conquering parties; and permanent settlement of people of northern descents in the conquered lands (see parts 2, 3 & 4).

Considering the above, it noteworthy to remind ourselves that "colonialism is based on unequal relationship of power between the colonizer and the colonized. And it is no divine mandate that the two sides of the power divide be of different races."[54] Teshale coined the phrase "Menelikan Christian-Amharic conquest."[55]

Perhaps, one of the main features of European colonialism in Africa and Asia was the prevalence of settler colonists. In Eritrea, the best cultivable lands were confiscated to realize Italy's desire to establish a "settler colony."[56] The British established "settlements of white colonists" in the confiscated lands in South Rhodesia (Zimbabwe), South Africa and Kenya. In Kenya, the whites settled in the "highly fertile regions."[57]

There is, however, a major difference between European and Ethiopian systems of settlements by 'settler colonists.'

European settlements were segregated and often whites only. Ethiopian settlements, on the other hand, were not segregated. In the words of Messay (1999), "Conquerors were not separated from the conquered." Europeans evicted natives from their lands and resettled them in reservations as British did in Kenya. Ethiopians did not evict natives; but they made them *gabbars* (peasant-serf sharecroppers obliged to pay mandatory tributes for their lands and produces; and required to provide corvee labor in the farms and households of their masters). Obviously, the Ethiopian settlement system proved to be highly effective and more profitable than the European style of settlement for several reasons. The eviction of natives from their lands quickly created resentments and rebellion against Italy in Eritrea (Michaela Wrong 2005, Bahru 1994, 2001). In Kenya evicted natives were huddled in reservation camps which created fertile ground for anti-British *mau mau* movement growth and recruitment of readily available disaffected masses.[58] In Ethiopia there was no room for such mass rebellion because control mechanism established against the locals through *gabbar* system was so tight and oppressive, which enabled peasant resistances and rebellions to be crushed effectively.[59] Each ga*bbar* (peasant-serf) household was assigned to a *gultegna*, a lord who has absolute control over his *gabbars*.

Pankhurst (1968) and Keller (1988) described that varying

numbers of *gabbars* were allocated to the landlords (*malkegna/gultegna*) in conquered lands where the latter had complete jurisdiction over the former. *Gabbars* were required to provide lifetime services to their masters;[60] with apparent semblance of black sharecroppers and plantation workers in the United States. Another reason for effectiveness of Ethiopian settlement system over Europeans was the former was self-sustaining in terms of generating free labor and revenue (tributes in kind or cash). Soldiers, rulers, *naftegna*, and priests in the conquered regions live off *gabbar* service, namely, labor, land, and tributes. As Donald Donham noted:

> Governors and soldiers thus became linked with a varying number of southern families who provided them with food through tributes, worked on their houses as personal servants, ground flour, carried water, built houses, fed mules, and generally did anything else that they could be cajoled or forced into doing.[61]

A *gabbar* (usually a household head male) and his family members were obligated to serve their master for lifetime in which if a *gabbar* dies, his son would automatically be enlisted to perform same duties.

Europeans did not have such a profitable, self-sustaining, and self-financing system of governance which, at the same time, also ensures effective controlling mechanism over their subjects. Therefore, their administrative costs had to be subsidized from the center (London, Paris, Lisbon, Rome, etc.). Pakenham (1991) comparing Menelik's conquest to the Europeans wrote: "It was imperial expansion and Realpolitik, African-style, and it brought greater rewards than any European war in Africa."[62]

The nature of conquests, the prevalence of permanent settler communities, and post conquest oppressive system of governance of the southerners (See chapter 7-9) made the Ethiopian situation not only complex and difficult to understand; but also, it created opposing and, sometimes, confusing views. Probably it is from this perspective that I. G. Edmonds, the author of *Ethiopia Land of the*

Conquering Lion of Judah, wrote: "While he fought European imperialism on one hand, he practiced African imperialism on the other hand;"[63] the notion echoed by the Oromo, Somali, Eritrean, Tigray, Sidaama, and other ethno-nationalist groups. Keller, in his book, *Revolutionary Ethiopia From Empire to People's Republic*, described it as follows:

> In addition to being seen as economically exploitative and politically dominant, the colonizers were seen as distinctively different in strict ethnic terms from those they colonized. When settlers and administrators from the core arrived in peripheral regions, they were accompanied by all of the elements of the Abyssinian cultural heritage. Language and religion played central roles in the process of colonization. ...the process of assimilation was extremely selective, affecting only a small segment of indigenous elites. The bulk of the colonized masses had no hope of ever-ridding themselves of the colonial bond."[64]

The prominent contemporary ethnographer of the south-central Ethiopian peoples, Ulrich Braukamper (2012), called it "colonialism" which "frequently surpassed the European imperialists in northeast Africa in their exploitation of the subjugated peoples." Empress Taytu's and Emperor Menelik's biographer, Chris Prouty (1986) called the conquests: "Menilek's Christianizing-colonizing objective"[65] The socio-economic and political legacy of such objective was further elucidated by Teshale: "It formed dual society: conqueror and conquered, victor and vanquished, civilized and barbarian, believer and infidel, clean and dirty, Amhara and "Galla (Oromo)."[66]

Chapter 2

Loose Definition of 'South' and 'Shewa'

For many people, the words 'South[67]' and 'Shewa' sound easy to grasp. As a result, many people, including academicians, use them carelessly and without much scrutiny. Defining 'South' and 'Shewa' is not as easy as they sound. They are not as simple as some would like think. Both 'South' and 'Shewa' are often described by different authors in different ways.

2.1. The "Old" and the "New" Shewa.

For most historians 'Shewa' is synonymous to the historical kingdom of Shewa; and the 'South' is synonymous to the present Southern Nations, Nationalities and Peoples Region (SNNPR). For others Shewa denotes to the province of *ye Shewa Teklai Gizat of* Haile Selassie era or *ye Shewa Kifle Hagar* of the Derg regime. Yet for others, it denotes to five administrative regions *(astedader kililoch* mentioned below) which were curved out of the former *Ye Shewa Kifle Hagar* in the latter years of Derg regime. Most writers, including Bahru, simply say 'Shewa' without bothering to specify it. Most Ethiopian historians and writers fall in these latter group.

Defining South is also as confusing. For example, Dr. Bahru's definition of the south goes as follows:

"እዚህ ላይ ደቡብ የምንለው የሸዋን መንግሥት ሳይጨምር ከዓባይ ወንዝ በስተደቡብና በዚያው አርከን የሚገኘውን ክፍል ነው። እነዚህንም ግዛቶች አንድ ከሚያደርጋቸው የጂዎግራፊ አቀማመጣቸው ባሻገር በጎንደር ዙሪያ ይሽከረከር በነበረው የዘመነ መሳፍንት ፖላቲካ አለመሳተፋቸው ነው።"[68]

("Here what we say south comprises regions south of the Abay River and areas along that line excluding the Shewa kingdom. Besides being contiguous, what makes them one was their nonparticipation in the politics of *zamene mesafint*, which revolved around Gondar.") *My translation.*

He used three elements to define South. One was excluding Shewa kingdom entirely from South. The second was a historical event -non-participation in *zemene mesafint* politics, and the third element was geography -contiguous region located south of Abay River. His definition, however, appears to have two shortcomings. The first was excluding Shewa entirely out of the southern region without specifically defining its boundaries and historical period. While *Semen/*North Shewa districts are predominantly Amhara and they are historical base of Shewa monarchs (Sahle Selassie, Haile Melekot, Menelik II, and Haile Selassie); other parts of Shewa (East, West, & South) are inhabited by various ethnic groups which had been incorporated by Menelik. Bahru's definition ignores the fact that administrative map of Shewa had been altered and reconfigured several times by Menelik II, and the regimes which succeeded him - Hailie Selassie, Derg, and EPRDF.

When Menelik submitted as a vassal to Yohannes in 1878, the official border of Shewa was limited to the areas between the Bashillo River in the north, Abay in the west and Awash River in the east and south.[69] Before and during this time, the Shewa kingdom led by its young king, Menelik, had successfully brought into its domain several territories of Shewa and Wollo Oromos and advanced further into the northern Gurage region. In the ensuing years, the Shewa kingdom exerted its control further over the Gibe & Wollega regions as well as in Arsi and Harar. Technically, the old Shewa kingdom or government ceased to exist, or rather morphed into Ethiopian government, only when Menelik became a *neguse negest* in March 1889. Until that time, it was officially a government of the Shewa kingdom, but it expanded further away from its traditional base in Ankobar. Therefore, excluding Shewa from south without specifying the period or defining its boundaries would lead to confusion.[70]

From the time Menelik became *neguse negest* to the early years of Haile Selassie's rule, i.e., from 1889 – 1936, the district of Shewa included areas between Wollo and the Awash River;[71] In the interim years of the Italian occupation, 1936 - 1941, Shewa was limited to the Italian colonial administrative areas of Addis Ababa and its vicinities.[72] During Italian occupation, the Kambaata-Hadiya region in south central Ethiopia, for example, was included in 'Galla (Oromo) and Sidamo' region with its capital in Jimma. After the liberation, Kambaata-Hadiya region's center Asela, in Arsi. In 1962, however, the Kambaata-Hadiya region was made one of the districts of Shewa Province.[73]

During Haile Selassie era Shewa was known as *ye Shewa Teqlai Gizat* and during the early years of Derg regime it was rephrased as *ye Shewa Kefle Hager,* which consisted of all districts of the Shewa-Amhara, the City of Addis Ababa, predominantly Oromo districts of Selale, Yere na Kereyu, Ambo, Nazret/Adama, Debre Zeit/Bishoftu, Menagasha; all of the Gurage lands, all of the Hadiya lands, all of the Kambaata lands, all of the Halaaba lands, all of the Tembaro lands, and all of the Silte lands..

As Professor Lapiso described, in terms of geographical markers, "between 1941 and 1986 Shewa was the name of the province located between Wollo, Abay River, Gibe River, Tiqur Wonz, and lower Awash Valley."[74] Thus, Shewa consisted of the historical Shewa-Amhara districts as well as the southern and Oromo regions and territories.

An accurate and best description of Shewa was that given by Arnold J. Toynbee in his book, *Between Niger and Nile*. Toynbee wrote, the "New Shoa had been added to the Old Shoa" which created the "Greater Shoa."[75] Ankobar centered 'Old Shoa" evolved with the expansion of its rulers and incorporated other areas ("New Shoa") and formed the "Greater Shewa." This fact eluded most Ethiopian writers and/or they consciously ignored it.

In the later years of Derg, ye Shewa *kefle hager* was divided into five *astedader kililoch* (administrative regions). They were: (1) *Semen/* North Shewa)- the Shewa- Amhara districts; (2) *Me'erab/* West Shewa which included the Oromo and Gurage districts; (3) *Debub/*South Shewa which included the Hadiya, Kambaata, Gurage, Silte, Halaaba,, Qabeena, & Tembaro districts; (4) *Misraq /* East Shewa which included the Oromo districts; and (5) Addis Ababa *astedader kilil,* the nation's capital. In other words, "from 1987-1991 Shewa was a name given to administrative region bordering Wollo, Gojjam, Illubabor, Sidamo, Arsi, Harrarghe, and Asseb administrative regions."[76]

After EPDRF seized government power in May 1991, it re-configured all Ethiopian regions based, primarily, on their ethnic composition and makeup. As a result, parts of the former Shewa provinces were allocated into three regions: North Shewa districts became part of the Amhara Peoples' National Region (APNR); central, eastern and parts of northern Shewa regions were included in Oromiya Region; and southern parts of the "Greater Shewa" regions became parts of the Southern Nations, Nationalities, and Peoples Region (SNNPR). To sum up, the South included parts of Shewa. More specifically, it included, what Toynbee called, the "New Shoa."

2.2. "Cultural South"

The second shortcoming of the definition of south mentioned above lies in its assertion that the regions which did not participate in the politics of *zemene mesafint* are regarded as south. This raises two questions. One is regarding Shewa and the other is regarding Wollo. The turmoil and upheavals of *zemene mesafint* era was, as a matter of fact, limited to Northern provinces of Begemeder/Gondar, Tigray, Gojjam and Wollo. Note that the Shewa kingdom or the "old Shoa" did not participate directly in the upheavals of the *zemene mesafinit,* the fact Bahru stated in his book. "South-east of the Abbay river, Shewa was comparatively insulated from the wars and politics of northern Ethiopia. Its successive rulers were steadfastly worked towards strengthening of the principality by conquering the neighboring Oromo lands."[77]

Shewa, just like some of the southern kingdoms, did not participate in *zemene mesafit* politics directly. We also saw above that the "New Shoa" was part and parcel of the South.

On the other hand, Wollo was an active participant of the *zemene mesafint* thanks to its Christianized Yejju Oromo dynasty which was centered in Gondar-Debre Tabor. The Yejju princes were not only participants, but also, they were movers and shakers of *Zemene Mesafint* era politics. After the end of that era, however, Wollo became a primary focal point of expansions and conquests by successive Ethiopian kings: Tewodros II, Yohannes IV, and Menelik II. One of the major participants of *zemene mesafit,* Wollo, was also one of the first targets of expansion. As a result, Wollo fell in the sphere of, what Dr. Teshale (1995) termed as, "cultural south." Hence participation in *zemene mesafint* politics per se is not good criteria to define the south.

According to Donham (2002), the "southern marchlands" stretched "roughly from the Abbay (Blue Nile) counterclockwise to the Awash River."[78] In other words, the South comprised regions conquered by Menelik II. Some historians preferred to describe the Ethiopian north-south in larger historical and cultural ties, and contexts rather than in geographical terms. Meredith (2005), for example, used such phrases as "inner core" and "outer regions" to differentiate between the historical north and south respectively.

> The inner core of the empire consisted of the mountains and plateau of central Ethiopia populated by Amharas and Tigreans bound together by ancient ties of history and religion. But the outer regions had been added by conquest during Emperor Menelik's reign at the end of the nineteenth century."[79]

The title of Dr. Donham's work, *"The Making of an Imperial State: An Old Abyssinia and the new Ethiopian Empire..."*[80] was self-telling.

Dr. Teshale, used innovative phrase, "Geez Civilization,"[81] to refer to Amhara-Tigre historical heritage, which is synonymous to Donham's "Old Abyssinia," and Meredith's "The inner core."

The word "Abyssinia" was used widely by western historians and writers to denote the northern Amhara-Tigre provinces. "Abyssinians" and its Arabic and Amharic derivatives, "Habesh" and "Habesha" respectively were used to refer to the people of Amhara-Tigre descent as opposed to the rest of the Ethiopian peoples. In the wake of the coup *d'état* sponsored by Shewa nobility and the Church to depos *Lij* Eyasu Mikael from power; an American Consulate in Aden had sent a lengthy confidential memo No.268, on April 23, 1919 to Washington D.C. The memo was about the over-all state of the country. In that memo, the consulate used such phrases as "true Abyssinians," "original Abyssinian," "original provinces," to refer to the northern Amhara-Tigray provinces; and "subject provinces," to refer the rest of the southern provinces. The memo further stated:

> Ethnologically and geographically Abyssinia seems to consist of the four original provinces of Tigre, Godjam, Amhara, and Shoa, and the people from these four provinces form the Christian, the military, and the ruling elements in present day Abyssinia. By conquest the original Abyssinia had been expanded to include a number of subject provinces..."[82]

Wollo was not included in the 'original provinces.' Professor Richard Pankhurst's book (1997) title used the phrase, "The Ethiopian Borderlands," to describe the peoples and regions which existed beyond the Amhara-Tigre spheres including native people of the north and northeast such as the ancient Cushitic peoples of Beja, Barya, Agew, and Afar in the north and north east; various Omotic, Cushitic, and Nilotic peoples further in the south, south east, and south west. In Pankhurst's book, the words "Ethiopia" and "Ethiopian" were reserved to the rulers and peoples of "inner core" areas.

Thus, attempting to define the South only in terms of geography or historical background may be somewhat misleading. Hence, Dr. Teshale's description of the south may help us to disentangle some of the complexities and help us to understand the South from geographical, cultural, and historical senses at the same time, rather than looking only at binary lens. He wrote:

> By South here is meant not a geographical South, but a cultural South. Accordingly, the Raya and Azabo, Oromo Muslims living in Wallo and Tigray, are the cultural South of Dabra Libanos, although they are geographically north of it.[83]

In this book, unless specifically mentioned, Shewa refers to the "Old Shoa," the small but important kingdom, aka, Shewa-Amhara, which was an epicenter of expansion led by Menelik II from mid-19th century to early 20th century. The 'Old' Shewa was also the home of modern-day Ethiopian monarchs: Emperor Menelik II, Empress Zewditu, and Emperor Haile Selassie I, and multitudes of nobility.

The South aligns with definition of "cultural south" when discussing conquests and their ramifications. Because 'cultural south' is not bound in contiguity, it allows us to discuss in a more general sense of shared historical and cultural legacies and ties. The South, in this book, is used in both geographical sense when mentioned specifically, and cultural sense when discussed in general sense. In both geographical and cultural senses, however, South denotes to the regions conquered by Menelik II during his reign as a king of Shewa and an emperor of Ethiopia. All peoples' in these regions are regarded as the Southern Ethiopian Peoples.

Chapter 3

Southern Societies Before Menelik's Expansion

"...before the conquest of Menelik in the late nineteenth century, the southern part of Greater Ethiopia was the scene of multidimensional interaction." - Donald N. Levine, *Greater Ethiopia: The Evolution of Multiethinic Society* 2nd ed. *1974:81*

"the origin and the political institutions of the early central and southern African civilization of Ankole-Rwanda and Zimbabuwe-Monomatope may be traced back to the kingdoms of southern and western Ethiopia - Damot, Enarya, Kaffa, Janjero, etc." - Richard Greenfield, *Ethiopia A New Political History.* 1975: 58

3.1. Historical and Paleontological Overview

"Where there are people, there is history." - Philip D. Curtin, *The Horizon History of Africa* 1971:8

3.1.1. Mosaic Heritage and Cradle Lands

One may wonder whether southern peoples had an organized system of governance and societal structures prior to their contact with the armies of Menelik II? Were there any meaningful aspects of civilizations? Was there a trade network among southern kingdoms and territories prior to conquest?

It is difficult to answer these questions accurately mainly due to lack of written records. However, there is a fair amount of record which, when pieced together, would give us highlights of conditions which had existed in pre-Menelekian South. Southern regions and peoples were generally depicted as ኋላቀር *(*backward), and አረመኔ (heathen) ጣኦት አምላኪ (idolaters). Hence conquests against them were often portrayed as a 'civilizing mission.'

The author of *YeAtse Haile Selassie Tarik (A History of Emperor Haile Selassie),* for example, wrote that Menelik **had** dispatched "ሊቃውንት" (highly educated, literally, 'scientists') from Gondar, Shewa, Wollo, and Tigray, that is, Amhara and Tigre priests, to the southerners and educated them. He made the heathen abandon idols and converted them into worshiping God and hence brought them into the family of God.[84] In other words, he equated it to the 'white man's burden' of 'civilizing mission.' If this were written by the nineteenth century white European, it would easily been dismissed and portrayed as being a product of a colonialist mentality. But it was written by an Ethiopian who was one of the top officials of Haile Selassie regime, a parliamentarian, high court judge, and longtime civil servant.[85]

The author did not invent such a narrative, though. Such narrative and rationale for conquests as civilizing mission was the single most important marker of "Geez Civilization."[86] This narrative mirrors Jürgen Osterhammel's (2014) "self-justificatory patterns" often used by "the invaders." Osterhammel's three self-justificatory patterns are "a missionary duty to civilize the "savages," "the right of the conqueror" and "the doctrine of *terra nullius,*"[87] which is discussed in chapter 5.2.

Brigadier General Mengistu Neway, who staged a coup against Haile Selassie in 1960 together with his brother, Germame Neway, stated that Ethiopian children were "taught unbalanced history" and were not taught a history of Kaffa;[88] by extension the history of southern peoples. Greenfield expounded it as follows: "In Ethiopia, the Amhara children who predominate in the schools do not learn of Kaffa before the time of incorporation into the modern Ethiopia by Menelik II at the end of nineteenth century."[89]

As historian Abebe Admasu articulated in his work (2014): "The past cultural, historical, social and political achievements of southern Ethiopian ethnic groups are not well researched...Historically, most attention was given to northern Ethiopia where the earliest states are located. However, the state formation of southern Ethiopia is of great interest but received much less attention."[90]

Because this and other reasons, Ethiopians were not taught about southern kingdoms and principalities at large. Most Ethiopians genuinely lack knowledge about their fellow Ethiopian socio-cultural and historical past, which I regarded it as heritage of national ignorance. Such heritage was rooted in the nation's establishment's obsession to focus solely on the so-called 'Solomonic Dynasty' and the history constructed around it (discussed in chapter 1.2. above). Hence, various cultures and civilizations which were parts of the Ethiopian mosaic heritage were sidelined, excluded, and remained unappreciated.

Such mosaic heritages, as discussed below, ranged from ancient cultures of Beja and Afar to wonders of Aksum and Agew (Lalibela); and from footprints of "ancestral Omo" and "remarkable Tiya" pillar sites of Gurageland. It also varied from a "highly sophisticated brand" of Konso "cultural landscape," and an "early megalith of Silte" and "megalithic builders of Hadiya. It encompassed the monoliths and stalaes of Gedeo, Sidaama and Borana, and the Halala Keela of Dawuro. It also ranged from "elegant architecture" of Kaffa to "highly organized polity" of Wolayta and the "wealthiest trade centers" of the Gibe states.

Some historians, however, equated the genesis of Ethiopian history and civilization only with Aksum and Aksumites. But, as Teshale (1995) reminded us: "To say that Ethiopian history starts with the Sabeans, and not the Agaw, Beja, etc....is tantamount to starting with the invaders."[91] In other words, long before Semites crossed the Red Sea into the present-day Eritrea, an indigenous civilizations had existed in the Ethiopian region. The southern peoples are part of that ancient Cushitic, Omotic, and Nilo-Saharan civilizations which prevailed in the region for centuries. Tekle Tsadik Mekuria and others claimed wrongly that Menelik's expansion to the south was to reclaim the territories ruled since Aksumite and Zagwe times. This forgets the fact that the "territorial extent" of Aksumite empire "at its largest was confined to what is now Eritrea, Tigray, Northern Wallo, and at times to parts of Arabia."[92] *UNESCO General History of Africa: Volume II Ancient History of Africa* described the extend of Aksumite kingdom as follows:

> Archaeology shows the Axumite kingdom as a tall rectangle roughly 300 kilometers long by 160 kilometers wide, lying between 13° and 17° north and 30° and 40° east. It extended from the region north of Keren to Alagui in the south, and from Adulis on the coast to the environs of Takkaze in the west. Addi-Dahno is practically the last-known site in this part, about 30 kilometers from Axum.[93]

Evidence of archaeological and paleontological findings of human existence and civilization in southern Ethiopia predated the Aksumite era. Professor Greenfield even suggested that the "mystical punt" land location may be, after all, somewhere in the south-western Ethiopia.

> ... a semi mythical source of gold and riches somewhere, in or near the eastern Horn of Africa. The author has referred elsewhere to stories of the existence of paved roads and tessellated pavements with stone sculpture and graffiti in the unexplored Manya plaines in south-west Ethiopia. If they exist, these ruins though probably of later origin, could conceivably be connected with the kingdom of Punt.[94]

The team of experts including an Ethiopian palaeo-anthropologist Zeresenay Alemseged published in the *Nature Journal* their findings of the "oldest direct-evidence of stone tool-manufacture" in Afar region of Gona "dated between 2.6 and 2.5 million years ago", in Bouri "approximately 2.5 million years ago" and in Dikika "stone-tool assisted consumption of animal tissues before 3.39 million years ago."[95] Jamie Shreeve, writing about Middle Awash area, noted that the area "is the most persistently occupied place on Earth. Members of our lineage have lived, died, and been buried there for almost six million years."[96]

Obviously the Middle Awash and the Lower Omo River Valley are best known to have been the cradle of humankind where Lucy and her descendants once walked and lived there. Hence, these areas are rich in ancient artifacts and hominid fossils.

> By nine thousand B.C. hominids flourished in the Omo River Valley...Those along the Omo River, apparently flourished perhaps due to the tropical climate provided by surrounding water and valleys. F.C. Howell's and Yves Coppen's finds along the Omo River and down the Lake Turkana describe an area rich with hominid fossils. Many varieties were found of the Australopithecus including the Robustus, and the Boisei. If Africa was the mother of all humanity, then the Omo River acted as a main artery.[97]

Archeologists and Paleontologists believed that the Omo River once flowed into the Indian Ocean before volcanic and tectonic activities severed it. As Reader (1999) wrote: "At times, the ancestral Omo flowed through the basin and east to the Indian Ocean (a connection which is confirmed by the presence in the Turkana deposits of fossilized ocean fish remains, such as the teeth of a stingray)."[98]

> At other times its waters remained in the basin like tangled braids of hair, meandering through gallery forests and woodland, creating flood plains and ephemeral lakes. The pattern of the waterways was dictated by tectonic and volcanic activity associated with the formation of the Rift

Valley...volcanic activity peaked around 1.7 million years ago, and lave flows accumulating along the eastern boundary of the basin severed the ancestral Omo from its Indian Ocean outlets.[99]

This reminded me of my own several hours visit to the Kenya National Museum in Nairobi more than twenty years ago, on January 3, 2000. I was particularly impressed on how the Museum had curated past and present history of the Omo River and Lake Turkana. "Geological studies show that in the past, the Omo River flowed through the Turkana Basin and then onto the Indian Ocean." Lake Turkana "continued to expand and contract in size during the last 1 million years" and, due to volcanic and geological activities the Omo River shrunk down to its present entry point at Lake Turkana. The museum also showed how various ethnic groups moved from "southern Ethiopian highlands" to Kenya and beyond. For instance, Plain Nilotes entered Kenya "around 1,000 A.D.," Highland Nilotes "around 2,000 years ago", and Eastern Cushites "about 14th century."[100]

In recognition of the discovery of ancient hominid fossils during the 1901 French Expedition and International Expeditions conducted from 1965 to 1975; the Lower Omo River basin was declared as the World Heritage Site in 1980. The discoveries were clear indicators of the earliest human settlements in the region at large. The Omo River arises from the Gurage Mountains in south-central Ethiopia and encompasses several regions and travels several hundred kilometers until finally drains into Lake Turkana at the Ethio-Kenya border. Although it was not highly publicized the Lower Omo and the Omo River produced several remarkable discoveries.

Hominin (of human lineage) fossils unearthed there between 1967 and 1974 consist of about 200 teeth, four jaws, a partial skeleton, parts of two skulls, and a leg bone. The various layers have yielded remains from a broad and critical span of time in human evolution.[101]

Some of the oldest fossils were also discovered in "different localities in the lake rudolf (turkana) section of the rift valley (omo, lothangam, kanapoi, and sites on the east side of the lake)."[102] Along Middle Awash and Lower Omo, the most recent discovery at Fincha Habera of the Bale Mountains solidified southern Ethiopian region's ancient history and human settlement. In an article titled: "Middle Stone age foragers resided in the high elevations of the glaciated Bale Mountains," the Science magazine in its August 2019 issue wrote: "Located in Africa's largest alpine ecosystem, the repeated occupation of Fincha Habera rock shelter is dated to 47 to 31 thousand years ago."[103] According to the Ethiopian Academy of Sciences website published article, at Fincha Habera, "scientists unearthed numerous signs — such as stone artifacts, burnt animal bones, clay fragments and a glass bead — that the rocky outcrop was once inhabited."[104]

3.1.2. Footprints of ancient civilization

People of the Beja and Agew descent were believed to have inhabited the region long before Semites crossed the Red Sea and settled there. Although archeologists "are more inclined" to state that the plough agriculture was a "direct consequence" of Sabaeans, as John Reader argued in his book, *Africa: A Biography of the Continent*, "...the plough may have been used, possibly even invented, by Ethiopians some time before the Aksumites were in contact with the Sabaeans of southern Arabia."[105] In other words, the plough was probably invented by indigenous people who inhabited the land before coming in contact with the peoples of the Semitic origins. In this regard, the work of Frederick J. Simoons, *Some Questions on the Economic Prehistory of Ethiopia,* is particularly interesting and worthy of reading. Professor Simoons argued that the "Ethiopianists" and "certain writers have credited various innovations to Semites without supporting evidence."[106] He suggested that "the Agow [Agew] or the northern Cushites had a plough - derived from the north end of the Red Sea - and practiced cereal cultivation involving teff, perhaps finger millet, sorghum, what and barely in pre-Semite times."[107] Simoons also posed a question: "Who domesticated the ensete?" and weighed the notion of *enset* domestication by Egypt and the reports by James Bruce and others of the presence of enset in northern Ethiopia; and concluded that the "Sidama people of southern Ethiopia are viewed as likely candidates in *ensete* domestication."[108]

> The evidence for ensete cultivation in ancient Egypt is weighed and judged inconclusive. The cultivation of ensete for food in northern Ethiopia is viewed as recent. The suggestion is made that cereal-plough agriculture pre-dated the Semitic invasion. The ancient Cushitic inhabitants of northern Ethiopia are seen as having been in an excellent position for contacts with countries at the north end of Red Sea, particularly Egypt, whence wheat and barely and the plough could have been introduced."[109]

Greenfield (1965) quoted Professor Oliver who suggested that the sources of southern and central African civilizations are the southern Ethiopian kingdoms.

> ...the origin and the political institutions of the early central and southern African civilization of Ankole-Rwanda and Zimbabuwe-Monomatope may be traced back to the kingdoms of southern and western Ethiopia-Damot, Enarya, Kaffa, Janjero, etc.[110]

Anthropologist Georges-Clovis Savard (1921-2012) lived and worked in Ethiopia from 1947 to 1971, taught at Teferi Mekonnen Elementary and High Schools, did anthropological research in Afar region, and taught Ethnology and Ethiopian Cultures at Addis Ababa University. In 1961 he published a long article titled *The Peoples of Ethiopia* in the *Ethiopian Observer* about existence of ancient Cushitic cultures and civilizations across the Horn of Africa and their divisions into separate groups and spreading into East Africa and beyond. He wrote of "existence of Neolithic agriculturalists who spread...from the Ben Shangul territory to the Lake Rudolf" (Turkana); and the Agau (Agew) who "demonstrated remarkable spirit of inventiveness" and who "discovered new varieties of the cultivated plants."[111]

> The Agew...also enabled some of the plants that grew wild, and originated a cultivation that has last till out day" finger millet (*dagussa*), *teff, enset*, cress, sunflower, coffee, *kat*, castor, etc. It appears also that the Agau domesticated the donkey and discovered how to breed mules."[112]

Traces of ancient human existence and civilization were found in wider areas in Southern Ethiopia. Findings of "the Wiltonian Industry"[113] in various parts of the South proved the existence of ancient civilization in the region. "Characterized by Micro lithic tools: lunates and thumb-nail scrapers, made of obsidian, it is found in numerous sites, from Harar to Sidamo, and from Yavello, through Moggio, Debre Zeit to the Dahlak Archipelago."[114]

> In 1928, Teilhard de Chardin discovered Porcupine Cave, a few miles south of Diredawa. Four later the cave, excavated by P. Wernert, was yielding the only well-identified prehistolric human remains found in Ethiopia. They consist of the right part of a mandible with molars and premolars. No one, it seems, doubts that this is a human jaw although it shows "archaic" traits: massive bones, absence of chin, very large teeth, etc.[115]

Ancient cave paintings depicting animals and people found in Lagaada, Hararghe highlands, and in Shabe, Sidamo, as well as ancient funerary steles found, in Arsi, Hararghe, and in the former South Shewa regions showed an existence of people who had practiced animal husbandry, agriculture, and handicraft around four to five thousand years ago. Such findings were unique in that they were found in regions not influenced by such ancient civilization Egyptians, Axumites, Romans or Arabs.[116] The "twelve sites at Konso-Gardula, or KGA" near Ethio-Kenya border, was attributed as great discoveries of ancient artifacts. KGA was "the oldest known hand ax site in the world" which was "dated between 1.37 and 1.7 million years ago."[117] In a logical southward dissemination of such civilization the "oldest stone tools, made some 2.6 million years ago" were discovered "from Koobi Fora on the east side of Lake Rudolf."[118]

Writing about ancient footprints of southern Ethiopian peoples and regions, the renowned African historian, Basil Davidson, in his celebrated book, *The Lost Cities of Africa* (1959) noted: "Southwards from Addis Ababa, in abrupt valley of the Sidamo and Borana that led down slowly into the choking plains of northern Kenya, one may come upon many stone monoliths that are carved to represent a phallus."[119] He emphasized the mysterious nature of symbols on stone monoliths and carvings.

> Sometimes these stones, ten or twelve feet high, bear engraving in lines and unexplained symbols; more often they bear nothing at all. They don't seem to have been burial stones. No one knows when they were built, the present population can say nothing about them. Alongside these tall granite monoliths, at other sites, are other kinds of standing stones, sometimes, engraved, sometimes not, perhaps contemporary, perhaps earlier. Often enough these are engraved with swords or daggers; but the daggers seem to be of a comparatively recent type, and there is nothing to suggest that this dagger-engraving on monoliths has any close parentage, for example, with the almost certainly much more ancient dagger-engravings of Bronze Age Europe at Stonehenge or Carnac, though the visible results are oddly reminiscent of each other.[120]

In conclusion, as Donald N. Levine, in *Greater Ethiopia,* noted, "before the conquest of Menelik in the late nineteenth century, the southern part of Greater Ethiopia was the scene of multidimensional interaction between"[121] various Cushitic and Omotic speaking peoples whose history and extent of civilization has yet to be studied and investigated.

Chapter 3.2. below highlights established kingdoms and long lines of dynasties existed before Menelik's conquest in several southern regions which also had an organized administrative and defense systems. It also shows the presence of various types of polities and communities, and active interaction between and among various peoples.

Here I would like to emphasize that the history, trade, and government of the southern peoples described below is only an overview. Thorough research is left for others to undertake. Each community of people deserves independent anthropological and historiographical studies. My inspiration here is merely to produce something which would serve as an introduction to scholars and students alike.

3.2. Southern Nations: History, Government and Society

> *"A functional and unique administrative system of the nation and the people was in our midst which we did not hear or we're unable to hear. That system is still here."* - Asafa Chabo, *Yetizita Feleg* 2016:89 My translation.

3.2.1. The Kingdom of Kaffa

We begin with the kingdom of Kaffa because its history and success represented the untold history of the southern peoples' at large. Although Kaffa was devastated and its inhabitants were decimated during and after the invasion, in some ways, we are fortunate to have its conquest history recounted by an eyewitness, Alexander Bulatovich. After getting permission from Menelik to be part of the expeditionary forces, Bulatovich travelled from Addis Ababa and arrived at ras Wolde Giorgis's headquarter in Bonga, where he enjoyed splendid reception. Then he was embedded with the armies and directly participated in an on-going conquest in the southwestern territories.

He served as an advisor to the *ras* and, at times, he was person-ally engaged in the fighting against the native peoples. At the end of his mission, *ras* Wolde Giorgis awarded him "the silver spear" of *Tato* Gaki Sherecho, which "he had thrown on the Abyssinian who had taken him prisoner." When he returned to Addis Ababa, he was awarded by Menelik, which he wrote: "the Emperor awarded me a gold shield – an outstanding military distinction, given only on rare occasions."[122]

Bulatovich arrived at Kaffa in January 1898, few months after it was conquered. Much of what we know now about the Kaffa king-dom's conquest and its aftermath came from his writings and diaries.

Professor Pankhurst noted that the first of long-line of Kaffa kings "reportedly came to the throne around 1390."[123] Since then Kaffa was ruled by successive dynasties whose "line of kings goes back to at least 19 generations from 1890."[124] Kaffa kingdom contin-ued to exist and function until the last king, *Tato* Gaki Sherocho, was conquered by the army of Menelik in September 1897.

In its heydays, "Kaffa subdued neighboring states, and formed out of them a powerful southern Ethiopian empire, known formerly under the general name of Kaffa."[125] The kingdom was ruled by a powerful *tato* who was most revered by its subjects. *Tato* Gaki built strong army and enlarged the kingdom's frontiers to include vassal kingdoms. He ruled them using a fairly, modern administrative mechanism which granted vassal kingdoms to retain their own inde-pendence. "Kaffa did not interfere in their internal affairs, demanding only payment of tribute and acknowledgment of their suzerainty."[126] Kaffa was divided into 12 regions, each with its own governor (*waraba* or *rasha*) appointed by the king; and their responsibilities consisted of administration of justice, provision of supplies for the militia in time of war. Each region is subdivided into smaller areas.[127] The Kaffa king or Kafino' Ta'to', was also known as Adi or "Majesty," and its crown was hereditary.[128] *Tato* ruled and run his government assisted by an advisory council of nobles known as *mikrecho*.[129] Kaffa allowed free merchants and had its own native religion and priests.[130]

A prominent Ethiopian historian wrote that Kaffa's "economy as in both Waleyata and Jangero, as well as among a number of Cushitic and some Semitic peoples of the south, was based on the cultivation of *enset*."[131] The accuracy of such generalized description, however, may be questioned for several reasons. First, it lumped up the economy of "a number of Cushitic and some Semitic peoples of the south" to a single source of *enset*. By doing so it did not take into consideration other sources of economy such as horticulture, livestock, trade, agriculture, and pastoralism which existed among various southern Cushitic and Semitic groups. Secondly, Kaffa's economy was reduced to only *enset* cultivation and to eating "roots" after the kingdom was conquered and severely devastated for its fierce resistance and refusal to peacefully surrender (See chapter 4.4.1. for conquest against Kaffa). As Bulatovich noted, the *enset* based Kaffa economy description may fit into the economic profile of post-conquest Kaffa.

> In the former times, the food of the Kaffa consisted of meat, milk, and porridge made of the seeds of various bread-grain plants. Nowadays, they eat almost exclusively bread made from the roots of a banana-like tree (that same musa enset), since that is the only food stuff they can obtain after the general destruction.[132]

Thirdly, Kaffa kingdom, as witnessed by early travelers, had enjoyed an extensive trade networks and flourishing industry and local economy uncommon even in most, if not all, northern regions. An Italian explorer Cecchi was one of the early foreigners who visited Kaffa and witnessed the extent of its trade. During his time Kaffa was engaged not only in domestic trade with neighboring states and kingdoms in the south; but also, it had trade contacts with foreign nations which enabled it to export its commodities.

> In Cecchi's time Kafa was the richest country in south-west Ethiopia. It was in direct contact with the kingdoms of Kullo, Konta, Wolamo (Wolayta), and had trade connections with the Somali coast, Zayla, Massawa, Suakin, and Gallabat. Its

chief exports were coffee, cardamom, civet, and ivory - apart,
that, from slaves.[133]

Honey was also one of the export items of Kaffa.[134] Professor
Mohammed Hassen wrote: "From Kaffa also came the best ivory,
musk and spices as well as a large quantity of coffee."[135] "Excellent
cloth and the best iron articles – spears and daggers – were made in
Kaffa."[136] Kaffa together with Gibe States was a magnet which at-
tracted Jabarti and Afkala traders as well as merchants from Gurage,
Hadiya, Kullo, Konta, Janjero, Tambaro, Wolayeta, Wollega,
Illubabor and others.[137]

Bonga, the capital of Kaffa, was a trade hub which was connected
to the Gibe State and beyond. "From Bonga, a number of small
routes branches off in different directions, all facilitating the flow of
goods into Bonga, from whence the fast moving Afkala merchants
brought them to Saqqa."[138]

The wealth obtained from its local economy and trade was also
manifested in its architecture. Bulatovich observed that the "buildings of the Kaffa are very similar to those of the Abyssinians, but
they [were] made more carefully and more elegantly;"[139] the palace
of the Kaffa king in Andarachi was "an enormous palace...the span
of each of the columns that support it was several times the reach of
both extended arms." After he personally witnessed the devastation
caused by *ras* Wolde Giorgis; he lamented: "Abyssinians, having torn
the city asunder, had to spend a long time trying to destroy this co-
lossal building, until they finally succeeded in burning it down."[140]

Kaffa was also known for its infrastructure, especially roads (*bocco*)
and bridges which were "made throughout the country by the king,
and their upkeep was the responsibility of an official called ade'ra'so."
In Kaffa: "Rivers were crossed by fords, *kim'a*, wooden bridges, *ya'o*,
supported on posts, and by suspension bridges, *kofo'*, made of wood
and liana."[141] Besides, "special roads were built for the king, along
which no one else could go. The *tato* had several residences in various places and lived in them for these times of year which for that
particular place were considered the healthiest."[142]

The Kaffa "state obtained its revenue from taxation and the customs dues on the prosperous trade with the Oromo states."[143] Kaffa's past industrial achievement and the destruction it suffered after its conquest was apparent.

> ...In the distant past, before its destruction and conquest by the Abyssinians, Kaffa was the industrial and commercial center of Ethiopia. Thanks to its wealth, to the fertility of soil etc....it had the reputation of being an almost fairytale country. It abounded in bread, mead, cattle, and horses, and with its tributaries, it gathered a huge quantity of ivory...A large part of the musk exported from Ethiopia was obtained in Kaffa. Excellent cloth and the best iron articles –spears and daggers- were made in Kaffa. But the circumstances changed, and the once flourishing and busy state is now completely destroyed and an almost deserted country.[144]

3.2.2. The Kingdom of Yam

The small, but powerful kingdom of Yam in southwestern Ethiopia was also known as Janjero. Yam was a well-established principality for centuries before its last king was conquered by Menelik armies in 1894. About 280 years before Yam was conquered, a Portuguese Jesuit missionary, Father Antonio Fernandez visited it. He was received by one of its kings in 1613.[145]

The kingdom of Yam was one of those small polities which existed about bigger kingdoms. But its rulers built a strong defense system, like that of Kaffa, which enabled it to repulse an early Oromo invasion; and later an expansion of Jimma Aba Jifar II. As Greenfield wrote, the Oromos "skirted around regions where the local leaders were too powerful, such as Kaffa and Janjero to the west of the river Gojab in the south-west."[146] Bahru wrote that the kingdom of Janjero was ruled by *amano*/king, whose government hierarchy included "state of council of twelve astessor, whose chairman (the *waso*) was highly influential, provincial governors (*erosha*) and district chiefs (*ganna*)."[147] Yam was at war with its neighboring kingdoms at times, especially with the Jimma Abba Jifar but it maintained its independence until it was conquered by Menelik II. Yam's "economy was based on land worked by a tribute-paying peasantry, with trade and crafts (more particularly iron-casting and weaving) playing a supportive role.[148] (See 4.4.2. for conquest against Yam)

3.2.3. Konso

Konso was recognized by UNESCO in recent years as a "cultural landscape" for its unique terracing and distinctive funerary practices and statues. Its distinctive cultural practices and a modern land management skill has a rich history, which dated back to 400 years.[149] A "distinguished historian of pre-colonial Africa," Basil Davidson wrote in the *Lost Cities of Africa:*

> Some of the most successful terracing of all may still be found in use and construction, for example, among the pagan Konso, a...people of the southwestern Ethiopia; here too the hills are contoured with an infinite number of meandering lines.[150]

Davidson added that "the art of building in dry stone - of building without mortar - is another ancient skill ... Konso still use it today."[151] Perhaps one of the least known fact about Konso was that it is a home of "the oldest known hand ax in the world." The *National Geographic* senior assistant editor in 1997 wrote that he was shown, by Ethiopian scientists at the National Museum in Addis Ababa, hand axes and tools collected from twelve locations at Konso-Gardula or KGA "...dated between 1.37 and 1.7 million years ago, making KGA the oldest known hand ax site in the world." He added that the team of scientists "returned two years later and collected hundreds of hand axes."[152]

Konso was conquered and ruled by *dejazmatch* Luel Seged in 1896 and by *fitawurari*, later *ras,* Habte Giorgis in 1997. As a Konso scholar and expert, Dr. Christopher Hallpike, in his book, *The Konso of Ethiopia: A Study of Values of an East Cushitic People*, stated "long before the Ethiopian conquest" Konso had been "an important trading center in the region" and "it was particularly known for its cloth, coffee, tobacco, and grain."[153] Konso's interactions involved merchants from Borana bringing "salt from the salt pan in the crater of Mt. Sogida near Mega, and of megada or...chewed tobacco;" and "attractive rarities... such as cowrie shells and conus shells for the ritual xallsha head ornaments" coming from Somali coast and "iron ore ...from Gofa to the north, and Burji pottery.[154] (See 4.4.6 for conquest info).

3.2.4. The Sidaama

Sidaama was "part of the great Cushitic civilization" which had its own "local system of governance inculcated in *halale* principle" and "*luwa* system which was based on consultative decision-making."[155] "Their territory is among the richest in Ethiopia with its large coffee and cotton plantations."[156] The Sidaama region, including neighboring Borana, had marks of their ancient culture represented with stone monoliths that are curved to represent a phallus, but "no one knows when they were built" and they "bear engraving in lines" and "unexplained symbols."[157] According to Davidson, the tall phallic statues and monoliths found in Sidaama region were also found in other parts of Africa.

> Perhaps the habit of distinguishing men by curving a phallic ornament on the foreheads of their funerary statues, practiced still in southern Ethiopia, goes back to a common source with comparable practices in West Africa. Perhaps the tall stone phalli of the Sidama, also in southern Ethiopia, are related to the menhirs of West Africa, the phallic gravestones of East Africa, and the phallic trinkets of...Rhodesia.[158]

For several hundred years, the economy of Sidaama was based on mixed horticulture and cattle breeding which for much of the last century shifted to farming.[159] Sidaama proper shouldn't be confused with the Sidama family language group, which consisted of Kambaata, Hadiya, Gedeo, Halaba, Tambaro, etc. For Ullendorff (1960) the peoples related to the Sidaama groups consisted of (a) *Sidaama-Kambata* which consisted of "Sidamo, Hadiya, Darasa (Gedeo), and Kambatta"; (b) *Ometo (or West Sidama)* which comprised "Welamo (Wolayta), Gofa, Zala, Basketo, Chara, Kullo, Konta, &c." (c) *Gimira-Maji* which included "Shakko, Bensho, Nao, and Maji."[160] The group listed in (b) and (c) are no longer classified as Sidaama language families.

Before they were reduced to their present-day areas because of invasions and subsequent assimilations by the Oromos since the 16th century; and later by Amharas since mid-19th century; the Sidaama family group of peoples used to inhabit in much larger regions (Huntingford (1956), Shack (1966), Henze (2000), Ullendorff (1960). Because of the major historical events mentioned above, they were "forced…into the region they now dwell."[161] G. W. B. Huntingford stated that they inhabited a much larger territory which stretched from Abay to Gojab; and lived in two states formerly known then as Bizamo and Damot. [162] "Bizamo lay between the Abay and the Angur, Damot between the Angur and the Gibe, while Gafat was farther east, probably between the Gudar and Muger rivers. All these are reckoned as "Kingdoms" by Ludolf, whose map of 1683 continues to show all of them south of Abay, as does Almeida's map of about 1640.[163] While several Sidaama family groups managed to survive and kept their identities, further south they were also assimilated by Amharas and Oromos. As Henze wrote: "The inhabitants of Damot were originally Sidama stock but appear to have been assimilated into the Amhara majority in Gojjam. Further south…Oromo migrants took over some but many Sidama groups and languages survived."[164]

It appeared that these Sidaama groups might also have lived even further in the north. One of the possible indicators, although not an evidence, was the existence of *ensete* at the present-day Amhara centers of Gondar and Gojjam. *Ensete* is a staple-food source of south and south-western peoples. Its existence in the north was witnessed by such early travelers as James Bruce and Almeida.

> *Ensete* appears in household compounds throughout the cen-
> tral and southern highlands, and curiously, in isolated areas
> of the Simen mountains. …Seventeenth-century Portuguese
> accounts, and later James Bruce, described ensete cultivation
> on the northern highlands especially around Gonder and
> in Gojjam. Almeida described it as "a tree peculiar to this
> country [i.e. Northern Ethiopia] so like the Indian fig that
> they can be distinguished only very near…"[165]

During the Oromo migration, peoples of the Sidaama family group had put up stiff resistance and successfully fend off the Oromos and hence they preserved their lands and identities (Hassen 1994, Levine 1974).

> It was only the Sidama countries south of the Gojab and
> extending east of the lakes (Zeway, Abaya, 'Camo) that
> successfully resisted them…At least, we do know that the
> Sidama south of the Gojab were never conquered by the
> Galla (Oromo). The pre-Galla (Oromo) population of the re-
> gion between the Abay and Gojab was also Sidama, but they
> were perhaps not so well organized or determined as their
> southern kinsmen, and entry into their country was easier,
> so that they fell prey to the Mocha Galla (Metcha Oromo)
> among whom they became eventually absorbed.[166]

Levine in, *Greater Ethiopia*, wrote how the Oromo expansion was stopped in the west and east. "On the west, Lacustrine and Omotic peoples such as the Konso, Derasa, Wolamo, Sidamo, Gurage, and Kefa stood their ground, effectively preventing an Oromo takeover; expansion on the east was checked by the Somali and the Afar."[167] Mohammed Hassan's description on how Sidaama family groups of eastern and western Cushitic peoples curtailed Oromo expansion is informative.

> As we have seen the Metcha spread over a wide area within three to four decades. Their campaign was stopped in the south by the people of Enarya, to the east by the people of Hadiya, Gurage, Kambata, and Jajero, to the north the Abbay provided a natural barrier which mitigated the effect of their sudden attack on Gojjam.[168]

Dejazmach Balcha Safo ruled over Sidaama, Gedeo and other neighboring peoples for several years. He monopolized the rich Sidaama-Gedeo coffee business which, in turn, created confrontation between him and the young Teferi Mekonnen, later Haile Selassie I. Eventually Balcha was removed and replaced by *ras* Birru in 1928 (see chapter 17). During Haile Selassie's reign, 'Sidamo' province was formed by merging several regions and peoples. The term "Sidamo," according to a Sidaama native and scholar, Seyoum Hameso, was "misrepresentation undertaken to suppress Sidama identity.[169] See 4.3.6 for conquest against Sidaama.

3.2.5. The Kingdom of Wolayta

Wolayta was one of the "highly organized polities"[170] existed in the south before it was conquered by Menelik in 1894/5. The Wolayta kingdom is one of the oldest kingdoms which traces its foundation to the beginning of the thirteenth century. Its last ruler, k*awa* Tona (Tsona) Gaga, was "the fourteenth monarch"[171] in the kingdom's well-established line of dynasties. Wolayta, led by its indigenous leaders, emerged as one of the powerful kingdoms.

Wolayta traded with Kaffa and Gibe States[172] and its currency, *dorma*, was circulated beyond its borders and was used by neighboring nations. When M. S. Wellby travelled through Wolayta in early 1898, about four years after it was conquered by Menelik, he saw dorma currency being used at the marketplace. He wrote,

A purchase was made by means of "dormas", A dorma is a thin piece of iron with one end bent, measuring about two feet long and once inch broad. Fifteen of them go to a dollar. For every transaction a small tax is exacted, either in the shape of a pinch of cotton or a piece of ginger.[173]

The Wolayta kings built defensive walls, ditches, and fortifications which were designed to defend their territories from enemy attacks and invasions, some of which, like the Ijago Keela/Walls are still visible [Greenfield, (1965), Hailu Zeleke (2007)]. The kingdom of Wolayta ended when it was conquered by Menelik II. But the Wolayta people did not give up their kingdom easily, and they defended their land and fought to the last minute until they were finally defeated when their king was captured, chained, and taken to Addis Ababa as prisoner (See chapter 4.3.5).

3.2.6. The Gurage

Broadly speaking, Gurage comprises several 'linguistically unintelligible' groups which occupied areas bounded by mountains and rivers (Awash, Omo, Gibe, and Wabi). According to Wolf Leslau (1956) "there are about twelve dialects spoken in the province of Gurage that can be divided into three main groups," namely, Eastern Gurage, Western Gurage and Northern Gurage.[174] Each of them is divided into several subgroups with its own developed and rich social-cultural systems, the detail of which is not the scope of this work. Although the "Gurage have no centralized institutional political power or leadership" in the past, they had organized system in which "power is vested in lineages" and where "descent groups display corporate rights, obligations and influences," and "the religious or ritual system is highly centralized; ritual officials sanction the authority of political elders."[175] Engdawork Nimane, who conducted research (2013) in *Sebat-Bet* Gurage also wrote that the Gurage "political system is characterized by its segmentary form, political units are relatively independent and positions with political units are attached to fields of clanship."[176]

However, the Gurage were believed to have occupied and inhabited the present region for a long time. Citing the sixteenth century Portuguese traveler, Richard Pankhurst tells us that Alvares described Gurages "as a freedom-loving people" and "none of them....were slaves," (which unfortunately changed since mid-nineteenth century when the area was subjected to widespread enslavement and raids.) Alvares also visited northern Gurage region and saw people who "lived in the vicinity of Awash River." During Alvares's time, they had "numerous excavations" and large caves where "twenty or thirty persons could find room inside with their baggage."[177] The eastern Gurage, especially Silte and "other neighboring regions," according to Pankhurst, had "numerous stone megaliths, smaller but no less interesting than the famous obelisks of Aksum" which were "believed to date from possibly the time of Christ."[178]

The World Heritage Site in Tiya is "among the most important of the roughly 160 archaeological sites discovered so far in the Soddo region...The site contains 36 monuments, including 32 carved stelae covered with symbols, most of which are difficult to decipher...and whose age has not been precisely determined."[179] Perhaps one of the most important contribution of Gurage, to the Ethiopian society at large, was the introduction of the concept and practice of communal self-help. Levine wrote: "The territorial and "project" *mahebar* were introduced into Ethiopian life by the Gurage: so, as far as present evidence indicates, were the *eddir* and the *equb*.[180] Like other societies, Gurages also have their own well developed customary and communal legal and conflict management systems. *Seera, yajoka,* various types of *Qyiça* customs can be cited as an example.

Although the northern Gurage region, Aymelel/Kistane, had a long history of interaction with Shewa beginning with king Sahle Selassie, Menelik's conquest against Gurage began in mid-1870s. However, due to stiff resistance in eastern and western Gurageland, the conquest was not completed until the end of 1880s (see 4.1.3).

3.2.7. The Hadiya

Hadiya is one of the well-known and oldest Sultanates which used to occupy vast territories and developed rich tradition. Richard Burton, who was the first European to visit Harar, claimed that Harar was the ancient capital of Hadiya. In his words: "The ancient capital of Hadiyah, called by the citizens "Harar Gay," by Somal "Adari," by the Gallas "Adaray, and by the Arabs and ourselves "Harar,"[181] He added: "The province of Hadiyah is mentioned by Makerizi as one of the seven members of the Zayla Empire, founded by Arab invaders, who in the 7th century of our era conquered and colonized..."[182]

The kingdom of Hadiya was one of the well-known kingdoms in medieval times. The Hadiya were believed to have occupied parts of the Bale-Arsi-Hararghe regions before they became insignificant in their ancient domicile on one hand and established themselves and persevered their identity in various parts of the country on the other hand. This involved greater population movements, absorptions, assimilations, expansion etc. Such historical events as the wars of Ahmad Gragn and the Oromo expansion, which had caused significant population movements, displacements, integration, and/or resettlements in Ethiopia, had also played considerable role in reshaping the history of Hadiya people. Ulrich Braukamper in *A History of Hadiyaa in Southern Ethiopia* (2012), wrote extensively on how the 16th century wars of Ahmed Gragn (Ahmed ibn Ibrahim al-Ghazi) could be attributed as one of the most important historical period in which several Hadiya groups had moved from their original homelands in the east and south-east and settled at their present day areas in south-central Ethiopia. The Oromo expansion was another historical event which resulted in some of the Hadiya groups absorption and assimilation in Arsi, Bale and parts of Chercher region of Hararghe as well as in their relocation into other areas.

The ancient Hadiya sultanate's rocky relationship with Ethiopian rulers was recorded by Arab historians and Ethiopian chroniclers as a tributary and as independent principality, the detail of which is not the subject of this book. But a historical marriage relationship entered between Hadiya-Ethiopian king is worth mentioning here.

One of the wives of the Christian ruler, Zareaa Yakob (Zara Yakob), was "Eleni, the daughter of the King of Hadiya," who "outlived Zara Yakob by a half a century and became one of the most influential women in Ethiopian history."[183] [We don't know her Hadiya native name, but her father was Gaarad Mehmad (Muhammed). Mehmad's son and Eleni's brother was Mahiko, (Mihiko, Mayuko). Mahiko rallied some Hadiya gaarads and rebelled against Zareaa Yakob. He was killed by his relatives who were Zareaa Yakob's allies.[184]] Eleni, however, "played a major role in Ethiopian state craft" and "helped bring together" the Hadiya and the Ethiopian ruling dynasties.[185] She "continued to be influential" during the reigns of Baede Mariam (1488-1478), Zara Yakob's son; Iskinder, Baede Mariam's son; Naod, 'Iskinder's half-brother'; and Lebne Dingel, Naod's son.[186]

As Henze noted: "From her childhood in Hadiya, Eleni retained awareness of the wider Muslim world and sought to achieve a degree of reconciliation and good commercial relations between the Christian kingdom and Adal."[187] She also realized that the Ethiopian kingdom needed help to counter ever-growing threat from Arab-Muslim forces. Thus Eleni "dispatched an Armenian named Mateus to Portugal to ask for help for Ethiopia in resisting Muslim pressure... Mateus...reached the court of King Manoel I in Lisbon in 1514, where he was well received."[188] However, when Portuguese mission arrived at Massawa in 1520 Lebne Dingel became "suspicious of the Portuguese motives." Eleni was retired by then. He denied their entry and the mission left the country. The "Queen Mother Eleni understood this ('Muslim threat'), but Lebna Dengel did not." Several years after he died, his son, Galawudwos, got Portuguese military support which helped to defeat Ahmed Gragn's forces.[189]

The Hadiya rulers rebelled and fought with Lebne Dengel. In mid-sixteenth century when Ahmed Gragn forces occupied most parts of the country, as Shinn and Ofcansky wrote, the Hadiya ruler became an ally and "provided Ahmed and his senior commander with a daughter and a sister respectively to cement the link."[190] After Gragn's defeat, Atse Gelawudwos had to use Portuguese military support to subdue Hadiya. Yet Hadiya rebelled.[191] "Queen Eleni had retired to her domain in Gojjam.," where she built a church at Martule Mariam which has symbols of sun and fireplaces in it. W. H. Jani (2015) regarded that the sun and fireplace symbols in Mertule Mariam Church had something to do with Eleni's ancestral religion of Fandano. She

> was converted Christian from the culture of Hadiya where Fandanism was originated...In relation to Fandanic Hadiya culture where the Queen originated, the fireplaces...found in the surviving structure could relate to Fandanic aspect fire ceremony linked to sun worship...some of the religious traits might have been practiced by the converted Christian Queen under cultural rather than religious basis.[192]

Evidences of Hadiya's ancient tradition can be seen in its relics in present-day Hadiya. Abdisalem Melesse Sugamo, in his study, *Ethno-archaeological Study of Megalithic Tradition in Southern Ethiopia: Muslim Megalithic Builders of Hadiya,* identified a total of "nineteen living megalithic traditions" in the forms of stelae and stone circles; which were identified as "anthropomorphic, phallic, figurative and monolithic types."[193] During pre-Menelikian era Hadiya merchants traded goods with Gibe states, especially with Limmu-Enarya.[194] Various Hadiya groups put up resistance but they were defeated and subdued. Particularly, Qebena-leader, Hassan Enjamo, who operated in Hadiya-Gurage regions had put up fierce resistance and halted Menelik's march of conquest. However, Hadiya was finally defeated after Menelik's "extensive military campaign against Hadiya between 1870s and 1890s."[195] (See chapter 4:2.4, 4.2.7, 4.3.4.)

3.2.8. The Kingdom of Kambaata

The Kambaata people were believed to have been settled at present geographical region for several centuries. Mount Hambaricho was the historical center of Kamabaata people, from which their original settlements "radiated" outward and to which they have common bond of connections and sense of belongingness. Kambaata, as David Shinn, put it, "was once an independent kingdom" and its "society divided into nobles, free commoners, artisans and slaves."[196]

Kambaata was mentioned in chronicle of *Atse* Yeshaq (1412-27) song. It was one of southern kingdoms with well-established monarchical system. The monarchy of Oyeta dynasty was first instituted in 16th century and operated without interruption until it ended at the last decade of ninetieth century. As Cohen stated "Kambata developed institutions of dynastic kingship and were ruled by a royal lineage that was only deposed at the time of the conquest of the area by Emperor Menelik's armies in the last decade of the nineteenth century."[197]

According to E. Cerulli (1956) Kambaata "had its own king... and in the 19th century Borelli recorded the names of the four kings" of Kambaata; and "Dilbato was the ruler in 1885."[198] Braukàmper wrote that the establishment of the last dynasty was "preceded by four kings (whose names are no longer known) from the...hinnira clan."[199] Even before monarchy was instituted, Kambaata society was led by a much venerated *Abba*, a Kambaata high-priest or a god-king.[200] "During the era prior to the establishment of the royal family, organized group of gods led by the king-god Abba was in charge of both secular and religious leadership of the Kambata society."[201] The Kambaata god, Abba, was officially worshipped by the entire Kambaata society for "595 years;"[202] and his office was the center of Kambaata society's unity and confederation. The Kambaata monarchs led confederation styled governance and administrative system known as *Sajje Gocho* (discussed below) which existed and operated until the 1974 Ethiopian Revolution. One of the distinctive features of the government of Kambaata kingdom was the co-existence of secular and spiritual systems of governance, namely the *Woma*/King; and *Abba*/the High Priest. As Jani noted,

> Within the circle of thirty gates, dual governance systems
> operated. The secular governance was controlled by the king

and thirty governors and the religious based administration was led by the state god and more than thirty ordinary gods. The king god remained the primary spiritual adviser of the king and leader of the gods.[203]

During Imam Ahmed ibn Ibrahim Al-Ghazi (Ahmed Gragn) wars, the invasion against Kambaata was led by Imam's commander and secretary, Abd en-Nasir in 1532. To defend their lands and themselves the Kambaata people fought against the powerful forces of Grang which was also supported by various allies. Ulrich Braukamper in *A History of Hadiyya in Southern Ethiopia,* wrote: "The rest of the Christian population of Kambata, in so far as they did not flee westward across the Gibe, could only withstand the Muslim invasion on the steep mountain massif of Ambarichcho."[204] Professor Richard Pankhurst wrote that the "Kambata people, and those of nearby Gafat, joined together to resist, but were easily routed. The Adal army killed many of the inhabitants of Kambata, and then imposed the usual poll tax."[205] Ulrich in *Die Kambata* (1983), further stated that Kambaata "became a battlefield" and it was "conquered from the southeast" and the "province suffered such heavy loss of life that it became in the course of sixteenth century an attractive target for invaders from southeast."[206] As Braukàmper stressed Kambaata not only survived the Gragn's era's heavy loss to its people and lands, but also it became a welcoming land to all people.

> From Hamalmal times onward, Kambata served as a refuge for political refugees and economically threatened groups from southern and northern Ethiopia...The Kambata people were famed for their sophisticated agricultural techniques and their surplus production; yet population pressure (itself a consequence of this agricultural success) presented a growing threat to their existence." [207]

Although the monarchy was from Oyata clan, the Kambaata government was structured to represent all tribes within its thirty administrative regions, known as *Sejje Gocho*, the Thirty Gates, which W. H. Jani referred to as "the Kambata of Thirty Gates." The Kambaata king credited for creating *Sejje Gocho* administrative system was *Woma* Anno who came to power in the early 1750s. Anno was also credited for state institutions and administrative structure of *Kokata* (General Assembly), *Womi Laha* (Crown Council), *Gochidanomat* (regional governorship), *Gaazena* (defense minister), *Elami Danna* (kinsmen leader), *Herra Danna* (hamlet/village leader)[208]

Administrative structures and institutions created by *Woma* Anno were consolidated during the reign of *Woma* Degoye (1810-45). Yet, Kambaata "enjoyed" what Braukàmper called "classical age" and Girma Zewude Anjulo called "the golden era" during the reign of *Woma* Dilbato Degoye (1845-92) when "the institutions of state[209] reached their highest stage of development" and "diplomatic and military measures led to a considerable extension of the area covered by the state."[210] Through marriages the Kambaata kings established strong relationships with neighboring peoples of the Leemo, Sooro, & Baadawaacho Hadiya, Tembaro, Halaaba, and Wolayta[211] the tradition of it dated back to the founder of the dynasty, Hamalmal who married Oyyata, daughter of Silte leader *Haji* Aliye and whose mother was from Endagagn. She became the founder of the Oyata dynasty which bore her name. Braukmaper described it as follows:

> The sons of hadjdj Aliye, born to a Gurage mother from Endagań, were named Allaqiiro, Abeechcho, Dilaapa, Samardiino, and Ajaamo, and his daughter was called Oyyata....Oyyata, the daughter of hadjdj Aliye, is insofar important in the history of southern Ethiopia, as she married Hamalmal,..governor of Kambata, and became founder of a new dynasty, which was named after her. This fact is extraordinary...[212]

Regarding their administrative structure Jani wrote: "Each of the thirty gates is triangular and each region is called gate. The term gate is applied for both physical gates and triangular regions. The appointed gate representative called Danna governed each gate region. Sub regions were governed by the representatives called Wanna. The Wanna reported to the Danna and the thirty Dannas in turn reported to the King."[213]

Merchants from Tembaro-Kambaata traded their products with the Gibe states, particularly with Saqqa, the capital of Limmu-Enarya, with which they were connected with trade/caravan routes.[214] For centuries Kambaata had long been governed by a traditional institution of *Seera*, "a code of conduct practiced and internalized" among members of society which regulates "relations between individuals, tribes and territorial units."[215] The *seera* institution consisted of (1) *kokata*, "the general assembly of all Kambata," (2) *gotcho,* thirty asymmetrically divided territorial units, (3) *muricho*, "sections and sectional leaders" appointed by the assembly of gotcho,, (4), *gogota* , "a traditional army consisting of males between 18 and 50 years of age," (5) *ilamo,* "a collective membership of a tribal group", and (6) *heera*, "the smallest unit of territorial organization…comprised of dozens of rural households."[216] Dr. Belachew Gebrewold in his research work: *An Introduction to the political and social philosophy of Kambata*, stated that the Kambaata aphorism or expression *mannu manna ihanohu mannienet* (Human being become human beings through fellow human beings) sums up "all realms of activities" and special significance of belonging to the community, and belief in a fellow human beings.[217]

The Kambaata king, w*oma* Delbato Degoye refused to submit to Menelik's armies and was determined to defend his kingdom. During the resistance fight the king, his cabinet members, and families were killed in 1892. After the conquest and incorporation of Kambaata "the new authority destroyed some of the institutions and transformed others. *Gogota* was of those institutions destroyed. W*oma* was transformed to *balabat*, *gotcho* to *sanghi-danomma*, *gotchi-danna* to *sanga-koro*, and *muricho* to *chikashum*."[218] (See chapter 4.3.3 for conquest against Kambaata).

3.2.9. The Afar

Afar has no contender as the most ancient land as it's the cradle of humankinds. The Middle and Lower Awash Valley were the birthplaces of 3.2 million years old Lucy; 4.4 million years old Ardipithecus ramidus "Ardi" adult female; and the 3 years old Dikaka baby which was 3.3 million years old.[219] As the National Geographic's, Virginia Morell beautifully put it, the "dry and sterile" Danakil is "a creative, hyperactive geologic wonder, its volcanoes, fissures, faults, hot springs, and steaming geysers all part of the birthing process of a new ocean."[220]

Professor Pankhurst even suggested that the Old Testament 'Land of Ophir' where King Solomon's ships 'sailed in search of gold, algum, or incense, trees and precious stones' may be our own Afar region.

> Trades such as that described in ancient Egyptian inscriptions
> continued into post-Pharanoic period and may have found in
> the Biblical reference to the commerce of the Land of Ophir.
> To it the ships of King Solomon (c.973=930BC) are said to
> have sailed in search of gold, *algum*, or incense, trees (con-
> ceivably myrrh or similar trees, and precious stones. Some
> historians have suggested that the word Ophir is related to
> Afar, the people and country of that name in north-eastern
> Ethiopia. This identification, which is by no means implausi-
> ble, would tend to confirm the long-established character of
> the Ethiopian region's foreign trade. If Ophir is in fact situ-
> ated in the area, it would indicate gold, presumably from the
> Ethiopian interior, and incense trees from the coastal stretch
> of Horn of Africa, were still being exported a millennium and
> half after the earliest Pharonic inscriptions – and indeed a
> thousand years before the birth of Christ[221].

The Afar country continued to produce rock salt in the medieval period, which was being transported and distributed into the interior "for both human and animal consumption" and a medium of exchange or as "primitive money."[222] Afar remained as a pivotal source of mineral both before and after the conquest. The Afar are born warriors who guarded the Ethiopian frontiers from foreign intrusions and incursion for centuries. They are real patriots who have strong and unwavering belief in Ethiopia sovereignty.[223] One of the many examples of Afar bravery and sacrifice was when they fought and destroyed the entire Egyptian army led by Swiss mercenary, Warner Muzinger Pasha, in Awsa in November 1875,[224] which aborted Khedive Ismail's major plot to instigate civil war between *negus* Menelik of Shewa and *neguse negest* Yohannes of Tigre.

The Afar sultan who led the attack against the Egyptian army led by Muzinger was Mohammed Hanfare Illalta, who also fought the Italians at Adwa alongside Emperor Menelik II. He was a grandfather of the longtime Afar ruler, the late *Amoyta* (Sultan) Alimirah Hanfare (1921-2011).[225]

3.2.10. The Gedeo

The Gedeo people are believed to have lived in their present localities for thousands of years practicing *Baalle*[226] a highly organized cultural and administrative system.[227] Prior to the conquest in the early 1890s they "lived in a federation of three territories called *Sasserogo*" *which* "shared one *Aba Gada*....and every eight years was passed to a new office holder in the next age set at a ceremony also known as *baalle*. According to Gedeo tradition, all leadership positions from Aba Gada at the top down to the office of *Hyiticha* were assumed at the *baalle* ceremony."[228] The Gedeo people are Cushities and belonged to Eastern Cushitic language family which consists of Sidaama, Kambaata, Tembaro, Hadiya, Halaaba.

One of the distinguishing features of the Gedeo people and their land is an abundance and richness with ancient cultural and archeological heritages of both tangible (staeles, caves, and rock arts) and intangible properties (folklore, dances, *baalle* system). The tangible heritage sites of the Gedeo included the Oddoola Galma Rock

Carvings, the Tutofala Archaeological Site which has 254 stelae; the Chalba - Tutiti Megalithic, which has "the largest reserve of stelae , that is, 1530 stelae...in only 21,600 m² area"; , the *Sade Sooddoota* Archaeological Site, which has 663 stelae, 409 of them standing and 252 fallen, and 56 of them is broken; the *Saakarro Sooddo* Megalithic Stelae Site, which has 43 phallic stelaes with "engravings unseen in other places"; and the *Songo* System, "the place where *Baallee* system is practiced."[229]

Beginning from the early years of Teferi Mekonnen, later Haile Selassie, Gedeoland known for its coffee production, had become a magnet which attracted government officials, nobility, and *naftegna*. The longtime governor of the then Sidamo province, *Dejazmach* Balcha monopolized coffee, introduced land measurement (*qellad*) in Gedeo and Sidaama, which expropriated fertile lands and pushed the Gedeo peasants further into the forest and periphery. His successor Desta Birru further reinforced the land measurement (McClellan (2002), Talbot (1952). The Gedeo people, never stopping claiming their land, and opposing expropriation and imposition of the *gabbar* system. They tried to appeal to the highest government level, but they were not heard. This led them to engage in popular resistances and rebellions where they were crushed by using disproportionate forces (See chapter 4.3.6 for conquest info and chapter 12.2 for Gedeo's resistances from the 1920s through the 1960s).

3.2.11. The Gibe and Western Oromo Kingdoms

The Gibe states of Limmu-Enarya, Goma, Guma, Jimma, and Gera were established as an independent polities between 1800 and 1835[230], and all of them were ruled by kings who "had the Oromo title of *moti* ("king" or "conqueror.")[231] Among the insignia and symbols of the Gibe kings are gold rings, gold earnings, the crown, the throne, silver bracelets, umbrella, and double-bladed spear.[232] Owing to its geographical proximity to south-western gold-producing area and itself being a gold producer; the Gibe region not only became "the main trading center" but it also "became one of the wealthiest trading centers of the Horn of Africa, famous for its slaves, ivory, and musk."[233]

One of the most familiar Gibe kingdoms in our times was Jimma, which was formerly known as Jimma-kaka. As Herbert Lewis, in *A Galla Monarchy Abba Jifar, Ethiopia 1830-1932* wrote, the territory of Jimma was conquered by Oromo in about 1750.[234] Before the Oromo arrival to the region, Jimma was believed to have been inhabited by Western Cushitic speaking peoples. The Jimma monarchy probably occupied the "former territory of Enarya in the northeast, Janjero in the east, and Kafa and Garo in the south and central regions."[235] The man who started the foundation of Jimma-Kaka kingdom was Abba Magal. When he died, he was succeeded by his son Sanna, who established the kingdom by 1830. He became the first king and was known by his war-horse name of Abba Jifar, which became the name of both the kingdom and the king.[236] Since its foundation until Abba Jifar II submitted to Menelik II in the early 1880s, Jimma was ruled by successive kings. The scope of trade and opportunities of profit-ability of the trade among the Gibe states was "widened" after the formation of the state of Jimma.[237] The well-known Jimma market of Hirmata and several other markets had attracted Indians, Arabs, Greeks, etc. who connected Jimma and its inhabitants to Arabia, Sudan, India, Europe, and other regions of Ethiopia."[238]

The Gibe states and their neighboring independent kingdoms of Kaffa and Janjero became a hub of trade and commerce which attracted traders from all regions of Ethiopia. Particularly the capital of Limmu-Enarya, Saqqa, "constituted the nexus" caravan routes and networked the southern kingdoms trade and commercial activities as well as traders from the north.[239] As Mohammed (1994) wrote several routes connected Saqqa to the Gibe states of Jimma, Gera, Gomma and Gumma which made it a busy trade center.

> Other caravan routes from Saqqa went to Janjero with its slaves and ivory and to Kullo, which, in addition to salves and ivory, provided Saqqa with mules and cotton. There were routes to Walayata, bringing precious skins, and to Gurage,

Hadiya, Gimira, Kambata, Meji, Konta, Tambaro, Gamo and Gardo. Another major route led to Wallaga, whence came most of the gold and where the Gibe merchants met with the Arab merchants from the Sennar. Slaves and ivory were brought to Saqqa along the route from Illubabor. There was still another caravan routes that went from Limmu-Ennarya across the Gibe river to Agabaja in Shewa, from whence it went to Wollo and beyond. This was the main route along which the rich coffee of the Gibe region went to Wollo, where it met the needs of the Muslim population in that land.[240].

The local industry of the Gibe states had produced such essential products as, "spears, knives, axes, hoes, sickles, and ploughshares from locally mined iron;"[241] "Industrial products of the Gibe region were exported in almost every direction and were highly sought after even among the Christians to the north."[242]

Like their Gibe counterparts, the Oromo states established in the present-day Wollega, adopted monarchical system of government. But they were established in the 1870s. Bakare established himself at Leqa, Nekemte, region. His son, Moroda Bakare, and grand-son, Kumsa Moroda (later Gebre Egziabher, the slave of God) would become influential figures of the western Oromo following incorporation of that region by Menelik II. Another influential figure, by his own right, was Jote Tullu, whose domain existed in Leqa Qellam, southwestern Wallaga. Like Moroda and Jimma Abba Jifar II, he also submitted peacefully to Menelik after being harassed by Gobana's mighty cavalry and army; and continued to play key role in the region and at the center after the region was incorporated. (See chapter 4.2.3. for conquest information).

3.2.12. The Dawuro

Before its incorporation into the Ethiopian state in 1891, Dawuro was an independent kingdom, which was ruled by its own kings. The title of a Dawuro king is *Kati*. The Dawuro kingdom and its kings were known for building walls and ramparts along their kingdom's borders which covered several hundred kilometers. Some parts of the Dawuro Walls or Halala Keela (Walls), are still intact and standing. Hailu Zeleke (2007) and Admasu Abebe (2014) research works had illuminated a light on these massive historical, cultural, and engineering heritages of the Dawuro people. Admasu noted that "this medieval historical contribution of the Dawuro society to Ethiopian civilization was either deliberately overlooked or unintentional ignored in the diversified nation-state structure."[243] Hailu, writing about the walls of Dawuro and Wolayta, also noted that the walls did "not yet get the attention of the researchers, wardens of cultural heritage, tourists and local elites. Thus, the walls are not yet incorporated into the identity of the peoples of the two zones in particular and of the Southern Nations and Nationalities in general."[244]

Citing the Ethiopian Ministry of Culture and Tourism report of 2010 Admasu wrote that the Dawuro "walls are three to seven rows whereas the length of a single row of the walls is estimated to be more than 200 km and the sum total of all the walls is about more than 1,000 km."[245] The engineering and construction details of Kati Halala Keela dry-walls was also fascinating.

> The dry stone walls are essentially separate but interlocking walls, tied at irregular intervals by longer rough or tie stones, and the middle is filled with small pieces of stones. The big and heavy basalt stones are laid at basement. Building up course by course, each new stones bridging the joint between the two lie beneath it. Most are pinned behind with smaller stones so that they stand solidly. No mortar or cement is used for bonding the dry stones walls. Appropriately dressed flat stones lie on the top and copestones stand upright along it. Small piece of stones are hammered down between the capstones, setting everything solidly in place. Carefully dressed, sharp and flat stones are placed towards the front sides on the upper part of the walls facing the enemy. Indeed, it is designed to easily crash the enemy who tries to break/

cross the walls. Hence, to make the walls strong enough and long lasting, the thickness and the height of the walls were well proportionate.[246]

The great Dawuro walls have seven strategically positioned main gates and they were manned by "soldiers day and night'; and they were used for the purpose of controlling "the flow of trade activities, the movements of people to and from the neighboring kingdoms." An illustration of one of the main gates, Daara Mis'a (Daara) gate, showed a check point at the entrance, a fortress in left and right side from within followed by a first and second watching towers.[247]

According to oral tradition and history of Dawuro people, the walls were believed to have been built by *Kati* Halala (c. 1757-1782) to "defend his territories from outside invaders," or the neighboring kingdoms; and the technique used to build the walls was part of ancient walls and fortifications building "techniques...developed by local inhabitants of southern Ethiopia."[248]

Dawuro was conquered by the armies of ras Wolde Giorgis in the early 1890s.

3.2.13. The Gamo-Gofa, Malo & Lower Omo Valley

Gamo people are organized in *deres*, which according to the Gamo native and scholar Assefa Chabo means a country; and there are about 40 d*eres* in Gamo region, each with its own *kawo*, who are "ceremonial" and "spiritual fathers of the *deres*[249]. Dena Freeman, the author of *Who are the Gamo? And who are the D'ache?* stated that "there are well over 40 communities, *deres*, in the Gamo highlands." Before sowing and harvesting begins sacrifices are first made by *kawo* for the whole *dere* and then by eka'*a*s (northern Gamo) or *sagga* (southern Gamo) for districts or sub-districts and then by households.[250]

Like many other southern societies, have a well-developed system of conflict resolution and "customary justice system "which comprised " *dere woga* (customary laws), *dubusha* (customary court/public assembly), and *derecima* (council of elders)."[251] The "dere woga is a body of norms and a set of moral values that provide a wider framework for social interactions and human conduct across Gamo communities." The *dubusha*, on the other hand, is "customary court' where conflicts are resolved" and "communal and topical issues are discussed and settled" at the community assembly.[252] The "*derecima* refers to a council of elders that plays an important role in settling different types of conflicts."[253] "The Gamo culture is bound intimately with the land" and they "have protected least 272 sacred groves" or sacred location which included *bossa* (burial grounds), *balee* (grasslands), *kashaa* (forest), *dubushaa* (outdoor assembly places), *boncho zummaa* (mountains), *boncho shafaa* (rivers), *kalloo* (pasture lands) and *bonchetida fultoo* (springs).[254]

The Malo, situated in Malo Kozo region of the Gomo Zone at SNNPR, in the former times "was an independent kingdom until the land was incorporated in the Ethiopian empire in ca 1890."[255] Some of the Malo clans who established Malo kingdom since eighteenth century were believed to have descended from Wolayta and Gamo.[256] In Malo kingdom the "whole territory was ruled by a single hereditary king or ritual leader called *kaate*."[257] Several kings ruled in Malo during the last dynasty and they were Madda, Tso'ona, Goba, Miza, Kantsa, Nika, Pola, and Kalsa.[258]

The Lower Omo Valley region, in which one of the oldest hominid fossils discovered, was designated as the World Heritage Site. Together with the Lower Awash Valley it is regarded as the cradle of humankind. The Omo Valley is also a home of indigenous people for which the Omo River served as "the lifeline." Some of the well-known indigenous Lower Omo Valley inhabitants included: Hamar, Dassanech, Arbori, Ari, Mursi, Dorze, Kwegu, Bana, Bodi, Bumi, Konsao, Kara, Suri, Tsemey, and the Turkana.

Table 1: Titles of rulers/leaders of southern kingdoms & territories

Region	Title of Ruler/ Leader	Region	Title of Ruler/ Leader
Aari	*Babbi*	Wolayta	*Kawo*
Afar	*Amoyta/Sultan*	Wollo	*Imam*
Kaffa	*Tato*	Gamo/Gofa	*Kawo*
Kambata	*Woma*	Malo	*Kaate*
Silte/Qebena	*Imam*	Hadiya	*Amano, Garad, Adil*
Gumuz	*Sheikh*		
Gibe States	*Moti/Abba*	Benishangul	*Sheikh*
Leqa/Qellem	*Moti*	Harar	*Emir*
Donga	*Hanagasa*	Dawro/Kulo	*Kati*
Sidaama	*Mootichcha*	Tembaro	*Woma*

Part II

Wars of Conquests: The Fate of Southern Peoples

"Hard times now ensued for all the states which made up the southern Ethiopian empire. A new phase in their history began."
– *With the Armies of Menelik II, in Ethiopia through Russian Eyes County in Transition 1896-1898*, Alexander Bulatovich *2000:217*

"...the Menelkan octopus spread its tentacles in all directions south, sucking up in the soft and crushing and "pacifying" the rebellious"
-Teshale Tibebu, *The Making of Modern Ethiopia 1896-1974*, 1995:39

Chapter 4

The Process of *Agar Maqnat*

'Wars of conquests' here pertains to the "two concepts" of the Amharic words of *agar maqnat and dar agar* as defined by Teshale (1995): *"Agar maqnat* refers to colonization, cultivation, (and Christianization) of the land defined as "empty," waiting to be made used of. *Dar agar* (frontier) pertains to the end horizon of the expansion, the boundary of colonization."[259] Although the lands subjected to Menelik's expansions were not 'empty,' they were targeted 'to be made used of' by the king of Shewa, and, later by the emperor of Ethiopia whether it was for their natural and human resources or otherwise.

Wars of conquests also pertains to the process of conquests and the method in which they were conducted. I believe *zemecha* is the one word which sums up all aspects of wars of conquest mentioned above. In it, it included a fighting force, weapons, commanders, logistics, orders of the *neguse* or *neguse negest,* targeted area for attack, the time (date, month, or season) of the planned attack, and sometimes the duration. In this regard, *Zemecha* was a well-organized expedition of conquests and/or raids by the armies of Menelik and his regional commanders. They were often carried out by Shewa armies in conjunction with the king's various commanders, and their affiliates and allies such as armies of the previously subdued regions and peasant armies of co-opted local leaders.

For instance, when Emperor Menelik decided to wage final assault on Wolayta kingdom, in addition to his own army, he mobilized the armies of *ras* Mikael Ali of Wollo, *fitawurari* Gebeyehu, *liqa mequas* (later *ras)* Abate Bowyalewu, *dejazmatch* Balcha Safo, *ras* Wolde Giorgis, and armies of Jimma Abba Jifar II. About three years later, when he ordered zemecha against the Kaffa kingdom, he deployed the armies of *dejamatch* Demessie of Wollega, *ras* Tessama of Illubabor, *ras* Wolde Girogis (appointed to be a governor of Kaffa), and armies of Abba Jifar II, Kullo and Konta. As Dr. Bahru wrote that the rulers of Jimma, Kullo and Konta served "as guides to break the intricate defense system of Kaffa." When *ras* Mekonnen, then a governor of Harar, was ordered to subdue Ben Shangul region, the armies of dejazmatch Demissie, *dejazmatch* Kuma Moroda of Leqa Neqemet and *dejazmatch* Jote Tulu of Leqa Qellam joined him.[260] It was common practiced for commanders and governors to mobilize previously conquered or surrendered peoples to fight against the communities who put up resistance. It was double Jeopardy for subjugated peoples. As it happened among the Oromo, Gurage, Hadiya, Silte, Kambaata, and southwestern regions, this often means people were compelled to fight against their own kinsmen or the neighboring peoples.

Once the area was conquered, garrison posts or *katamas (katama* came from Amharic word *keteme,* meaning settled) were established in strategic locations, often on hillsides, which served not only as command posts, but also as the points from which the process of permanent occupation and settlements would diffuse. Teshale described them as follows: "Here were *kattamas* of Christian warrior-settlers of predominantly Amhara extractions that were imposed on the local population."[261]

The Shewa armies "consciously selected as routes for their wars of conquest in southern Ethiopia the elevated zones along the escarpments of the Rift Valley and avoided as far as possible any undertakings in the sparsely populated lowlands."[262] Such strategy took into consideration the potential for the invading armies to plunder targeted communities for its upkeep and for procurement of logistics. Elevated and populated zones were also ideal choices to replenish resources and to establish garrison posts for permanent settlements. Menelik's *zemechas were* ended by incorporating various peoples and lands in the south, south-west, east, and north-east and south-central regions; and by establishing administrative centers in all corners. International borders were demarcated, and treaties signed with colonial powers of the time -British, France and Italy. Hence, modern Ethiopian state.

From the time it started when he was a ruler of Shewa kingdom (1865-1889) until it was successfully completed while he was a *neguse negest* of Ethiopia (1889-1913, Menelik's project of *hager maqnat* lasted nearly half a century.

During these times, his seats moved southwards from Ankobar to Entoto I, Entoto II, and finally to Addis Ababa (Finfine). He made the small kingdom of Shewa the center of the empire and the source of imperial powerhouse. He married[263] Woizero Bafana Wolde Michael, who had eight sons and daughters from her previous husbands and who was "twice his age," and who orchestrated a coup against him. He fathered Zewditu, Shewaraga and Asfa Wossen (died) out of wedlock with a "variety of women" until he finally married and settled down with Taytu Bitul; who also had been married to four husbands before she met him. He also transitioned from a young guy who had no experience when he assumed power in Shewa and who was "completely ignorant of the Shewan political and religious scene" to a pragmatic, shrewd, and skilled politician and matured statesman who garnered international respect. He showed openness for modern ideas, created the first cabinet, and, toward the end of his life, designated an heir for his throne.

Through all these changes and developments, the status of conquered lands and peoples *did not* improve. In fact, it moved from bad at the beginning of conquests to worse after his death. When it came to conquered regions, he left everything where it was. After his death, southerners found themselves at the worst place than they were during reign.

From the beginning, the methods and tactics used (discussed

in chapter 5) during the *agar maqnat* process were designed on causing maximum devastation on targeted communities to force quick and immediate surrender. They achieved their goal and ensured complete surrender. But that was only the beginning of the long and endless ordeal. Overnight southern peasants found their status changed from free people to *gabbars —peasant-serfs randomly allocated to* the soldiers, civilians, and clergy to provide lifetime covee labor in the fields and households of their new masters and also to pay tributes in kind and/ in cash. They became subjects of constant raids which ended in enslavement and plunder. In short most of the south and south-west became the American 'wild west' (see part III).

As I mentioned in the Introduction, the Ethiopian history was devoid of the true accounts of *agar maqnat* process and the realities of post-conquest South. Only the sanitized versions were reproduced and made to recycle. This book is by no means capable of presenting a comprehensive historical account of *agar maqnat*. Against the background of limited materials and resources, however, the author had invested a lot of time and energy to conduct an extensive archival research to gather relevant information and to present an evolution and progression of *agar maqnat* process. Hence an all-inclusive original work.

For the convenience of our discussion, I divided the conquest periods into four major phases: *Initial Phase of Conquest, The Second Phase of Conquest, The Third Phase of Conquest,* and *The Final Phase.* Attempts were made to group the conquered kingdoms and territories in the chronology of conquest/submission periods. However, the conquest periods/phases are not mutually exclusive. Rather, they were overlapping in most cases. It was not uncommon to conduct *zemechas* simultaneously in various parts of the country, often after the *kremet* or rainy season. For instance, in Gurageland, Arsi, Wolyata, Kaffa, Sidaama, Kambaata, Qabeena, Hadiya, etc. due to resistances and/or rebellions, the *zemechas* did not go smoothly as intended. In other words, several years had lapsed between the initial invasion and the eventual conquests and pacifications.

4.1. Initial Phase of Conquests 1866-1881

The Initial Phase of Conquest covered roughly fifteen years' period (1866-1881). This period covers Menelik's formative years as the *negus* of Shewa. After he escaped from captivity in Meqdela in June 1865, as an heir of Haile Melekot, he seized power and became Shewa *negus* in August 1865. The young Menelik aided with firearms and supporters of his late father, crushed power-contenders and consolidated his power. Then, he embarked on expanding the domains of the small but strong Shewa-Amhara kingdom.

Following the death of Tewodros in 1868, he saw an opportunity of northward expansion. But a powerful warlord, Wag Shum Gobaze of Lasta emerged and extended his influence into Begameder, Gojjam, parts of Tigre and parts Wollo, and crowned himself as *neguse negest*, Tekle Giorgis. He posed a threat to Menelik's otherwise independent Shewa. Menelik skillfully maneuvered Tekle Giorgis and escaped from potential attack. Another powerful warlord and contender from Tambein, Kassa Mercha, equipped in modern rifles and better trained fighters, defeated Tekle Giorgis and crowned himself as *neguse negest* Yohannes IV. He extended his rule over former domains of Tekle Giorgis. Fortunately for Menelik, Yohannes had enough troubles at his own home base and at coastal areas from foreign incursions to keep him busy. Menelik used this time for his own advantage. He intensified expansion in Shewa. More importantly, he extended his powerbase into the Wollo country and established his control as far as Meqdela. But Yohannes forced him to relinquish most of those areas in 1878. In that year, Menelik was also coerced to submit as a vassal to Yohannes. The latter took away most of Wollo from Menelik and gave it the man he forcefully converted and baptized, *ras* Mikael, the former Mohammed Ali Abba Bula. Barely three years later, following the Battle of Embobo, Yohannes again took away some of the Wollo areas and gave it to his son, Areaya Yohannes. Menelik learned that he had no chance of controlling the traditional power base of Amhara-Tigre in the north. After realization of the facts on ground, "Menelik therefore had to concentrate on the south." [264]

During the initial phase, Menelik and his armies conquered the neighboring Oromo territories in Shewa, parts of Wollo in the north, parts of Mecha country in the south-west, and parts of Gurage, the Silte, and parts of the Hadiya territories in south-central Ethiopia.

4.1.1. Shewa-Oromo

The first targets of Shewa's outward expansionary conquests were the Shewa Oromo territories. I would like to note here that territorial expansions and conflicts between Oromo and Amhara in Shewa did not begin by Menelik. It had been ongoing for centuries beginning from the time the two groups settled in the same neighborhood. One group raiding the other's territories, and vice versa was not a strange phenomenon. The power balance kept tipping toward the Shewa-Amhara since they began possessing modern firearms. Menelik's grandfather and the first *negus* of Shewa, Sahle Selassie, extended Shewa's domain southward. His "expansion was directed initially against the Tuulama Oromo and Argobba."[265] In the early years of 1840s William Cornwalis Harris, the British envoy in Ankobar, witnessed raids by Sahle Selassie's army against the neighboring Oromo groups and described it graphically, which is beyond this topic's discussion. In short, raids and counter raids were frequent during Sahle Selassie's reign. During the initial years of Haile Melekot, Menelik's father, the Abichu Oromo group "attempted to retake Tegulet and marched on Ankobar"[266] but they were repulsed.

McCann wrote that "the initial 'conquest' of Ada by expanding Shewa state must have taken place at some point in the late eighteenth century" but the relationship was "under no more than a loose tributary relationship" which "seems to have continued into the second quarter of the nineteenth century."[267]

The man who became an invaluable asset for Menelik from the onset of his early years in power to the next twenty years was Gobana Dache.[268] Gobana, a Shewa-Oromo, was a military tactician and experienced warrior best known and feared for his cavalry. He joined the young Menelik soon after he returned from captivity.

However, as Darkwah (1975) tells us he was not stranger to the Shewa royal house. Before he joined Menelik, he was at the service of the Shewa royal family, including Menelik's grand-father, Sahle Selassie, Menelik's father, Haile Melokot and even Bezabih.[269] For Gobana's life and legacy see chapter 17.

Using mainly Gobana, Menelik set in motion his initial expansion into the neighboring Shewa-Oromo clans, tribes, and territories. Campaigns against the Shewa- Oromo groups were still underway by late 1870s when Gobana was leading *zemechas* against "Gulele, Yaha, Wachacha, Bambici and Metta" in May 1878.[270] Menelik "through the influence of Gobena" scored sweeping victories over several Oromo groups of Meta, Gulele, Wachecha, Mount Ziquala, Lake Zway, Ambo and other Oromo.[271] Gobana devised smart political strategy of forming the Shewa-Oromo Confederation which played crucial role to win over several groups and which was also used as a prototype for further expansion into Mecha countries and beyond.

4.1.2. Wollo

After eliminating threat from his usually hostile neighbors next door, Menelik directed his army to other powerful Oromo groups in the north; the Wollo-Oromo.[272] Gobana played role in Wollo expansion, although Menelik's Shewa army were the main actors in Wollo front.

The Wollo expansion was met with drawbacks. In August 1870 Abba Wattaw (Yimam Ahmed) fortified himself in Meqdela. "While Menelik (was) dealing with this problem in Wello, other Oromo burns [ed] Angolala"[273] but attackers were dealt with. In January 1871 Menelik left Gobana "as his deputy in Shoa" and campaigned in Wollo; by February it was declared that "Wello and Shoa are united under one elfin" (elfgn); but "it will take six more years before unity is achieved."[274] In January 1873 Menelik "invaded Wello with large army" and in May he gave Bafana's (his wife's) daughter to Imam Mohammed Ali, the future *ras* Mikael of Wollo "as a peace offer."[275] In September 1876 he appointed Worqit as governor of Meqdela and Wole as a governor of Yejju and captured Wataw, who had been in rebellion. He also honored Mohammed Ali in Wore Illu and awarded "Amhara titles on Wello chiefs and named Mohammed Ali the head of Wello and Amhara provinces."[276] Here what Menelik did was contrary antithesis to Yohannes's active policy of proselytizing Wollo Moslems into Christianity. Yohannes's policy were unpopular in Wollo and Menelik was exploiting those weaknesses to his own benefit.[277] But Wollo will become restive once again when he Imam Mohammed rebels against Menelik and burnt Wore-Illu in May 1877. Menelik led expedition against Mohammed Ali but failed to capture him.[278] Mohammed Ali joined the more powerful Tigrean lord, Yohannes, who later ordered and presided over his conversion to Christianity.

Wollo was sandwiched between the powerful Tigrean armies of Yohannes IV in the north and Menelik's growing Shewa-Amhara power base in the south. Besides, past historical narratives of the Christianized Yejju Oromo's dominance in the imperial politics of the north had created a common understanding between Shewa and Tigre rulers to suppress Wollo. For the next several years Wollo was at the frontline of conquests, resistance, and rebellions. It became both a battlefield and a "buffer zone" between the Tigreans and Shewans tacit, but omnipresent and potent power struggle. As mentioned above Wollo's sour relationship with the Amhara-Tigrean powerbase had been simmering below the surface since Gonadarian and *zemene mesafint* times. It reached an intolerable level following Tewodros's ascension to power. By the time of his death,[279] regardless of his extreme measures against Wollo, it did not produce what he needed. His failed mission of converting Wollo from Islam to Christianity was, however, carried on with vigor by Yohannes and his fanatic edicts[280] of conversion or facing severe consequences. Such ultimatum, among other things, resulted in the conversion of Oromo-Muslim leaders, Imam Mohammed Ali, and Yimam Ahmed, who were Christianized and renamed as Mikael and Haile Mariam respectively. Those who refused to renounce their faith were "exiled" to such faraway regions as Sudan, Gurage, and Arsi. Yet "large number of inhabitants resisted" and continuation of repression increased the rebellion, which was "finally suppressed by the intervention of both Yohannes and Menelik, and after a campaign characterized by devastation and massacre."[281]

Just like Wollo's citizens who walked carefully between the two opposing faiths; Wollo rulers also calculated their decisions of submission or rebellion depending on the political and military strength of the dominant ruler as well as on the opportunities at hand. Mikael Ali first submitted to Menelik and then rebelled and submitted to Yohannes and served him faithfully until the emperor's death in March 1889. While Mikael and Worqit allied with Yohannes; Mestawat and her son, Haile Mariam, aka, Abba Watow, allied with Menelik.[282] Following Yohannes's death Mikael submitted to Menelik and was brought to Shewa orbit permanently. Their relationship was finally cemented by marriages of conveniences.[283] He emerged as a powerful political figure after his son, Eyasu, inherited Menelik's throne. He was crowned by his son, as the *negus* of Wollo.

Due to Wollo's vicinity and strategic location Menelik invested several years to fully bring Wollo into his dominion. "Between 1868 and 1876 he succeeded to bring Wollo under his control."[284] Soon after conditions on the ground changed dramatically. Yohannes confiscated large parts of Wollo from Menelik and dimmed his chances of expanding to the north. Menelik had to wait years until he became a *neguse negest* in 1889 to assert full control over Wollo and the rest of northern provinces.

4.1.3. Guragelands

Gurage was one of the earliest southern regions which faced Menelik's invasion in 1875. Some scholars stated that Gurage was "permanently conquered in 1875."[285] Contrary to such assertions, a conquest of Gurage lands was not completed until "the second half-of 1889."[286] Gurage resisted and fought back the invasions. Menelik personally led military expedition against Gurage three times in four years. The first expedition was in May-June 1875, the second was in October 1876, and the last one was in autumn of 1879.[287] The 1875 incident by Menelik armies was the "first raid upon the Chacha Gurage people." Menelik "raided again for slaves and cattle in October of the following year.²⁸⁸ When Menelik's army conducted campaign of conquest against Cheha Gurage in 1876, it "ended in embarrassing defeat"²⁸⁹ because "only one-third of Menelik's force returned to Shewa, the other being killed or captured and sold to slavery by the Muslims."²⁹⁰ "Alqa Zannab..died on that occasion...Many *mekwan-nent* also died...Many Amara people...sold...to Kamta [Kambata] and Welamo [Wolayta]...The negus also returned in sorrow and entered Lečče"²⁹¹ [Liche]. Rosenfeld (1976) called that expedition, "it is a failure."²⁹² Menelik, however, did not give up. He continued further conquest of the region.

The Silte, Ennaqor, and other Gurages, including the Qabeena and some Hadiya groups submitted without fight, although Qabeena would engage in rebellion and resistance a few years later. The leader of Ennaqor, imam Imerkiiso sent horses for tribute.²⁹³

It should be noted that northern Gurage, particularly Eymalel (Kistane) region, due to its proximity to Shewa, had been raided since Menelik's grand-father's time for booty and slaves. As a result, Eymalel fell under Shewa's influence for a longer time than the rest of Guragelands and hence adopted Christianity.²⁹⁴ Menelik appointed *dejazmach* Germame over the subdued parts of Gurage. According to Professor Greenfield, Germame refused the Gurage, and was given lands in Bishoftu and Adama, instead.²⁹⁵ The part of Gurage Germame was appointed, most likely, might be the northern Gurage region which submitted 'peacefully.'²⁹⁶ Their submission, according to Bahru Zewde, was due to their "relative geographical proximity, and their religious affinity with Christian Shewa" and also due to "the threat of the Oromo that surrounded them."²⁹⁷

Various western Gurage groups had formed a 'confederation' of tribal groups known as *Sebat-Bet*, the Seven Houses. "On the eve of Menelik's conquest of the region, however, "the *Sebat-Bet* Gurage had politically been disorganized" and it "did not imply political unity of the seven groups under one head of state with a political power along with state machinery."²⁹⁸

Menelik established a garrison in Soddo and appointed the first governor, Mashasha Seifu as a first governor, who was later replaced in 1866 by *dejazmach* Wolde Ashagre who "carried out further campaigns of conquest to the south from his residence at Waliso."[299] Western and some of the eastern Guragelands, however, continued their resistance well into the late nineteenth century. Chief Bacci Sabo (Shaabo) of Chaha and Umar Baksa of Qabeena led the rebellion,[300] which got steam under the leadership of Hassan Enjamo who operated in Gurage-Hadiya lands. The resistance "movement swept across a large part of western Gurage" and it "had elements of a Hadiya-Gurage coalition" which was "finally crushed" by the armies of *ras* Gobana[301] (see 4.2.4 below).

In general, resistances were more pronounced in *Sebat Bet* Guragelands and in Qabeena region. The *Chaha* resistance in western Gurage had persisted for several years. They "were subjugated only after some fierce fighting"[302] for the last time by Habte Giorgis. "*Fitaurai (fitawurari)* Habta Giyorgis, under orders from Menilek, finally put down the rebellious Gurage where Ras Gobana had failed in several previous attempts."[303] *Chaha* was eventually defeated and "subdued after fierce engagement."[304] Habte Giorgis was rewarded mightily. The *Chaha* people not only lost the battle but also, they lost "over two-thirds of the most fertile land" of *Chaha Woudema* which was "decreed private property of *Fitaurai*" as gift for his victory[305]. William Shack described the reaction of Gurage people and the extent of "the annexation of Chaha woudema" as follows:

> This vast expanse of land that Gurage sometimes call the 'Plains of Atat,' extends from the Ghibie River to the Megacha-Gotam tributaries on the east, and northwards to the Uabi River basin. It has been apportioned entirely out of Chaha lands since the defeat of the *sabat bet* in 1889, and its annexation is bitterly remembered by the Chaha. From Government's point of view this was presumably the most favorable section of Gurageland. Its large flat plains were more suitable for plough cultivation, which would be employed by

Ethiopian military colonies, than the more mountainous terrain elsewhere; it afforded direct access to Addis Ababa. Its annexation was a penalty levied directly against the Chaha for leading the *sabat bet* to resist Government aggression. But to the Gurage, political subjugation and tribute and land apportionment are separate and distinct issues' the latter creates a deficiency in the amount of available land that becomes more pronounced with each generation. Annexation of land, Gurage argue, should not be made a penalty of defeat in warfare. Hence, in consequence of these issues, Chaha woudema is sparsely settled; it contrasts sharply with the densely populated areas elsewhere in Gurageland.[306]

Habte Giorgis, was also "appointed Governor of Gurageland;" in addition to his other positions. In his long-term strategy of "preventing uprisings of Gurage," he had "Shoan military colonies planted in each tribe of the *sabat bet;*" and enforced subjugation. After his death, Haile Selassie gave the *Chaha Woudema* land to his own son, Crown Prince Asfa Wossen Haile Selassie;[307] the Chaha land loss became permanent.

4.1.4. Gibe States

The Gibe states region (Jimma, Gomma, Gera, Gumma, Limmu-Enarya,).and the western Oromo kingdoms in Wollega were penetrated by Gojjam's Tekle Haymanot prior to Menelik. But the penetration was based mainly on plunder and on mild tributary relationship. Menelik set his eyes on those regions mainly in pursuit of rich natural resources and control of well-established trade centers. Such interest in the region, mainly economic, became a catalyst for rivalry and armed conflict between Gojjam and Shewa rulers. By 1881 Menelik controlled most of the former Gibe states. Soon a major conflict would erupt between the two regional rivals- Gojjam's Tekle Haymanot and Shewa's Menelik- which eventually propelled the Shewa ruler as a sole dominant figure in the region.

4.2. Second Phase of Conquests 1882-1888

What I called the second phase of conquests covered a period of six years (1882-1888). During this short period, Menelik scored great victories which included his decisive victory over *neguse* Tekle Haymanot of Gojjam. This had removed his potential rival and put him as a sole actor in the south and south-west. Utilizing *ras* Gobana's skillful combination of diplomacy and destructive war tactics, he 'peacefully' subdued Leqa-Nekement and Leqa-Qellam Oromo rulers in Wollega and Aba Jifar II in Jimma. He broke down the Arsi-Ittu Oromo stiff resistances and conquered them. He then marched to Harar and defeated Emir Abdullahi's weak army at the Battle of Chelenqo. His Harar victory enabled him to control the trade route to the sea which, in turn, enabled him to direct all trades through Shewa and revitalized the sagging economy. He consolidated his hold on the former Gibe states. He subdued various Hadiya groups and also completed conquests of the Chaha-Gurage and Qabeena; who put up stiff resistances. Conquests against some of these lands had begun during the initial phase and, due to resistances and rebellions, they lingered on. Another important achievement of this period was establishment of a brand-new capital, Addis Ababa (formerly Finfine), further south of Shewa's traditional bases of Ankobar, Liche, & Entoto.

It was one of the most productive periods in which Menelik's power was elevated and his scope of wealth enlarged greatly. As a result, he emerged as the most powerful *negus*, who positioned himself as a clear threat to the *neguse neg*est to the north..

After the conquest of Harar (1877), there was no major *zeme-cha* by Menelik for about three years, although his generals continued skirmishes and fighting elsewhere in the newly conquered territories. Three probable factors may be responsible for the lull. The first probable reason may be related to Menelik's deteriorating relationship with Emperor Yohannes. The latter was aware that Menelik had been making back door deals with Italians and *negus* Takle Haymanot, building armies and became nominal vassal by not paying his tributary dues regularly. But he was preoccupied in attempting to curb Italian incursions in the north and dervish attacks in western Ethiopia. Secondly, the armies of Menelik were stretched out in his various conquest ventures. He appeared to have been consolidating them to defend Shewa should Yohannes marched south to punish him. By 1888 Yohannes devastated Gojjam and intended to conduct a similar campaign against Menelik. But it was aborted due to the more urgent situation caused by Mahdists. Thirdly, previously conquered regions from Gurage to Arsi to Bale had continued to pose threats by putting up resistance and revolts. He mostly likely wanted to end such threats during the interim period. By the end of the period he crushed resistances and rebellions in previously conquered regions.

4.2.1. Gojjam

The turning point for Menelik's unrestrained conquest endeavors began after his decisive victory over Gojjam's *ras* Adal Tessema, crowned as *negus* Tekle Haymanot by Emperor Yohannes IV in January 1881. Menelik's Oromo general, Gobana, who was in the mission of plunder in the south-west clashed with another Oromo general, Darso, who was leading the army of Gojjam on a similar mission of plunder in the south-west. In the face of Gobana's large cavalry and better equipped army, Darso was forced to hand over the booty and retreated. "Humiliated Tekle Haymanot" sent a reinforcement army led by his son, Bezabih, but he too had to retreat from Gobana's army.[308] Both Menelik and Tekle Haymanot claimed the region was theirs. As a matter of fact, it belonged to neither of them at the time.

Yohannes bestowed the title of king of Kaffa and Gojjam on Tekle Haymanot hoping to create a wider area of influence for Gojjam's ruler as a counterbalance to Menelik's growing influence. Zewude Gebre-Sellassie wrote that Menelik was unhappy about Yohannes' intention and this was what led Menelik organize Gobana's expedition to the region in the first place - to create a "pretext for conflict" with Gojjam's ruler.[309] Just like Yohannes gave nominal title of 'king of Kaffa' to Tekle Haymanot, Menelik also gave nominal title to Gobana as a king of Kaffa. Neither Tekle Haymanot not Gobana (Menelik) ruled Kaffa, which remained an independent kingdom for more than fifteen years after the Battle of Embobo. (see chapter 4.4.).

If we were to believe Tekle Tsadik Mekuria's version of the story, Tekle Haymanot, sent an infuriating verbal message to Menelik in which the former portrayed the Shewa *negus* as a coward who would come up with excuses to avoid war. He reportedly did not want to send a letter because he reasoned that Menelik would read and shred it; and then pretend that he had not received any. Therefore, he chose to send a verbal message and instructed his messengers to tell Menelik in front of his courtiers and attendants such that he would be ashamed to retreat from a call for a battle. Offended by Tekle Haymanot's arrogance and lacking a way out of a sticky situation, Menelik not only agreed to fight but also declared: "Gojameis have no territory at all beyond Abay River."[310] My translation.

Thus, the stage for a battle was set. Both parties mobilized their armies. "The Gojjam army [was] larger than the Shoan, but less well armed."[311] Gobana achieved great diplomatic success in convincing Moroda of Neqemt to "remain neutral"[312] and not to aide Gojjamies. The Shewa army also got a boost from a Wollo Oromo leader, who joined the Shewa king with her own and her son's[313] armies. More importantly, Menelik joined the formidable Gobana's Oromo armies at Nono. Gojjam and Shewa armies converged in Wollega country and fought a bloody war at Embobo[314] on June 5, 1882. Gojjam's army was routed. On his diary of January 11, 1898, Bulatovich wrote that *ras* Wolde Giorgis and other military men (participants of Embobo battle) "remembered…about the battle of Embobo" in which they reminisced how "Ras Gobana…just arrived in time, attacked the Gojjam from behind and the enemy turned in flight" and saved the Shewa army from defeat.[315]. An Ethiopian biographer of Menelik, Paulos Gnogno, wrote that the Shewa army was rescued from defeat because of the Mestawot's (Wollo Oromo leader) army and cavalry which Menelik deployed at a decisive moment and it helped him to score decisive victory over Gojjam.[316] Tekle Haymanot was wounded, captured, and taken to Shewa as a prisoner of war together with his followers.[317]

Menelik's victory euphoria was somehow overshadowed by Yohannes, who was infuriated because his unruly vassals disregarded his order to desist from fighting and to wait for his mediation. Yohannes ordered Menelik to hand over Gojjamie prisoners and all captured weapons. Menelik complied and surrendered firearms together with his prominent prisoner, *negus* Tekle Haymanot. Yohannes reinstated the latter and re-established the status quo.

Nevertheless, the Battle of Embobo accomplished two things. First, Gojjam never recovered from that humbling and humiliating moment. Takle Haymanot and successive Gojjamie rulers had to accept grudgingly Shewa's hitherto dominance henceforth. Secondly, the Embobo victory opened the doors for Shewa's conquests wider than ever before. After Embobo, in the words of Teshale (1995), "... the Menelikan octopus spread its tentacles in all directions south, sucking up in the soft and crushing and "pacifying" the rebellious."[318] Gobana was let loose coercing the rulers of south-west regions into peaceful submission or facing the wrath of his destructive force.

4.2.2. Kingdom of Jimma

The rich kingdom of Jimma was his next target. Abba Jifar II[319] came to power in 1878, after his father, Abba Gommol, died. He was only seventeen years old.[320] Abba Jifar II seized power in Jimma at a time when the Gojjam and Shewa-Amhara rulers were determined to assert their powers over the neighboring lands and peoples. Both rulers were competing to control the south-west. Both deployed powerful Oromo generals- Gobana and Darso – to coerce into submission the Oromo kingdoms, which were richer and wealthy but weaker militarily.

> Shortly after Abba Jifar became king, Gojami forces came
> to the region...and caused great deal of destruction in the

neighboring areas..By 1882 the rival Showan forcers of Menelik II, under the command of Ras Gobana, had come to this area.[321]

Gobana's forces were "armed with rifles... Abba Jifar, realizing his predicament, agreed to pay tribute to Menelik and to aid his forces in return for Jimma's continued internal autonomy." Abba Jifar II, submitted peacefully after being coerced by Gobana, which established Menelik's rule over Jimma. Although the kingdom of Jimma remained under the influence of Gojjam and Shewa for several years, several sources indicated that Abba Jifar II officially submitted in 1884 (Marcus, 1995, Lewis, 1965). Due to its rich trade and natural resources Menelik made Jimma *maed bet*. Then Abba Jifar became a good client, who "regularly paid tributes, generally managed to escape Menelik's anger and enthusiastically aided Menelik in his wars" against other southern polities which refused to submit peacefully such as Kullo, Wolayta and Kaffa.[322]

4.2.3. Kingdoms of Wollega

Rulers of Wollega, Moroda Bakare of Leqa, and Jote Tullu of Qellam, were persuaded by Gobana to submit peacefully in exchange for internal autonomy. Gobana also convinced Moroda to "remain neutral" during the battle of Embobo. Moroda not only remained neutral during Shewa-Gojjam battle; but also, he rallied "several Oromo rulers of the region," for which he was "recognized as a sole ruler of his territory"[323] Following his submission, Gobana reportedly arranged a meeting between Moroda and Menelik where the former asked for a private meeting and was granted. He took a "small bag of gold" and asked Menelik if he wanted Wollega's gold go directly to him or to others, in this case to Gobana. The choice was obvious. Gobana was sidelined from becoming a middleman. Menelik declared, "Moroda's land should belong directly to *maed bet*, with no one in between."[324]

Gobana's influence and presence, however, persisted. He

helped Moroda to expand his territory by conquering the Nole Kabba- Nejjor, Arjo and Sibu regions.[325] Upon the death of Moroda, his son, Kumsa, replaced him and was Christianized as *Gebre Egziabher*, the slave of God. Gebre Egziabher continued paying tributes to the center. The tribute, however, kept increasing from time to time until it became a burden on him and his people.

> The tribute was gradually raised. It amounted to 300 weket in 1903 and was pushed to 1,000 by 1905. At the same time, a certain amount of honey and ivory was sent to Addis Ababa yearly; 1,000 thalers 'in lieu of honey' was sent in 1905. The honey tribute was raised to 600 large earth ware pots (*gundo*) by 1906 and increased to 1,000 by 1925. The tribute was often accompanied by 'gifts' (*meteyaya*) ranging from 20 weket in 1903 to 100 in 1906. Furthermore, after Gebre Igziabiher had been charged with the collection of tribute from the 'Arab country' (Bela Shangul) in 1903, he was taxed both in gold (600) *weket* and ivory (100 tusks) on this last territory.[326]

In addition, starting in the 1900, the "northern soldiers" were settled in Gebre Egziabher's domains. Thus "he was asked to pay 10,000 thelars for their provisions... which...was later raised to 23.000 thalers."[327] The sudden increase was the work of *ras* Tessema Nadew "starting in 1910...the newly-appointed regent, ras Tessema, added to the existing tribute a sum of 13,000 thalers as a provision of the northern troops (*gondere*) stationed in the region, the burden of these imposition on Gebre Igziabher's financial resources appears to have been heavy indeed."[328]

Triulzi's research showed that Gebre Egziabher kept sending letters to Menelik, and, after his death, to Eyasu, and then to Teferi Mekonnen. He continued "lamenting" about increased taxes and tributes and their adverse consequences on his people. In his November 1917 letter to Teferi Mekonnen "he complained that his own people were leaving his country 'because the tribute was too much and the country [had] turned into a desert.'[329]

4.2.4. Qabeena

The Hadiya region fell under the target of Shewa forces south-ward expansion since they began establishing themselves in northern Gurage in 1875. As the neighbors of Gurage, the Qabeena "were the first Hadiyya group to be affected by the military expansion."[330] The Qabeena relationship with Menelik's army had passed through two distinct phases. The first phase involved peaceful submission and agreement to pay tributes. The second involved revolt and resistance. The Qabeena leader, Umar Baksa,[331] submitted and campaigned alongside Menelik's army during the 1876 campaign Chaha, Muher, Yacharat and Ennamor; and paid tribute in 1877.[332] Influenced with internal and external factors, Qabeena's politics changed its course. New leaders adopted new policies of shifting away their allegiance to Menelik and declaring *jihad* against what they regarded as Christian armies. Around 1880 Umar Baksa was replaced by Hassan Enjamo,[333] charismatic leader who rallied followers around religious line and steered Qabeena into rebellion and resistance. Internal condition involved Qabeena's rejection to Umar Baksa's new leadership style. He "become proud and arrogant" to his people and "no longer wanted to speak to them face to face" and hence "he was eventually expelled"[334] The Wollo Moslem refugees and the news of the success of Mahdists in Sudan can be viewed as external conditions which influenced Qabeena leaders.

In June 1886 Qebeena waged a surprise attack at "garrison in the area of Waliso and killed *qegnazmatch* Wube Argano, amongst others" which led Menelik to dispatch *dejazmatch* Wolde, *dejazmatch* Germame and *balambaras* Mekonnen to the region.[335]

Hassan Enjamo rallied his people but others under religious ban-ner; and emerged as a powerful resistance leader against Menelik's incursions and occupation in the region. Umar Baksa also joined him in the resistance. As Shack (1966) noted Chief Bacci Sabo [Shaabo] of Chaha and Umar Baksa of Qabena were leaders of the rebellion. Umar had declared Qabena independent and ruled it as such.[336] Qabeena's revolt swept the region under the leadership of Hassan Enjamo, who "succeeded in bringing the territory from Amayya to East-Gurage and the major trade routes from south-western Ethiopia to Shewa under his control."[337] His "followers ravaged the areas west of the Gibe River" which forced *dejazmatch* Walde to "retreat to a fortified *katama*."[338] Bahru described it as follows:

> The western Gurage...were subjugated only after some fierce fighting. The subsequent rise of a Muslim revivalist movement led by Hassan Enjamo of Qabena, to the north-east of the Gibe river, posed a serious challenge to Shewan authority on the eastern side of the Gibe river. Inspired by Muslim refugees from Wallo, and with possible connections even with Mahdist Sudan, the movement swept across a large part of western Gurage and was attended by a fast rate of Islamization. [339]

The connection of the Qabenna with "with Mahdist Sudan" would not be in terms of getting fighters or arms. Together with the stories of Wollo Muslim's persecution, a plausible connection was what "they heard of the military successes of the Mahdists in Sudan and this propaganda obviously inspired them to try to break the power"[340] of the occupation. "In July 1888, the Qabeena defeated an Amharic (Amhara) army, killed its commander *dejazmatch* Garmame and most of the soldiers in the battle and carried of 400 rifles;" and "with this victory Hassan Enjamo stood at the pinnacle of his success."[341] The Qabeena situation concerned *negus* Menelik. At this time, he had a lot of worrisome conditions at his hands. His relationship with Emperor Yohannes was worsened especially after the latter discovered his two vassals -Gojjam's Tekle Haymanot and Menelik - plot against him. Menelik was expecting that Yohannes's devastating plunder like's like that of Gojjam. He was preparing to defend Shewa. And yet, "Menelik no longer wanted to underestimate

the fighting force of the Qabeena and summoned *ras* Gobana Dači…
to suppress the insurrection at the region of upper Gibe."[342]

One of the least known aspects of Hassan Enjamo's leadership
was his foresight to create a united front against the northern armies
after his realization that no single southern nation or leader can stop
Menelik's expansion. With this insight, he took initiative to invite
southern kingdoms and territories to convene and form military alliances. He reportedly sent invitation to *kawo* Tonna Gaga of Wolayta,
moti Abba Jifar II of Jimma, *tato* Gaki Sherecho of Kaffa, *woma* Dilbato
Degoye of Kambata, leader of Masqan Imam Duno, leader of Silte
Sedisso, leader of Chiron Lalelo, leader of Wulbarag Shafi Lafebo,
leader of Azarnet Gonfamo, leader of Enaqor Ali, leader of Hadiya
Leemo Arsie, leader of Shashogo Abagada Alamo, and leader Halaba
Imam Nunede.[343] Leaders of Wolayta, Kaffa and Jimma reportedly
declined to accept the invitation and stated they can fight by their
own. The rest responded positively. The leaders or their representatives
convened together. Hassan Enjamo laid out Menelik's strategy and the
need to form a united front. He also reportedly asked them to convert
to Islam, which hindered most of them from joining him. Only a few
accepted it.[344] So his grand plan was not materialized.

According to Bahru (1991) "Hassan Enjamo's force, which had
elements of a Hadiya-Gurage coalition, inflicted a number of defeats
on the Shawan forces, until Menelik's general, Ras Gobana, took
the field in 1888 and finally crushed the movement."[345] Although
Gobana was ordered and he had begun mobilizing his forces against
Qabeena; there were several reasons why he was not in hurry and
unenthusiastic about it. Citing Cerulli (1922) Braukamper (2012)
wrote that Gobana was previously defeated "four times" by the forces
of Hassan Enjamo which was composed of "Hadiya, Gurage and
Oromo fighters."[346] By this time Gobana was getting older and was
in his mid-sixties. When Gobana was summoned for the Qabeena
campaign, he was in the western front where he successfully fought
against Mahdist incursions in the Wollega front and defeated them
(see chapter 17). Going from one battlefront to the other, especially
to the place he had experienced fierce resistance previously may not

be motivating. "Moreover, Gobana obviously lacked the motivation to embark on a campaign to rescue his adversary Wolde Ashagari (Ashagre) and therefore carried out this order with decided tardiness."[347] Yet when he finally engaged the Qabeena forces and he dealt them a final blow.

"In the first half of 1889, the Šawan commander-in-chief finally advanced with his strong forces against the Qabeena, defeated the djihad fighters who had been stimulated to undertake a desperate resistance, and subjugated the entire territory...Umar Baksa was taken prisoner and Hassan Enjamo fled."[348] The final battle took place at Jabdu, near Waliso" and "one of the sons or close relatives of ras Gobana fell (died) in this battle."[349] Hassan Enjamo was found nowhere. Whereabouts of Hassan Enjamo was known and Abba Jifar of Jimma was suspected of giving sanctuary and he was taken to Ankobar prison. But the charge was "unfounded", and Abba Jifar returned to Jimma.[350]

On June 30, 2018 I was shopping books in Addis Ababa at one of the Churchill Godana bookstores. I initiated conversation with the person in the store who, I found out later, was the owner of the bookstore. I mentioned to him that I am in the process of writing a book on Ethiopian history of mid nineteenth century and early twentieth century which emphasizes on Southern Ethiopian peoples. Several minutes into our conversation, he shared me important information about Hassan Enjamo. According to my informant, "Hassan Enjamo did not die in battle...one of Gobana's son was killed in the battle. He died of malaria while he was heading to Jimma. Hassan Enjamo was buried in Sebba, Qabeena which is near to my house. He was buried at Zenabanner, Seba...Hassan Enjamo's daughter Emha Ebrar died during my lifetime. Emha Ebrar's mother, woizero Ginni was a native of Chaha, Gurage."[351]

4.2.5. Arsi -Ittu

Arsi in the early 1880s became a target of plunder and occupation. While Gobana and his famed cavalry were busy subduing vast territories in the southwest and western regions; Menelik's core Shewa-Amhara forces were marshalling incursions into Arsi. In the expedition of the 1880 the "army spent the rainy season in Dabba-Gojjo and returned to their country with a huge booty of cattle."[352] Harold Marcus described it as follows: "In 1880-1881 Menelik sent a large expedition into animal-rich Arsi, which returned to Shewa reportedly with one hundred thousand heads of cattle."[353] The goal of Menelik's *zemecha,* including the one he led "in person" in January 1882, "was looting rather than permanent occupation."[354] More expeditions were launched in 1883 and 1884. Unlike the previous expeditions which were aimed on "only plundering raids, the third expedition's objective was permanent occupation."[355] Expeditions also targeted Chercher territory known for its rich agricultural resources and inhabited mainly by Ittuu-Oromo.[356] Strong resistance put up by Arsi and Ittuu groups not only posed challenges to Shewa arm, but also to the life of *negus* Menelik. For instance, during the December 1883 battle Menelik "barely managed to escape with his life."[357]

Zewude Gebre-Selassie, in his book, *Yohannes IV of Ethiopia: A Political Biography* wrote: "By 1885-6 Menelik was completing the long and bloody conquest of Arussi…He made two new appointments for the Arussi and the eastern lowlands. The command of the Ittu (often known as Tchertcher) went to *dejazmatch* Wolde Gabriel Abba Saitan and that of Arussi (Arssi) to Menelik's uncle, Ras Darge."[358] Menelik finally launched what, Abbas Gnamo called "The Extermination Phase"[359] in 1886. He "decided first to conquer Arssi Oromo. They were well organized and able to put an army larger than the Shoans' into the field."[360]

Marcus wrote:

> in June and May [Menelik] had accompanied him {Darge} to his new domains…. During the rainy, season, when communications between Arussi and Shewa were difficult, the Galla rebelled again. The Shoans sustained some bloody defeats before Darge was able to break the back of the organized tactics; they abandoned the land, moved into sanctuary

in the far south, and followed a scorched-earth policy. The resulting lack of food played havoc with Darge's army. With his forces thus weakened, the ras called on Menelik for reinforcements to end the struggle against the rebels, who had sworn an oath to die rather than surrender.[361]

They put up fierce resistance. They "made a surprise attack on Dejazmatch Wolde's camp and killed 2,000 men. As a result, Menelik's devastation of the area increased...there was mass looting as far as the Wabi River."[362] The Arsi were finally defeated mainly due to the overwhelming firepower and due to its "internal divisions."[363] Regardless of their defeat and imposition of *gabbar* system, Arsi "remained unreconciled to the rule of northerners and resisted assimilation." The resistance was fueled not the least because of the religious element. The followers of Sheikh Hussein declared 'jihad.'[364] Furthermore, they were able to draw support for fighting from Muslim groups as far as Guragelands. Chief Bacci Sabo [Shabo) of Chaha and Umar Baksa of Qabena besides rebelling against Menelik, they also sent their followers to fight in Arsi. In Shack's words, "Gurage were allies of Arussi against Shoan forces led by Ras Darge."[365]

> The Arsi resistance north of the Wabi Shaballe was organized primarily by six war commanders: Lenjiso Diiga from Kolooba clan in Arba-Gugu, Koffe Shamoo (Weege) in the Lake Zway territory, Oagatoo Biinno (Adaree) in the Muneessa territory, Intalilli Soole (Ataaba) in Robee/ Diida'a, Goobana Robee (Heebano) in Gada and Gatiso Balango (Haballo) between the Kambata Mountains and the Sidaaama aeas of residence."[366]

Pankhurst (1968) noted that one of the first steps taken in Arsi after the conquest was "extensive appropriation of land." Large estates were allocated to the emperor. Lands of those who died without heir and the lands belonged to the "rebels" were also expropriated.[367]

Not long afterwards, Menelik anxious to consolidate his rule, allocated malkannas, or administrative officers, to the province, and assigned to each of them a specific number of *gabbars* who were obliged to give them service and provisions. Later, when the fertility of the areas became known, other settlers arrived from various area of the Amhara, Galla, and Gurage country. Many of these immigrants after paying tribute to the *malkanna* for two years were recognized to have acquired their land as rist, or inheritable property. Lands were allocated on the basis of *gashas*.... merely measured by eye, *ayn gamad...* Three-quarter of the land, according to Brotto, was in one way or another allocated to Government employees, soldiers, nobles and ecclesiastics and one-quarter to the balabbats. ...Many of the Amhara recipients, however, preferred to sell their land to the local Gallas, insisting at the same time on gabbar service ...the guarantee of tribute....An ordinary soldier, depending on the length of the service, was allowed two or three gashas.[368]

The conquest of Arsi, paticulary Ittu (Chercher region) opened up the door for Shewa's march to the east.

4.2.6. Harar

Harar became Menelik's next target after Arsi. But the Harar occupation plan was in the making for a long time. Menelik had been preparing to take over Harar since Egypt ended its ten-year colonial occupation and evacuated in 1885. Part of his preparation involved gathering actionable intelligence. For this purpose, he sent spies into the walled city.

One of such spies was Atsme Giorgis who, "began his career by carrying official correspondence between Menelik II and his governors." So, he was someone already trusted with high level confidential official business. "The emperor also ordered him to conduct a survey of the political-military situation in Harar in preparation for a military campaign against that town. Disguised as a Moslem merchant, Atsme lived in Harar for three months compiling his report for Menelik II.[369]

Emir Abdullahi, who came to power after Egyptian evacuation, was not considered a strong leader. His military was already weakened during the previous incursion. Harar was attacked after Egypt's evacuation by the order of Emperor Yohannes.[370] A Shewan army led by Wolde Gabriel was, however, "cut into pieces by Emir Abdullahi's...troops"[371] and dispersed. After that Wolde Gabriel became less favorite in the king's circle."[372]

Menelik was well prepared for the final assault. He reportedly marched against the Emir with "40,000 cavalry and foot soldiers."[373] Others estimated the Menelik's army between 9,000 and 10,000 riflemen; and the Emir's forces at 3,000."[374] On Christmas day the Emir attacked the Shoan army. He assumed that Menelik and his army would be distracted with Christian holiday celebrations. But he found out quickly that his calculations were quite wrong when he realized that his enemies were well prepared. Harar army was defeated at the Battle of Chelenqo and the Shewa army "captured 2 cannon and some 600 good rifles." The war was a costly one, particularly for the Hararis. "A bloody battle took place in Tyalanka (Chelenqo) in which 11,000 Hararis and Gallas (Oromos) were killed. Abdullahi, who had taken refuges behind the city walls, was captured and brought back in chains to Entoto."[375] Menelik entered Harar and was rewarded with great booty.

On entering the city of Harar he is said to have seized a further 4 Krupp cannon, 3,000 shells and 600,000 cartridges. British sources, however, put the Emir's force at only 1,200 muskets, adding that though this ruler had endeavored to make Ramingotns they were very weak and prone to burst. The booty, however, was undoubtedly considerable: Rimbaud states that Menelik found 3,000,000 cartridges in the city; he adds that the Ethiopian ruler was hence so well supplied that he was no longer willing to purchase ammunition, a fact which the poet knew to his cost as he was then engaged in supplying Menelik in big consignment including 8,000 Ramingtons. The French man subsequently reported that Menelik on his triumphal return to Entoto had been followed by two Krupp cannon each carried by twenty men, and that "large quantities" of arms and ammunition had been born on a "long stream" of carts.[376]

Unlike the Oromo campaigns where a "great quantities of cattle and movables were taken;" Zewde Gebre-Sellassie says "there was no pillage" in Harar because Menelik wanted to gain confidence both from Hariri trading communities as well as the Europeans.[377] Instead of pillage, he imposed "financial levy of 7,000 thalers"[378] on the city. The conquest of Harar gave him great advantage over his adversaries, including Yohannes IV. It enabled him, among other things, to control a more secure trade route from Shewa to the sea. In the ensuing years, Menelik directed all trade activities from south, southwest, and central Ethiopia to go to Shewa and then to Harar. Pankhurst wrote that occupation of Harar:

> facilitated his communication with the coast which were now under secure control from Shoa; the route furthermore was reduced from 50 or 60 days to only about 35 and passed through more peaceful country than that inhabited by the Dankails who had sometimes interfered with communication by way of Assab. The extension of Ethiopian rule in the direction the French Somali Protectorate had the additional effect of provoking the Italians to redouble their commercial activity in the fear that trade would otherwise be dominated by the French...[379]

Although building churches was widespread practice immediately after conquests, in Harar it had special significance. After Menelik finished his preparation to take over Harar, he sent a letter to Emir Abdullahi to peacefully submit and to pay annual taxes. Abdullahi responded that he "know no master." Menelik again sent an order for his submission. The response he got was one of clear defiance which undoubtedly led Menelik to respond in kind. Emir Abdullahi "sent Menelik a Muslim dress, turban and prayer carpet with the message, 'when you are a Moslem, I will consider you my master.' Menelik replied, 'I will come to Harar and replace the Mosque by a Christian Church —Await me.'[380]

Menelik kept his word and easily defeated the weak Emir's army, appointed his cousin, the young[381] *Balambaras* Mekonnen as a governor and promoted him to *dejazmach*. Menelik "ordered a number of detachments and reinforcements from his own army and other commands to remain in Harar with now *dejazmach* Mekonnen.[382] Mekonnen expanded his domain far away from the walls of the city and incorporated the Oromo and Somali lands and territories. As Mosely put it: "Mekonnen brought with him from Shoa an entourage of Shoans and Amaharas who took over the key positions in the city and the province...Ras Makenon built a Coptic Church for himself and his Christian followers in Harar."[383] He confiscated lands and distributed them for soldiers and *naftegna*. In *Contemporary Ethiopia*, Talbot (1952) compared land ownership before and after the conquest; and wrote that during Turkish-Egyptian occupation the land in Harar and its vicinities was "left in the hands of the inhabitants."

> During the Turkish occupation of the province of Harar, the Harar plateau, including the districts of Harar, Garamulate, Wabarra, Jijjiga and Gursum, were measured in units called 'shibata,' the size of which varied from district to district. The land was left in the hands of the inhabitants, mostly Gallas. When His Highness, Ras Makonnen...took over the administration of there, land was required for settling his men and for other administrative purposes. A considerable amount of ...land was utilized for these purposes, and he, in addition, sequestered a portion from a landed gentry of each district. These persons were permitted to retain one-quarter

of their land and the remaining three-quarters were distributed among the soldiers.[384]

Having appointed his cousin Mekonnen over Harar; and his uncle Darge over Arsi; and Wolde Gabriel, another Shewan, over Bale; Menelik returned to his capital triumphantly in early 1887. During this period, Menelik moved his capital from Ankobar to Entoto I and then Entoto II. By 1886/87 Addis Ababa became his capital. It was an ideal location for his southwardly expanding domains. More importantly, it was situated, unlike Ankobar, further south from the reach of Yohannes, should he try to invade Shewa.

4.2.7. Hadiya

4.2.7.1. Maraqo/Libidoo

The conquest of Gurageland placed the Hadiya as the next target of occupation. The Shewa army's conscious choice of 'elevated zone's and populated areas as its routes for its southward expansionary conquest created two paths. The one expansion path which directed to the south led through the Arsi highland east of the Lake Region, while the second passed along the western escarpment in the Gurage Mountains and led into the territory of the Hadiyya proper."[385] The Libidoo was the first Hadiya group to face "the first attack in 1876," but "successfully repulsed the invaders," after which "they had been considered such a strong opponent that Menilek decided to lead the campaigns against the Libidoo between 1880-1886. The Libidoo "put up fierce resistance under their war commander Lachchebo Ajjaachcho."[386] As it was witnessed in several other places,

> Despite their bravery, they could not withstand the three-pronged assault of the "Menilek-Amhara" from Soddo, Selte, and the Lake Zway area, and were forced to retreat southwards. One contingent of the invading army was commanded by ras Gobana, the bulk, however, were under the

personal commando of the Šawan king...The battles against
the numerically and materially vastly superior foe in which
Lachchebo and most of the Libidoo warriors are said to have
lost their lives, took place between Butajira and Qoshe."[387]

Among the survivors some joined the Arsi-Oromo and the other
Hidiya groups but "the rest yielded and sent *wolab garaad* Miseebo
Burqaamo as negotiator to Menilek" for surrender. The conquerors,
driven by the instigation collaborating groups of Libidoo's traditional
enemies; subjected them to "decimation;" and hence, "many of the
Libido captives were allegedly murdered and part of the people deported to Kimbibit [Qimbibit] and UndotWaša in Ankobar."[388]

> Only a minority of those abducted and taken to the harsh
> highland area survived resettlement and forced labour and
> were able to then return to their homeland in the course
> of the next twenty years. Hardly any other ethnic unit of
> southern Ethiopian had suffered such decimation in relation
> to its population as the Libidoo. To escape from extermina-
> tion, some of their warriors under the command of Miseebo
> Burqaamo...joined the Habaša troops and participated in the
> later campaigns against the Hadiyya groups living further
> south as well as the Walatytta and Sidaama....the interpreter
> of daġġazmač Walda Aššagari [Ashagre) on his campaigns
> against the Sooro, Leemo and Shaashogo is said to have been
> a Libidoo captive.[389]

4.2.7.2. Shaashoogo

While Menelik was leading the final conquest expedition against
the Arsi in 1886, ras Gobana marched from Silte and Libidoo southward and invaded the Shaashoogo unexpectedly. He overrun and set
up camp at Musaageesa. A "relatively small group" of Shaashoogo
was no match for the enemy who came with superior firearms.
After 'skirmish at Shaamo" they surrendered and negotiated tribute

payment through *abagaaz* Geedo Bashiro.[390] The Shaashoogo did not
meet their promised tributes. Five years from their initial conquest,
in 1891 *dejazmatch* Wolde Ashagre led the invasion. The Shaashoogo,
however, refused to pay tributes and decided to fight. They moved
their livestock, women, and children to "hardly accessible bush
areas." Taking lessons from the Libidoo and Arsi, they got " rid of
shields recognized as useless in the face of rifle bullets" and planned
for "close combat" in order to exploit the time 'in between the fu-
sillads when the enemies were reloading their guns."[391] The strategy
worked for their advantage.

> After heavy losses on both sides, the Habaša troops with-
> drew from the marshy, malaria infested Shaashoogo terri-
> tory in May 1891, but returned with strong contingent once
> more in October after the rainy season. During this cam-
> paign the Shaashoogo were finally defeated and a large part
> of the tribe taken captive. One year later a new expedition
> under *daǧǧamač* Wadaǧǧo, a son of *ras* Gobana Dači, sealed
> the henceforth administrative integration of the Shaashoogo
> in the Ethiopian state[392].

After the conquest *dejazmatch* Wodajo appointed *abaagaz* Hosiso
as a balabbat of Shaashoogo. *Abaagaz* Geedo Bashiro was killed, the
motive of which "remains unknown." After Hosiso, his nephew,
Umaakko, took over the *balabat* position, which remained in their
family line through the 1970s.[393]

4.2.7.3. Leemo & Sooro

The northern peripheries of Leemo Hadiya had been "ravaged" by
the army of *ras* Gobana in 1886 "on a plundering raid" after it "defeated a local defense contingent under *adil* Adaa." *Dejazmach* Wolde
Ashagre also plundered the Sooro territory. Since then the northern
army had been organizing itself. By 1890, they were in the position
to "realize their plan to conquer the relatively strong Leemo, Sooro

and Kambaata peoples."[394] In 1891 "with the backing of numerous auxiliaries from Gurage, Libidoo and Shaashoogo" *dejazmatch* Wolde led expedition "to subjugate the Leemo, Sooro and Kambaata." The Leemo fighters and the Baadogo under *adil* Ineea, understanding the might of invading forces, resorted to use guerilla warfare. While the resistance was ongoing, *dejazmatch* Wolde appointed a Leemo man, Hemachcho, to *balabat*, which the Badogo and Endagn also acknowledged. New fortified garrisons were established in Bulbuula and Damaalla. Leemo "entered into a coalition with the Habaša… and acted as auxiliaries for further wars of conquest."[395]

After subduing the Leemo, *dejazmatch* Wolde Ashagre turned his attention towards the neighboring Sooro. They avoided open engagement after they made 'realistic assessment of…superiority of the enemies' weapons… and "largely fled into the barely accessible lowland regions at the Omo, from where they could put up resistance." The devastation of Sooro was milder than other similar *zamachas*. The Tembaaro, however, suffered "considerable loss of life." During this time, the former leader of Sooro, *adil* Adaayee Agaago, died. His son, Annoore negotiated with the victors. He was appointed as a *balabat* and "together with other five officials,"[396]

4.3. The Third Phase of conquest (1889-1895)

At the beginning of this period Menelik's lifelong ambition was fulfilled. Following the death of Yohannes in the Battle of Metemma, his vassalage not only ended but himself became a *neguse negest*, an emperor of Ethiopia. He was now *Jan Hoy*, His Majesty. Several years ago, when he was a Shewa *negus*, he ordered a *neguse negest* seal to be made and had begun using it for his official domestic and foreign correspondences. Emperor Yohannes killed that title in 1878 and compelled him to use only a *negus* of Shewa seal.

Fate, luck, and his supper cunny performances may have played a part in fulfilling his long-awaited dream unexpectedly. After hearing the news of the emperor's death, he quickly moved north and asserted his power. After their king's death, the armies of Tigray were in a total disarray. Yohannes's last-minute designation of his illegitimate son, *ras* Mengesha, as an heir to his throne only increased dissent and friction within the province's elites and potential power contenders, which all worked for Menelik's advantage. It was also during this period that he signed a fateful Wuchale Treaty[397] on May 2, 1889, which drove him and the nation into the war within less than six years.

During the early years of this period, he firmly consolidated his power in all parts of the country, except in Tigre where Mengesha was vacillating between submission and declaring himself *neguse negest* (or at least he expected to be a *negus* which Menelik was unwilling to consider). Unlike previous periods, during this period, he was in a position to mobilize any ruler from northern provinces to fight along his armies. It was also at the beginning of this period that Italy occupied Asmara (1890) and established a colony of Eritrea.

The third phase of conquests lasted roughly six years (1889-1895), in which he conquered vast and fertile lands, which included heavily populated and cotton-producing regions stretched from Kambata-Sidama-Gedeo to Wolayta-Gamo-Gofa to Yam-Kullo-Konta, and to Boroda and Koysha.

The Kambata – Sidama-Gedeo and Walyata- Yam zones were densely populated and known for their fertility and natural resources. Particularly, the Wolayta-Gamo zone was "heavily populated and a fertile cotton-producing region" about which "Menelik told Capucci that there were more people living in Welamo (Wolayta) than between Shewa and Massawa."[398] Pankhurst citing Hudson wrote that "...enormous areas" of Kambatta, Welamo (Wolayta) and Boreda were "extra ordinary fertile."[399] Conquests of these regions came just in time to respite northern regions which were suffering for four years (1888-1892) of the Great Hunger, known as *kefu qen,* Rinderpest reportedly brought by Italians in Massaw decimated the cattle and hence hunger and famine to all northern provinces, including the Shewa kingdom. Eagerness to feed their starving soldiers and to share a war booty was, as Bahru noted, the main reason why almost all Menelik's armies and prominent warlords, including *ras* Mikael of Wollo, *liqa mequas* Abate, *fitawurari* Gebeyehu, *dejamatch*

Blacha and others marched south to fight against Wolayta (see 4.3.2. below). Conquests of these regions tremendously strengthened the emperor's ability to gain more resources, logistics of war including conscription and mobilization of tens of thousands of peasant armies from the newly conquered regions to fight against Italy in Adwa.

4.3.1. Bale

Bale had become a natural target of occupation ever since the Arsi, Ittu regions were conquered. But protracted uprisings in those regions and elsewhere delayed its complete conquest. Hence, it was "only in 1890...ras Darge...begin with the conquest of the Bale area" when he "left the garrison in Shirka...and led a protracted campaign (*zemecha*) to the south-east from October 1891 to July 1892."[400] At Fugag the Arsi "put up strong resistance and defeated" the vanguard army but they "were decisively beaten at Waabee Guraandaa (Gaasara district in Bale) and were no longer in a position to stop the Habaša advance."[401] Bale "was attacked from two directions: by *ras* Darge from the north and *dejazmach* Wolde Gabriel...from the East."[402] When Menelik called ras Darge in 1892 for other duties at the center, Darge " appointed his son, Asfaw Darge, governor of the newly conquered territories."[403] In the same year the resistance leaders,

> Aliyyu Tolaa (Illaannii) and Shayimo Kimoo (Wolashee) laid down their weapons in eastern Bale. In Gololcha territory dejazmatch Walde Gabreil Abba Saytan waged he campaign and captured the Arsi leaders Abdullah Kasim (Yabsaana) and Argoo Yimar (Gololcha) and accepted their surrender before ehe proceeded via Dabbu Jaara to Ginnir... The Oromo of that region...fled...without putting up resistance ... The hill of Ginnir...selected as the residential site for eastern Bale because of its strategically convenient position. Asfaw Darge had quarters built there near present-day Gobba."[404]

Bale's conquest was slow and was totally conquered around 1897. As Abbas Gnamo, noted in his book, *Conquests and Resistance in the Ethiopian Empire 1800-1974: The Case of Arsi Oromo,* both Bale and Arsi regions fell under the control of *ras* Darge family and the officers associated with them.[405]

4.3.2. The Kingdom of Yam

Menelik ordered his cousin, *dejazmatch,* later *ras,* Wolde Giorgis to conquer the small but independent kingdom of Janjero. Wolde Giorgist marched together with Abba Jifar of Jimma and subdued. "With Abba Jifar's help, Walda-Giorgis overran much of the tiny, independent...kingdom of Janjaro from October 1890."[406] When Abba Bagibo realized his defeat, he "fled to Gurage" country, but eventually he made "an act of submission to Menelik in Addis Ababa."[407] During his submission, king Bagibo (also known by some as (Abba Gosaso) appealed to Menelik in person to make his kingdom not subjected under other rulers but to "directly answerable" the emperor. Bagebo "obtained a written promise of immunity...On 9 February 1891 Antonelli and Salimbeni [Italy's representatives in Ethiopia] witnessed Menilek's hearing of the petitions brought in person by the king of Janjaro" and "the prince's territories being restored to him"[408] Abba Bagebo's son, Abba čabsa was Christianized as Gebre Medhin and became a Yam balabat when Megesha Wube was a governor in 1928.[409]

4.3.3. Halaaba

Halaba was targeted for conquest in 1891/92. It was the period known in Ethiopia as a ye *kifu qen* or great famine which was mainly caused by rinderpest, which devastated livestock in the country. It was during this time, the conquest against Halaaba was waged. Invading armies were "strengthened by Gurage and Leemo auxiliaries advanced into the lowland east of Bilate; and the *zemecha* was led by *dejazmatch* Wodajo Gobana, "whose father several years before had executed a plundering raid through this territory."[410] Halaaba "together with neighboring Arsi clans under the leadership of Bare Kajawa, put resistance in part." It was no match with the weapons of the invading armies and accepted its defeat and sought "for peace after a short time."[411]

4.3.4. *The Kingdom of Kambaata*

Professor Pankhurst (1968) wrote that the occupation of Kambaata had begun in 1890. Others such as Ulrich Braukamper (2012) suggested that the initial *zemecha's* against Kambaata might have begun as early as 1887. By this time, the Shewa armies were in control of Gurgelands and much of the neighboring Hadiya territories. *Dejazmatch* Wolde Ashagre oversaw the newly conquered Gurage and Hadiya lands but his garrison was still in Woliso. Inevitably, the kingdom of Kambaata would be on the next listed targets. However, the actual occupation did not start and *Woma* Dilbato was still in charge. Conditions within the kingdom were not at their best. According to Kambaata sources, at the time of northern incursions, a faction within royal families began collaborating with the forces of Menelik; which were already at the doorstep of Kambaata. Reportedly there was also some dissatisfaction of subjects toward their *woma*. (Girma Zewude (2010 E.C., Yacob Arsano 2002). These were favorable conditions for the invading armies.

A contingent was reportedly dispatched to the king demanding Kamabaata's surrender. *Woma* Dilbato Degoye (1845-92) and his cabinet consulted on the impending danger. But they made it known their refusal to surrender the kingdom and their intention to resist the invasion. This triggered the invading forces to devise a better strategy and plan.[412] Equipped with modern weapons and aligning with a collaborating faction leader, they conducted a surprise attack and surrounded the Kambaata king, his families and cabinet members. In 1892 *woma* Dilbato "was captured and killed together with his advisors."[413] In the words of Braukamper, the "Ethiopian soldiers had liquidated King Dilbato and quite a number of his relatives and dignitaries on the campaign against the Kambaata."[414] Among those killed together with King Dilbato were *Ashina* Hageyo (chairman of the crown or king's counselor), *Serecho* Dimbiso (the Kambaata spiritual leader), governors of Yebu, Geyoxa, Eneno, & Awutena *gochos* (regions), royal family members – Sakelo Dilbato (son), Sedebo Degoye (brother), Kumalo Waqo, (uncle) etc. There were also several cabinets members, and many other ordinary Kambaatas.[415] The invasion against Kambaata was led by *ras* Tessema Darge Sahle Selasie and *ras* Mengesha Atkim.[416] As Professor Richard Pankhurst summed up: "In 1890 the occupation of Kambaata was began and was completed in 1893."[417] Although *woma* Dilbato was killed in 1892., Kambata was not pacified until the following year (see chapter 10).

According to Zewdue Girma, a Kambaata culture and history researcher and author, woma Dilbato's famed horse might have been taken as a war booty to Addis Ababa and rewarded to the Emperor Menelik, who reportedly used it frequently for various *zemechas*. Kambaata elders and oral history recounted that the horse portrayed at Menelik's equestrian monument in Addis Ababa in front of the Qdus Giorgis Church resembled the stature and size of the war booty of the *woma* Dilbato Degoye's horse.[418] Taking war booty of defeated enemies was the most common practice. When Alexander Bulatovich finished his south-western conquest adventure, he wrote that *ras* Wolde Giorgis: "overloaded me with gifts...He gave me his marvelous mule, taken from the prince of Gofa, a horse with silver dress, the silver spear of the captive of the king of Kaffa..."[419] After the Emir of Harar was defeated, the victorious Menelik, among other things, took with him caged birds and leashed dogs.

4.3.5. Tembaro

The Tembaro land was targeted for invasion by Menelik's army in 1891/2. The Tembaro people, like their neighboring peoples, decided to resist the invasion. Led by their *womma* Choforro and such leaders as Akko, Sageto Mandaqe and others; the Tembaro people engaged in resistance. However, like other southern peoples they were defeated by the power of firearms, which was unknown there. After conquest Choforro was made "the first Amhara style balabat" and then new rulers and landlords began to settle in Tembaro region.[420]

4.3.6. Baadaawacho -Hadiya

In 1893 it was Baadaawacho's turn to face the invasion. As in before the Ethiopian army had continued widely deploying fighters from previously conquered lands against the newly targeted communities. In other words, using kinsmen against kinsmen, and neighboring peoples against their neighbors. Dejazmatch Wolde led the conquest and passed from the direction of Daato Mountain and passed the hills and reached toward Baadaawacho, who were "the only Hadiyya group left who were not under...Ethiopian Empire."[421] Then Baadaawacho heard unexpected news regarding the destruction of their ally. Then,

> the news came that the Ethiopian soldiers had liquidated [killed] King Dilbato and quite a number of his relatives and dignitaries on their campaign against the Kambaata, it had such a shock effect[422] on the autonomous Hadiyya, that they decided to resolve [their] sworn enmity with the Walayta and beseeched an alliance with this powerful southern neighbor. [423]

During the initial skirmishes with the invading armies, Baadawaacho's *anjaanchcho* Kabiisso was killed, which also "contributed to their decision to seek an alliance with the Walayta."[424] In their alliance with Wolayta the "Baadawwaachcho had almost completely evacuated their territory and withdrawn behind the fortification walls of the Walaytta."[425] However, the Baadawaacho did not restrict themselves to the fortification walls only. They adopted guerilla tactics and "repeatedly attacked from the dense bush areas around Qorga."[426] During their alliance with Wolayta: "Three Hadiyya military commanders fought with their warriors on the side of the Walaytta:

Gatiso Balango (Haballo and south-western Arsi), Sandaabo Bijaamo (Daawwe) and Fagiisso Goddee (Waageshmanna)."[427] Even though the Baadawaacho fought at the frontline more aggressively, they and their ally, Wolayta, were finally defeated by Menelik's armies which enjoyed both numerical and firearms superiority. Baadawaacho sent a delegation with two fattened oxen to Menelik, who then camped at mount Damoota, and "by this act they announced their subjugation."[428]

4.3.7. The Wolayta Kingdom

During winter of 1890s Menelik ordered his "favorite, R*as* Mangasha Atikam, from his governorship of Amhara Sayent...to the south in order to feed his men...the smaller...but exceedingly prosperous, Omotic kingdom of Wallayta was assigned as prey for this hungry host."[429] *Ras* Managasha Atkim mobilized his armies south. Together with the armies of *ras* Tessema Darge and Bashah Aboye, they conquered the kingdom of Kambata and moved onto the neighboring Wolayta. While the Hadiya groups of Limu, Shashogo and Soro; and the neighboring Halaaba and Kambaata were defeated from 1886-1893; anther Hadiya group, the "Badawacho astonishingly formed an alliance with Wollamo (Wolayta) to fight the Amhara."[430] (See Badawacho above).

Wolayta like the neighboring Kambaata and other southern peoples did not have firearms. However, "they had become expert in building trench fortifications against the Oromo cavalry...The new king, *kawo* Tona Gaga...repulsed Mengesha Atkim's invasion."[431] Rosenfeld tells us that it was in November 1890 that "Mangesha-atikim (Atkim) attempts but fails to subdue Walamo"[432]

Wolayata posed great challenge to the emperor and it "remained the greatest unconquered prize in the southwest after Kafa."[433] *Dejazmatch* Tessema Darge led *zamacha* in 1891 into Wolayta but he "was defeated and could only beat a retreat through Timabaro with great difficulty."[434] Another zemecha was ordered. But, "The Wallayta drove back another invasion a couple of years later led by

Ras Gobana's son, Wodajo."[435] In 1893, *fitawurari* Teklu established a garrison post north of Baadawaacho at Qata hill, which served "as base camp for the deployment of troops" and played "an important role for the conquest of adjacent territories in the south."[436]

Menelik continued working to bring about solution to the challenge posed by *kawo* Tona (Tsona) Gaga; who "had come to power because of a tide of popular support" from Wolayta people and was also able to mobilize "the Kullo and Konta peoples, to the west of Walayta, to rise against Menelik's authority."[437] Now, Menelik was determined to conquer it. There was also an economic reason for the conquest. As Chris Prouty (1986) stated:

> The real reason [for occupying Wolayta], was that it was a heavily populated and a fertile cotton-producing region; Menelik told Capucci that there were more people living in Welamo (Wolayta) than between Shewa and Massawa. It was inevitable that Welamo (Wolayta) be brought under Menelik's hegemony.[438] [*parenthesis by me*]

According to Vanderheym, who accompanied Menelik into Wolatya conquest, some of the reasons included: "to take revenge for the preceding defeats, expectation of particularly rich booty and to eliminate once and for all the threat...by Walayta."[439] Bahru stated that the socio-economic condition of the country at the time made the conquest attractive and urgent in the wake of . For four years (1888-1892) of debilitating Great Hunger, *kifu qen*, particularly in the Northern provinces.

The final campaign against Wolayta was led by Menelik himself. To defeat Wolayta and to share from its rich war booty, according to Bahru, almost all famous Menelik's generals and leaders participated: *ras* Mikael of Wollo, *fitawurari* Gebeyehu, *liqa mequas* Abate Bwayalew, and *dejazmach* Balcha Safo. In addition, *ras* Wolde Giorgis and Abba Jifar of Jimma also participated. In Bahur's words: "What had happened/followed was not a battle, but extermination."[440] According to Rosenfeld (1976) ras Alula, and Haile Mariam also participated in addition to those listed above. Ras Wolde Giorgis also "attacked Walamo from the rear."[441] As Vanderheym (1896) described that along the Ethiopian army a "considerable contingents of Gurage, Leemo, Sooro, Shaashoogo and other ethnic groups participated as combatants."[442] Compelling previously conquered people to fight against other people who put up resistance was a common practice and, probably, a hallmark of Menelik's southern conquest strategy.

Wolayta was attacked from various directions simultaneously by several armies equipped with modern weapons. When Menelik became emperor in 1889 he "had at least 60,000 guns of all kinds, one million cartridges and about one million percussion caps, and many barrels of gun powder."[443] By the time of Wolayta conquest in mid-1890s, Menelik was in a position of mobilizing up to 100,000 troops with rifles.[444] Such was the magnitude of firepower *kawa* Tona and the people of Wolayta stood against, in addition to numerical superiority of fighters Menelik deployed. Rosenfeld (1976) and Braukamer (2012) described that Menelik left Addis Ababa for the Wolayta campaign on November 15, 1894.

> The imperial army apparently followed the old trading route which led along the western slope of the Rift Valley, reached to Libidoo plain via Geja (Gurage-Soddo), advanced from there south-west through Selte and Walbarag, and camped in Kambaata at a place with hot springs ['situated at Mt. Daato']. From there the main body of the Habaša troops marched via Shonee to Qorga in the Bilate lowland.[445]

Rosenfeld wrote that he "met with Tessema Darge at the border of Arussi and Walamo and receives large quantity of cattle to feed his soldiers on expedition...December 11-15, Walamo are slaughtered by the thousands; many captives are brought to Addis Ababa; captured cattle are divided among the soldiers."[446]

> King Xona [Tona] took a stand with his main body of fighters at Gasseena near today's town of Boditte, while groups

of Baadawwaachcho warriors, whose main knowledge of the territory provided them with an advantage, enabled them to delay the enemy's advance by drawing the Christian Ethiopians into smaller-scale skirmishes...Menilek personally led the decisive campaign taking his main body of troops out of the Shoneearea towards the Walayta position of defense in Gasseena. West and east of the main army, smaller contingents of soldiers advanced from Ilgiira on the southern edge of the Kambata Mountains and from the Duquna range against the enemy. Simultaneously, the Ethiopian troops invaded the Walayta territory from across the Omo River and began to raid the enemy at the rear. The Walayta and Baadawwaachcho could not withstand the cumulative force; after putting up valiant resistance, their fighting force was utterly crushed.[447]

Regardless of its antiquated weapons, they fought to the end. They most probably utilized similar warfare tactics like their "ancient defense works which they built to repel the Arusi."[448] Travelling from Addis Ababa Captain Montagu Sinclair Wellby arrived at Wolayta in 1898, few years after it was conquered. He saw that some of tactics used by Wolayta against Menelik's armies did "still exist everywhere." He wrote:

> These are successive rows of little pits, dug in close proximity to one another, and resembling our military obstacles. They were constructed by ...Walamo (Wolayta) to baffle King Menelik's cavalry when he took the country about four years ago, and, to judge from their awkward-looking appearance, they must have done good work.[449]

The armies of King Tona reportedly used bee colonies against invading forces. In the early 1980s a Wolayta native once told me that the Wolayta arm had used swarms of bees as a weapon against the invading armies to create chaos and confusion and 'it worked' in Wolayta's favor.[450] Despite their fierce resistance, the power of modern firearms of their enemies, Menelik's long time methodical planning, and strategy had brought them down. They were finally defeated. As Bahru rightly put it, the Wolayta people did not have a means of withstanding such well-armed and well-coordinated attacks for a long time.[451] Even after Menelik overwhelmed him with superior fighting forces and weapons, *kawo* Tona did not surrender. He resolved to resist. He fled to Borodda, a neighboring country. In December 1894 he was wounded and captured in Borodda."[452] Then he was chained and taken to Addis Ababa as a prisoner of war.

The casualties were extremely high on both sides. 118, 987 people were killed or wounded from the Wolayta side and 80,000 killed or wounded from the imperial side.[453] As Harold Marcus put it, Menelik "added to his empire a large, rich kingdom, with the acquisition of much booty and glory."[454] Conquered Wolayta was, however, devastated, and depopulated. Horror met its people. It became a victim of the imperial armies' usual *zemecha* tactics[455] of burning houses, destroying crops, killing males, taking women and children to captivity together with war booty and prisoners of war. In Prouty's words:

> The slaughter was terrible and description by Guston Vanderheym, who accompanied the army, did much to tarnish the image of a beneficent monarch that Menelik had enjoyed in France. One old warrior Vanderheym that it was the worst carnage he had ever seen. The women and children captives forced to carry the severed genitals of their husbands and fathers, though Vanderheym said that Menilek tried to forbid these atrocities. Soldiers snatched infants from their mothers' arms to relieve them of a burden that might slow them down on the march back to Shewa. Menilek's Christianizing-colonizing objective was achieved but at a terrible cost.[456]

Besides atrocities, Wolayta was devastated and plundered. Bahru Zewde summed it up as follows: "the Wolayta *zemecha* was unlike

any other *zemecha* and it probably had no parallel for its atrocities."[457].
"On January 18, 1895 on Timket (day) Menilek enters capital with
about 18,000 Walamo slaves; Tona submits at the ceremony... on the
19th Vanderheym (was) expelled for writing about Menelik's Walamo
expedition."[458] Without counting all the cattle that was slaughtered
and taken by various armies; "the cattle he [Menelik] took back to
Addis Ababa numbered 36,000."[459] Survivors of the war, including
King Tona, were ordered to convert. "After he had been baptized"
kawo Tona was returned to Wolayta, and "Christianity was imposed
on everyone. Legend has it that 11,000 people were baptized in
one day."[460] According to Rosenfeld (1976) "King Tona of Walamo
(Wolayta) is interned in Shoa" in September 1903.[461]

The conquest of Wolayta opened doors wide for Menelik's armies
to march against the adjacent **Gamo, Gofa, Borodda, Malo,
Koysha** and other kingdoms and territories. Some of them were
already penetrated from the south-west by the armies of *ras* Wolde
Giorgis. Some of them were now brought into the empire. The last
war against Wolayta was not limited to Wolayta proper. On the
contrary, it took place in the larger region as the conquering armies
converged on from various directions. As described above *kawo* Tona
fled from his main base at Gasseena to Borodda country and was
taken prisoner there.

4.3.8 Sidaama-Gedeo

The present day Sidaama – Gedeo region was conquered by the
armies of Menelik II from 1893-1897. After Menelik's commanders
"had secured their position in Bale, they proceeded with the occupation of Sidaamaland from 1893 onwards." The Sidaama conquest was
led by *dejazmatch* Bashah and *ras* Leul Sagad. But the Sidaama people
resisted the occupation. As a result, "it took more than three years
for the Sidaam-Guǧǧi-Oromo...to be worn down to the point where
they gave up resisting and acknowledged the Empire's sovereignty."[462]
After long and protracted wars, the Sidaama and the neighboring
people came to terms that their traditional weapons were no match

to the modern refiles. "In 1897, the hitherto independent peoples of the area which later became known as Sidamo-Borana Province submitted largely without a fight."[463] As Shinn and Ofcansky wrote: "Until Menelik II conquered them at the end of the 19th century, the Sidama are believed to have had kingships."[464] Although Sidaama was first conquered mainly by dejazmach Leulseged, the most familiar name often associated with Sidaama conquest was its longtime governor, *Dejazmach* Balcha.[465] He established a garrison and named it, *Hagere Selam*, the land of peace. The territories of Sidama together with those of Gedeo, Wolayta, and others were later collectively known as the Sidamo province. Sidamo became a magnet for settlers who were attracted by its fertile lands as well as by its most valuable commercial commodity – coffee - which, ironically, increased misery and exploitation of the autochthonous people. Pankhurst wrote:

Land tenure in Sidamo underwent a significant change during Menelik period. Giaccardi declaring that "a real system of military colonization" was established. Setters, he says, included soldiers of the time of Menelik and their descendants, as well as troops brought in by later rulers such as Dajazmach Balcha, Fitawurari Beru and Ras Desta.[466]

Dejazmach Balcha was credited to have started *qalad*, a land measurement using a rope, in Sidamo; which was used to distribute lands mainly among his followers. The main opposition came from early settlers and followers of *dejazmatch* Luel Seged, who fist conquered Sidaama; who complained that most of the land was given to late comers. They even appealed to the emperor (The native people whose lands were taken were not in the equation). Balcha's successor, in addition to continuing implementation of land measurement, "introduced a consolidated tax assessed at a flat rate of 28 dollars a *gasha*."[467] In his formative years the young Teferi Mekonnen, the future emperor Haile Selassie I, was appointed as a district governor in Darassa/Gedeo region. For about two years he administered "through officials already in office as he himself was still in his teens... He no doubt accumulated a considerable amount of wealth there."[468] Most probably he came to appreciate Sidamo's rich resources during those years of his nominal governorship. Teferi deposed Balcha in 1928 and replaced him with a loyalist Shewan, *ras* Desta. After he became emperor, Sidamo fell under the monopoly of imperial families, their associates, and absentee landlords. In 1935 Birru was replaced by Haile Selassie's own son-in-law, *ras* Desta Damtew, who married Tenagne Worq Haile Selassie. Lands in Sidamo were expropriated and distributed among the beneficiaries of the imperial apparatus and a *gabbar* system was instituted.

A Sidaama native once told me a true story of a Sidaama man (*gabbar*) who was assigned to farm fields and do all kinds of chores at his master's household from Monday through Friday every week. Then the man went back to his home village and worked for himself on Saturdays and Sundays. But he must be at his master's house on Monday morning, which also requires a long journey. The man had to execute so many things in less than two days. He was obliged to plough and plant at night in the dark while his wife carried torch light alongside him. The man was so overwhelmed and exhausted with his endless obligations such that he did not have time or energy to have pleasure with his wife. He even did not have time to groom himself and hence, his pubic and armpit hair grew like an afro. The Sidaama *gabbar* story has striking similarities to the dreaded *gabbar* system, practiced elsewhere in the south. The Maale informant described the following to Donham Donham:

> ...the load on gebbar was a heavy one. For a week at a time, the gebbar lived in his master's house, cut firewood, brought water, farmed the master's fields, and cared for his mule. He had to cook his own food and to sleep outside on straw. At the end of the week, another gebbar arrived and the first left —carrying a sack of grain that his wife would grind and that he would return when he came for the next week of service. In addition, he had to pay four Maria Theresa thalers a year for his master's 'salary'(*demoz*), a large gourd of honey worth approximately three thalers twice a year on holidays, and five thalers whenever his master went on a long journey.

Not surprisingly, many Maale chose to move away rather than endure such extractions.[469]

4.4. The Final Phase (1896-1906)

What I called the Final Phase of conquests began shortly after the Battle of Adwa in late 1896 and was completed in the early years of 1900. Menelik's crushing victory over Italy in Adwa garnered him more modern weapons into his arsenal. Above all, it earned him more recognition and respect from world leaders. Colonial powers, which tacitly approved Italy's ill-fated adventure and which were tip-toing along Ethiopian borders, suddenly enlisted the victorious Menelik as their partner. Many countries began establishing their diplomatic missions in Addis Ababa. Italy was compelled to swallow bitter pills of truth to accept annulation of the Wuchale Treaty and to fully recognize Ethiopian independence.

During this period, the ambivalent Tigre ruler and vassal, Mengesha Yohannes, was deposed by use of force and exiled to Ankobar prison. This effectively ended beneath the surface hidden rivalry of Tigre-Amhara power struggle in favor of the latter. It was also during this period that Menelik signed international treaties of border demarcations with colonial powers –Italy, France, Britain - which occupied neighboring countries. Menelik was at the apex of fame, power, and success.

With more deadly weapons at hand and a morale boost in the rank and file of his military; Menelik calculated the time was right to subdue regions which remained outside his reach until now. He dispatched his most able generals, namely, *ras* Wolde Giorgis Aboye, *ras* Tessema Nadew, *dejazmatch* Demessew Nessibu, *ras* Mekonnen Wolde Mikael *ras* Hapte Giorgis, *dejazmatch* Leul Seged and their deputies into frontier areas to incorporate several pockets of territories and kingdoms which still did not recognize his rule.

The first three generals were ordered to go to the south-west, ras Mekonnen to the west, and Hapte Giorgis and company headed to the south. As a result, the kingdom of Kaffa, frontier area up to Lake

Turkana, Benishangul, parts of Illubabor and other frontier areas, Borana, and Maji were conquered.

4.4.1. The Kaffa Kingdom

During this period Kaffa was the biggest target of conquest. Conquering Kaffa was in the making for a several years because for "over a decade, the ancient kingdom had defied the claims for suzerainty first of Gojjam and then of Shewa."[470] From the early 1880s onwards Menelik's attempts to subdue Kaffa had failed several times. This was due to a well-organized resistance put up by Kaffa and its king, *Tato* Gaki Shericho, whose tactics were often one step ahead of invading forces. Thus, Kaffa became one of the last major southern kingdoms left unconquered. Menelik ordered *ras* Wolde Giorgis to subdue Kaffa and its powerful *tato*. But, as in before, Kaffa refused to submit and resorted to fight back. Bulatovich put Kaffa's resolve as follows: "To Kaffa... there remained only to submit voluntarily or be subdued. But Kaffa decided to defend its independence to the very last."[471]

Tato Gaki, who became a king in 1890, was in power for seven years only. But he had already repulsed several attempted invasions led by Ras Gobana and others.[472] Kaffa was known for its bravery and fortifications. Greenfield wrote: "The trenches and fortifications of the Kaffa kingdom, which is said to have once stretched from the Sudanese lowlands to the Rift valley lakes, may still be seen in places."[473] Kaffa was "populated by a strong people, imbued with love for their fatherland and an enterprising, war-like spirit, occupying an advantageous central position, protected by forests and mountains"[474]

This time, however, the Kaffa king was strategically in a weaker position than before for two main reasons. First, Kaffa's neighbors were now occupied by Menelik; and they were ordered to march against it in conjunction with the armies of Menelik. Another major disadvantage for *tato* Gaki was that he had no guns and his enemies had marshalled mighty forces which were equipped with modern weapons. Yet tato and his people refused to surrender solely depending upon their own resources and determination.

> The Kaffa are bold dashing horsemen. Their horses are
> rather tall…horses serve exclusively for military purposes….
> The weapons of Kaffa include a throwing spear, which has
> a very beautiful form and in sometimes decorated with an
> intricate point, and a dagger worn in the belt. Round leather
> shields serve for defensive armaments.[475]

Determined not to repeat the mistakes of the past failed incursions, this time, Menelik decided to confront Kaffa with overwhelming force. He ordered combined forces of *ras* Wolde Giorgis, who was "designated governor of Kaffa in advance;" *dejazmach* Demissew, governor of Wollega, *dejazmach* (later *ras*) Tessema, governor of Illubabor; Jimma Abba Jifar II; the ruler of Kullo; and the ruler of Konta.[476] The objective was to encircle Kaffa from all directions and to quickly defeat *tato* Gaki and his people. The co-opted rulers of Jimma, Kullo, and Konta mobilized fighters from their respective regions. They were also "serving as guides to break the intricate defense system of Kafa."[477]

> In Novermber 1896 *ras* Wolde Giyorgis, the first of the three
> particpants in the campaign, marched into Kaffa from Kulo
> with 10,000 men and, putting to fire and sword everything
> on the way, arrived at the city of Andrachi, the capital of
> Kaffa, which he build a fortified camp….Having consolidated
> his position in Andrarchi, ras Wolde Giyorgis divided his
> army into large detachments, and sent them out in various
> directions. These detachments laid waste the country, ravaging it for a radius of tens of versts (seven miles), taking
> prisoner the women and children who were hidden in the
> forests, and setting fire to everything that could burn.[478]

These forces encircled Kaffa from all directions and waged scorched-earth tactics. Yet, it proved difficult to defeat Kaffa and to capture its king. Gaki and his people continued fighting utilizing their forests, and their "trenches and fortifications,"[479] and their "love for their fatherland and...warlike spirit."[480] The war dragged on for several more months.

> ...the final campaign had lasted for eight months before the last Kafitcho emperor... was sent as a prisoner in golden chains to Ankober. ...The tale is told that on the way, as he rode behind Ras Wolde Giorgis over a bridge across the Gojeb River, he hurled his royal ring into the water with the words, "The Empire of Kaffa has come to an end. There will never be another emperor of Kaffa! The emperor's ring shall rest in the bed of the river.[481]

When Gaki Tato was captured, his crown. Golden throne, golden whip *(alenga),* two war drums (one made of silver and the other made of copper) were also captured.[482] Kaffa was conquered. The conqueror, Menelik's cousin, *ras* Wolde Giorgis Aboye, established his base at the *tato's* capital, Andarachi. And *tato* Gaki Sherocho "spend the rest of his life in miserable captivity."[483]

About five months after the capture of *tato* Gaki, Alexander Bulatovich entered Kaffa to join *ras* Wolde Giorgis on his next planned expedition of conquest to the south-west. He was amazed by the beauty of Kaffa country. He wrote: "In nature some kind of joy of living was felt - a surplus strength hidden within it. The charming beauty of the place carried one off to some place far away, to a magical world."[484] In contrast to the "charming beauty of the place," he also saw the grim reality of wanton destruction of property, strewn human bones everywhere, and the absence of native population in places they had formerly inhabited. On his January 8, 1898 diary, he wrote:

> But instead of the poetic circumstances of a fine story, [of Kaffa's beauty] before us appeared the dreadful signs of death and destruction. Amid the green grass, the white of human bones shone here and there. Settlements were nowhere to be seen —only thick weeds, growing on plots of recently cultivated earth, bear testimony of the people who once lived

here. An evil fairy of war destroyed them and scattered their bones across the fields. The closer we came to the capital of Kaffa, the more noticeable became the signs of recent battles. Near the town itself, clearings were completely strewn with human bones...”[485]

Bulatovich entered the town of Andarachi "at five o'clock in the afternoon" and met *ras* Wolde Giorgis. Unlike the misery of locals Bulatovich witnessed, ras Wolde Giorgis and his followers were enjoying abundance. He was served for dinner with "various dishes prepared in European manner." His servants received from *ras* "a bull, several rams, bread, beer, mead, pepper sauce, etc." After slaughtering a bull and rams, they feasted while enjoying tent campfires and songs. The warm reception made him forget his 42 days journey from Addis Ababa to here.[486]

During his stay in Andarachi from January 8-22, 1898 he gathered information about Kaffa's past and investigated present conditions. He wrote about the harsh tactics used by *ras* Wolde Giorgis's army during the battles and how the *ras* oversaw the destruction of Kaffa. Bulatovich wrote:" The palace of the Kaffa King, erected on top of one of the highest hills, was burnt down on orders from Wolda Giyorgis."[487] He added:

> The main capital was the town of Andrachi, in which an enormous palace was located: the span of each of the columns that support it was several times the reach of both extended arms. The Abyssinians, having torn the city asunder, had to spend a long time trying to destroy this colossal building, until they finally succeeded in burning it down. In front of the palace, there was a large open space. Those who came to court had to dismount here and go the rest of the way by foot.[488]

As professor Richard Greenfield noted Wolde Giorgis also had "Bonga, the site of the former royal capital, burnt together with the palace after the conquest.[489] Chris Prouty, the biographer of Taytu and Menelik, summed the Kaffa military expedition as "the genocide that had characterized Ras Welde Giorgis's conquest of Kaffa."[490]

Twelve years after *tato* Gaki Sherecho was captured and sent to prison, an Austrian ethnologist got permission from Menelik in 1909 and visited the former king of Kaffa.[491] The Kaffa king was transferred from Ankobar prison to "Dessie where he lived in poverty in the house of Ras Mikael."[492] After Eyasu seized power he allowed Gaki Sherecho to be taken to Addis Ababa. Tato Kaficho died there 1919.[493] On his January 24, 1898 diary Bulatovich wrote that he met the "wives" of Tato Gaki at the summit of Mount Bonga-Beke, where they were kept "under strict surveillance." He spoke with *tato*'s "young...beautiful" wife who answered his "questions quite naturally, and behaved reservedly, and with extraordinary dignity."[494] On his diary of the same day, he wrote the following about *tato*'s ex-wife.

> She is the daughter of the king of Kusho, one of the former tributaries of Kaffa. She got married at the age of 12. She is now 25, and the 13 years of her marriage were for her, in her words, continuous happiness. The king loved her more than all his other wives and adorned her and dressed her more richly than them and more frequently than any of them summoned her to himself. She loved her king, was depressed without him, and asked me if I had seen him, if he was healthy, if he had already died in confinement. She spoke with amazing simplicity, remembering her former life with regret. The whole time, there was an imprint of deep sadness on her face.[495]

4.4.2. *Gimira*

In 1897 Gimira was conquered by *ras* Wolde Giorgis whose army caused devastation and mass enslavement. Bulatovich, passed through Gimira region and wrote his observation:

> Bordering Mocha from the south, the Gimira tribe rep-
> resents a different type than the rest. ...They are involved
> in agriculture. By the testimony of the Abyssinians, all these
> tribes are very brave and warlike, and adults never surrender
> themselves into captivity —only women and children fall into
> the hands of the conqueror.[496]

Gimira's contact with *ras* Wolde Giorgis's army was the beginning of its depopulation and misery. R*as* Tessema also conducted raizzas against Gimira. Overall situations kept going worse for Gimira's native population. In the early 1900s the heir of Menelik, *lij* Eyasu Mikael, went on hunting and killing expedition against indigenous people. In addition to those killed and displaced, he drove 40,000 Gimiras into slavery out of their homelands[497] (See chapter 8).

4.4.3. Illubabor

Parts of the western Ethiopian region, which later became Illubabor, had been conquered after the mid-1880s where *dejazmach* (later *ras*) Tessema Nadew was appointed as its ruler. In 1898 Menelik gave order to Tessema to lead Ethiopian army to assist French colonial mission and to join with the mission's leader, Major Marchand at Fashoda, Sudan. Tessema, with Menelik's approval, used the moment to conquer the territories along Baro all the way to the frontier of Sudan. Dejazmatch Tessema ruled with heavy-handedness. During his *zemechas* of conquests and governorship, thousands of natives were killed, displaced, or driven out from their homelands and taken into slavery. *Ras* Tessema was not secretive about his actions. On the contrary, he "openly declared in 1897" how he had conducted his business in that part of the country: "Up to now I have made war to kill, ravage, pillage and collect beasts and slaves."[498] Besides human toll suffered by native people, *ras* Tessema, as Pankhurst noted, also caused great devastation in the region's wild game.

...in Ras Tessema's province in the south-west no less than 300 elephants were killed every year, which would have meant an annual ivory production of some 12,000 kilos...A considerable decline in wild life was also taking place in far south and west, and was due...to those who killed for profit, as well as to the introduction of firearms.[499]

Ras Tesema ruled the region until 1909 when he was transferred to Addis Ababa after the emperor appointed as a regent to *lij* Eyasu Mikael. His son, Kebede[500] Tessema, replaced him as governor of Illubabor. Tessema's relative dominated the Ethiopian government both during Menelik's as well as Haile Selassie's reigns (see chapter 15.4).

4.4.4. *Ben Shanguel, Aqoldi (Assosa) & Khomosha*

Ben Shanguel/Bela Shangul, Aqoldi (Assosa) and Khomosha regions were conquered by military operation led by *ras* Mekonnen Wolde Mikael. He was supported by Wollega's governor, *dejazmach* Demissew as well as Wollega's co-opted leaders, Jote Tulu and Kumsa Moroda.[501] Menelik sent Mekonnon to Ben Shangul who joined forces with the troops of Demissew.[502] After waging devastating campaign and subduing it, in May 1898 *ras* Mekonnen returned from Ben Shangul to Addis Ababa[503] *He* "annexed the north-western corner of the present-day Wellega to Menelik's domains."[504] During that conquest he drove the captured natives as prisoners of war into the interior. When Italy's colonial governor of Eritrea, Martini, visited Addis Ababa in 1906, Menelik received the Italian administrator of Eritrea with an elaborate and huge military parade. Among those performing the parade were "Shanqila (Berta people) captured" during conquest and brought to the interior, and some of them trained" in military.[505]

After Ben Shangul's conquest "three ruling shaykhs" (sheikhs) were deported to Addis Ababa. And the governor of Wollega region, *dejazmach* Demissew, was appointed as an "over-ruler" of Ben

Shangul.[506] Triulzi wrote about *ras* Demissew's exploitative rule in Ben Shangul: "The first five years of Shewan-Amhara direct rule over the region, it was reported, had 'made wilderness of Bela Shangul.'"[507] Starting in 1903 Ben Shangul fell under Wollega's Kumsa Moroda, who ruled it until 1908 when "the three Bela Shangul rulers"were released from prison in Addis Ababa and restored to power.[508] Due to its wealth in gold, Ben Shangul joined the ranks of Wollega and Jimma as *maed bet*, whereby tributes were made directly to the emperor. Shiekh Khojali (Hojale) in later years would become a constant visitor of Haile Selassie's palace, paying his tributes in gold and slaves.[509] During 1897/98 campaign Shiekh Khojale secretly allied with *ras* Mekonnen giving him "a liberal supply of gold to win his favor" and provided intelligence to *ras* Mekonnen which became "instrumental in reversing the earlier successes" of other sheikh's such as Sheikh Abd al-Rahman Khojale and Sheikh Mohammed Wad-Mahmud.[510] Regardless he served about a decade in prison in Addis Ababa together with the other two sheikhs and was released together with them.

4.4.5. Borana, Konso, Gidole, Burji

The Konso-Gidole-Burji lands were conquered and brought under imperial rule by the armies of *dejazmach*, later *ras,* Luel Seged in 1896. He "invaded Burji, and then came across the Sagan valley to Konso where he subjugated the regions of Garati, Takati, and Turo before going to Gidole."[511] Autochthonous people put up resistance against the occupation. After his Borana *zemecha* fitawrari Habte Giorgis's "army then moved north and passed through Konso, via Turo, in August."[512] Habte Giorgis marched to Konso–Gidole region to provide "reinforcements for a military operation that was already well underway." by *dejazmatch* Leul Seged and others.[513] According to Shin and Ofcansky, Konso was defeated after "imperial troops destroyed two Konso towns that resisted."[514] This author is not sure whether the town were destroyed by the forces of *dejazmatch* Leul Seged or *fitawurari* Habte Giorgis. One of the largest *zemecha* was carried out by *fitawurari*, later ras, Habte Giorgis against the Borana. In June 1897 *fitawurari* led an expeditionary army of 15,000 which "passed to the east of Lakes Abaya and Shamo, until it reached Sogida in Borana country on 31st July...established a garrison at Mega."[515]

Writing about Menelik's post Adwa conquests against the southern and south-western regions, Thomas Pankham noted:

> The next year, 1897, Menelik sent out his Shoan armies on a new war of conquest against the Keffa of the south-west and the Galla of the southern borderland. These unfortunate neighbours, who had only a few hundred muzzle-loaders, between them, were no match for Menelik's warriors armed with magazine rifles. Tens of thousands of blacks were killed or sold into slavery. Their cattle and gold were looted, their land parceled among the Shoans. Soon Menelik's empire was double the size of Yohannes's empire at its peak. It was imperial expansion and Realpolitik, African-style, and it brought greater rewards than any European war in Africa. With gold looted in Kaffa and the south, Menelik was able to re-equip his army, start the process of modernizing his ancient state, and thus the dominance of Shoa far into the twentieth century.[516]

Table 2: Southern polities, their rulers before conquests[1] & years of conquests.[2]

Kingdom/Land Year Conquered	Native King / Leader	Kingdom/ Land Year Conquered	Native King / Leader
Afar 1896	Mohammed Hanfare Illalta	Geleb (& Omo Valley) 1897-1900	--
Anyuak 1897	---	Gimira 1897	---
Aari -	Babbi	Gofa 1893-4	Kawa Kamma?
Arsi 1886	Elected *haaxe/ moote*	Goma 1879-1887	Aba Boka
Assosa 1897-8	Khojali al-Hassan	Guma1878-2	Aba Jobir
Bako 1889	---	Guma-Gumuz1889	Hamadan Abushok
Bale 1891-2	---	Gurage 1875-88	Baccii Shabo (Chaha), ...
BelaShangul 1897-8	Abd al-Rahman	Badawacho 1894	Gatiso Balango & others
Borana 1896-7	Gada System	Leemo -1886 1st 1891 2nd	Adil Ineea Hamacho
Boroda 1894	----	Halaba 1891/92	Imam Nunde died 1885
Bosha 1883	----	Harar 1887	Abdullahi
Burji 1896-7	----	Gidole 1896	---
Dawuro/Kullo 1890-93	Hanagasa Gansa	Illubabor 1889	Fatansa Illu
Dasanetch/ Galeb1889	----	Ittu 1885-7	---
Ennarya 1879-1884	AbaGomboli	Janjero/Yam 1890-1	Abba Gosasa, -Aba Bagibo
Gamo 1893-5	--	Konso 1896	Sakalla

---

1   Some of the southern societies were governed by traditional/generational leaders and religious figures, while others were ruled by well-established monarchical dynasties.
2   Year of conquests were poorly documented and conflicting in some cases. Regardless of my best attempt to get it right, a year of conquest for some kingdoms and territories may be a year a conquest started or ended.

Kingdom/Land Year Conquered	Native King / Leader	Kingdom/ Land Year Conquered	Native King / Leader
Gedeo 1892-3	---	Konta 1889	Belete-Menota
Kaffa 1897	Gaki Sherocho	Koysha 1894	---
Kambaata 1890-93	Dilbato Degoye	Jimma-Kaka 1884	Tulu (Aba Jifar II)
Shaashogo 1st time 1886. 1891 2nd time	Geedo Bashiro; Hosiso	Maraqo/Libido Miseebo Burqamo	Lachebo Ajaacho
Sooro 1st time 1886. 1891 2nd	Adaaye Agago Anore Adaaye	Silte 1876-8	Ormoora
Khomosha 1898	Muhammad Wad-Mahmud	Mecha 1879-84	---
Leqa Nekmete 1882-3 Leqa Qellam 1882-3	Moroda Bakare Jote Tulu	Tembaro 1891-2	Chofforo
Limmu-Enarya 1879-81	Aba Gomol	Ogaden 1890-97	Clan leaders
Maale 1897-8	Aregude	Qabeena 1876 1st 1888 2nd	Umar Baksa, Hassan Enjamo
Malo 1890	---	Gera 1879-84	----
Maji 1898	---	Sidaama 1892-97	
Wolayta 1894	Tona Gaga	Tulama 1879-82	---
Wollo 1866-78	Worqit/Mikael-Mestawat/Haile Mariam	Majji, Bako, 1898	

Sources: Richard Pankhurst, *Economic History of Ethiopia 1800-1935 (1968)*; *The Southern Marches of Imperial Ethiopia* (2002), Alexander Bulatovich, *Ethiopia through Russian Eyes, Country in Transition 1896-1898* (2000), Bahru Zewude, *A History of Modern Ethiopia 1855-1913*; (1991); Chris Prouty, *Empress Taytu and Menilek II: Ethiopia 1883-1910 (1986)*; Lapiso G. Dilebo, *Ye Ethiopia yegebbar sereat na jimer capitalism 1900-1966*; Harold G. Marcus, *The Life and Times of Menelik II Ethiopia 1844-1913 (1995)*; Anthony Mockler, *Haile Selassie's War,* (1984), Chris Prouty Rosenfeld, *A Chronology of Menelik II of Ethiopia 1844-1913 (1976), Ethiopian Border States* http://www.worldstatesmen.org/Ethiopia_states.html accessed on 5/24/2003; Ulrich Braukamper, *A History of Hadiyya in Southern Ethiopia* (2012). Table and compilation is by me.

4.4.6. Tigray's Final Submission

Although the relationship between Shewa and Tigray ruling houses was rocky at times, the Tigray province had maintained internal autonomy and was ruled by Mengesha Yohannes from March 1889 until 1898. Beginning from the time he assumed power as an heir Mengesha's journey, however, was not an easy one. He was conflicted between submitting to Menelik and maintaining his father's title of *neguse negest* and declaring himself as such. But he did not have the capability to overcome Menelik's overwhelming power. The army of Tigray was in disarray after the Battle of Metemma. Several powerful figures within Tigray challenged Mengesha's legitimacy as an heir. He had to fight with some of them to consolidate his power. He vacillated between submissions and rebellions. Italians continued playing a subversive role to create rift between Mengesha and Menelik. In May 1891 in his letter to Dr. de Martino, he used "King of Kings of Zion, King of Kings of Ethiopia"[517] seal to describe himself. He refused to come to Shewa for submission. At the beginning of 1892, the relationship between him and Menelik got worse and war seemed imminent. But in February Menelik decided against declaring the war. By April of that year Mengesha was carrying "imperial red umbrella" and "people address Mengesha as *jan-hoi*."[518] But in September he "announces he will submit to Menelik" which Alula and Sebhat opposed.[519] At April of 1894 he was on the way to Shewa with 6,000 men. Alula and Hagos were with him and he entered Addis Ababa on June 2nd. The "submission ceremony" was held on June 9th in which he was "pardoned with reproaches" but "denied title of *negus*,"[520] which will become a bitter pill for Mengesha to swallow in the ensuing years.

Attempts were made to mend the relationship between the two power-contending royal houses of Shewa and Tigray by arranging marriage between Mengesha Yohannes and Taytu's niece, Kefay Wole. The marriage project was engineered by *Etege* Taytu. She made sure that a highly publicized marriage was accompanied with myriads of gifts. For the next few years, after that marriage, there was not much problem between the two sides. It seemingly brought a temporary fix. Mengesha led the Tigray army and fought against Italian aggression in the Battle of Adwa alongside Menelik. In post Adwa, however, the Shewa-Tigray relationship began showing cracks. Mengesha vacillated in his loyalty to the emperor and showed insubordination. Priests and other intermediaries shuttled from Shewa, carrying special messages from Taytu and reminding him about the marriage, the wickedness of Satan, to stop listening to wicked people's advice, and so on. Regardless, Mengesha made clear his insubordination.

History repeated itself. The marriage project failed to bring any meaningful remedy; another reminder of spectacularly failed arranged marriage between Menelik's daughter, Zewuditu, and Yohannes's son, Areaya in early 1880s. Neither Areaya's, nor Mengesha's marriages produced desired results because they did not address a much deeper, underlying cause which persisted between the two houses: *power rivalry and deep-rooted distrust.* Menelik could have bestowed a *negus* title on Mengesha just like he allowed *ras* Hailu of Gojjam to become *negus*. In other words, to retain his father's *negus* title. But Menelik did not trust Mengesha. Menelik maintained a good relationship with Italian colonial office in Asmara and made sure that Mengesha did not get support from them. Eventually, he dispatched large armies of his cousin, *ras* Mekonnen and others to the north. By an apparent military power display, Menelik forced Mengesha out of his father's domain and exiled to Ankobar prison, where he died in 1906. He was replaced by *ras* Mekonnen of Harar for a short time, and later by Wole Bitul. To tame it further, the province was divided into three Tigray native rulers appointed by Menelik. Tigray was eventually brought into Menelik's hands and Shewa's power base was reassuringly secured in the north.

Table 3: Northern Rulers &Years of Submission to Menelik II

Region	Year of Submission	Native Ruler
Gojjam	1889	*Negus* Tekle Haymanot Tessema.[3]
Quara, Enfaz, Lasta, Begemeder Semein,	1889 1889	*Dejaz*.Meshesha Tewodros.[4] Gessess Wolde Hana,[5] Wole Bitul, Mangasha Atikim.[6]
Tigray	March 1890 1st sub–mission, 1894 formally submitted.	*Ras* Mengesha Yohannes.[7]

3   His given name was Adal Tessema. He was made *negus* by Yohannes IV in January 1881. Menelik let him retain his negus title. He died in 1901, but his families ruled Gojjam until the Ethiopian Revolution with few exceptions of intermittently appointed Shewa-Amhara governors, who also faced opposition from the people and were removed.

4   Meshesha was *Atse* Tewodros's elder son who was "out of favor with his father." In 1865 he helped Menelik & Shewans escape from Meqdela by leaving "gates of the fortress...unguarded" (Prouty 1986:6). Menelik made him ras in 1889.

5   Gessess was a son of a younger sister of Empress Taytu. Wole was Taytu's brother.

6   Mangasha Atkim was a Gojjamie and Menelik's favorite.

7   Mengesha was an illegitimate son of Emperor Yohannes IV by his brother's (Gugsa's) wife. He was legitimized & made an heir by the Emperor at his deathbed in March 1889. Until that day, he was regarded as Gugsa's son. Some powerful men in Tigray refused to recognize him as an heir which created chaos and disarray. Ras Mengesha and Alula Aba Nega refused to submit to Menelik. Menelik's refusal to make him a *negus* angered him. He vacillated between loyalty & rebellion until he submitted under Menelik's imminent threat of military action. He fought Italy in Adwa along Menelik's side. Soon after he rebelled. He was removed and exiled to Ankobar prison, and he died there in 1906.

Chapter 5

Tactics of Menelik's Armies and Rationale for Conquest

"Tessema Nadew announced a new Menilekian policy. 'Up to now I have made war to kill, ravage, pillage and collect beasts and slaves. Now His Majesty Menilek wants no more of this kind of aggression.'" - Chris Prouty, *Empress Taytu and Menilek II: Ethiopia 1883-1910.* 1986:206

"Whenever the army surged forward, there was the utmost devastation; houses were burned, crops destroyed, and people executed." - Harold G. Marcus, *The Life and Times of Menilek II, Ethiopia 1844-1913,* 1995:67

5.1. Tactics of Menelik's Armies

"We land here and here and here. Then march down here and up there, uniting the armies. Rich country... We live on the land, burning and pillaging if the inhabitants don't give us what we want. A little dose will tame them. We'll sweep all before us." -Hermann Hagedorn, *Makers of Madness (1914)*

For anyone who studied Menelik's southern marches of conquests of the late nineteenth century and early twentieth century and the subsequent tactics undertaken during those military expeditions; the resemblance between the *Makers of Madness* play scene quoted above and the tactics and objectives of Menelik's conquests was unmistakable. As in the play, the main objective of the "imperial march" was subduing the "rich country" with expressed goal of conquering ("we'll sweep all before us") and permanently settling and controlling the vanquished ("to live on the land"). This plan necessitated employing scorch-earth tactics ("burning and pillaging") against those peoples who resisted and/or refused to submit peacefully ("if the inhabitants don't give us what we want").

Various authoritative sources such as Pankhurst (1968), Darkwah (1975), Prouty (1986), Marcus (1995) and others described the heavy-handedness and devastating methods of invasions and tactics used by the imperial army. The tactics were designed to subject targeted communities to severe punishments and harsh treatments. While several historians mentioned some of the tactics and strategies employed by the armies Menelik, in one way or the other, the biographer of Emperor Menelik,, Harold G. Marcus (1995) did thorough investigation of the "devastating" tactics of the armies were from mobilization to the initial military reconnaissance stage to the battles and afterwards. Here I used generously from his work.

Once Menelik decided to conduct *zamacha* (expedition of conquest/raid) against certain region, the king's decrees were announced in public places "a month or fifteen days before the departure." Not heeding the kings order would result in severe consequences of confiscation of all belongings and properties. On set time all would flock to a designated area, "from time to time new forces joining the main army...This mob of soldiers, animals, retainers, wives, slaves, priests with portable church altars and religious objects...encamped...The king occupied the central position."[521] The reconnaissance detachment would be deployed first.

> Once in enemy territory, the *fanno*[522] moved one or two days
> march ahead of the main force, devastating the deserted

countryside. During the first skirmishes between patrols, the invading army took prisoners for questioning. Those who refused to disclose the enemy's where-about and where the cattle were concealed were shot immediately, as warning to the remaining captives. Co-operative individuals were well treated, given new clothes and a horse, and acted as guides for the Shoans. Once the critical intelligence had been obtained, the invaders were ready to attack[523]

As we shall discuss later in this chapter and elsewhere in the book, such tactics were used time and again to gain cooperation, to coerce submission, to make a lesson to others, and to maintain control. Harold described the next phase of attack and the tactics associated to it which is more harsh and severe than the reconnaissance phase. During this phase, the army marches forward "to an assault line" and regroup. "Menelik will be in the center surrounded by his young favorites (the *balamwal*) and his various personal guards." He will order the assault, which will go on for "eight or ten hours," after which "the soldiers began to return to the camp with herds of cattle and groups of women and children: captive able-bodied males and the elderly were killed."[524]

The severity of the *zamacha* was aimed at the eradication of all resistance. Harshness was particularly prominent when a long series of campaigns had been required, where resistance had taken a heavy toll of Shoan troops or where the kings' prior offer of honourable submission had been rejected. Whenever the army surged forward, there was the utmost devastation; houses were burned, crops destroyed, and people executed. Two or three violent attacks occurred during any one campaign until the camp overflowed with booty and prisoners. Only when the remaining enemy authorities decided to surrender did the commander-in-chief halt the assaults. After a formal act of submission, looting and burning were forbidden for a people now Menelik's subjects.[525]

Now the enemy was subdued and conquered. Menelik "assigned a Shoan nobleman with his retinue and some colonists to reorganize and administer the ravaged land, while the main force returned home" carrying and overburdened with war booty and captive people, now slaves. "Once in safe territory the booty was divided, and the king received one-half to two-thirds of the total. The victorious re-entry into the capital was solemn and brilliant, accompanied by much pageantry."[526]

Such tactics and strategies of destruction and devastation were widely used, particularly, in the regions which resisted or attempted to resist the invasions. R. H. Kofi Darkwah, in his authoritative book, *Shewa, Menelik and the Ethiopian Empire 1813-1889* (1975) wrote that "a considerable number of enemy was killed off during campaigns. It...was usual for the Shewans to burn down the whole villages."[527] What happened to those who escaped the killings and burnt villages? Their fate was slightly better than the dead. They fall into one of the two options left to them. Darkwah wrote that those who were captured would be taken to Shewa as prisoners of war (slaves); and those who escaped the capture would become *gabbars* for the conquering forces. He wrote:

> ...those who survived the campaigns...some were taken captives to Shewa where they were recruited to swell the royal troops and also the troops of the governors...Those who survived the campaigns but escaped capture remained on land to pay tribute to the conquerors and to form a peasant-soldier division of Shewa army.[528]

Bulatovich based on the account of the former participant of *ras* Gobana's army described devastating tactics employed against 'un-submissive tribes.' "Approaching the domain of an unsubimissive tribe, the Ras surrounded the border by night. At dawn, his huge horde was already flying like the wind in the all directions, destroying everything that fell in its path.... At the decisive moment, he set his reserves in Motion."[529]

As the governor of Illubabor, *ras* Tessema Nadew, had openly acknowledged in 1897 that an official Menelikan policy was waging the
"war to kill, ravage, pillage and collect beasts and slaves."[530] Thomas
Pakenham noted that the French envoy "was told by an Ethiopian
that one of Menelik *rases* had sent cavalry to burn the villages in a
wide circle around, killing the menfolk and enslaving the women and
children. Then he would move his camp and repeat the process."[531]

Menelik's occupation of the south through a series of military
expeditions, according to Richard Pankhurst, had "produced much
devastation," which, in addition to creating casualties and "destructions of housing", had caused "extensive seizure of cattle, grain, and
slaves."[532] As an adopted tactic, Pankhurst stated that, the troops
fire shots and the natives would run away from their homes and
village; and then the troops would loot all their grains.[533] Thanks
to Bulatovich, who was embedded with *ras* Wolde Giyorgis's army
during south-western conquests, we have a great deal of information about unfortunate fate of the people of southwestern region.
Bulatovich wrote:

> In November 1896 Ras Wolde Giyorgis, the first of the three
> participants in the campaign, marched into Kaffa from Kulo
> with 10,000 men and, *putting to fire and sword everything on
> the way*, arrived at the city of Andrachi, the capital of Kaffa,
> which he build a fortified camp. Tato Chenito [Sherocho]
> retreated...Having consolidated his position in Andrarchi,
> Ras Wolde Giyorgis divided his army into large detach-
> ments, and sent them out in various directions. These de-
> tachments laid waste the country, ravaging it for a radius of
> tens of versts(seven miles), taking prisoner the women and
> children who were hidden in the forests, and setting fire to
> everything that could burn."[534]

The result of such scorched-earth tactics was the obvious one:
Wanton destruction and mass killings which Bulatovich wrote in
Kaffa on his diary of January 8, 1898:

…before us appeared the dreadful signs of death and destruction. Amid the green grass, the white of human bones shone here and there. Settlements were nowhere to be seen –only thick weeds, growing on plots of recently cultivated earth, bear testimony of the people who once lived here. An evil fairy of war destroyed them and scattered their bones across the fields. The closer we came to the capital of Kaffa, the more noticeable became the signs of recent battles. Near the town itself, clearings were completely strewn with human bones…[535]

The other tactic often practiced by Shewa army was overcoming the enemy with an overwhelming force. This was exactly what happened to the regions which repulsed previous attempts of conquests or put up stiff resistances.

In order to defeat *tato* Gaki Sherocho of Kaffa, Menelik mobilized the forces of *ras* Wolde Giorgis, *dejazmach* Demissew, *ras* Tessema, and the armies of Kullo, Konta, and of Jimma simultaneously, encircled and caused massive devastation.[536] Likewise Menelik defeated *kawa* Tona of Wolayta by mobilizing nearly all the armies of the empire; which included his own personal army, the armies of *ras* Mikael Ali of Wollo, *liqa mequas* Abate Bawyalew, *dejazmach* Balcha Safo, *ras* Wolde Giorgis Aboye, and armies Abba Jifar II of Jimma.[537]

What made Menelik's conquests unique was permanent occupation of conquered lands and establishment of garrisons, or *ketemas* (towns) in apparent departure from his predecessors. Prior to Menelik, the conquerors would leave the area after taking war booty and subduing the conquered to tribute payments. It was "rare" for conquerors to occupy conquered lands permanently. But it was not unknown. There were several examples of new *ketemas* which were "built in each newly conquered district and given to Shewan subjects for occupation."[538] Darkwah wrote: "This…was how Harr Amba, Kundi, and Ankobar itself had originated in the eighteenth century; similarly, this was how Angolola and Cholie, in the Soddo country, grew up in the reign of Sahle Selassie, and Liche and Addis Ababa in the reign of Menelik."[539]

5.2. Rationale

Menelik's invasions were driven primarily by the 'might is right' approach. To use Teshale's description it was carried out using the "language of gun." Besides, the rationale for conquests included, what Jurgen Osterhammel called the "three self-justificatory patterns" which "invaders marshal...separately or together as need dictates." The three 'self-justificatory patterns' are: "1. the right of the conqueror, which may simply declare existing occupation rights to be null and void. 2. the seventeenth-century Puritan doctrine of terra nullius, which regards land populated by hunter-gatherer or herdsman is "ownerless," freely acquirable, and in need of cultivation. 3. the missionary duty to civilize "savages," often added afterward as a secondary ideology or post festum legitimation of coercive dispossession."[540]

Obviously, the notion of *'terra nullius'* was one of the "fictitious empty land"[541] reasons given to wage wars and to justify the task of *agar maqnat* in Ethiopia. Once the areas were subdued and brought under imperial control, the policy of "the right of the conqueror" entitled imperial forces and administrators to expropriate conquered lands and resources. Conquered lands in the south automatically belonged to the king, who can distribute them solely on his whims and wishes. It also entitled them to categorize the people in the conquered territories as subjects who would be distributed to the settlers-soldiers as *gabbars*. Following at the footsteps of military, the Orthodox Church, duly supported by the state, was at hand to build churches and to convert the natives; thereby fulfilling its sacred 'missionary duty to civilize "savages."

Conquered lands and peoples, therefore, were now "freely acquirable" and "ownerless." Thus, existing native land rights and centuries old inheritance rights were declared "null and void." The lands were apportioned among the northern authorities (governors, local administrators, clergy, *naftegna* (settler-soldiers and peasants). The settlers and military administrators were allocated *gabbars* (peasants) in accordance with their ranks and status (see part three).

Chapter 6

Major Factors Contributed for Menelik's Military Victories

"...in Abyssinia, more than even in most places, might is right," - Lord G. Edwards, *With the Mission to Menelik 1897.* 1898:150

"War is war...the more the one with superior strength can defeat his enemy, the better."-Alexander Bulatovich, *With the Armies of Menelik II, Ethiopia through Russian Eyes,* 2000:371

"They ('Assili' people) entreated me to make my home amongst them, and teach them the art of manufacturing guns, so that they might become as well armed as the Habesha. Then they could fight them, whereas now, without guns, they acknowledged their inability of accomplishing anything." Montagu Sinclair Wellby, *Twixt Sider and Menelik: An account of a year's expedition Zeila to Cairo through unknown Abyssinia,* 1901:189

6.1. The Modern Firearms Factor

Menelik...still ruler of Shoa was fully conscious of the decisive importance of fire-arms...considered their import a matter of life and death" Richard Pankhurst, *Fire-Arms in Ethiopia (1800-1935),* Ethiopian Observer 6(2), 149.

Firearms were introduced into the northern Ethiopian region by Turks and Muslims in the sixteenth century. They were later brought by Portuguese who came in aid of Ethiopian king against the invasion of Gragn Ahmed.[542] The Shewa kingdom possessed firearms and king Sahle Selassie (1813-1847) got "increasing quantities" of firearms as gift. However, firearms in Shewa were "relatively scarce until the time of Menelik."[543] As John Illife in *Africans: The History of a Continent* put it "the possession and use of modern firearms had played significant role for Menelik's success and victories."[544]

When Menelik seized power in Shewa, he did not start it from scratch. Rather, as an heir of the Shewa dynasty, he had inherited an organized system of government in which firearms were pretty much in use for expansion dating back at least to his grand-father's reign. Sahle Selassie "in the early years of 1840s," had possessed "muskets, percussion caps, pistols, and cannon."[545] King Sahle Selassie, according to a European who "lived in Shoa from 1842-1843… had…more than 1,000 fire-arms, a figure which was confirmed by Krapf."[546] As Pankhurst noted, soon after he became a Shewa king, Menelik "at once appealed to the French for arms" because he "was fully conscious of the decisive importance of fire-arms" and "he considered their import a matter of life and death."[547] In 1867 he had 2,000 - 3,000 muskets and many of his rifle men were Gondares.[548] Pankhurst thought the reason for majority of Gondares to become Menelik's rifle men was because the people from that city were more familiar with firearms.[549] In addition to using "private traders" for arms procurement, by mid-1870s Menelik established contacts with Egypt's Ismail Khedive and Italy, and requested for arm supplies.[550] "The first thing he wanted from the Europeans therefore was an unlimited supply of firearms."[551] By 1872 when a French man, Pierre Arnoux, was in Shewa.

> At this time the army numbered 40,000 and was composed equally of cavalry and infantry. Less than one-quarter were armed with fowling pieces, matchlocks, and percussion guns of various types…When Arnoux equipped one hundred of the royal guards with rifled carbines, the king exclaimed,

'Ah! If only I had ten thousand men like that.'Arnoux replied
that with French instructors and arms of from Europe, his
army soon would improve...Europe, where Anoux was authorized to act as Shoa's representative.[552]

From various sources Menelik had "received substantial foreign aid in the form of military and technical assistance inviting
Europeans to his court to assist in the training of his men. With the
support of armaments and expertise, atrocious wars were conducted
against relatively less armed"[553] peoples of the South, most of them
were only armed spears, shields, clubs, and sabers.

Italy's representative in Addis Ababa, Count Antonelli, reported
in November 1887 that Menelik "had perhaps 50,000 men armed
with rifles of which 12,000 were modern."[554] The firearms factor was
apparent in enabling him to defeat some of the fiercest resistances
such as that of Arsi which was conquered in 1886/87; and Harar in
early 1887.

By this time, in addition to Wollo & Shewa Oromo regions, he
controlled the rich Gibe states in the south-west, Leqa and Qellem
in the West, large parts of Gurage and Hadiya in the center, and Ittu
and Harar in the east. The resources he controlled in the conquered
regions brought him more wealth. This, in turn, enabled him to purchase more modern weapons. The conquest of Harar, for example,
had opened the safest and shorter trade route to the sea and facilitated
weapons imports.

By 1889, shortly before he began his *zemecha* to conquer southern
kingdoms of Kambata, Sidama, Gedeo, Wolayta, Gamo, Gofa, Kulo,
Konta, etc..; he "had at least 60,000 guns of all kinds, one million
cartridges and about one million percussion caps, and many barrels
of gunpowder."[555] By mid 1890s, Menelik's firearms power had
grown exponentially. In addition to his bodyguards of 3,000 he was
in a position of mobilizing up to 100,000 irregulars with firearms.[556]
By then only Menelik and Mahdists alone in all Africa were armed
with machine guns.[557] Mohammed Hassen (1994) understandably
lamented about "the absence of firearms in the Gibe region and

Wallaga and the slowness of…Oromo leaders to adjust themselves to the use of such weapons" which resulted in obvious "weakness of the defense system" of those regions.[558] The same argument could be made about other southern kingdoms as well.

> During the second half of the nineteenth century, the Amhara polity to the north had access to a large quantity of modern European weapons of destruction which drastically topped the balance power in its favor. Never since the first half the sixteenth century had such a radical change in the balance of power occurred in the Horn of Africa and with such speed as it did during the second half of the nineteenth century. The new weapons not only made victories easier for the Amhara, but also enabled their leaders to set up administrative and military colonies Oromo territory at a long distance from their home base.[559]

M. Sinclair Wellby (1901) described how the Asilli people in the southern frontier region had clearly understood the role of firearms as war game-changer. They asked him to teach them how to manufacture modern weapons. "They entreated me to make my home amongst them, and teach them the art of manufacturing guns, so that they might become as well armed as the Habesha. Then they could fight them, whereas now, without guns, they acknowledged their inability of accomplishing anything."[560]

What the Asilli people faced at the turn of the century was the fate of all other peoples who were subdued several years before them as a result of the power of modern firearms. Uri Almagor's research: *Institutionalizing a fringe periphery: Dassanetch-Amhara relations*, demonstrated a game-changing capacity of firearms possession even in ruler-subject relationships. "The first encounter of the Dassanetch with the Amhara was violent and traumatic; troops brought destruction and death to people who were powerless to retaliate."[561] Such a role of one side dominance changed "within two decades of occupation," when "the Dassanetch were equipped with firearms and soon emerged as a dominant fighting forces," and hence the probability of "Dassanetch raids terrified Amhara soldiers."[562] As Almagori put it:

> This mutual fear of confrontation formed the basis for an uneasy balance of power. Both sides realized that they were more or less evenly matched and that any attempt at using force would be met with resistance. This realization served as a means of control, for it implied a rule of deterrence. Slight deviations from this rule (arms searches, the Dassanetch breaking into a military depot in Kalem to steal food, arms, and ammunition) were condemned by the injured parties, but were also tolerated as part of the game, as an acceptable show of force. Such tacit agreement was exemplified in way taxes were collected. The Dassenetch knew that tax evasion would provoke violent countermeasures; on the other hand, Amhara officers knew that punitive action would only invite violent resistance. Therefore, both sides have to come to terms. The Dassanetch paid less taxes than the Amhara had expected to collect and employed delaying tactics that drew out payment for years on end; the Amhara governor accepted whatever payments were made and refrained from resorting to force in order to increase his revenue.[563]

Such tolerance and "mutual fear of potential violence" was completely absent when unarmed and 'powerless' communities attempted to resist well-armed and powerful forces. Even many years after initial conquest, subject communities remained helpless when they were subjected to extreme forms of subjugations. In Maale not paying a preferred type of tribute (ivory) was sufficient enough to take away their children as slaves.[564] In western Ethiopia inability to pay tribute resulted in taking away children for slavery.[565] In Aariland: "Failure to pay tribute and to perform labor service resulted in slavery. Many Aari (mostly women and children) were taken away as domestic slaves because Aari families could not afford to pay the tribute or to perform the labor services."[566] The same was true in Gimira and elsewhere.

6.2 Gobana & The Oromo Factor

*"Ras Gobana, supported by numerous Galla (Oromo) nobles and sol-
diers, in fact carried out much of the conquering other Galla (Oromo)
tribes for Menelik."* Donald N. Levine, *Wax and Gold*, 1974, 85

By any measure, Gobana Dachie was a power behind the success
of Menelik conquests. This was particularly true at the onset of
the young Menelik's expansion ventures. Gobana was astonishingly
successful in subduing various Shewa and Wollo Oromo groups
and tribes. He expanded his success further into Mecha countries
by conquering Oromo kingdoms and territories in south-west and
western regions. He used both persuasion and coercion - carrot
and stick approaches -in order to gain submissions. In other words,
rewarding those which submitted peacefully and destroying those
which resisted or refused to join him. In addition to several initial
conquest missions, his renowned cavalry was dispatched to various
areas, including to south-central regions of Gurage-Hadiya-Wolayta,
to put down rebellions and to crush fierce resistances.

As Levine put it: "Ras Gobana, supported by numerous Galla
nobles and soldiers, in fact carried out much of the conquering
other Galla tribes for Menelik."[567] Lapiso G. Delebao summed up
Gobana's preeminent role as Menelik's leading general in breaking
down centuries old Oromo threat against Shewa. In Lapiso's words:
"This formidable Oromo warlord brought southern Oromo...under
the Amhara in five years, a mission that Amhara kings and warlords
tried and failed in 400 years."[568] On one hand, Gobana's unique role
in Menelik's empire building endeavor earned him accolades from
some Ethiopians who see him as a hero; and, on the other hand,
he became a prime target of attacks from others, particularly from
Oromo nationalist groups, who see him as a traitor and sell out. Here
I refrain from delving into his service and controversies as I briefly
discussed them in chapter 16.2.

The Oromo disunity has long been discussed by historians. This
has been displayed in Ethiopian political scene ever since the Oromo

expansion set on from their "homeland...in southern Ethiopia, somewhere between the middle lakes of the Great Rift Valley and the Bale
plateau."[569] In late nineteenth century the top generals who were instrumental for Amhara and Tigrean kings were Oromos. Ras Darso,
general of *negus* Tekle Haymanot's army of Gojjam, ras Gobana, the
ablest general of Menelik's army, and ras Mikael Ali, staunch ally of
neguse negest Yohannes IV were Oromos. The latter fought along with
Yohannes and then he joined Menelik's camp following the death
of Yohannes in Metemma. "Exploiting the internal division of the
Arsi," ras Darge Sahle Selassi "inflicted a shattering defeat on them at
the Battle of Azule, in September 1886."[570] Some Ethiopian scholars
such as Dr. Messay Kebede (1999) went to the extent of saying that
Menelik's southern conquest was to bring unity among Oromos because of the inability of the Oromos and their gada system to bring
about unity amongst themselves. While such claim is merit less and
based on gross generalization, undoubtedly, existence of regional,
cultural, and religious diversities among the Oromos made them
vulnerable and disunited.

6.3. Newly conquered lands and their resources

> *"As King of Shoa, Menelik had exploited the south and south-
> west to purchase weapons; as emperor, he used its wealth to bol-
> ster the north's sagging economy, and to ensure the continuation
> of Amhara-Tigrean political and cultural hegemony."* Harold
> Marcus, *The Life and Times of Menelik II: Ethiopia 1844-1913*
> 1995:140

Menelik controlled vast resources – natural and manpower – in the
conquered lands. It contributed significantly to further his conquest
endeavors and to strengthen his power in several ways. (1) It enabled
him to control export-commodities (coffee, gold, civet, wax, ivory,
slaves, ghee, gum and so on) which became vital revenue sources.
Growing demand in the world market for such commodities further
opened his appetite for more conquests and for strengthening the

existing ones. (2) Menelik redirected southern trades routes into Shewa. By doing so, he further increased Shewa's trade, which, in turn, increased revenues from taxes. (3) Previously submitted and conquered regions became sources of conscriptions to field new fighters and swell up various armies of his loyal generals.

He was also skillful in deploying existing armies of previously subdued rulers such as those of Jimma, Leqa, Qellam, Kullo, and Konta against stronger rulers which resisted occupation such as Wolayta, Kaffa, and Ben Shangul. Abba Jifar II was a prime example in this regard. As Herbert S. Lewis, in *A Galla Monarchy: Jimma Abba Jifar, Ethiopia,* wrote:

> Abba Jifar regularly paid tributes, generally managed to escape Menelik's anger, and enthusiastically aided Menelik in his wars against Kullo (1889), Walamo (1894), and Kafa (1897).[571]

(4) Constant and reliable flow of commodities and tributes from the South brought greater wealth, which enabled him to purchase more weapons and pay off debts such as arms loan from Italy.[572] Harold G. Marcus wrote that "the king began to acquire modern weapons with the revenues derived from the south-west. Both goods and slaves were used as exchange... Many slaves were however supplied by him from the tribute received from the slaving countries of the south-west, primarily Jimma, Laka, Guma, and Gera."[573]

In addition to commodities, taxation from subject regions especially from regions designated as *maed bet*, became the main source of revenue for Menelik. It also remained as a revenue source for the regimes which succeeded him. According to Herbert S. Lewis, who cited Cerulli as his source, Jimma Abba Jiffar's: "annual tribute to Shoa was MT[8]*$87.000 plus MT$15,000 for the army of the empire but Lipsky puts the figure at MT$200,000."[574] (5) Distribution of expropriated lands from conquered regions became a magnet attracting northern settlers to the South. Settler communities, in turn,

8   Maria-Teresa thalers

helped the new administrative system efforts to take root in three ways. First, northern settlers who were mainly based in garrison towns helped to further consolidate subdued areas as administrative and auxiliary bodies. Armed peasant–settlers, *naftegna,* also served as a fighting force when needed. Secondly, they became agents of cultural diffusion to disseminate Amharic language and Orthodox Christianity, which resulted in what Messay (1999) termed as: "Rapid Ethiopianization and Christianization of the southern populations"[575] Thirdly, conquered regions not only became self-sustaining economically, but also they became catalysts for overall growth and expansion of socio-cultural and political power of the center. It is from this perspective that Harold Marcus wrote:

> As King of Shoa, Menelik had exploited the south and south-
> west to purchase weapons; as emperor, he used its wealth
> to bolster the north's sagging economy, and to ensure the
> continuation of Amhara-Tigrean political and cultural
> hegemony."[576]

The volume of Menelik's purchase of weapons kept growing and growing. His constant need for more resources and revenues exacerbated the exploitation. "Always in need of money, he allowed his southern domain to be ruthlessly exploited for livestock, and for slaves for export across the Red Sea."[577] Table 4 below shows how natural resources from the South had become a major source of revenues for the emperor. The table, however, shows *only a one-year (1899-1900)* export which passed through Addis Ababa. The volume and magnitude of export revenues would have been huge if cash amounts for all commodities were given and exports via other routes were included.

Records of Ethiopian commodities export through Djibouti shows that by 1932 coffee export had increased to 11, 412,000 kilograms, wax increased in 1934 to 400,000 kilograms and civet in 1910 to 422,000 kilograms. On the other hand, due to excessive hunting and poaching, the elephant population was exterminated from some regions. Thus, ivory export fell sharply to 64,000 kilograms in 1912.

It plummeted to 3,000 kilograms in 1930. Two years later in 1932 it fell to 300 kilograms only. By 1934 there was no ivory export. The civet export followed similar patterns. It fell from 422,000 kilograms in 1910 to 185,000 kilograms in 1918 and to zero from 1919 to 1934. (Pankhurst, 1968).

Table 4: Export commodities via Addis Ababa 1899-1900.[578]

Commodity	Origin of the commodity	Total amount	
		Weight in ounces	Maria Theresa
Gold	Ben Shangul	8,000	224,000
	Wollega	8,000	220,000
	Dubbe	10,000	280,000
	Shanqella	4,000	112,000
Total		**30,000**	**856,000**
Ivory	Kaffa	----	----
	Wallaga	----	----
	Hillu	----	----
	Shanqella	----	----
	Walamo/(wolayta	35,125 Killo	600,000
	Kambaata	----	----
	Wurru	----	----
	Arussi/Arsi	----	----
	Sidamo/Sidaama	----	----
Coffee	Enarya	----	----
	Limmu	----	----
	Jimma	3,405,000 --	----
	Hillu	5,107,500 kilos	600,000
	Kaffa	----	----
	Gumma	----	----
Salt	Boromeda	500,000 pieces	125,000
Civet	Kaffa		
	Wollega		
	Jimma	850 kilos	75,000
	Limmu	Chiefly from Kaffa	
	Hillu		
	Harjo		
TOTAL			**1,603,500**

6.4. The Adwa Victory

The Adwa victory over Italy was credited for a big momentum for Menelik's final conquest marches carried out from mid-1896 onwards. The victory in Adwa had raised his fame and stature to a higher level at international level. After Adwa Ethiopia's independence was recognized by many countries. "In 1897, a year after the victory in Adowa, missions were sent to Menelik's court by the Turks, Russians, Italians, the Sudan Dervishes, the British, with two from the French."[579] His prestige was also elevated to a higher level within the country. He re-armed his already better armed forces with most modern weapons seized from defeated Italians and immediately deployed it to further conquests. He directed his generals to subdue the frontier regions in the south, south-west and west.

This unleashed what I called the final phase of conquests (see chapter 4.4.). From mid-1896–1906 various kingdoms and territories of Kaffa, Illubabor, Ben Shangul, Borana, Maji, and the Lower Omo region were conquered. It was also after Adwa that Menelik decided to bring down the Tigre ruler, Mengesha Yohannes, who had been vacillating between rebellion and loyalty. Mengesha, who led the Tigre people against the Italian invasion and fought alongside Menelik in 1896, was exiled to Ankobar prison in 1898.

6.5. Foreign Military Powers and Advisors

The fifth and often overlooked factor in advancing Menelik's conquests was the role played by European citizens and nations. In this regard Europeans who arrived at Shewa as missionaries, adventurers, traders, military advisors, and representatives of their countries had all played a role in helping Menelik procure firearms, in serving as military advisors and trainers and in helping establish contacts with their respective nations. Shewa's association and contact with foreigners dated back to the era of Menelik's grand-father, Sahle Selassie. Menelik was pragmatic and acutely aware about advantages of modern military training and modern weapons. During his

Meqdela years he witnessed Tewodros trying to achieve these things, though he was unsuccessful in getting them as he had wished for. Menelik also witnessed how the British easily defeated Tewodros during Napier's expedition thanks to the superiority of their modern weapons. In post Meqdela he also saw how Kassa Mercha of Tigre, after gaining British weapons, easily defeated *negus* Tekle Giorgis who had emerged as the most powerful ruler in the Amhara region.

It was because of such awareness that the possession of firearms became a "a matter of life and death"[580] for him; and "the first thing" he wanted Europeans in his domain to do for him was to get him "unlimited supply of firearms"[581].

> Even before he became emperor, Menelik invited Europeans to his court to assist in training his men. These trainers mainly French and Russians, and their activities were largely confined to instructing Ethiopian soldiers in the use of certain types of weapons. Some of these individuals even accompanied Ethiopian military units as advisers during campaigns of conquest in the south...there was some effort to train Menelik's soldiers in the organization, strategy, and tactics of European militaries.[582]

Thus in 1877 a Frenchman named Pottier was employed in training a group of Shewan youths in European military techniques. Pino, another Frenchman, was a regular officer in the army which was commanded by Ras Gobana. Swiss engineers, Alfred Ilg and Zemmerman were employed on, among other things, building bridges across the Awash and other rivers to facilitate movement within the kingdom.[583] Some Europeans even took part in the military expeditions. Rosenfeld noted that in January 1898 "Four doctors including Schhusev, and Boulatovich joined Wolde Giorgis"[584] in the south-west.

Of course, when we speak of foreigners who served Menelik, the famous Swiss citizen, Alfred Ilg, comes to mind. During several years of his service, he served the king at various capacities such as working as 'Counselor of the State', as personal envoy to European nations, making arms deals & shipments, and making treaties and negotiations.[585] In the early 1900s a French man, M. Leon Chefneux, was also serving as a "Counsellor of State to the Emperor."[586] In the late 1890s there were two Russian military advisors, Babichev and Leontiev who lived in Qulubi, Hararghe. They were awarded the Ethiopian military titles of *dejazmatch*, and *fitawurari* respectively for their service.[587] When the American government envoy, Skinner, visited Addis Ababa and met Menelik in 1903 there was a "Swiss officer was in command" of training palace artillery troops, and a Frenchman named M. Sourvis, was "the official interpreter and private secretary of the Emperor."[588] Another foreigner, Mr. Dyuba, "a French deserter, a former lieutenant of a cuirassier regiment"[589] was at Menelik's service in late 1890s.

The Russian colonel, Alexander Bulatovich, was perhaps one of the most prominent foreigners who participated directly in the conquest process. He recounted his experiences and adventures in his two books: *From Entoto to River Baro*, and *With the Armies of Menelik*. The latter was about his marching with the army of *ras* Wolde Giorgis, during which time he provided valuable service in conducting reconnaissance, mapping areas, and, in some instances, engaging in combat activities. Paul Henze, in the *Layers of Time*, wrote that Bulatovch had "constructed a series of forts in the southwest which earned him praise from Menelik."[590] Another Russian Nikolai Leontiev was Menelik's favorite. Menelik gave him "territory in the far southwest to develop" and he "remained in Ethiopia for several years."[591] Prouty wrote that Menelik "had granted unspecified lands" to Leontiev who brought from Europe "small army" which, together with "300 soldiers" Menelik assigned, had engaged in sacking, killing, and taking booty from people and the lands where he became a governor.[592]

Part III

Post-Conquest South

"Emperor Menelik's campaign had caused tremendous loss of life. It had caused property destructions. It affected the dignities and liberties of various peoples.' It had stopped the development of their languages and cultures'. All these is undeniable fact." Translated from Amharic by me. Tesfaye Mekonnen *Yedres Le Baletariku* October 1992:29-30.

❖

L ife in post conquest south for conquered peoples was more than unpleasant. It was unpredictable, dreadful, and cumbersome. Southerners found themselves in a vulnerable condition when everything around them suddenly changed. Their system of governance which existed for generations was dismantled and scrapped. Their own rulers, kings, and traditional leaders lost their power. New rulers took over every aspect of the administrative system. New rules were implemented. Their native leaders were given new duties of facilitating the jobs of new rulers - they were made intermediaries.

Lands became *ye negus meret* (king's lands) or *ye mengist meret* (government lands) and were distributed as *gult, maderiya, samon*, etc. Rist (family land inheritance) was abolished and replaced with a *gult* system. Southern peasants/farmers were transformed into *gabbars,* *s*erf-tenants. They were assigned to a master/*gultegna* for lifetime service of paying tributes and providing free labor in the households and farm fields of their masters. The "northern settlers who had acquired tributary rights over southern peasants, the *gabbar,* ended up owning the land altogether, through purchase from distressed *gabbar,* or through forcible seizure."[593]

Southerners, as discussed in this and next chapters, had faced pillaging, subjected to decades of subjugation, and became victims of, in the words of Mecklberg, "government-backed businesses" of slavery. Slaves, along coffee and ivory, became one of the most lucrative commodities. Because of that widespread slave raids, slave-trade, and enslaving practices prevailed. Some southern regions "were reduced virtually to producing slaves"[594] and became "a hunting ground for humans as wells as animals"[595] Native communities were removed forcefully from their homelands by armed slavers, soldiers, and government officials *en masse* and taken to Addis Ababa and to the northern regions. Some were sold into slavery. Others were distributed for domestic servitude. This, in turn, caused massive depopulation in several south-western regions. [Wellby (1901), Bulatovich (2000), Pakenham (1991), Pankhurst (1968), Thesiger (1987) and Starrett & Steffason (1976), Bahru (1991), Braukamper (2012)]. These realities of the post-conquest South, however, were barely investigated or even mentioned in the history books written by most Ethiopian scholars. Most historians primarily focused their attention on presenting and preserving sanitized Ethiopian history.

This book, however, does not delve into the broader themes of subjugation, pillaging, depopulation, or slavery which merit further research by career academicians. My aim here is just to highlight the scope of subjugation, pillaging, slavery, and depopulation which existed and persisted in post-conquest South.

Chapter 7

Subjugation and Pillage

"Tens of thousands of blacks were killed or sold into slavery. Their cattle and gold were looted, their land parceled among the Shoans. Soon Menelik's empire was double the size of Yohannes's empire at its peak. It was imperial expansion and Realpolitik, African-style and it brought greater rewards than any European war in Africa. With gold looted in Kaffa and the south, Menelik was able to re-equip his army, start the process of modernizing his ancient state, and thus the dominance of Shoa far into the twentieth century." Thomas Pakenham, *The Scramble for Africa: The White Man's Conquest of the Dark Continent from 1876-1912,* 1991:486

"Paternalistic and arrogant, Abyssinians looked upon and treated the indigenous people as backward, heathen, filthy, deceitful, lazy, and even stupid...Both literally and symbolically, southerners became the object of scorn and ridicule." Gabru Tareke *Ethiopia: Power and Protest: Peasant Revolts in the Twentieth Century* 1996:71

What made the overall post-conquest South conditions unique, even in comparison to some of the European colonies in Africa, was an absolute authority vested in the hands of the imperial auxiliaries (governors, soldiers, settler-civilians) on one hand; and the condition in which conquered peoples at large were reduced to servitude, second-class citizenship, and slavery on the other hand.

Subjugation of the conquered people was undoubtedly supported with the "administration strategy in the south" which "was not oriented towards integration and equal development within the Empire, but towards exploitation for the benefit of the conquerors."[596] Adverse consequences of such strategy in socio-economic and cultural lives of conquered peoples at large could only be understood with comprehensive and independent investigation, which is beyond the scope of this work. Levine in *Wax and Gold* (1961) termed such consequences as "the drawbacks of Amhara dominance,"[597] which he further explained:

> During the great Amhara expansion under Menelik (1889-1913), many peoples were maltreated. Independent tribesmen were reduced to slavery; unique cultures were decimated; proud kings were dragged in the dust. Those who held down the Amhara position in these occupied territories seized land from the indigenous peoples and exploited them much as would any invader. The unfavorable reputation of the Amhara in the non-Amhara provinces has been due largely to the example of these governors and soldiers whose worst impulses were at times allowed free play.[598]

An influx of settlers from northern provinces into southern regions was common and had become an ever-increasing phenomenon. In September 1890, three years after Harar was conquered, for instance, ras Mekonnen brought with him so many "newcomers" from north, which Caulk, citing ras Mekonnen's biographer, Haile Giorgis, put it as follows: "So numerous were the newcomers who had attached themselves to his train -Tegrayan and Amhara from Gojjam, Lasta, Bagemder as well as Shawans – that his clerical biographer writes that on setting off, "the people of Shawa said: "The whole world has followed him.""[599]

> When an Italian newspaperman, Edoardo Scarfoglio, arrived in Harar early in May 1891, he heard, that no fewer

than two to three hundred thousand people had poured into the new province since its conquest in 1887. He was told that this flow had become a flood after the cattle plague had broken out throughout northern Ethiopia from the middle of 1888.[600]

As Bahru noted, new settlers and settlements in the south had "eased the congestion in the *rist* lands of the north," and also "it transposed the *gabbar-malkagna* relations to most of the newly incorporated regions."[601] Easing the burden on one section of the country meant loading it on those who were already overloaded – exacerbation of exploitations and dispossessions.

The *gabbar* system varied from "mild" at the onset of conquests in some regions to "notorious" in other areas. Generally, as it was seen in Maji and elsewhere in the South. As Garretson (2002) in his excellent research discussed it, *gabbar* related oppression progressed to the worst

> In case of Maji, it seems to have been relatively benign in the early years of imperial rule, but it grew in. By the 1920s and 1930s it was perhaps the most notoriously oppressive gebbar system within the Ethiopian empire. The individual gebbar was initially similar in a very general way to a serf in Eastern Europe, but by the 1930s some districts were reduced virtually to producing slaves, and only after World War II was there a change to tenant system.[602]

Conquered peoples were obliged to carry out large scale and cumbersome duties ranging from construction projects of churches and towns to working in mining fields and performing tasks related to *zemechas*. For instances, in 1901 when Emperor Menelik and Empress Taytu came up with a plan to build a brand new capital city at Addis Alem, Menelik had brought in "some 20,000 Oromo workers to build houses and an imperial residence in a unique style, based on the palace of Versailles,"[603]France. After most buildings were completed, unfortunately, he abandoned his plan of moving into Addis Alem. He then turned the royal residence into a church and decided to build a road to link Addis Ababa to Addis Alem.[604] So in 1903 he asked provincial governors to contribute workers for the road work. "20,000 workers supplied by *ras* Mekonnen and by other chiefs."[605]

Officials in the south were accustomed to governing southerners unjustly and arbitrarily. As Wilfred Thesiger[606] and others testified, subject people were treated as second class citizens and slaves. based on his father's documents, he described in his book, *The Life of My Choice*, the extent of pillaging and enslavement of southerners. "In the subject provinces of south, governors and their armies of occupation pillaged the land and sold the inhabitants into slavery. The soldiers that leave a province sweep up all they can and those that can enter the rest."[607]

Particularly in the west of Omo river region, "the higher state officials considered it their right to when being transferred to another province to force as many of their subordinate peasants as possible to go with them."[608] One such "sweep up" and pillage occurred in 1910 when *ras* Wolde Giorgis Aboye, Menelik's cousin and governor of the south-western regions for 13 years, was transferred to the north as a governor of Begameder. Wolde Giorgis and his deputy, *dejazmach* Damte, using government power and resources plundered and pillaged the region they had ruled for many years. Then they forcefully removed indigenous people from their homelands and carried them off to the north as slaves.

> Dejazmach Birru Haile Mariam was appointed to replace ras Welde Giyorgis in Kefa and Maji, he took up his new post within a month of the departure of Welde Giyorgis and dejazmatch Damte. The change-over was a catastrophic for Maji's people and economy. Maji's whole garrison was withdrawn, and dejazmatch Demte took with him not only his and ras Welde Giyorgis' troops but some of the imperial soldiers as well. These soldiers in turn collected as many

of the gebbar as they could to take north as slaves, or else raided the neighborhood – especially the Boma plateau – to get more cattle, sheep, and any other movable booty they could capture. Maji and its immediate surroundings were denuded after Demte had left in June 1910. One estimate said that the population of Maji dropped from thousands to a few hundred in 1925[609].

The survivors of *ras* Wolde Giorgis and *dejazmach* Damte's reign of subjugation and extreme exploitation had faced similar ordeals because the new governor's dynasty became "the most powerful" and "entrenched" in Maji.

> ...dejazmatch Birru [Haile Mariam] was recalled to Addis Ababa. More important, was the fact that his son Desta Birru and the soldiers remained. They were the most powerful, entrenched, stable, and long-lasting factor in Maji's unfortunate history, from 1910 to at least 1936. Even by 1924, out of a total of 66 principal officers in the Maji area, 41 were still surviving officers *of dejazmach* Birru.[610]

What Habte Giorgis Denegde did to the Gumuz people was consistent with the actions of ras Wolde Giorgis and his successors in the southwest. "At the beginning of the century, *fitawrari* Habta Giyorgis transplanted Gumuz people...from north western Ethiopia to the neighborhood of Qabeena in the Upper Gibe."[611]

What was even more disturbing was that the condition not only remained in place but also, they continued getting worse. Soldiers and armed peasants, generally known as *neftegna,* were engaged in hunting people for fame and for fun sports. Bulatovich on his May 5, 1897 diary wrote the following about hunting natives for "amusement."

> We marched to the very borders of Gimira. The soldiers said Farwell to war, and those who for the whole march had not

succeeded in killing anyone...*established a special sport.* When the detachment abandons a bivouac, they hide in lean-to cabins and wait for when the natives come to the abandoned position, and then shoot at the natives from ambush.[612] Italics added by me.

Years later the practice not only persisted but also widespread. Bahru also reiterated the accounts of the early travelers and eyewitnesses of late nineteenth and early twentieth centuries on how the southerners were killed arbitrarily for fun and rounded up for mass enslavement.

Military commanders and soldiers alike did not consider that they had responsibilities of justly administering and protecting the peoples of the newly conquered territories from the enemy. Instead they saw them as (animals) which they could drive as they wished. Therefore, southwestern Ethiopia particularly became a ground where a human being would be hunted down like a wild game.[613]

Widespread practices of enslavement, constant raids, hunting innocent people for amusements and fame were more than just random acts. Ras Tessema Nadew, Governor of Illubabor and western regions, "announced a new Menilekian policy" to the French expedition team in Gore in late 1897 as follows: "Up to now I have made war to kill, ravage, pillage and collect beasts and slaves. Now, His majesty wants no more of this kind of aggression."[614] The practice, however, did not stop and it continued unchecked and unabated long after Menelik's death. Raids were often carried out by those who were part of government apparatus: local officials, armed peasants, soldiers, and slave traders.

Captain Montagu Sinclair Wellby entered the country legally from the east (Hararghe region) and travelled through southern regions shortly after Menelik's conquest and proceeded to Sudan. He documented several compelling eyewitness accounts of miseries, mistreatments, displacements, and stories of killings in his book, *Twixt Sider and Menelik: An Account of a year's expedition from Zeila to Cairo through unknown Abyssinia,* which was published in 1901. When he visited Harar, he was received by *Ras* Mekonnen. He came across a group of Oromos who were trying to reach *ras* Mekonnen to file their complaints and to seek justice from the governor.

> As soon as the Ras prepared to move off, certain Gallas (who are the inhabitants and former possessors of Southern Abyssinia) rushed forwards, crying loudly, "Abeit!" "Abeit!" which means "Justice!" "Justice!" but for the most part they were promptly collared and roughly handled by the soldiers, who gave them a dose of what they considered "Abeit."[615]

When Wellby travelled through Gamo, Lower Omo Valley, and Lake Rudolf (Lake Turkana) regions, he witnessed the plight of subjected people was even worse.

> I sat down with these citizens of Alibori and listened with interest to all they had to say. They explained to me how they had formerly been the wealthy owners of many head of cattle, whereas to-day they had scarcely any to speak of, and were consequently dependent for their living upon the fish they caught… for the Abyssinians had raided them no fewer than seven times.[616]

The natives narrated to him difficulties they faced and their failed endeavors to reach out to the officials to try to come up with solutions.

> Although they themselves were anxious to arrive at a friendly understanding with the Abyssinians, and were prepared to pay whatever taxes were right, still they were never allowed a chance of doing so. Sometimes they had been even gone out to meet the Abyssinians, taking with them the property they

were willing to give them, but had only been mercilessly shot down. ...unfortunately [they] had now no chance of riding, as all their donkeys had been carried off. Their pitiable story was probably true, for their statements, as far as could be gathered, were corroborated by my own men who had been over to the tribe.[617]

While Wellby was passing through "the Tochi valley," he witnessed starved people and recorded the following sad incident after he saw how the natives rushed down to eat his dead horse.

A certain number of Shangkallas were living on land about these hills, though many of them, I was told, had been killed off by the Habesha. These survivors were in an extremely poor way, living in simple hovels, owning neither cattle nor crops; so when they learnt the death of my pony, they swooped down like carrion birds to feast on the foul, putrid flesh.[618]

Wellby heard several complaints of killings, constant raids, and pillage from all tribes he came across the southern frontier lands. "The Asilli of the district in which I happened to be, complained bitterly of the treatment they suffered at the hands of the Habesha, telling me how ruthlessly they had been shot down, and their cattle carried off."[619] Wellby's travel through the south was authorized by Menelik who provided soldiers to accompany and escort him. Several cattle and sheep were given to him together with hundreds of *southerners* to carry and transport his heavy supplies.

My caravan, by this time, might almost have been called an imposing one, for, in addition to my sixty animals and forty odd men, there were quite two hundred Gallas[620] laden with supplies for us, a flock of sheep, and nearly thirty head of cattle, as well as the fifty soldiers, many of whom were mounted, and their large crowd of Galla bearers. ...Most of my Galla bearers ...scarcely ate enough to keep a cat alive[621]

Assigning southerners to foreigners and foreign adventurers to carry luggage and supplies was a common practice. Bulatovich's diaries provided several instances of indigenous people being used as his *ashkars* (servants) for carrying and transporting heavy supplies and luggage throughout his journeys from Addis Ababa to the southwest, west, and to the coast on several occasions. Other travelers also documented similar stories.

When Menelik granted permission in 1897 for the French colonial expedition team travel from Ethiopia to Fashoda, Sudan; Bonchamps "persuaded Menelik to let him have guides and the letter of introduction to the local Governor of Gore,"who was *ras* Tessema Nadew. He got what he asked for; and they began their journey from Addis Ababa. Bonchamps started his journey "from Addis Ababa with three ardent French companions and an escort of 100 surly Ethiopians... The surly Ethiopians, forced to carry six tons of stores, soon became mutinous."[622] He described that the land is "a green wasteland" and seven years ago "Menelik's conquering army had swept through these green upland valleys, dotted with Galla (Oromo) villages and rich in grain and cattle."[623]

> Now there was hardly a trace of huts, people or animals. Bonchamps was told by an Ethiopian that one of Menelik Rases had sent cavalry to burn the villages in a wide circle around, killing the menfolk and enslaving the women children. Then he would move his camp and repeat the process. ... the green valleys would not remain empty long. There would be setters from the east, Menelik's Shoan soldiers, paid off with Galla lands."[624]

Poor Ethiopians, because of bearing excessive burdens, became "mutinous" and some of them deserted. But the Frenchman asked Menelik again. The latter granted permission for rulers of the western region to provide support for the French mission. While French might have been happy for being granted all assistance they needed, for the local population it meant more trouble and suffering. "The new letter from Menelik meant that dozens of Gallas (Oromos) were forced to serve as escort. Many deserted. Others tried to desert but were recaptured and flogged with cowhide wipes. Many died of fever or starvation in the swamps along the south bank of the river."[625]

Southerners were also made to be subjected to pillage and arbitrary rule by foreigners. Menelik granted lands and appointed a Russian, Colonel Nicholas Leontiev, governor and awarded the title of *dejazmatch*. Another Russian, Babichev was given *fitawurari* title.[626] Menelik "had granted unspecified lands to govern in June 1897" to Leontiev at "the province of northeast of Lake Rudolf,"[627] now Lake Turkana. David Mathew (1947) tells us that Leontiev brought gifts to Menelik which the emperor liked. "Colonel Leontieff now brought a great diamond and the Order of Catherine of Russia in brilliants, gifts from the Tsar Nicholas. They adorned the ring finger and the breast of the Emperor Menelik."[628] Rosenfeld, in *A Chronology of Menelik II of Ethiopia* (1976) also described that Menelik was wearing the ring Leontiev brought him. Leontiev established close friendship with Alfred Ilg, which enabled him to get the emperor's favor. After receiving granted land, Leontiev went back to Europe. When he returned to Ethiopia in 1899, he brought with him an army of foreign mercenaries. Menelik also provided 300 soldiers to him. Leontiev used his mercenary army and Menelik's soldiers to terrorize the local population in the south.

> He went to see his shareholders and returned to Ethiopia the following year with a small army of assorted French, Russian and Senegalese. These were joined by a detachment of Menelik soldiers and two Croatians, the Seljan brothers. From June to October 1899, Leontiev's expeditionary force did what all of Menilek's colonizing armies had done: sack, kill and take booty. ...Menilek assigned them 300 soldiers and they went with Leontiev to the southwest. When Leontiev left, the Seljans stayed as "governor," with Menelik's permission, until late 1901.[629]

Prouty noted that "Leontiev delivered a large booty to Addis Ababa."[630] Following the emperor's example, in 1909 *ras* Wolde Giorgis, governor of the south-western provinces of Kaffa, Maji and others, "gave a monopoly of Maji's most lucrative export, ivory, to an Indian...to increase his revenues."[631] Pankhurst (1968) wrote that such actions coupled with introduction of firearms led to the extermination of elephants and wildlife in many parts of the country. The degree of devastation and pillage varied from place to place. Hence, the people of Wolayta, Kaffa, Gimira, Maji, Berta, and other south-western and southernmost territories were frequently subjected to well- organized slave raids and servitudes.

They often resisted and tried to defend themselves where and when they could. But their spears, shields, and clubs were far inferior when compared to modern firearms. They lost the battles and were forced to accept their subservient positions. Others had to abandon their homelands and villages of their forefathers; and fled as far away as they could. They ended up settling in territories beyond the reach of authorities. Some like the Borana, Gabra, Geri, and other peoples of the frontier areas crossed the border into the then British East Africa Territory. According to Wilfred Thesiger,

> By 1913 conditions on the boundary between Abyssinia and the British East Africa Protectorate, later known as Kenya, had become worse than usual, with frequent incursion by well-armed gangs of Abyssinians raiding for slaves and ivory. My father was therefore anxious to travel Nairobi and discuss with the Governor measures to prevent these raids, as well as the possibility of delimiting the frontier and finding an answer to the demand by the Abyssinian Government for the return of the Boran and Gabbra tribesmen who had migrated in large numbers into East Africa after Menelik's conquest of their homelands.[632]

In the south-west razzias not only existed, but also intensified. Thus, Boranas, Gabra, and others remained in Kenyan side of the border under the British protection and they made their home there. Today they inhabit Marsabit and Northeastern Districts of Kenya.

The Gumuz "lived in the higher country of what is now central and southern Gojam in the eighteenth and nineteenth centuries."[633] But in search of safety, the Gumuz, fled into a hostile and inhabitable lowlands, which are often infested with malaria and other tropical diseases.

> In response, the indigenous population of the new western periphery frequently moved into the remoter areas (usually low-lying) of greater safety. In such 'reception areas', newly defensive social systems developed. The south bank of the Blue Nile in Wellega is such a 'reception area', and within it the immigrant Gumuz have created, partly through the repeated making of exchange marriages among themselves, a distinctive society marked off by defensive political hostility, endogamy, and various barriers.[634]

The Gumuz were given a derogatory name, Shanqilla, which they "have adopted as a self-name ...to refer to all their various sections, as against highland peoples."[635] They found themselves even in difficult situation which placed their very survival at stake mainly due to sex slavery which targeted their women and children. Wendy James wrote:

> In the exaggerated forms of exploitation that developed in the western periphery the predatory expansion of the state affected particularly women and children of the subjugated populations...it is noted that the demand for *women* slaves was relatively high; and in the system whereby the local population was divided up for allocation for military colonists as gabbar there is some evidence that the sexual access among the rights an owner of gebbar might expect."[636]

Subjugation of the Gumuz, like some of the southern indigenous peoples, was multifaceted and persistent. As described above in this chapter *fit*. Habte Giorgis forcefully removed the Gumuz people when he was transferred and took them with him.

Retreating to lowlands was not unique to the Gumuz. Other minority groups had already adopted such practices. In 1848 Walter C. Plowden[637] observed that the Weyto people were living around Lake Tana in "unhealthy" areas where fever was prevalent. An introduction and implementation of *gabbar* system stripped off *rist* rights and subjected southerners to serfdom, tenancy, and slavery. Gabru Tareke in his book, *Ethiopia: Power & Protest: Peasant Revolts in the Twentieth Century*, summed up that the southerners were "...looked upon and treated...as backward, heathen, filthy, deceitful, lazy, and even stupid.... Both literally and symbolically, southerners became the object of scorn and ridicule."[638]

An example of Gabru's assertions was witnessed by Bulatovich in 1898 when he was embedded with *ras* Wolde Giorgis's expedition in the south-west. He described an eyewitness account on his January 7, 1898 diary how contemptuously the soldiers treated native people.

> Soldiers who have assembled for the march treat the local populace rather impetuously. For example, they consider it their undisputed right to take everything edible from those they met...the soldier took from him a gourd of mead and a piece of bread – in a word, everything that caught his eye. And the soldier's wives kept pace with their husbands in this behavior. I happened to see how one of them, a small and frail Abyssinian woman, for some offense hit in the face a big, strong [man], who in response only mournfully lamented..."Forgive me, forgive me, madam." Even my *ashkers* became imbued with this military spirit.[639] [man] *added by me.*

Montagu Sinclair Wellby also witnessed such incidents and stories of soldiers and officials looking down upon subject peoples and mistreating them. In one of those instances, Wellby wrote that the people of "the Hammer Koki district are of the poorest description imaginable, and it is difficult to understand how some of them

manage to exist at all. Whatever they have had has been taken from
them, and there is no doubt that some of the petty Abyssinia shums
treat the Shangkallas of these parts in a very discreditable manner."[640]

He went on describing another such instance of how these indigenous people used to be self-sufficient with their livestock before
the conquest and how they were reduced eating "grasses" and living
on catching fish.

> In order to supplement this scanty fare, they move down to
> the riverside and catch fish, besides collecting certain eat-
> able grasses that grow on the banks. Formerly, they were
> the owners of many head of cattle, but now all have been
> raided by the Abyssinians. At nightfall they brought for our
> animals grass which they had cut from some distance off,
> and in return for their trouble I presented them with cloth,
> much to the disgust of the Habesha soldiers, who, acting
> up to their traditional habits, had taken advantages of the
> strength of our combined force, and seized some sheep from
> the harmless natives. I was very angry with them and pro-
> tested against such cowardly behavior. ...They agreed that
> it was always the custom of the Habesha to loot the Gallas
> [natives] of these parts."[641] Parenthesis added by me.

The condition Wellby, Bulatovich, Newmann, and others observed at the end of nineteenth century not only persisted; but, also
the situation got worse for the natives from the beginning of the
twentieth century and well into the next several decades.

Chapter 8

The New Slavery

"He was indirectly Ethiopia's greatest slave entrepreneur and received the bulk of the proceeds, along with a tax for each slave brought into Shoa and one for every slave sold there. It was not until his other resources had grown considerably that Menelik could attempt to eradicate the trade." - Harold Marcus *The Life and Times of Menelik II: Ethiopia 1844-1913* 1995:73

"In the subject provinces of south, governors and their armies of occupation pillaged the land and sold the inhabitants into slavery. The soldiers that leave a province sweep up all they can and those that can enter the rest." - *Wilfred Thesiger The Life of My Choice*, 1987:45

8.1. Slave Trade in Ethiopia: An Overview

"Ethiopia was one the favorite hunting ground of slaves to provide the insatiable need of the Arab and Ottoman worlds for their harems, bureaucracy, army, and menial jobs." Teshale Tibebu, *The Making of Modern Ethiopia 1896-1974* 1995:66

Slavery in Ethiopia was neither started by Menelik, nor was a new practice. The practice of enslaving prisoners of war had existed for many centuries, at least beginning from the time of Aksumite rulers. *Fitah Negest*[642] endorsed enslaving captives of wars and hence, the practice was institutionalized and embraced by the establishments, namely, the church and state. As noted by Bahru (1991), Pankhurst (1968) and Tibebu (1995) owning slaves became a symbol of status and prestige in Ethiopian society. Hence organized raids and warfare became the most common method of getting slaves[643] by kings, rulers, and slave-merchants. Soon slaves became one of the most lucrative export commodities. It resulted, among other things, in depopulation of the targeted ethnic groups. As Kevin Shillington (2012) wrote it also had unintended consequences with far reaching political and cultural implications.

> The principal Ethiopian export was captives taken from southwest of Lake Tana and sold into slavery in Egypt and western Asia. It has been estimated that in the reign of Sarsa Dengel as many as 10,000 captives a year were sold to Turkish on the Red Sea coast. The removal of so many people from the southwest merely eased the further expansion of the Oromo from the south.[644]

Most Ethiopians, if not all, assume that slave trade happened in West Africa or elsewhere, but not in Ethiopia. They often speak of slaves shipped out of West Africa into the Americas and Caribbean. They were and are oblivious of their own national heritage in this regard. This was mainly because they were not taught that Ethiopians were sold into slavery *en masse*. It would be shocking news for many Ethiopian to hear that their country was one of the top slaves exporting countries in the world. According to the research conducted in Harvard University: *The Long-Term Effects of African's Slave Trades*, and published in the *Quarterly Journal of Economics* on February 2008, "Ethiopia and Sudan are also among the top exporting countries because they were the primary suppliers of slaves shipped during the Red Sea and Saharan slave trades."[645] Between 1400 and 1900 Ethiopia was the fourth largest slave exporter in the world after Angola, Nigeria, and Ghana in that order. During that period, Ethiopia's estimated slave export was 1,447,455 slaves, of which 633,357 were exported via Red Sea and 813,899 were Trans-Saharan.[646] The figure would most likely be higher than that. As cited by Teshale, Pankhurst estimated that 1, 250,000 slaves were exported from Ethiopia within just a half century, 1800-1850.[647] This would mean an average of 25,000 slaves per year.

Several historical accounts indicated that buying and selling Ethiopians at established domestic market centers was widespread practice. Richard Pankhurst's book, *A Social History of Ethiopia: The Northern and Central Highlands from Early Medieval Times to the Rise of Emperor Tewodros II* offers greater insight about the extent of slavery and slave trade in Ethiopia. Pankhurst stated that Roge and Abd-al-Rasul were "renowned slave markets" in 'Old' Shewa; and Tigre and Shewa had had considerable slave population.

In early 1840s when the British envoy, William Cornwalis Harris, was in Ankobar, he witnessed a very large of slave population providing various services of servitude to *negus* Sahle Selassie: "300 grinding-women, an even larger number of girls fetching water, and several hundred more engaged in the brewing of beer and mead,...considerable number of males employed in transporting wood," who were "originated largely from the south and west."[648] Mockler wrote that in 1866 "thousands" of Ethiopians[649] were "being sold each year, five hundred on some days at the market in Gallabat alone" which "Muslim dealers collected their supplies at Zeila and Tajura for shipment to markets in Egypt, Arabia, and Turkey."[650] The slave trade was run mainly by local chieftains, sheikhs, and rulers in south-west and western regions.[651] It would soon become one of the lucrative revenue sources for the Shewa king. Not surprisingly slave trade brought Christian rulers and *jabarrtis* (Muslim & Arab merchants) together. The unity between the two groups was crucial to run the trade smoothly as one served as supplier and overseer; while the other undertook the business of buying, managing the caravan to the coast and selling them at the coast and beyond.[652]

8.2. The New Slavery

> *"Tens of thousands of blacks were killed or sold into slavery.*
> *Their cattle and gold were looted, their land parceled among the*
> *Shoans."* Thomas Pakenham, *The Scramble for Africa* 1991:486

In this work, my discussion about slavery in Ethiopia is limited to the practice of enslavement in post-conquest South, that is, during and after those areas were conquered and incorporated. The methods in which slaves were procured involved organized raids and razzias with soldiers, armed settler-peasants, slave merchants as well as central government officials and agents. In conquered regions peasants who failed to meet their tribute payments obligations were themselves taken as slaves and/or desperately saw their children being taken as slaves.[653] From mid-19th century to early decades of the twentieth century, slave trade in Ethiopia became, to use Alexander Meckelburg's phrase, a "government-backed business." It is from this perspective that I chose to use the term *The New Slavery* in order to help us to differentiate it from the practice of slavery and slave trade existed in Ethiopia for centuries.

The slave-trade and enslavement practices in Ethiopia will need systematic scholarly investigation, which is beyond the scope of this work. Here I attempt to highlight the prevalence of "government-backed business" of slavery in post-conquest South to achieve three simple objectives. The first objective is to highlight the existence of widespread and entrenched slave-trade in Ethiopia which was also embraced by the establishment and its affiliated institutions. The second objective is to try to demonstrate that extensive enslavement practices in the South were byproducts of the conquest and the victims of such practices were mostly, if not all, were the southerners. In doing so, I hope to initiate constructive conversations toward nation building. Until now, it remained a very 'sensitive' topic from which even academicians shy away. When they write about it, they tend to focus on slave trade practiced in the south-west and western kingdoms before Menelik's conquest (Bahru 1991, Teshale 1995) and they ignore the prevalence of slavery in post conquest era. It would not be understatement to say that the topic is a taboo among Ethiopian academia. It was from this background that Meckelburg wrote: "As in African studies in general, in Ethiopian studies in particular, research on slavery was mostly treated with caution if not omitted all together.[654]

Several years after incorporation, *balabats* of Jimma, Ben Shangul, Gubba, Leqa, Gera, and Guma had continued practicing slavery, i.e., enslaving their subjects and paying tributes to Addis Ababa with slaves. In the southwest and western parts, local co-opted leaders were obliged to pay specific type of tributes. If they fail to comply, children or family members were forcefully taken as slaves.[655] The third objective is to highlight adverse effects of slavery in the South which left some defenseless indigenous communities drastically de-populated, and "almost exterminated," to use Pankhurst's phrase (see chapter 9).

During Menelik's reign slave markets continued to operate and slaves were supplied for both domestic and international markets.[656] Domestic slavery was practiced widely and became a means of gain-ing wealth and higher status in the society – the greater the number of slaves one owns, the higher the privilege and status enjoyed in the society (Bahru (1991), Pankhurst (1968), Teshale (1995), Garretson, (2002).

As Pankhurst (1968), Bahru (2001), Bulatovich (2000) noted some regions of the South became a harvesting as well a hunting field of slaves. Government officials, starting from the emperor and empress at the top to various functionaries at provincial, district, and local level were engaged in and benefited from slavery and slave trade as discussed below in this chapter.

In his research paper: *Slavery, Emancipation, and Memory: Exploratory Notes on Western Ethiopia,* Alexander Meckelburg, had concluded that "slavery in western Ethiopia was thus for a long time a government backed business."[657] As a matter of fact, it was also a "government backed business" in other parts of the South from which powerful of-ficials and those in the establishment had profiteered. Harold Marcus wrote that Menelik II himself had made slavery one of the profitable commodities for his own personal gains.

> The slave trade provided the biggest profits, though the king did not participate directly, always leaving the seamy side of the business to his Moslem agents at Abdul Resul. The supply came through warfare or from Jimma, which in 1884 submitted to Menilek in return for autonomy...Abba Jifar's exploitation of slaves supported his court and government and paid Menilek his tribute. Similar situations in Leka, Guma, and Gera benefited Menilek, who also taxed sales of slaves in Shewa or their transit through the province or both.[658]

In 1882 Menelik defeated his rival, *negus* Tekle Haymanot of Gojjam, at the Battle of Embobo in Wollega. The battle fought over territorial control of rich resources of the south-west and western regions which, among other things, included slaves and slave trading centers. According to the *London Anti-Slavery Reporter* estimate in 1884 "almost eight thousand slaves were still being exported from Ethiopia, and that King Menelik received, as the price of his connivance, one slave for every ten exported."[659] Therefore, it wouldn't be surprising that Menelik himself was regarded as "Ethiopia's greatest slave entrepreneur and received the bulk of the proceeds, along with a tax for each slave brought into Shoa and one for every slave sold there."[660]

Richard Pankhurst's description in the *Economic History of Ethiopia 1800 – 1935* may shed more light into the degree to which slavery was entrenched in Ethiopian society from top-down.

> Menelik and Taytu owned 20,000 slaves at the palace in Addis Ababa and a further 50,000 elsewhere, while Ras Walda Giyorgis had 20,000, Ras Tassama 6,000 and Ras Mikael 1,000, Ras Wale of Semen also had a large number, but Ras Habta Giyorgis was a poor man with only 500. A

generation later Ras Tafari Makonnen was said to have 7,000 and Ras Haylu also very many...[661]

When Gubba in western frontier was brought into Ethiopian control, in 1898 "a thousand slaves were sent from Gubba in tribute"[662] and "two thousand slaves were demanded in 1910."[663] In "1910, a visitor to Tajura found that the export trade was alive and well... Moreover, this included a small proportion of castrated boys."[664] The American Consulate in Aden sent a lengthy memorandum to Washington D. C. on April 21, 1919. The theme of the memorandum was "*General Social and Economic Situation in Abyssinia.*" "Most of the slave raiders," according to the memo, were soldiers, whose actions were sanctioned or tolerated by their superiors.

> ...most of the slave-raiders are... Abyssinian officers and soldiers...These officers and soldiers will obey their immediate chief as long as he doesn't interfere too much in their wrong practices. It is the general opinion in Abyssinia that the Abyssinian soldiery will not give up the practice of taking, and of keeping or selling slaves... and the Abyssinian government is apparently unable to use or command the necessary force....[665]

The same memorandum also stressed that the victims of slave raids were southerners because: "Much of the present slave-raiding is said to occur among the Boran people in southern Abyssinia, in Kaffa province, and in the region of Lake Rudolph [Lake Turkana] on both sides of the frontier;"[666] and most of the Ethiopian "serfs are not true Abyssinians, but are members of the Galla (Oromo), Dankaali, Somali, and other subject tribes conquered... by the Christian Abyssinians."[667]

There were several ways in which the southerners as well as other Ethiopians would become a slave. One way was battles and raids. The other way was a tribute system where people (slaves) are paid as tribute to a landlord or a king.[668] Vanquished people became targets of being rounded up and captured as slaves. As evidenced in Wolayta, Kaffa, Ben Shangul, and south-west, the regions which resisted Menelik's conquest were more likely to produce more prisoners of war, that is, more slaves. A Gamo native and scholar, Assefa Chabo, wrote in his memoir:

> War was a number one source of slaves. Because Menelik is-
> sued a decree to sell and exchange (prisoners of war), 30,000
> Wolamo (Wolayta) were removed from their homeland. Go
> to Addis Ababa Fit Ber. Surroundings of Menelik's palace is
> Wolamo (Wolayta) residential areas. Go to Holetta, Gojjam,
> Gondar, Wollo, Tigre. You will find a Wolamo (Wolayta)
> and Wolama's (Wolayta) residential areas.[669]

Oscar Neumman, after getting permission from Emperor Menelik, travelled through the south and southwest into Sudan in 190. He published his travel account in *The Geographic Journal* published by The Royal Geographic Society in 1902. In a long article titled *From the Somali Coast through Southern Ethiopia to Sudan*, he wrote that in the provinces of Kosha and Konta "the slave trade is in full-swing. At the large weekly market, you can see -besides cotton, coffee, flour, goats and children- children sold in small or large lots."[670] While passing through Kaffa, Gimira, Shako, Bench lands he observed: "I never saw a woman either in Shakho and Binsho (Bench) probably because they are first placed in safety as the object most desired by the Abyssinians," for slaving and therefore hidden as a measure caution from being victims of slave raiding; and "the Shakho (men) are always lurking in the bush."[671] Heading westward toward the Sudanese border area he found "Anyuak, poverty stricken through many Abyssinian raizzas, live hidden away in small islands in these swamps. A large part of the people had migrated westward and live in a state of semi-slavery under the protection of the more powerful Neuer near the Egyptian fort of Nasser on the Sobat."[672]

In general, during conquests and slave-raids, men were more likely to get killed than taken as slaves. In those instances, captured slaves were mainly women and children who would end up being taken north, or distributed among soldiers, and used for various domestic services elsewhere, or sold away [See Marcus (1995), Pankhurst (1968), Darkwah (1975), Bulatovich (2000)]. Pankhurst wrote:

> Menelik's army captured 18,000 slaves, one-tenth of which were considered as the Emperor's booty, the rest as the property of his soldiers. Slaves, he adds, were at this period given as presents from one chief to another almost like visiting cards. A British diplomatic report for 1895 stated that 15,000 slaves were captured in Wellamo [Wolayta] and that persons obtaining them were subjected to a tax of a dollar per slave.[673]

Pankhurst cited eyewitness account of a French journalist, Vanderheym, who joined Menelik's army during the Wolayta expedition of 1894, and who himself took eleven slaves.[674] One of the high-profile slave-raid involved Menelik's grand-son and heir, *Lij* Eyasu Mikael. He "travelled to south-western Ethiopia for …elephants and their ivory as well as slaves."[675]

Thousands of southerners who were captured by *Lij* Eyasu from their homelands were driven *en masse* to the interior. Those who survived death and miseries and who were not sold were distributed from royal households to *mekuanents* to the churches and monasteries to the foreigners in Ethiopia as gifts or bartering objects.[676]

As noted elsewhere in the book early travelers, including Bulatovich, reported eyewitness accounts of devastation occurring to the conquered people of Kaffa. Achame Shana, a Kaffa scholar, wrote that "more than 160,000 people" were sold into slavery from one region of Kaffa alone in just the first decade after Menelik's death.

> Between 1912-1924, as the Northern Ethiopian grip on Shekacho society tightened, the people lost control over their land and resources. The Shekacho aristocracy was eliminated and the common people were uprooted; hunted down

and sold into slavery. It is estimated that more than 160,000 people were sold into slavery from Shekacho region of Kaffa alone.[677]

As mentioned above, *Lij* Eyasu conducted raids against various defenseless natives of the south-west in 1909 and again in 1912. He captured forty thousand innocent men and women from various localities and regions; and drove them north. Many died of illnesses and hunger during their long and miserable journey to Shewa.

> The prince (Lij Eyasu) ...sent a gift of 200 slaves from Gimirra as early as 1909, and, according to Merab and De Coppet, conducted a series of razzias in 1912 in Jimma, Kaffa, Gimirra and the Anuak country, capturing 40,000 slaves of both sexes, half of whom died en route of smallpox, dysentery, hunger and fatigue.[678]

Bahru called Lij Eyasu's 1912 slave raid against the Gimira an "inhuman expedition".[679] As Pankhurst stated Eyasu gave some of the native slaves to soldiers and officers who participated in hunting and capturing. He distributed others as "gifts" including to "monasteries and churches;" and kept thousands for himself

> Iyasu was ... able to give away thousands, one or two to ordinary soldiers, 50 or 100 to more important officers, and an even larger number to his father Ras Mikael. Gifts were also made to a number of monasteries and churches. The prince is reported to have kept for himself 10,000 or 12,000 slaves whom he established near his palace. Hudson notes that 8,000 slaves were taken in Gimirra, the soldiers being allowed to retain one in every three for themselves.[680]

Just as Emperor Menelik and Empress Taytu were the top slave owners and beneficiaries of slave trade; the top church leaders (Abune & Echege) were also among such beneficiaries.

> Slave owning immediately prior to World War I was, according to Merab, still widespread, and was practiced even by Greeks and Armenians as well as by the Abuna, the Egyptian head of the church, and the Nebura Ed, or ecclesiastical governor of Aksum.[681]

Giving away slaves as gift objects or using them as bartering items was also common in the royal household of Shewa even before Menelik was born. William Cornwallis Harris was shocked when Menelik's grandmother offered a Gurage slave girl named 'Hubsheeri' (Abshero?) to barter her with a "salad oil." He also noted that a court official offered him a male slave "as a Christmas gift," and they were puzzled when he refused to accept such a 'gift.'

> Not long after Her Majesty's arrival, she sent me an unfortunate child, recently purchased from a Gurague slave caravan, with a request that Hubsheeri might be exchanged for some clear salad oil which had met with special approval "for medicine for the face;" and great surprise was elicited by my reply, "that such a course of proceeding would involve disgrace and criminality, in as much as the unchristian-like traffic in human beings was held in abhorrence beyond the great water." But in this matter the Emabiet was not singular. Certain of the Courtiers, who considered themselves under obligation, had previously tendered us "strong Shankela slave" as a Christmas gift; and all had been equally at a loss to comprehend our motives in refusing.[682]

As Mohammed Hassen (1994) described the practice of bartering and giving slaves as a gift was also common among the Gibe States.[683]

In the post-conquest era, the South became a source of slaves and a hunting field for slave-raiders. In addition, it also became a poaching and indiscriminate hunting field of wildlife. While hunting and razzias had resulted in depopulation of both wild games and humans on one hand; they also became means of wealth for the powerful and privileged class, on the other hand. Bahru wrote how conducting slave raids and hunting elephants for ivory had become quickest means of accumulating wealth for the Ethiopian nobility.

> Merchants and hunters had figured out a means of quickly enriching themselves by conducting slave-raids and poaching elephants for tusks there (in the southwest) and by bringing them back with them. The upper class /nobility became owners of thousands of slaves. Exchanging slaves as gift objects also became customary practice. In short, the number of slaves an officer owned had become a yardstick of measuring one's status and place in the society." [684]

Pankhurst, citing Montandon, wrote that "the entire Shanqella populations of Gimirra were either slaves or serfs."[685] Toward the end of the first decade of twentieth century, more than one out three residents of Addis Ababa was a slave or house-servant. In other words, in 1900 E.C. (1908) slaves and house-servants constituted 33% (20,000) of the total population of Addis Ababa. Accordingly, the proportion of southerners in Addis Ababa was large. Out of 60,000 residents of the city in the same year, Oromos were 20,000, Shanqila 15,000, Amhara 14,000, Wolayta 5,000, Gurage 2,000, Tigre 1,000, and others 3,000.[686] Excessive supply of slaves made it possible not only for "many Europeans" to own slave, but also for "the servants of European households."[687] During the first decade of twentieth century, "slave trade came to replace ivory as the basis of the economy of the south-west."[688]

Half-hearted efforts to ban slave trade were going on since Menelik's times. But the practice persisted. In 1924 a "Bureau for the Liberation of Slaves" was created which "established many branches in the interior, particularly in the areas infested by slavers, such as Gore, Gondar, Kaffa and the frontier of French, Italian and British Somaliland."[689] But the prohibitions effort remained nominal and impractical. Just like the edict of Atse Tewodros[690] before it, government actions and attempts of abolition of slave trade appeared to be ironic. For example, the edict[691] issued on October 2, 1909 urged that "runaway slaves must be restored to their masters with in eight days, and those who cannot find their masters are to report to Wolde Gabriel."[692] Haile Selassie's government took steps to abolish slavery, but its actions were puzzling and as mentioned above it was ironic. On one hand, it was engaged in issuing permissions to buy slaves legally from *Tsehafe-Tizaz* (Minister of Pen) and to receive them as gift objects. On the other hand, it was punishing ordinary individuals caught in selling slaves.

> The trade was, however, still officially forbidden, persons violating the law being publicly hanged, and open slave markets being things of the past. It was, nevertheless, legally possible, according to Mareb, to buy slaves by permission from the Minister of Pen or the Interior, or to obtain them as gifts from the sovereign or important chiefs.[693]

As Meckelburg tells us the regent *ras* Teferi Mekonnen, regardless of his own proclamations to prohibit slave trade, was himself one of the receivers of slaves for tribute payments

> Despite several proclamations to abolish slavery after the rise of ras Teferi Mekonnen (the future Haile Selassie I) in 1927, ras Tefari received slaves through Khojali. Sheikh Khojali, who increasingly stayed in his palace in Addis Ababa, handed over affairs to his son Al-Rashdi Khojali, who was reported to have "millions of slaves."[694]

In addition to razzias, taking children as slaves became widespread practice in both western and southern Ethiopia, particularly from people who either "were unable to pay their tributes,"[695] or who were unable to pay a specific type of tribute such as ivory in the case of Maale people.[696] Maale king Arregude, who was appointed as *ballabat,* did everything he can to fulfill orders which came from his masters. He even "accompanied and assisted northern soldiers on several campaigns to subjugate peoples to the south of Bako."[697] But that did not satisfy the officials.

> After he became king, Arregude was held responsible for collecting tribute. If he could not give ivory, then Arregude was required to give children as slaves. The Maale king of course hated the enslavement of their children.[698]

Seeing their children taken as slaves became unbearable to Arregude and his people. So, he ventured to travel to Addis Ababa to appeal directly to Emperor Menelik to end the practice of taking their children as slaves in the pretext of not giving ivory.

> Arregude's role in it, even under the coercion of imprisonment, must have threatened to undermine his political position in Maale. In daring and successful journey in about 1906, Arregude travelled to the north all the way to Menelik's court to protest against the taking of Maale children. According to the story Maale leaders still tell, Menelik asked what he give in tribute instead of slaves. Arregude replied that he would ivory, honey, cattle, and goats. Menelik assented and Arregude took a letter from the emperor to the governor of Bako instructing the latter not to take slaves from Maale.[699]

Note that Menelik ordered to stop taking slaves from Maale only, but not from other neighboring ethnic groups. "Although a few slaves continued to be taken from time to time [from Maale], their number was slight compared to those from neighboring countries like Bako and Shangama, where cattle, for instance, were in far fewer numbers."[700] The fate of Aari people of the former Gamo-Gofa Province was like that of Maale when it came to taking people as slaves for defaulting on tribute payments. Alexander Naty in his research work (1994), *The thief searching (Leba Shay) institution in Aariland, Southwest Ethiopia, 1890s-1930s*, wrote extensively about "the powerlessness and

helplessness" of the Aari people of people in the face of their subjugation to slavery in the name of "civilizing mission which included the
concept of law and order" (leba shay institution) and in the pretext
of not paying tribute. He wrote:

> The military encounter between the Aari people and the
> imperial Abyssinian army during the late nineteenth cen-
> tury resulted in the defeat of the Aari and the introduction
> of hitherto unknown forms of socioeconomic and political
> relations between the agents of the Abyssinian state and the
> conquered population. With the conquest, an institution of
> serfdom *(gebbar sirat)* was introduced in Aariland whereby
> local families had to pay an annual tribute (in cash and in
> kind) to the soldier-settlers (neft'ennya). In addition, mem-
> bers of households had to perform labor services for the
> soldier-settlers. Failure to pay tribute and to perform labor
> service resulted in slavery. Many Aari (mostly women and
> children) were taken away as domestic slaves because Aari
> families could not afford to pay the tribute or to perform the
> labor services[701]

Naty posed the following question. "What was the reaction of
the Aari people to the removal of their society as domestic slaves
through the practice of leba shay?" And he answered it as follows:

> In general, they were quiescent. The traumatic experience
> of the conquest resulted in the development of a sense of
> powerlessness and helplessness. They coped with postcon-
> quest trauma through a revitalization movement which was
> known as the ak'aat k'all (voice or word of the ancestors).
> However, sometimes, the Aari people protested violently
> against slavery. The Aari former Baaka chiefdom, for exam-
> ple, rebelled against their ritual king Banzi who collaborated
> with the soldier-settlers in the enslavement of Aari children
> and women. This rebellion resulted in the installation of

Guri as a legitimate ritual king of the Baaka. According to informants, Guri protested slavery by appearing tot the court of Emperor Menelik in Addis Ababa.

To sum up, despite edicts to abolish slavery, the practice persisted through the 1930s[702]. According to the British Anti-Slavery and Aborigines Protection Society report issued on April 8, 1932, out of the seven – eight million Ethiopian population "there were at least two million slaves in Ethiopia."[703]

Chapter 9

Depopulation

"Southwestern Ethiopia became a hunting ground for humans and as well as animals. ...Members of the upper nobility came to have thousands, and sometimes tens of thousands of slaves at their disposal...The process was attended by massive depopulation in the south-western provinces." - Bahru Zewde, *A history of Modern Ethiopia 1855-1974* 1991:93

"A local permanent population simply doesn't exist." Bulatovich wrote after staying in the former Kaffa capital Andarachi "from January 8 to 22, 1898." - Alexander Bulatovich, *Ethiopia through Russian Eyes*, 2000:226

One of the many negative consequences of organized raids was the removal of native peoples from their homelands, to which south and south-western Ethiopia became a living laboratory of drastic depopulation. Writings of European travelers and diplomatic correspondences regarding slave raids and slavery in Ethiopia provided scanty, but valuable information on this subject.

Bulatovich arrived in Kaffa about five months after it was conquered and occupied by *ras* Wolde Giorgis army. Upon his arrival Kaffa had caught his attention in two major ways. One was "the charming beauty of the place." The second was the "dreadful signs of death and destruction." He described it devastation of Kaffa as follows:

Amid the green grass, the white of human bones shone here and there. Settlements were nowhere to be seen —only thick weeds, growing on plots of recently cultivated earth, bear testimony of the people who once lived here. An evil fairy of war destroyed them, and scattered their bones across the fields. The closer we came to the capital of Kaffa, the more noticeable became the signs of recent battles. Near the town itself, clearings were completely strewn with human bones.[704]

Bulatovich, in his diaries wrote that the armies of *ras* Wolde Giorgis "laid waste the country, ravaging it…taking prisoner the women and children who were hidden in the forests, and setting fire to everything that could burn."[705] When he visited the then capital of Kaffa, Andarachi, in January 1898, all he saw and found was the occupying forces of *ras* Wolde Giorgis and auxiliary civilians who came as part of the conquering armies. He did not find an indigenous population in their former capital. After that observation, he wrote that the "local permanent population simply doesn't exist."[706] He declared that Kaffa, "the once flourishing and busy state is now completely destroyed and an almost a deserted country."[707]

Describing about human toll of the conquest and subsequent occupation of the first 15 years in Kaffa, Achame (2006) noted that "between 1897-1912…It is believed that tens of thousands of people lost their lives."[708] Pankhurst, in his book, *The Ethiopians, A History*, wrote that Menelik's conquest to Kaffa had resulted "by much bloodshed, which resulted in considerable depopulation of the area."[709] Pankhurst also wrote that Kaffa's "population having been "almost exterminated."[710] The 1919 diplomatic memo of the United States Consulate in Aden had painted even darker picture on how Kaffa, once "rich" and "industrious" kingdom had been "converted in a few years" into the "land of wilderness" where "only a few people were remaining."

The large and rich province of Kaffa is said to have been converted in a few years, from a land of industrious people producing great quantities of agricultural and pastoral products, into a land of wilderness with only a few people remaining, and these spending their time hidden in the jungle to escape the notice of raiding, or marauding bands of so-called Abyssinian soldiers.[711]

As quoted by Pankhurst "the British Minister in Addis Ababa wrote of "gradual depopulation of the slave-producing districts"[712] in the south and south-west. In places like Kaffa and other regions of the south-west the process and speed of depopulation was shocking and drastic.

> …. the population of Kaffa declined from 250,000 to 10,000, Shoa-Gimirra from 9,000 to 2,000, and Maji from 45,000 to 3,000. Athill said the population of Kaffa was reduced by two-thirds, while Montandon claimed that of Gimirra was reduced from almost 100,000 to no more than 20,000 and possibly even 10,000.[713]

Perhaps one of the graphic descriptions of depopulation was given by an eyewitness account of a certain Darly who visited the southern frontier districts which Richard Pankhurst quoted as follows:

> Contemporary observers suggest that the slave trade resulted in some areas in a substantial decrease in population. Darly referred to "hundreds of square miles" on the Kenya frontier as "utterly depopulated." Describing a region which ten years earlier had been prosperous and where there had been much terraced agriculture, he declared: "To-day it is possible to march through this district for days without meeting a single human being; the terraces are still there, but the people who should be sowing and reaping are either dead or slaves in the capital. The whole countryside is abandoned to the jackals and the hyenas."[714]

Bonga, one of the capitals of *tato* Gaki before the conquest, had suffered complete destruction and was "deserted" until it was "re-occupied after the Italian occupation."[715] In Bonga "8,000 slaves were sold every year" at the end of the century.[716] By 1938 the total population of Bonga was 3,000, of which the native Kafa were only about 200.[717]

Maji was another victim of predatory governance. One of "catastrophic" period in Maji occurred when *ras* Wolde Giorgis and his deputy *dejazmatch* Damte were transferred to the north after thirteen years of iron-fist ruling of the entire south-western region. The governors and their soldiers "collected as many of the *gebbar* as they could to take north as slaves, or else raided the neighborhood...to get more cattle, sheep, and any other movable booty they could capture" which "denuded" Maji and its surroundings.[718]

Successive governors of Maji such as *dejazmach* Birru HaileMariam, his son, *dejazmach* Desta Birru, *fitawurari* Meshesha, and *dejazmach* Mekuriya continued practicing example set by *ras* Wolde Giorgis and *dejazmatch* Damte.[719] Garretson wrote about *dejazmach* Mekuriya's and his wife's raids: "The departing governor, dejazmach Mekuriya, raided Maji and its surroundings and made off with some 18,000 cattle and 50,000 sheep. His wife, *weyzero* Asselefech, carried out at least one raid against the Tishana, obtaining 93 slaves."[720]

Thus, out of "about forty thousand in 1910"[721] the "population of Maji dropped from thousands to a few hundred in 1925."[722] Some ethnic groups from frontier areas such as Borana, Gabra and others fled further and further away from their homelands into the British East Africa (later Kenya) to escape enslavement and to make themselves inaccessible for slave-raiders. Enslaving expeditions and raids were not only common in particular in the south-western Ethiopia which in Bahru's words, "became a hunting ground for humans and as well as animals" and in which "members of the upper nobility came to have thousands, and sometimes tens of thousands of slaves at their disposal" and which resulted in "massive depopulation in the south-western provinces."[723] Bahru mentioned one example of an "inhuman' slaving expedition carried out by the designated heir of Menelik's throne, *Lij* Eyassu Mikael, one of the several examples of 'government backed business' of slavery.

> In one slaving expedition alone- the rather notorious campaign of 1912 conducted by Lij Iyyassu himself – about 40,000 Giira in south-westrn Ethiopia were uprooted from their homes and dragged across the country to the capital [Addis Ababa]. Half of them reported to have died on the way, from various epidemic diseases. Some of the survivors were settled to the north-west of Iyyasu's palace at Seddest Kilo in Addis Ababa, in what came to be known as Gimira Safar. Similar tales of dislocation exist about the province of Kafa and Maji. Culturally, too, slavery and the slave-trade accentuated the differences between the central and the peripheral nationalities.[724]

Decades of organized slaving *zemechas* (expeditions and raids) by various government backed officials and armed groups persisted during regimes which succeeded Menelik, and the outcome was obvious: forced dislocation, displacement, mass enslavement and depopulation of native peoples. Martin Meredith's (2014) explanation of conduct and behavior of slave traders of West Africa might as well be pertinent to the situation existed in Ethiopia.

> In some cases, rulers of an expanding state regarded enslavement of a conquered population as a useful means of increasing their wealth and status and building armies; in other cases, slaves were simply a by-product of political conflict which could be turned into to profit.[725]

Chapter 10

Resistance, Rebellions and Counteractions

"...To Kaffa...there remained only to submit voluntarily or be subdued. But Kaffa decided to defend its independence to the very last." - Alexander Bulatovich, *With the Armies of Menelik II, Ethiopia Through the Russian Eyes*, 2000:217

"In the South, Abyssinian settlers holding large estates relied heavily on the armed strength of the state to keep their restive peasants under control." - Gebru Tareke, *Ethiopia: Power & Protest, Peasantry Revolts in the Twentieth Century*, 1994:49.

"The history of Ethiopia itself is marked by a succession of long uninterrupted rebellions, local autonomy and conquests by the monarchy."- Irma Taddia, *Eritrean Studies Land Politics in the Ethiopian-Eritrean Border Area between Emperor Yohannes IV and Menelik II, Aethopica* 12 (2009) 62-63. International Journal of Ethiopian and

Discussing the difference between wars and raids, Robin Hallett wrote that wars:

may be distinguished from raids in one or more ways, the greater the number of men involved, the longer duration

of the campaign, or the more enduring and decisive consequences of the conflict. Wars of conquest can only be
waged by a polity with organization elaborate enough to
maintain the army in the field and to possess some means
of controlling, for its own benefit, the conquered territory.[726]

According to Hallett, war of resistance is an "instantaneous reaction of certain societies to the threat of conquest," and revolts, on the
other hand, are "the latter reaction to foreign domination."[727] Most
of the southern peoples put up fierce resistance to Menelik armies'
wars of conquests during their initial contact. Post conquest resistances and sporadic revolts by conquered peoples persisted, although
they were crushed down quickly. The degree of resistances and revolts varied from one area to the other depending on the presence
or absence of such factors as access to firearms, level of organization,
geographical locations, and religious affiliations or lack of. For our
convenience of discussion, I classified the types of resistances that
existed during and after conquest into three broad and loose categories: war of resistance, migration, and embracing new identity. The
later was manifested in the form of seeking and embracing alternative
religious or faith affiliation.

Of course, the most common form of resistance was a war of
resistance which was undertaken by nearly all communities in the
south, south-east, and south-west save some areas which submitted
peacefully. Among those who chose to resist the invasion, some were
defeated quickly. Some resisted for years. But all were finally defeated
thanks mainly to modern firearms of Menelik's armies, which most
southerners did not possess and/or possessed very few outdated ones.

An exception in this regard was Emir Abdullahi of Harar whose
forces were armed with relatively modern firearms and cannons.
Unlike most other kingdoms and territories, Harar was familiar with
firearms for several centuries. It was once a capital of Ahmed Ibin
Ibrahim Al-Ghazi or Gragn Ahmed, whose forces were armed with
rifles. Because of its vicinity to the coast, Harar also had attracted
merchants, including arms traders and dealers. Above all, it was

occupied by Egypt for ten years. Egypt was equipped with modern weapons at the time. When Egypt ended its occupation and evacuated Harar in 1885, it left behind some of its weapons to the ruler of Harar. But the emir's firearms were no match both in quality and quantity to those of Menelik's army.

At the Battle of Chelenqo, which determined the fate of the Emir, Hararis were easily routed. 11,000 Hararis and Oromos were killed; Emir Abdullahi was captured, chained and taken to Entoto.[728] The relatively easy victory over Harar was a much-needed relief for Menelik. Few years earlier in Arsi he faced stiff resistances and "some bloody defeats."[729] Besides, in 1883, Menelik 'barely escaped with his own life."[730] The people of Arsi lacked centralized leadership and firearms as that enjoyed by Shewa. But they "were well organized and able to put an army larger than the Shoans' into the field,"[731] which became a challenge from early 1880s until Arsi was defeated and subdued in 1886. In its opposition to embrace the Christian faith of the north, Arsi embraced Islam (Ulrich 2002, Abbas Gnamo 2014). Islam then became a rallying factor for resistance, and it brought supporters and fighters from other regions such as Guragelands.[732]

The war of resistance and later the revolts put up by *Chaha* Gurage and by Qebena was one of the underreported stories regarding southern conquests. Menelik's early incursions to Gurage started in 1875, in which the northern Gurage[9] (Kistane) region was brought into Shewa domain. The next year, 1876, when the Shewa forces engaged in further conquest, they met not only strong resistance but also, they had an "embarrassing defeat."[733] Only one-third of Shewans returned alive and the other two-thirds were either killed or sold into slavery.[734] In the latter years, the Gurage resistance led by *Chaha*'s Chief Bacci Sabo, Qabeena's Umar Baksa and others went on until it was finally broken in 1888/89.[735] Related to this was Hassan Enjamo of Qabeenna who led fierce resistance in Hadiya-Gurage areas.

Hassen Enjamo realized the importance of forming an alliance

---

9 It should be noted here that the Eymelal region of Gurage has had direct contact with Shewa from the time of Menelik's grand-father, Sahle Selassie.

to fight against the powerful forces of Menelik and he took initiative to call upon leaders of southern kingdoms and territories to create a united front. To form such an alliance he reportedly sent invitation to kawo Tonna Gaga of Wolayta, *moti* Abba Jifar II of Jimma, *tato* Gaki Sherecho of Kaffa, *woma* Dilbato Degoye of Kambaata, leader of Masqan Imam Duno, leader of Silte Sedisso, leader of Chiron Lalelo, leader of Wulbarag Shafi Lafebo, leader of Azarnet Gonfamo, leader of Enaqor Ali, leader of Hadiya Leemo Arsie, leader of Shaashoogo Abagada Alamo, and leader Halaba Imam Nunede.[736] Leaders of Wolayta, Kaffa and Jimma reportedly declined to accept the invitation and stated they can fight by their own. The rest responded positively. The leaders or their representatives convened together. Hassan Enjamo laid out Menelik's strategy and the need to form a united front. He also reportedly presented conversion to Islam as a condition to create stronger alliance, which hindered most of them from joining the alliance. Only a few accepted it.[737] So his grand plan was not materialized. Hassan Enjamo, however, "posed a serious challenge to Shewan authority on the eastern side of the Gibe."[738] He inflicted damages on Shewa forces and put up fierce resistance until he was finally defeated thanks mainly to ras the army of *ras* Gobana.

The offer to surrender was rejected by Kambaata because they declared that they will not recognize any king other than their own.[739] Kambaata decided to fight and resisted the invasion. But it was defeated. In 1892 *woma* Dilbato was "captured and killed together with his advisors."[740] Kambaata staged sporadic attacks and resistance in such places Wonjella, Fereqessa and so on. However, it was eventually contained and hence completion of the occupation in 1893.

One of the fiercest resistances Menelik faced in the mid 1890s occurred when he marched to subdue the Wolayta kingdom. To avenge previous defeats and to ensure victory, Menelik in 1893-94 mobilized the largest armies he ever mobilized until that time. Arguably, it may be the largest in the entire history of "The Southern Marches of Imperial Ethiopia", which might only be rivaled by the marches against Kaffa in 1896-97. The Wolayta conquest led by the emperor himself comprised his personal armies, the armies of *ras* Mikael of Wollo, *liqa mequas* Abate Boyalew, *dejazmach* Balcha Safo, *fitawurari* Gebeyehu, *ras* Wolde Giorgis Aboye, and Abba Jifar II of Jimma.[741] It was vast army equipped with modern weapons. Regardless, *kawa* Tona Gaga and his people, although they were armed only with traditional weapons, fought to the end. Wolayta's complex defense network coupled with *kawa* Tona's ability to mobilize the Wolayta and the neighboring peoples of Kullo and Konta enabled him to put up fierce resistance. The war caused tens of thousands of casualties on both sides. *Kawo* Tona was wounded and captured, which brought an end and a final defeat to Wolayta. Its defeat paved a way for further conquests of the neighboring peoples of Gamo, Gofa, Koysha, Boroda, and so on. (see chapter 4.4). Afterward, the whole region was devastated, and their inhabitants became booties of war. Mass enslavement ensued (see chapter eight).

Few years after Wolyata was crushed, Menelik's show of forces on one hand and the native people's stubborn resistance on the other hand was displayed in Kaffa. It had previously repulsed attempts of conquests by Gojjam and Shewa forces since the mid-1880s. Now, however, Menelik was determined to bring it down for once and all. Favorable conditions were on his side. This included thousands of modern weapons captured from Italy in Adwa, higher moral and support, domestic and international fame he garnered after crushing the Italians in Adwa. Above all, Kaffa's neighboring countries were under his control. Kaffa was encircled. Yet Menelik did not leave anything to chance.

He ordered armies of *ras* Wolde Giorgis, *dejazmach* Demesew, *dejazmach* (later *ras*) Tessema to converge on Kaffa. The armies co-opted leaders such as Abba Jifar II of Jimmy, and the rulers of Kullo, and Konta kingdoms were also ordered.[742] But *Tato* Gaki Sherocho and the people of Kaffa refused to surrender. Bulatovich wrote: "Kaffa decided to defend its independence to the very last."[743] After more than eight months of scorched-earth tactics which involved "setting to fire everything that could burn,"[744] Gaki Sherocho was finally captured and tied with his own gold chains, and taken to

Addis Ababa by *ras* Wolde Giorgis. He was exiled to Ankobar prison. The defeat of Kaffa ushered two important historical events. First, it removed the last and the strongest southern kingdom and its resistance. Thus, it facilitated further incorporations of the southwest and frontier areas. It also ushered a new chapter of enslavement and drastic depopulation in the region at large (see chapters 8&9).

As mentioned above, the second form of resistance against incorporation involved migration. There were two aspects of migration. One involved crossing the border into the neighboring countries (Wilfred Thesiger, 1987). Some communities in the south and southwest, particularly those who lived at the frontiers, such as Borana, Gabra, Somali clans, Hamar, Anuak, Nuer, etc. fled into Kenya and Sudan, both of which were under British colonial administration. While some of them resettled permanently, others returned later. The other form of migration involved leaving their homelands and moving to a less desirable, less accessible lowlands and semi-desert areas. The purpose of such migration was less accessibility to the new administrators and slave raids. Some communities such as the Gumuz "frequently moved into remoter areas (usually of low-lying) of greater safety."[745] Montague Sinclair (1901) and others who travelled in Ethiopia toward the end of nineteenth century and beginning twentieth century witnessed native people fleeing their villages to escape from the reach of new administrators (see chapter 7).

Due to proximity of international borders, "if Ethiopian officials grew too exploitive, local peoples could simply cross over into the Anglo-Egyptian Sudan, British Kenya, or Italian or British Somaliland." The new masters sometimes had less or no control over the people living around international borders. "In Borana, for example, Amhara soldiers who manned posts in the lowlands kept slaves from the highlands to cultivate for them (it was impossible to press the surrounding pastoral Borana Oromo into the *gabbar* system). Periodically, these slaves escaped across the border into Kenya where the British, always willing to make the point that Ethiopians would be better off under Britain, allowed them to settle in Marsabit."[746]

The third form of resistance witnessed in post-conquest era involved conversions to new religion – Islam & Protestantism- or embracing traditional indigenous faith & rituals. This was adopted in apparent refusal to accept what they regarded was a state religion. This was particularly evident in Arsi where Islam emerged as a dominant religion during post-conquest years. The new religion provided a ground for opposition, organization, and for creating a sense of identity. (Ulrich Braukamper (2002), Abba Gnamo (2014). As in Arsi, some of the fiercest resistances against the center also occurred in areas dominated by Islam such as those in Wollo, Gurage, and Hadiya lands. As Donham in *Old Abyssinia and the new Ethiopian empire* described it, as an "attempt to resist cultural incorporation":

> Islam became attractive way for some southern peoples to reestablish their identities...In other areas, Protestantism offered same possibility...Mekane Yesus Church in Wollega and the Sudan Interior Mission in Welaita are two examples. More dramatic was the spread of possession cults...these cults seem generally to have taken root in those areas of the south closer to the Shewan core rather than on the far periphery.[747]

In various parts of the South, resistances and revolts persisted, although sporadically, well into the dawn of the Ethiopian Revolution of 1974. This was mainly driven by an iniquitous *gabbar* system which imposed the most oppressive system upon the conquered peoples. Among other things, the system compelled local people to pay tributes in cash or in kind, and it required peasants to provide corvee labor for households and farms of their allocated masters. Excessive exploitation engendered by such a system reduced indigenous people into serfdom and enslavement. In Maale, Aari, Majji, Gimira, and other south-western regions children and women were taken for slavery from their families who were unable to pay tributes or who did not fulfil required labor to their masters. Moreover, the natives were forcefully removed from their lands and driven into the interior as slaves by organized slave raids which often involved government officials (See chapter eight). At the end of the first decade of the twentieth century, the people of Maji revolted and waged armed resistance against the *gabbar* system and against raids by government officials[748] who seized slaves.

> Further to the north two figures arose to challenge the geb-bar system more forcefully. The first Mwanga, was leader of the people of the Boma plateau as well as some within Maji; the second was Serie; leader of the Belodya; the original in-habitants of Maji province. Mwanga had led resistance in the area for about thirteen years and had a following of 400-500 rifles. His headquarters were on the highland sources of the Akobo river, and he was accepted as the leader of the Tid and highland Murle, as well as some other groups within Maji proper. Serie built his base in the northern reaches of Maji but also had followers from the neighboring provinces of Gimira and Golda to the north and west. His following was much larger, estimated at 3,000 by Darley...Serie forged a brief alliance among 'all the remaining Shangallas against the Abyssinians', isolating and defeating military posts be-tween garrisons of Maji and Kefa.[749]

After the death of Serie the resistance sporadically continued. It was given the name Tishana. By mid 1930s the third Tishana revolt was going on in Maji as the "Tishana refused to submit to the gebar system."[750]

Expropriation of farmlands and coffee growing areas coupled with imposition of the *gabbar* system led the Gedeo people to engage in organized resistance for several decades. Gedeo can be cited as one example in which "competition for resources" (coffee) led to resistances, which in turn, triggered counteractions against it. In the 1920s and 30s Geodo *balabat*, Chimburu Shunde, appealed to the local administrators. When his appeal was ignored:

Chimburu travelled to Addis Ababa to present his case. He was kept in waiting indefinitely and ultimately, he returned to Sidamo…but clearly the government's position was never reversed…Chimburu's resistance continued into the administration of *ras* Birru…Chimburu's recalcitrance…brought him a public lashing and subsequent imprisonment at the provincial capital, Agere Selam. The balabat instantly became a local Gedeo hero.[751]

Charles W. McClellan's excellent research title, *Coffee in centre-periphery relations: Gedeo in the early twentieth century*, is self-revelatory of the resource control struggle that existed within the government bureaucracy on one hand; and between the government officials and the Gedeo people on the other hand.

Consequently, Gedeo never really gave up the struggle to regain 'their' land. From the start, physical resistance was one response to their dispossession. Violence in the1920s was focused against the surveying teams [*qalad* measurement]; during the Italian occupation and again in 1960, 1968, and 1974, it was directed against northern settlers and their property. But none of these efforts proved victorious against superior military odds.[752]

As Bahru (1991), Gebru (1996), McClellan (2002) discussed in detail the root causes of such peasant rebellions of the Raya Azabo in the early 1940s, the Yejju uprising toward the end of 1940s and again in 1970; the Gedeo rebellion of the 1920s, 30s and in 1960; and the uprising of the peasants in Bale from early 1960s to the end of the decade were associated with the legacy of conquests: expropriations and alienation of peasants from land, excessive exploitation of *gabbar* system, and ill-governance and lack of willingness on government side to redress injustice

Chapter 11

"Lands of the Cross"

"The effective colonizers were not the Spanish sea captains and conquistadors but the friars and monks who built churches and created parishes and schools." - The Oxford History of the Twentieth Century (Ed. by Michael Howard & Wm. Roger Louis), 1998:93

In Eritrea *"colonial education was largely delegated to both Catholic and Protestant missionaries." The Ages of Empires,* Edited by Robert Aldrich. 2007:258

"The warlords were serving the church by fighting the heathen. The fate of their military expeditions, on the other hand, was assisted by the prayers of the accompanying clergy." Donald Levine, *Gold & Wax* 1961:174

Menelikan Ethiopia...baptized its cultural mosaic with the holy waters of...its tabot Christianity on one hand and, the Amharic language on the other. It declared both to be the sole official seals of its identity. Teshale Tibebu, *The Making of Modern Ethiopia 1896-1974,* 1995:49

In the early 1840s William Cornwallis Harris, the British envoy at Sahle Selassie's court in Ankobar, Shewa, accompanied the king and his armies in one of the *zemecha* against neighboring Oromos. It was a gruesome scene of battle where Harris saw "in every direction the blood-stained ground was strewed with the slaughtered foe" and "mutilated corpse." After witnessing it, he described Sahle Selassie's army: "soldiers of the cross;" who were driven by religious motive of driving off of the heathen.[753] A decade and half later *Atse* Tewodros II defeated the armies of the *negus* Haile Melekot of Shewa and sub-dued the kingdom. Then he attempted to introduce a land reform in Shewa as he did in other northern provinces. Tewodros's initiative to tackle the monopoly of lands by the church and clergy by distributing it to the peasants and his peasant-soldiers irritated the Shewa priests.

In September 1857 the king's chronicler, recorded arguments between the clergy and the king. The clergy asked the king to be allowed to continue owning lands as they had been in the past. Tewodros highlighted the existing problem of the Church monopoly of the land and his rationale for distribution. The king asked: "What shall I eat and give to my soldiers?" "You have taken all the lands, calling them 'lands of the Cross,'"[754] the title of the chapter. Any discussion about Menelik's southern expansions and incorporation cannot be complete without discussing or at least mentioning its inextricable phenomenon, the "lands of the Cross."

Menelik did not dare to mess with the Church and its entrenched in-terests for good reasons. First, he learned good lesson from the 'mistakes' of Tewodros. He knew how the Ethiopian Orthodox Church (EOC) worked hard to enable rebellion and to undermine the king's credibil-ity. The second reason was the existence of strong support in Shewa for Emperor Yohannes and Empress Taytu among the EOC establishment for Yohannes and Taytu were more pious and hardliners than him. Moreover, Menelik knew that religious matters were among the top priorities of Yohannes's national agendas. Last but not the least; Menelik understood that getting Church support was vital for his success.[755] He must have known that his grand-father, *negus* Sahle Selassie, "undertakes nothing without first consulting the superiors of the Church, and is deterred from changing of residence, or from projected military expe-ditions."[756] Hence, Menelik understood that the Orthodox "Church can still make or break a leader, and …even try to play the king maker."[757]

The symbiotic relationship between the church and state in Ethiopia was summed up by the head of EOC Patriarch, Abune Tewophilos, who in April 1962 said: "'In Ethiopia the Church and state are one."[758] As observed by Levine in *Wax and Gold*, the two powerful establishments worked hand in hand in "reciprocal dependence" to advance each other's interest. "Far from opposing warfare, Ethiopian Christianity served rather as an inspiration and justification for wars... The warlords were serving the church by fighting the heathen. The fate of their military expeditions, on the other hand, was assisted by the prayers of the accompanying clergy."[759]

The Church, "in some cases...was more powerful than the state."[760] Thus, there was no reason for Menelik to get into endless intrigues with the very institution which would accompany the fighting king and his armies, give them spiritual blessings, moral justification and mandate for conquering the '*aramane*' (heathen) and 'Islam.'[761]

Menelik had also another strong incentive not only to support the Church, but also to please it. Unlike Tewodros's limited domain of arable lands, thanks to vast conquered territories, lands were in excess in Menelik's Ethiopia. In the same way they saw their armies and nobility, "Menelik and Haile Selassie saw the clergy as having a crucial role in the consolidation of the bureaucratic empire through proselytizing Ethiopian Christianity among the conquered peoples."[762] To this end vigorous policies were adopted and "provincial governors were encouraged by the Crown to give out large tracts of land to the Church as inducement to aid the colonizing mission."[763] As was the tradition, "building of churches was among the first things done... in the conquered areas."[764] During his research in Gurageland Shack (1966) found out that the EOC followed in the footsteps of the military and built "many new" churches "to provide places of worship" for the settler communities,[765] which equally applies to other lands in the South. Establishing churches was followed with "generous portions of land in all districts" being provided "as *samon*, or *samon gult* land," which, in Kaufler's words, made the Church being viewed as "just another instance of foreign domination and exploitation."[766]

Darkwah (1975) noted that building churches in conquered lands served "dual purpose.".

> The Churches which were built in the newly-conquered districts were meant to serve a dual purpose; first, to provide for the religious needs of the Christian Amhara who settled in those provinces as troops and colonists; secondly, to facilitate the conversion... Christianity.[767]

To this end, the Ethiopian state provided:

> support and helped the establishment of churches and the attendant religious infrastructure e.g. monasteries, cemeteries, and theological schools in the occupied lands of the subjugated ethnic groups. The state also provided lands and other forms of property so as to enable the church to finance its spiritual activities.[768]

Not surprisingly, the EOC itself became "one of the greatest landowners and is allied with ultra-conservative feudal landlords."[769] This was particularly true in the conquered lands because "the largest Church holdings could be found in the south" and the Church together with the "nobility and the imperial bureaucracy...held special rights to the land and to the fruits of the labor of those who worked the land."[770] Donald N. Levine summarized the nexus between the Ethiopian state and Church as follows:

> In general....the clergy and nobility worked to further each other's interests. The nobility supported the clergy by giving endowment to churches and monasteries, setting up churches in newly conquered lands, and observing religious ceremonies as state functions. The clergy, in turn, served secular authority by providing a communications network for relaying and supporting official policies, excommunicating enemies, and providing counsel and morale in connection

with military expeditions. Altogether, there was an easy commerce between the two elites. They felt common cause in their responsibilities and privileges vis-à-vis the masses.[771]

Though the relationship was based on mutual benefits, the clergy "occupied a privileged position" because they were "possessing the power of excommunication" and were "in charge of the spiritual welfare of the conquerors, and of those conquered.[772] Kaufeler noted that the EOC was "among the beneficiaries of conquest'" which held "a prominent position" in the south and for which "generous portions of land in all districts were reserved."[773]

The number of Orthodox churches in the South was fewer as compared to those in the Northern provinces of Amhara and Tigray. However, in the South the *fewer EOC churches had occupied much larger areas of land* whereas *many churches in the north owned fewer lands* as the following figures illustrated.

In 1957 E.C. (1964), for instance, 95 churches in Hararge occupied 2,734 square km. of land, 58 churches in Bale occupied 2,148 sq. km., 124 churches in Sidamo occupied 954 sq. km., 105 churches in Gamo Gofa occupied 378 sq. km., 136 churches in Illubabor occupied 349 sq. km., 207 churches in Kaffa occupied 264 sq. km., 274 churches in Wollega occupied 260 sq. km., 193 churches in Arsi occupied 122 sq. kilometers. On the other hand, in the northern provinces of Begemdr/Gondar 2,260 churches occupied only 33 sq. km of land, 2,635 churches in Gojjam occupied only 23 sq. km, 2,090 churches in Tigray occupied only 32 sq.km, 2,404 churches in Shewa occupied only 35 sq. km., 1,496 churches in Wollo occupied only 53 sq. km., and 760 churches in Eritrea occupied 155 sq. km. of land.[774]

Gilkes (1975), described the "number of *gashas* of measured land owned by the Church" based on the data collected from Central Church Treasury, in six provinces (Arsi, Gamo Gofa, Kaffa, Shewa, Wollega and Wollo). In these provinces Church owned land was 21,961 measured *gashas* which breaks down as follows: Arsi 3,126, Gamo Gofa 1,051, Kaffa 1,460, Shewa 12,311, Wollega 2,583, and

Wollo 1,430. The information from the Ministry of Land Reform, however, showed the number of measured *gashas* the church owned in Arsi and Kaffa was 9,696 and 1,992, respectively.[775]

The wealth earned from landholdings often benefited the top hierarchy of the Church, mainly Patriarchs, some of whom often put the interest of their native country, Egypt, first. For instance, in 1903 after the Shewa Patriarch, Abune Mattewos, returned from foreign trips to Ethiopia, it was discovered that he "had also used his trip out of country to move funds back to Egypt. His income from taxes on church land, ordaining deacons and priests, blessing *tabots* and conducting arbitrations had made him a rich man."[776] Trampling over Ethiopia's interest, Abune Mathewos signed a document which "validated jurisdiction of the Coptic Church of Egypt over Der-es-Sultan" monastery in Jerusalem which Ethiopia had claimed hers. Disappointed by Abune Mathewos's scandal, Menelik "dismissed him from his position and confined him to his residence for this conspiracy and for arrogating a capacity which he does not possess." Empress Taytu was even "furious" and she argued unsuccessfully for his replacement,"[777] that is, to send him back to Egypt.

As far as the Church's mission for conquered peoples was concerned, from mid-19th century onwards the EOC played a similar role to that it had previously played among conquered Falashas and Muslims in the fourteenth and fifteenth centuries.[778]

> Along with Amharic, acceptance of the Orthodox religion became the primary informal requirement for full incorporation into Abyssinian society. Whether or not conquered peoples became completely Amharized, they were often forced to abandon their animist beliefs and to adopt Christianity. Religious conversion was supported by the state, but the major responsibility for this activity was left with Abyssinian clerics[779]

John. McCann, in *The People of the Plow* (1995) explained various political, economic, and socio-cultural elements introduced and, in some cases, imposed in the South which proved to be game changers as far as advancing government's policies was concerned.

> In the periods of imperial expansion military conquest pro-
> duced new *gult* grants which expanded imperial revenues
> and increased the pool of loyalists who owed their economic
> and political base to imperial indulgence. That expansion
> also brought with it Ethiopian Orthodox Christianity, con-
> vention on social property, forms of taxation, and an overar-
> ching political culture. Incorporation of new areas…involved
> military conquest and also the expansion of Christianity,
> language, social institutions… The initial military conquest
> settled northern soldiers on new lands and provided patri-
> monies for new churches to serve them."[780]

Another area where the Church played a continually active role was carrying out mass baptisms and conversions of subject peoples. Herbeson (1988) noted that conversion to Orthodox faith was an "important indication of assimilation to the culture of conquering Amhara and the qualification for sharing local power with them."[781] Motivated partly by huge material rewards, such as land endow-ments, the Church took it as its primary duty and worked actively along the conquering forces on enforcing baptisms and mass con-versions both on local leaders, *ballabt*, as well as on ordinary citizens, which Empress Taytu and Emperor Menelik biographer termed as "Menilek's Christianizing-colonizing objective."[782] For instance, af-ter Wolayta was conquered, forced mass conversion was carried out where "Christianity was imposed on everyone" and hence "11,000 people were baptized in one day."[783]

There were historical precedents for this. Menelik's predeces-sors, Tewodros and Yohannes, issued edicts to forcefully convert Wollo[784] Oromo and the edict was carried out accordingly. Following Yohannes's order, the Wollo Moslem-Oromo leaders, Mohammed Ali Aba Bula and Yimam Ahmed, were 'baptized" and renamed Mikael and Haile Mariam respectively.

Converts were prescribed baptismal names (*yetimqet/ yekristina sem*), which would become their official name. It places them in the path of learning and adopting a new faith, customs, and manners (culture) in lieu of their former ones. Following the conquests, with exception of the few,[785] almost all conquered southern kings, leaders, and *ballabats* were baptized and given Amharic names. Such method of assimilation triggered some to ask:

> To be an Ethiopian, to be entitled to treatment as a citizen, meant to be a Christian. It was not possible for a person to be a Christian and still be a "Galla" (Oromo). Perhaps it was this problem which included all others. Would it be possible for the Church to accept the people in the south and west as Christians without forcing them to lose their ethnic identity?[786]

Practically speaking conversions were regarded as prerequisites for assimilation, and advancement in the society. Arsi could be cited as a case in point here. It put up stiff resistance during marches of conquests but was subdued (see chapter 4.2.). In the ensuing years and decades, however, Arsi had gone to a "total conversion to Islam."[787] According to Abbas (2014), "the only Arsi Oromo balabats who attained the rank of Awraja...governors –Fitawrari Wolde Mikael Buie and Fitawrari Bekele Ogato – were able to do so because they were converted to Orthodox Christianity. They were the only Arsi to rise up to this intermediary administrative post since the conquest of Arsi in 1886 until 1974."[788]

The prevalence of correlation between conversion and advancement in Ethiopian society; and the corresponding rationale behind it was eloquently and honestly stated by Ethiopian political scientist and a Gojjam native, Teshale (1995):

> Once an "infidel" was baptized and took a Christian name, he was eligible to join the Christian Ge'ez civilization. In some cases, baptism went along with the granting of high official

status in the imperial power hierarchy. In this way, "infidels" were assimilated into the high culture of Christian civilization, replacing their 'primitive barbaric" culture by a "civilized" Christian culture. For the "barbaric infidels" the road to civilization passed through tabot-Christian assimilation.[789]

Obviously, conversions coupled with loyalty opened a door of assimilation because a convert is now Christian and no longer *aramane*. In Menelik Ethiopia, as Teshale summed up, "*tabot* Christianity" and "Amharic language" constituted an official seal of Ethiopian identity.

> Menelikan Ethiopia…baptized its cultural mosaic with the holy waters of…its tabot Christianity on one hand and, the Amharic language on the other. It declared both to be the sole official seals of its identity. Its throne was the exclusive possession of the Christian descendants of the House of Solomon and Saba…All those outlandish to its religious –cultural universe that happen to live inside Ethiopia were declared unfit to rule.[790]

The "informal requirement" of conversions, however, were often met with passive resistances in the conquered regions. For example, as Bahru wrote it, when Christianity was imposed on Wollo by Tewodros II and Yohannes IV respectively, the Wollo people "conformed outwardly, praying to the Christian God in the day time and to the Muslim Allah at night."[791] Likewise, most southerners 'accepted' the new faith nominally and acted Orthodox outwardly. Most of them, however, encouraged pretensions and outwardly conversions, and using language with hidden meanings which cannot be easily deciphered as the following Sidaama poem[792] illustrates.

> *Xomi yihro Xomi*
> *Meenê Gedoni, dogo moni?*
> *if he says fast, fast*
> *in your home, is there a road?*

Fasting is an integral part of the Ethiopian Orthodox faith, where believers and converts were expected, as a religious dogma, to abstain from dairy products on the Church's calendar fasting holidays as well as on Wednesdays and Fridays. The first line of the poem reminded the Sidaama to pretend accepting priests' order of fasting and avoid upfront confrontation. The last line held the crux of the message. It informed the Sidaama of keeping their own practices and beliefs to themselves in their households for no road passes through their homes and, therefore, no one would know what they were doing in their private spaces.

Noting the existence of active and passive resistances in the conquered region, Darkwah wrote: "Although Amhara priests and monks followed each campaign it did not appear that much was done beyond establishing churches in the conquered provinces. This explains why several decades after the conquest Christians continued to be in the minority in these provinces."[793] Likewise Pierre Guidi, quoting Sabine Planel, wrote that "Orthodox Christianity was the "Church of the town" and Protestantism the "Church of the fields."[794]

Part IV

"Mixed System" of Governance in Ethiopia

"the administrative strategy in the south was not oriented toward integration and equal development within the Empire, but towards exploitation for the benefit of the conquerors."
Ulrich Braukmaper, *A History of the Hadiyya in Southern Ethiopia*, 2012:293

Chapter 12

"Dual Society"

In the southern provinces the administrative pattern was different from the very beginning after their occupation by Menilek."
Ulrich Braukamer, *A History of Hadiyya of Ethiopia*, 2012:287.

12.1. Mixed System of Land Tenure and Governance

Alongside with the creation of the modern Ethiopian state, an
equally important legacy of the 'marches of conquests' were the
creation of subjugated masses in the south, south-central, south-east,
and southwest. In the wake of the conquests, millions of peoples in
the south became subordinate citizens. Herbeson (1988), wrote in
his book, *The Ethiopian Transformation: The Quest for Post Imperial
State*: "Menelik imposed an imperial political economy upon his
new subjects" and "became the possessor of the conquered lands."[795]
In most regions, ancestral lands were expropriated and "assigned as
gult or private tenure, by grant or sale, to local administrators, those
emigrating to the south from overcrowded regions of the ancient
empire to the north, soldiers, and northern aristocrats.[796]" They were
distributed as *ma'ed bet, gult, samon, madeira, etc.* among authorities of
central government, regional and local rulers and their numerous
delegates such as the Church, soldiers, and *naftegna.*. Expropriation
of vast fertile lands was akin to the actions of European powers in
Africa and elsewhere.[797]

German social anthropologist, Heinz Kaufeler, had observed that "conquests provided many Abyssinians with the opportunity to acquire riches and improve their status. Many Amhara originating from poor peasant families became landlords in the conquered territories."[798] With imposition of *gabbar* system, the status of southern peasants changed from free people to tenant-serfs who were obliged to pay tributes and to provide free labor in the farms and households of their masters. "The common soldiery and ordinary naftegna were allotted between two and ten gebbars each."[799] But in the southwest "the minimum number was ten farmers per soldier; and... officers with rank of *balambaras, qannazmatch,* or *grazmatch* were often allotted between fifteen and twenty peasants."[800] According to Pankhurst the lands were distributed to the soldiers and officers based on their ranks. The higher the rank was the greater the amount of lands apportioned.

> *hamsa alaqa* or captain of fifty men, was allowed five gashas...a *mato alaqa*, or chief of hundred men, received ten gashas...and a *shambal* commanding three hundred men had twenty *gashas*. A significant feature in the Arussi situation was thus that a large proportion of the population became gabbars and were obliged to give service to soldiers quartered in the area. Cerulli says that between the Awash and the Albaso plain "each family of soldiers thus has a Galla family who is expected to cultivate the land free of charge." The gabbar had to work for the slidier a certain number of days in the week.[801]

Ministry of Agriculture records showed that those with higher positions were allotted greater numbers of *gabbars*: governors received up to the hundreds, each district commander received thirty to eighty, each officer received seven to ten, and each soldier received two to five *gabbars*.[802]

Besides suffering under the exploitative *gabbar* system, the South, as Bahru noted, "became a hunting ground for humans as well as animals. Ivory and slaves became the two precious commodities."[803] Tens of thousands of indigenous people, particularly in the frontier areas, were captured, sold into slavery, and distributed in the households of nobles, governors, churches, monasteries, and even Europeans in Addis Ababa.[804] Hence, the nation's leaders from Menelik to Haile Selassie became beneficiaries of the southerners' enslavement. For instance, Emperor Menelik II and Empress Taytu Betul owned 70,000 slaves in Addis Ababa and elsewhere.[805] As Marcus wrote Menelik was one of the prime beneficiaries of slavery in Ethiopia: "He was indirectly Ethiopia's greatest slave entrepreneur and received the bulk of the proceeds.[806] What was even more horrifying (See chapter eight) was the practice of taking away children as slaves from parents who "were unable to pay their tributes," or who cannot pay a preferred type of tribute such as ivory.[807]

Slavery and enslavement not only prevailed widely but the practiced also sanctioned and carried out by auxiliaries of the government, including the leaders at the top. Perhaps, one of the worst events in the post conquest South had occurred in what Bahru called "inhuman expedition" against the Gimira people and it was carried out by Lij Eyasu in 1912. He captured 40,000 natives as slaves and drove them north.[808] Although Haile Selassie took steps to abolish slavery; he, however, continued receiving slaves as a tribute from, among others, Sheik Khojali of Ben Shangul/Assosa,[809] and others. He also created a situation where slaves could be bought legally by permission from the Minister of Pen, *Tsehafe-Tizaz*, or obtained as gifts.[810] Constant razzias, displacements, and 'wild west' style of governance prevailed in the South. This resulted in drastic depopulation of some ethnic groups in the south-west (See chapters 7-9). The *gabbar* system, as an institution of enserfment had discriminated, degraded, and deprived most southerners of their equal citizenship status and placed them at a subordinate position.

As Ethiopian political scientist succinctly summed up imperial conquests and subsequent policies implemented in the south had "formed dual society: conqueror and conquered, victor and vanquished, civilized and barbarian, believer and infidel, clean and dirty,

Amhara and "Galla"(Oromo).[811] Gebru (1996) echoed similar views about post-conquest south:

> It is evident that formidable cultural and psychological bar-
> riers separated conqueror from conquered. ...northerners in
> general tended to be paternalistic, despising, and debasing
> local traditions and cultures. Exhibiting different manners
> and habits, the new rulers, were not without pretensions to
> a "civilizing mission." They tried, much like the European
> colonizers of their times, to justify the exploitability of the
> conquered peoples by stressing the historical inevitably and
> moral validity of occupation...Paternalistic and arrogant,
> Abyssinians looked down upon and treated the indigenous
> people as backward, heathen, filthy, deceitful, lazy and even
> stupid – stereotypes that Europeans colonialists commonly
> ascribed to their African subjects.[812]

For southerners' respite from serfdom and slavery was brought, ironically, by colonial administrators. The "*gabbar* system introduced during Emperor Menilek's time, which had degraded the majority of the subjugated peoples to a kind of bondsmen...was abolished,"[813] during Italian occupation The colonial administration "not only re-lieved compulsory labor service" to the peasants but also it "awarded the land cultivated by them which became their own property."[814] During the occupation period:

> compulsory labour and the frequent arbitrarily set special trib-
> utes fell away, the fixed tax rate demanded by the Italians lay
> considerably below that of the Habaša regime. The new rulers
> were anxious to win the sympathy of the subjects of their colo-
> nial empire and therefore kept the tax rate as low as possible...
> the Italians let the property tax...to fall except for the tithes.[815]

Just like they ended *gabbar* system, "colonial rulers emphatically fought against slavery and the slave trade with drastic punishment

of death by hanging...generally freeing slaves and facilitating social training for those freed"[816] Accordingly "freed slaves in cen-
tral-southern Ethiopia were allocated land."[817] They also did something important.

> Among the southern peoples, the Italians tried to work to-
> wards a return to local cultural traditions which sometimes
> went as far as revitalization of almost totally forgotten insti-
> tutions and customs which were awakened in the memory of
> the older generation...Civil rights matters and crimes right
> up to involuntary manslaughter through hunting accidents
> were preferably left in the hands of traditional jurisdiction.[818]

After the liberation Emperor Haile Selassie "could not risk"
to restore the *gabbar* system. But his administration "signified an
extensive return to the circumstances that had existed before the
Italian occupation"[819] as political and economic power in the south
remained a monopoly of non-southerners. Hence emergent modern
Ethiopian state, as in the old one, adopted overtly a single system,
but practically two separate systems of governance for the northern
and southern regions.

In the northern provinces of Begemeder, Gojjam, Tigray, parts of
Eritrea, Shewa and Wollo; the *rist* system of communal land ownership was maintained. In this system anyone belonging to family/kin-
ship "held the right to possession of land" and rights of inheritance.
In the Greater South, on the other hand, the state "claimed ultimate
ownership" of all lands and it expropriated and distributed vast and
fertile tracts of lands "among royalty, officialdom, soldiery, and clergy
from the north." Thus, the indigenous people were reduced to the
"near-enserfment...as tenant laborers for northern settlers and their
local allies."[820]

The "Northern provinces of Tigray, Begamedir, Gojjam, Wollo
and Shewa had a communal system of land ownership *(rist)* "which
ensured right to share the land with anyone who could establish his
or her "ancestral link." Whereas, in "the other parts of the country

(South) the prevailing land tenure system was private ownership of land where the problem of tenancy was extensive."[821] As a result, in the Northern provinces "the problem of tenancy was marginal, affecting 15-25% of the population," whereas in the South "the problem of tenancy was extensive, affecting 80-85% of the farmers. The remaining 15-20% accounted for owner-farmers and farmers with other contractual agreements."[822] In other words, nearly 100% southern peasants were tenants. Comparative view of the tenancy percentage in the north and south will give us a clear picture of disparity that had existed between the two regions.

Based on 1963-1967 Central Statistical Office data, Teshale (1994) showed that tenancy is predominant in the southern regions. Arsi had 52% of tenancy, Gamu Gofa 45%, Hararge 54%, Illubabor 75%, Kaffa 67%, Shewa[823] 62%, Sidamo, 39%, Wollega 59%, and Wollo 32%. In contrast, the percentage of tenancy in Begemeder for the same period was only 15%, Gojjam 20%, and Tigre 25%.[824] Most of the lands in the south were monopolized by a few landlords and nobles. For example, "Ras Mesfin Selashi... has 50,000 gashas (2 million hectares) in Kaffa and Illubabor, plus substantial estates in Shewa and Hararghe."[825] In Hararghe province 25 people [controlled] 74.6 percent of the land."[826]

Lands owned by ruling classes and religious establishments in the south from 1941 - 1974 amounted to 4,828,560 hectares.[827] Adding further strain, southern provinces and peoples were subjected to land taxes from which the Northern provinces and peoples were exempted. This became evident after the rural land tax law, proclamation No. 8 of 1942, was issued:

> ...the northern Teklai Gizats (Governorate-Generals) Begamdir, Gojjam, Tigray where the land tenure system was communal, revolted against the implementation of the proclamation.... The rebellion was pacified by another proclamation (No. 70 of 1944) that excluded all those regions where communal ownership of land was in practice from the application of the 1941 proclamation. In fact, the proclamations

shifted the tax burden to peasants where communal ownership was not in practice [to the South]. The Church, as a big
landowner, and those regions of communal land ownership
resisted and blocked any attempt by the government to cor-
rect the inequity in the rural land tax.[828]

Southern peasants, who were subjected to reckless and arbitrary
tribute payments, had also bore the "shifted...tax burden" from regions whose communal land ownership (*rist*) system remained intact.

An additional tax, to support the garrisons in the south, was
paid by the local peasantry directly to the military and, for
convenience, can be classified as the naftanna-gabbar system. Throughout all the conquered provinces, this personal
method of transfer payments was customary.[829]

Beginning at Menelik era, the South had become the main source
of revenue. By 1893, for example, it became clear that the majority of
Menelik's supplies and wealth "no longer originated in the north."[830]
Tributes from the north were nominal as Marcus described it below.

Dejatch Belay of Semien brought five rifles and five poor
rugs; Dajatch Birru of Wag remitted ten rifles; and Dajatch
Meshesha Tenyaneh of Balasa presented seven rifles; and
Naggadras Kenfi, who controlled the markets and tariffs of
Begemder, paid only one mule load of local cloths.... Menelik
accepted this *meagre tribute and returned far more valuable
gifts to his impoverished underlings.* In contrast, the governor
of territories between Licha [Leqa] and Wallega gave 500
ounces of gold and a supplementary amount of grain and
ivory.[831] Italics added.

Another area of governance disparity between the northern and
southern provinces was administrative duality adopted by successive
Ethiopian regimes.

In the Greater South governors and rulers from provincial level to the district and sub-district level came, in the words of Gilkes, from "outside;" whereas provincial and local offices in the Northern provinces were held by local appointees. In the words of Dr. Messay Kebede, in the south: "people who were ethnically different from the southern peoples were placed on top of the social hierarchy, whereas in the north no such ethnic disparity existed."[832] He added: "The well-founded nature of this mixed system cannot be seriously disputed. It ensured control until deeper forms of integration and Ethiopianization became effective." [833] As Braukamper emphasized during Haile Selassie era "in as much as nearly all state officials positioned in the old or newly-established southern administrative divisions were of Habaša descent."

The disparity between the north and south was even more evident when we look at the appointments of *awraja* (district) governors.

In Northern provinces most governors came from within, whereas, in the Southern regions an overwhelming majority came from outside. For instance, if we look at the *awraja* governors in Tigray, "between 1944 and 1966, 72 per cent came from Tigre itself, and 28 per cent from outside." Wollo had "68 per cent local appointees." In Gojjam some 52 per cent of the *awraja* appointments come from local mekwanint."[834] Figures of Begemder were unavailable, but "the collateral descendants of the Empress Taytu…have continued to hold on to important positions…the greatest members of the family…have been used for positions outside the province."[835] The Shewa -Amhara provided "the largest percentage of officials in all positions. Not surprisingly the percentage of *awraja* governors drawn from the province is the highest – 83 per cent."[836]

How about the south?

"In contrast with the predominantly local figures at the *awraja* level in the northern provinces the reverse holds true for the southern regions. The figures for *awraja* governors between 1942 and 1967 are Wollega- 26 per cent local and 74 per cent outsiders; Illubabor – 20 per cent and 80 per cent;

Kaffa- 29 per cent and 71 per cent; Sidamo- 19 per cent and 81 per cent; Arussi- 10 per cent and 90 per cent; Hararge 26 per cent and 74 per cent."[837]

12.2. Gojjam: A Poster Child of "Mixed System."

12.2.1. Governors, Tax and Land Policies

As shown above, the prevalence of governance disparity between the north and south was undeniable. In this regard, the northern province of Gojjam can be cited as a poster child for the "mixed system" of administration and governance in Ethiopia.

In 1889 n*egus* Tekle Haymanot of Gojjam submitted to Menelik II after the latter became *neguse negest* following Emperor Yohannes's death in Metemma. Menelik allowed Tekle Haymanot to keep his title of *negus,* the only one[838] to be granted such a title in the country at large. Until his death in 1901 Tekle Haymanot retained complete internal autonomy in Gojjam. His son, Ras Hailu, also ruled Gojjam "virtually autonomous for more than two decades;"[839] again there was no other region in the country which enjoyed such autonomy. In early 1932 Emperor Haile Selassie prompted his relative *dejazmach* Imru, a Shewa-Amhara, to *ras* and appointed him as the governor of Gojjam. Imru wrote in his memoir, *Kayehut Kemastawusewu,* that he refused to accept the position because

Ras Imru wrote in his biography that he made his reluctance to accept the appointment known to Haile Selassie via verbal message (palace couriers), in writing and in person. But the emperor refused to reconsider his decision and appointed him. At the time ras Hailu Tekle Haymanot, Gojjam's hereditary ruler, was removed from Gojjam and imprisoned due to his role in helping *Lij* Eyasu escape from Fiche prison.[840]

In spite of the fact that Ras Hailu had also been indicted for misgovernment nearly all his sub-governors were kept on after his removal, even though quite a number of them were close relatives of the Ras and equally guilty of this extortion.[841]

Imru's appointment triggered opposition because he was viewed as an "outsider." Gilkes (1975) noted: "The appointment of Ras Imru as the new governor of the province was not as well received, for he had no connection to the province…he faced considerable difficulties."[842] Imru implemented several developmental projects. Yet, Gojjamies still did not accept him. He shared his frustrations to Gilkes:

> Ras Imru told me of the difficulties he had and still experiencing with officialdom of Gojjam and Agaumeder…Its people are steeped in the old traditions…customs of…slave trading and owning, official bribery and highway robbery…Ras Imru seemed surprised to meet with so much obstruction.[843]

While Imru was a Gojjam governor, fascist Italy waged war on Ethiopia in northern and southern fronts. Ethiopians rallied around the emperor and marched to fight against fascist invasions. Gojjam armies headed to the northern front under *ras* Imru. However, in December 1935, the Gojjam army led by Gessesse Belew, a grandson of *negus* Tekle Haymanot and a nephew of ras Hailu, deserted from Gondar, and went back to Gojjam "to try and seize power there."[844] In March 1936, *ras* Imru, telegraphed from Gondar the following message to Haile Selassie, who was then at Dessie: "The greater part of the Gojjam troops have deserted and refused to fight except in their own province. The few who remain have been corrupting even our own personal following."[845] Imru wrote in his memoir that "very many" people deserted with *dejazmatch* Gessesse Belew and *fitawurari* Ayalew. Imru initially left Gojjam with "more than forty thousand" people. But when counted his army "few days" after desertion "half is gone." By the time fighting became hopeless and they began retreat, he was left with "not more than three hundred people."[846] The story did not end with desertion. Gessesse Belew "besieged the

Shoan garrison (central government administrative center) in Debre Markos."[847] *Bracket added by me.* Hence, amid the war Haile Selassie was compelled to send part of the army to Debre Markos to contain rebellious Gojjamies. He dispatched, "Nevraid (nebureed) Aregai with a thousand men over from Wollo and Dejaz Habte Mariam Gabre Egiziabher (Kumsa) up from Lekempti (Leqmet) with another thousand to relieve the small Shoan garrison at Debra Markos, now being besieged by Dejaz Gessesse Belew."[848] Although Ethiopians fought gallantly, Italy gained victory mainly because it used mustard gas and aerial bombardments.

Emperor Haile Selassie fled the country and Italians entered Addis Ababa. The French journalist who was present at Graziani's celebration ceremony at the palace in Addis Ababa witnessed that *ras* Hailu was the most notable of the "Ethiopian dignitaries" who submitted to Graziani and "raised their right arms in the Fascist salute."[849] They "conferred the title of *negus* on him"[850], and he became "the chief collaborator with the Italians after the conquest of Ethiopia."[851] Gojjam's EOC Patriarch, Abba Abraham, also pledged allegiance and collaborated with the Italians; "the only bishop to collaborate with the invaders."[852] Henze wrote that "Ras Hailu his (Graziani's) favorite, Aba Jobir of Jimma another. Both facilitated Italian penetration of the west and southwest."[853] Graziani later wrote that *ras* Hailu "was the man in whom I put my confidence. He became my councilor."[854] (By the way, *ras* Hailu was not the only high ranking official to collaborate. Several other officials and groups of people in all sides of the country had actively collaborated). After the liberation, *ras* Hailu was placed under house arrest in Addis Ababa for his collaboration (he died in 1951 in Addis Ababa). However, his cousin, Hailu Belew, was appointed as a governor of Gojjam (1942-46). As noted below, he would be appointed for the second time.

Emperor Haile Selassie knew that some of the reasons for instability and rebellion in Gojjam was associated with opposition to tax decrees issued him. So, one of the tactics Haile Selassie used to appease Gojjam was by showering them with pricey gifts. The emperor "visited Debre Markos, in mid-1944...accompanied by the distribution of large sums and the gift of 100,000 $MT (approximately £9,000) for distribution to the poor;" and also announced, "the land tax of proclamation of 1942 was amended for Gojjam (as well as Begemeder and Tigre...) the future land tax was to be collected...at the pre-Italian levels."[855]

In 1950 *dejazmach* Kebede Tessema, Governor-General of Gojjam, faced opposition partly due to his non-Gojjamie background (a Shewa-Amhara) and partly because he attempted to enforce tax rate raise "from low pre-war level." To appease rebellious Gojjamies, as Bahru noted, Haile Selassie "was forced to reduce the new tax rate by third, removed Kabbada, and reinstalled the hereditary governor, Haylu Balaw. Part of the animosity the Gojjame felt for Kabbada probably emanated from his being a Shawan origin."[856] This was Hailu's second round appointment (1951-56).

After him a Shewa-Amhara, Tsehayu Enqu Selassie, was appointed as a Governor-General of Gojjam. Gojjam's regionalism persisted during his governorship as well. Gojjamies again opposed him for being an outsider and for attempting to enforce agricultural income tax. Armed rebellion spread in several districts led by those who "bestow upon themselves titles such as that of *l'ul* and *fitawrari*." Once again, "in clear contrast to the way it was handled in the Bale rebellion...the government was far more accommodating over the Gojjame demands."[857]Tsehayu Enqu Selassie was removed from Gojjam and he was sent to Kaffa. As a Governor-General of Kaffa he subjected powerless and unarmed natives of Kaffa to an extreme exploitation and inhuman subjugation for several years.[858]

Gojjamies opposition of the tax decree was driven by a fear that the government might take away their *rist* rights and treat them as the "colonized people" of the south, which Gabru described as follows:

> What the tillers wanted to avoid was the dreaded fate of their
> southern counterparts. In their view, if southerners had been
> disinherited, it was because they were colonized people. But
> the Gojjame were free citizens, and the basis of their freedom
> was the heritage of collective ownership of land.[859]

When the "elders" of Gojjam "unequivocally stated before the emperor in 1950, they told Haile Selassie:

> "we are to be deprived of our tradition rights. There is no rist without liberty and no honor without rist..to institute in its place *something similar to the system now operative in the frontier lands occupied by force* [the South]...and *to contemplate governing Gojjam like them* [Southerners] *is...to institute a system of oppression in our land*...the Governor's intention is to govern Gojjam like an occupied territory.[860] Brackets & italics added by me.

12.2.2. *Belay Zeleke*

Many writers and even reputable historians focused mainly at the unfortunate execution of Belay Zeleke and ignored to expound the underlying reasons which led to his confrontation with the emperor in the first place. They also ignored Haile Selassie's 'accommodating' policies, Gojjam's rebellion and rebel leaders like Belay Zeleke which sharply contrasted with his policies against rebellions in the southern regions.

Belay Zeleke was a renowned patriot in Gojjam who led strong resistance against the occupation of Italy. He was not born of Gojjam's ruling families. As a matter of fact, his father was a shifta, a man who made his livelihood on highway robbery and banditry. According to oral history I gathered, he was a first generation Gojjame because 'his father was a Wolloye,' a Wollo native. One of my informants and the man I considered a reliable source was Assefa Tarekegn, a former Ethiopian journalist and a Wollo native. In December1999 Assefa told me the following story about Belay Zeleke's family background, which I wrote down in my notebook at the time.

> The name of Belay's father was Zeleke Endale. He was a native of Çeqeta (Cheqeta) in Wollo Borana. Zeleke murdered someone in Wollo and fled with his wife to Gojjam and

lived there as a shifta. Let us speak the truth. Belay Zeleke
descended from Wollo Oromos, who are Oromigna speakers
and who still live in Çeqeta. Belay's father and mother are
Wolloyes. Belay Zeleke's son, Aschenq Belay lives in Mekane
Selam, capital of Borana Saint District.[861]

In addition to his earned fame due to his patriotism, he also became famous because he married a daughter of *fitawurari* Admasu, a
nephew of ras Hailu (Gilkes 1975:181). The combination of these two
factors made Belay "a person of soaring ambition,"[862] which eventually caused his undoing. It was often said that he bragged: "*Enate
Belay belagnalech*" (My mother named me Belay (one who is superior
than others) and, hence, he would not be subordinate to anyone.

In recognition of his patriotic resistance against Italians, "Belai,
a son of *shifta* had been rewarded at the return of the Emperor by
being made a *Dejazmatch* and Governor of Bichena."[863] At the same
time Haile Selassie made him a *dejazmatch* and governor; the emperor
also rewarded three men from Gojjam's ruling family (relatives of
ras Hailu). Accordingly, "Dejazmatch Haile Belew was made a Ras
and Governor-General of Gojjam, Mengesha Jambere was made
Bitwoded and Deputy-General of the province, Negash Bezabeh was
made Bitwoded and President of the Senate."[864]

For a man of 'soaring ambition' this was unacceptable. Gilkes
(1975) wrote that Belay "was disgruntled by the fact that the three
other leaders had received greater position... Belai felt strong enough
to disobey orders both from the Governor-General and from Addis
Ababa [Haile Selassie] in 1942."[865]. Gabru's (1996) described it as
follows: Disgusted with both the office and the title given to him
in the post liberation administrative reorganization, Belai made the
ill-fated decision to defy the government by turning to banditry."[866]

His defiance was short-lived. *Bitwoded* Mengesha Jambere. the
Governor of Gojjam, "moved against him with over 3,000 men,
Belai found himself deserted and was forced to surrender. He was
brought to Addis Ababa and imprisoned along with two grand-
sons of Hailu, Dejazmatch Mammo and Dejazmatch Kebede Haile

Mikael."[867] Belay and other high-profile prisoners of Gojjam ruling families escaped from the prison and headed to Gojjam. Reportedly Haile Selassie had:

> severe fright when both Dejazmatch Mamo Haile Mikael, with his brother and half-brother, as well as Dejazmatch Belai with his brother, broke out of prison, killing a guard in the process. They were captured after only three days, on their way to Gojjam."[868]

Apparently Belay kept giving more reasons to his enemies to make their cases against him because "before his captors he is said to have enraged the emperor by remarking that 'God created every one of us, but did not appoint anyone to rule.' By contesting the diving basis of kingship, Belai provided his persecutor with additional reason to sentence him to death by hanging."[869]

12.2.3. "accommodating" vs. "wrath"

The central government, as Bahru (1991) and others, wrote had used different methods of handling the rebellion of Gojjam on one hand, and that of the Bale rebellion of 1963-1970, and the Gedeo rebellion of 1960, on the other hand. The former was described as 'accommodating' and 'appeasing.' In the latter's case the government used the might of its forces which 'vented their wrath' on the rebellious peasants.

In Bale the government "launched massive operations involving the army, the police, the territorials, the settler militia (*nach labash*) and volunteers (*waddo zamach*)."[870] Gebru's (1996) meticulous research showed that "State forces…vented their wrath on the farmers by callously destroying their hamlets, animals and crops. They slaughtered as many cattle, goats, and sheep as they could consume and turned over the rest to the state, which, in turn auctioned them at abnormally low prices."[871] During the two years "period 1968-70 alone, by official accounts, over 60,000 cattle (slightly over 4 percent of the livestock in Bale), 18,698 camels, 7,060 pack animals, and 22,215 sheep and goats were confiscated.[872]

Such devastation was followed by appointments of officials of northern descent, unlike Gojjam were locals were appointed. For example, "in 1973 in El Kere where the crisis had begun…all senior officials, including the district governor, were of Amhara-Christian origin."[873] Recognizing different ways in which rebellions in Bale and Gojjam were handled, Bahru cautiously described it as 'accommodating,' "In clear contrast to the way it was handling the Bale rebellion…the government was far more accommodating over the Gojjame demands."[874] Unlike "a vendee revolt," of Gojjam, to use Gebru's phrase, "the Bale rebellion was primarily a reaction to local needs and pressures."[875] In the words of Bahru:

> the connection between peasant exploitation and rebellion was more direct…The institution of the qalad in 1951 had had the effect of reducing many peasants to the status of tenants. The peasants' inability to pay the increased taxes accompanying new land measurements in 1963 had led to large-scale alienation. The conditions of peasants were worsened by the multiplicity and venality of government officials. The imposition of Christian settlers over a predominantly Muslim population also engendered religious antagonism. Settler arrogance, as well as political and economic domination, reached its peak under the administration of Fitawrari Warqu Enqwa-Selassie, whose appointment as provincial governor in 1963 might be said to have triggered the rebellion.[876]

The story of Bale's uprising and the heavy-handedness of government was repeated during the uprising of Gedeo people. The Gedeo people became landless due to land grabbing by settler communities, nobilities, and royal families. "The Gedeo uprising of 1960 had its genesis in land alienation. The coffee-rich lands of the district had invited a veritable land grabbing rush among the northern nobility and gentry. Amongst those involved was the emperor's daughter, Princess

Tenagnawarq."[877] As a result," many Gedeo had been reduced to tenancy. The economic exploitation of the Gedeo was coupled with the degradation of their culture. ...the Gedeo uprising was preceded by futile appeals and petitions to higher authorities."[878] Due to unwillingness of authorities to hear their appeals and to address their concerns, the Geodeo took the last resort measure. They revolted against the oppressive *gabbar* system and expropriation of their lands.

> The peasants then challenged the oppressive system by refusing to pay the *erbo*, the quarter of his produce that a tenant was expected to pay the landlord. The clash with authorities began when the peasants went on to collect the coffee without waiting for the assessors who could customarily determine the amount of *erbo* to be paid.[879]

Rebellion and resistance for the Gedeo people was not new. The 1960s rebellion, as a matter of fact, was a continuation of their resistance and rebellion of the 1920s and 30s. Before they engage in rebellious activities, they exhausted peaceful means of appeals from local level all the way to the emperor's court in Addis Ababa. But their concerns and appeals were ignored and pushed them to try to take their own actions (See chapter ten). Now, although they were unarmed, unlike Gojjam, they were tricked into peaceful resolution and brutally attacked.

> Armed mostly with spears and swords, Gedeo peasants confronted a well-equipped enemy composed of landlords and government troops. In the first clash, eighty-eight peasants were killed as against three from government side. In the final engagement at Michille, the peasants were lulled into discontinuing fighting by conciliatory gestures from the government envoy...Taking advantage of this the government troops stepped up their offensive, killing over a hundred peasants and destroying much peasant property...The defeat of the peasants was total.[880]

While Bale and Gedeo rebellions were met with severe punishments and devastation, in Gojjam the government gave several "concessions". In Gojjam the government dealt with armed rebellions leniently. The government was "accommodating." It "abandoned" the new tax, waived tax arrears from 1950 to 1968, and transferred "many government officials" (non-Gojjamies) to other regions,[881] and replaced them with local officials. Gojjam barely paid tax, although the tax levied on Gojjam and other northern provinces was lower than the tax rate in the south. For example, in 1968 the total tax assessed in seven districts of Gojjam was ETH \$306,283.90; out of which only ETH \$42,910.00 was collected, which means ETH \$263,373.90 remained uncollected.[882]

Hence, Gojjamies continued to live without sharing the "tax burden" of southerners and were financed by others for their own province's administrative expenses. As Bahru noted the province was not self-supportive in terms of generating revenue from within. "The government had scarcely been able to collect taxes there in the post-Liberation period: the amount collected was so low that it could not even cover the salaries of local officials."[883] In addition, the Haile Selassie regime rewarded Gojjam because it refinanced and allocated "a relatively higher expenditure in the province of Gojjam , during the 1965 and 1971 fiscal year."[884]

As was evidenced in Gedeo region and elsewhere in the South, madeira lands of *naftegna* were given permission to be converted into rist lands, which McClellan (2002) put is as follows:

> The soldier-farmers of an earlier era were being transformed into farmer-soldiers...After the war [the Italian], the transition was fully completed. At that time, settlers in the south were allowed to convert a portion of their *maderia* into *rist*. With this measure, the tenancy system became full-blown; for the first-time settlers gained heritable rights to land and thus were free to buy or sell it[885].

Part V

"Shewanization of the Empire" and the Enduring Legacies

"As King of Shoa, Menelik had exploited the south and south-west to purchase weapons; as emperor, he used its wealth to bolster the north's sagging economy, and to ensure the continuation of Amhara-Tigrean political and cultural hegemony."
- Harold Marcus, *The Life and Times of Menelik II: Ethiopia 1844-1913* 1995:140

"Menelik's reign not only made Shoa the most dynamic region in the country, it had also consolidated Shoan political dominance over Ethiopia. Shoans have extended their influence from their own to Harar and throughout the south...The Shoa elites could not be expected to let their dominance be dissipated. The reassertion of Shoan leadership ...was to last for almost sixty years."
- Paul Henze, *Layers of Time: A History of Ethiopia* 2000:194–5

Chapter 13

Dominance of Shewa-Amhara Ruling Class

"Not Surprisingly, since it was the Shoan empire of Menelik that made the conquest, the administration of these territories fell almost entirely into Shoan Amhara hands." - Patrick Gilkes, *The Dying Lion: Feudalism and modernization in Ethiopia* 1975:49

13.1. Menelik's Inner Circle

Alexander Bulatovich in his two books[886] provided valuable information about the inner workings of Emperor Menelik and his regime. Bulatovich was part of the Russian Red Cross mission which arrived at the country shortly after the Battle of Adwa. He soon earned Menelik's favor mainly because of his military background, his participation in the campaigns of conquests and his Russian Orthodox faith. Menelik's desire to establish cordial relationship with Czar Nicholas also played a part for his favorability. Between 1896-1898 Bulatovich met Menelik several times and was given unlimited access and travel opportunities into western and southwestern regions. During the south-west conquest, he was embedded with *ras* Wolde Giorgis's army and served as an advisor. He was also engaged in reconnaissance and, in some instances, in actual fighting alongside *ras*'s army. Bulatovich tried to learn as much about organization of

Menelik's government, military structure, and "Abyssinian customs." He was a keen observer and his writings gave us some insight into the emperor's inner circles. He noticed that Menelik and his "closest" officials were members of influential association called "Makhuber (Mahbere) Zamariam," "Society of Mary."

The "Society consisted of the Emperor and eleven of his closest *balamuals*" with whom "the Emperor eats on the floor from one basket with the rest of the members of the Society."[887] Bulatovich listed the members of Mahbere Zemariam: "The main members of this society[888] were *Ras* Dargi (Darge), *Ras* Makonnen, *Afa-negus* Nasibu, Ras Wolda Giyorgis, *Ras* Mengesha Bituaded *(bitwoded)*, Dajazmatch Ubye (Wube), Dajazmatch *(later ras)* Tessema, *Dajezmatch* Haile Mariam, *Likamakos (liqamaquas)* Abata, and *Alaka* Gebre Silassie."[889] In addition to the *Mahbere ZeMariam's* monthly gathering, the emperor also dines with his "very closest associates" such as *"Ras Darge, Ras Makonnen* and other balmuals" several days a week when he dines with Empress Taytu.[890] The common denominator among the officials who dined with the emperor was that they were *Shewans related to him by blood and/or by family ties..*

As Menelik's domains expanded further south, so did Shewa's royal seats move southward from the hills of Ankobar and Angolola to Liche, Entoto I, Entoto II, and finally to the fertile valley of Finfine.[891]renamed Addis Ababa, new flower. Menelik's southward incursions and expansions were directly associated with the availability of vast lands, lucrative trades routes, and natural resources. As Kaufeler noted, "Most of the beneficiaries of the great expansion in the late 19th century was Shoan Amhara. The expansive push had out from Shoa, and in the reign of Menelik this province had become the seat of imperial power."[892]

In conquered regions, Shewans predominantly held top military and civilian positions. After Menelik became *neguse negest* in 1889, "the Shewan system was extended to cover the whole empire" which Darkwah aptly termed it as "the Shewanization of the empire"[893]. Gilkes (1975) called it "the Shoan empire of Menelik."[894] Henze noted that during Menelik's reign Shewa became "the most dynamic region in the country" and "consolidated…political dominance over Ethiopia" and the Shewa–Amhara "have extended their influence… throughout the south."[895]

The process of "Shewanization" expanded hand in hand with the expansion of conquered territories, which, during Haile Selassie era, ultimately resulted in Shewa's undisputed dominance over the entire nation's political, economic, and intellectual life.

13.2. Haile Selassie I: The Legacy Relay

Haile Selassie's road to the imperial throne was through the 'Old Shoa' and not through Harar. He was rooted in *Menz* and *Minjar*. His father, *ras* Mekonnen, was a powerful Shewan and Menelik's cousin, Sahel Selassie's blood relative. He monopolized rich resources of Hararghe (lands, chat, coffee, ivory), owned customs & *naga-drases*, and controlled an important sea trade route from Harar-Zeila. Hence, he was "believed…to be richer than Menelik."[896] With the emperor's blessings, he built a vast & loyal army which made him an enormously powerful man in the empire.

Teferi Mekonnen was an heir of his father's *habtna tor* (wealth and army). When he was barely a teenager, he was appointed as a governor of Selale, Sidamo, & Harar (all while he was living in the palace in Addis Ababa). Rapid deployment of army (and flow of money) from Harar, as *ras* Imru recounted in his memoir, enabled Teferi to maneuver around and to survive during his regency years. It was also because of his Shewa root that the establishment (Shewa nobility & Church) rallied around Teferi and concocted plot against *Lij* Eyasu, whose father was a Moslem- Oromo-Christianized Amhara; and whose mother was an illegitimate child. Teferi cruised through ranks and titles: *Lij, dejazmatch, ras, negus* & *neguse negest*.

Teferi Mekonnon inherited Menelik's throne and became Haile Selassie (Power of Trinity) I. He later embellished himself with real and fictious grand titles which, among other things, included: *Elect of God, Lion of the Tribe of Judah, His Imperial Majesty King of Kings, custodian of the Seal of Solomon, Order of Queen Sheba, and Order of*

Menelik. He was also *a Field Marshal of the Ethiopian Army, Admiral of the Navy, & Marshal of the Air Force.*

During his 58 years reign as *alga worash*/regent (1916-28), *negus/* king (1928-30), and then as *neguse negest*/king of kings (1930-1974); Shewa established itself as the undisputed powerhouse of Ethiopia. He built upon the strong foundation his predecessors laid on. Its key player status was exhibited in high level positions disproportionally dominated by Shewans in administrative, political, and cultural (literature, writing) fields.

During the Haile Selassie era the dominant legacy of his forefathers had spread through the empire, percolated into government institutions, and established deep roots. It encompassed the nation's as well as the citizens' life. He achieved this primarily by installing his loyalists at all levels of the government. He sought absolute loyalty and allegiance from all his officials and civil servants. Loyalty was a litmus test, an unwritten law all should adhere to. His unflinching determination to seek obedience and loyalty made him lean on fellow Shewans. Henze remarked that "Haile Selassie era has often been characterized as a period of Amhara rule."[897] But it was not any Amhara. It was primarily the Shewa-Amhara. Gebru rightly stated that the "Shewa Amhara were favored heavily in the ...imperial system."[898] Messay (1999) called it "the Shewan tribalism of Haile Selassie."[899] Even among the Shewa-Amhara, the Menz remained as the nucleus of ruling class and dominated the center. .

As Donald Levine wrote in *Wax and Gold,* "Menelik and his successors filled the government with people from their home area; numerous higher officials of the imperial Ethiopian government are also of Manze origin."[900] The level of "Shewan tribalism" grew to such an extent that "during the period 1942-66 Shoans occupied 62 percent of the senior posts in the imperial administration."[901] Rothchild in his book, *Managing Ethnic Conflict in Africa: Pressure and Incentives for Cooperation,* noted that the nation's bureaucracy from top officials to the provincial governors were mainly occupied by Shewans. He wrote that Haile "Selasie who concentrated power in the bureaucracy at Addis Ababa, recruited an estimated 60 to 70 percent of the high central government officials and provincial governors from among the Amhara of Shoa Province for his cadre of rulers."[902] By any standard this is extremely high percentage..

Haile Selassie concentrated multiple cabinet posts in the hands of few Shewan prominent officials. Among the many who dominated the Ethiopian government bureaucracy during Haile Selassie reign, the following few can be cited as an example.

Wolde Giorgis Wolde Yohannes (1901-1974) was born in Bulga, Shewa. Because he was the emperor's confidant, he was appointed to run multiple government institutions simultaneously. He was *Tsehafe Tizaz* (/Minister of Pen) from 1941-1955. Meantime, he was also a Minister of Interior for six years (1943-1949) and Minster of Justice from 1949-1955; then, Governor of Arsi (1951-1960) and Governor of Gamu Gofa (1960-1961).[903] According Bahru he was "the *de facto* prime minster" when Mekonnen Endalkachew was a prime minister and was "the most powerful man next to the emperor."[904]

Mekonnen Endalkachew (1890-1963) was one the powerful Shewa aristocrats and a relative of another powerful Menelik's official; *ras* Tessema Nadew. He was a nephew of ras Tessema and grew up at Menelik palace. He was married to Emperor Haile Selassie's niece, Yeshashwork Yilma and was made *bitwoded,* the favorite, the title reserved for select few loyalists. He was appointed by Haile Selassie as Minister in London, then Minister of Interior, Governor of Illubabor, and the first Prime Minister of Ethiopia, a position he held from 1943 until 1957.[905]

Another family of Shewans who dominated Haile Selassie's government cabinet were the three sons of Habte Wold: Akililu Habtewold, Mekonnen Habtewold, and Akaleworq Habtewold. They were introduced to Haile Selassie by *Tsehafe Tezaz* Wolde Giorgis Wolde Yohannes. Haile Selassie educated and appointed them in various ranks. Mekonnen Habte Wold was a Minister of Commerce, Minister of Finance (194-1958) and Minister of Agriculture. With the help of his older brother, Mekonnen, Akililu Habte Wold "emerged at the forefront of Ethiopian politics". He was made Deputy Prime Minister (1957-1960) and became Prime

Minister of Ethiopia, a post he held for 14 years (1961-1974. Akale Worq Habte Wold was made deputy *Tsehafe Tizaz* and then Minister of Education.[906] John Gunther in his book, *Inside Africa*, described that "these three brothers (Mekonnen Habte Wolde, Akililu Habte Wolde & Akale Worq Habte Wolde) comprise three-eighths of the total cabinet "[907]positions.

Endalkachew Mekonnen (1927-1974) was son of Mekonnen Endalkachew, Ethiopia's first prime minister. Endalkachew was a born aristocrat who grew up in the center of power and privilege and was educated in Oxford. Like his father, he too was made a Prime Minster of Ethiopia.

Ras Imru Haile Selassie was Haile Selassie's first cousin and his confidant. He was appointed as a Governor-General of Hararge, Wollo and Gojjam provinces. After the liberation he was appointed as Crown Councilor and ambassador to India, United States, and the Soviet Union.[908] His son, Mikael Imru, who was educated at Oxford, was appointed by Haile Selassie as deputy Secretary of Agriculture (1958-1959), as a diplomat in Washington D.C. (1958-1961) and in Moscow (1961-1965), Served as Ethiopian Foreign Minister "few months between these diplomatic posts"; and then he worked at UNCTAD in Geneva (1965-1968), Minister of Trade and Industry and Prime Minster of Ethiopia, after *Lij* Endalkachew.[909]

What was even more revealing was that these officials were preceded and/or succeeded by officials from same the region since the beginning of the Menelik era. As Kapuscinski wrote in detail in *The Emperor: Downfall of an Autocrat* (1983), Haile Selassie personally decided, selected, appointed, dismissed, and reappointed all officials from cabinet ministers' level down to school principals and hospital and hotel managers.[910] Professor Donald Donham noted that the Emperor was directly involved in the appointments of governors to the *awraja* level in which "Shewans predominated."

> Haile Sellassie was personally involved in appointing and reappointing governors down to the level of awraja (sub provinces), of which there were approximately one hundred.

Given the emperor's base within the Shewan establishment, it is not surprising that Shewans predominated in these and other appointments. In the years from 1941 to 1966, for example, the Shewans appointed to the rank of vice-minister or above was a remarkable 62 percent.[911]

As Gilkes in his epic work (1975) described, the military appointments also showed predominance of Amhara. "Certainly, among the officer corps Amharas are preponderant. An analysis of appointments at the level of Divisional Chief of Staff and above between 1941 and 1966 produced the figures – 62 per cent Amhara, 15 per cent Oromo; 9 per cent Eritrean; 5 per cent Tigre; 9 per cent others."[912] The table below shows ethnic origin of Ethiopian army officers make up in 1970 & 1972..

Table 5: "Army Officers – Origins"[913]

Rank	Origin	1970	1972
Lt. Colonel and above	Amhara	75	65
	Tigre/Eritrea	10	8
	Oromo	12	21
	Others	3	6
Below Lt. Colonel	Amhara	65	60
	Tigre/Eritrea	10	=
	Oromo	25	30
	Others (includes Tigre/Eritrea		

Some Amhara scholars not only dismiss the notion of Amhara domination of the Ethiopian government during successive regimes of Menelik II, Haile Selassie I, and Mengistu Halie Mariam; but also they even go to the extent of denying the Ethiopian monarchs themselves belonging to Amhara ethnic group.[914] Dr. Bahru emphasized that during post liberation era Haile Selassie "continued his pre-war policy of recruiting men of low and humble background to ensure their loyalty"[915] disregarding the fact that he did not 'recruit men of low and humble background' from any other region of the country, not even from other Amhara provinces.

13.3. "Doling out" Conquered lands

As Menelik's domains moved from Shewa's historical center in Ankobar and Angolola to the south, conquered lands were expropriated and came under direct control of imperial agents and military rulers. Expropriated lands "went not only to the important generals but also to ordinary soldiers and lesser officers, many of whom settled in these provinces or were appointed to some position or garrison duty there."[916] Because "the Shoan empire of Menelik that made the conquest, the administration of these (conquered) territories fell almost entirely into Shoan Amhara hands."[917] In other words, all the lands belonged to the emperor; and the Shewa rulers and emperor's appointees had jurisdiction over those lands and peoples. Along with controlling lands and administrative apparatus, Shewa's traditions and instruments of government (military, land tenure, customs, religion,) were exported to conquered lands.

One of the earliest large-scale land expropriations and share out among Shewans occurred in Addis Ababa where "large areas of land" was distributed among the top Shewa nobilities and "important personalities," including those affiliated in marriage with the king.

Professor Richard Pankhurst, in *Economic History of Ethiopia 1800-1935*, described some of the nobilities and officials who had received lands and whose new land ownership title was published in 1886-7 by Addis Ababa Municipality. The main recipients were *etege* Taytu Bitul, *ras* Darge Sahle Selassie, *ras* Mekonnen Wolde Mikael, *afe negus* Nesibu, *echege* Gebre Selassie, *fitawurari* Hayle Mariam Wolde Mikael (brother of *ras* Mekonnen), *dejazmatch* Wolde Gebriel, *dejazmatch* Germame, *ras* Mikael, *dejazmatch* Tasew, *bajerond* Fikre Selassie, *tsehafe te'ezaz* Gebre Selassie, *ras* Nadew, *dejazamatch* Biru Haile Mariam, *ras* Abate, *negadras* Agedew, *dejazmatch* Wube, *fitawurari* Gebeyehu, *ras* Wolde Giorgis Aboye, *azaj* Gizaw, *ras bitwoded* Tessema Nadew, *fitawurari* Aba Koren, *dejazmach* Bashah Aboye, *ras* Leul Seged, and *liqamequas* Adnew.[918] In the ensuing years:

> As more lands conquered, Menelik doled out land in con-
> quered areas as private tenure, and gult tenure holdings. He
> gave land and access to tribute to soldiers who helped him
> conquer the land; to setters and local notables, *balabats*, who
> helped him administer it; to members of the nobility and
> royal family's as gifts.[919]

The emperor's apologists, in their attempts to rationalize treat-ment of subject people and expropriation of lands, tried to dilute the facts on the ground and portrayed expropriation of lands in the conquered areas as a random act of "theft and swindle" rather than both systemic and systematic act of the conquerors.

> Let it be noted that the expropriation of land occurred after
> the conquest and according to a procedure akin to theft and
> swindle rather than to imposition of the indefeasible right of
> the conqueror. This trait alone tells a good deal about the
> non-colonial intention of the southern expansion.[920]

Due to surplus conquered lands Shewa nobilities had to pick and choose the lands and the people they wanted to rule over. Such was the case with *dejazmatch Girmame*, one of Menelik's closest *balemuals*. After the conquest of the Guragelands, Menelik gave Gurage over to Germame. But he "refused the overlordship of Gurage. Then Menelik divided the Guragelands into five negarit (military) admin-istrative regions.[921] For Germame, in lieu of Gurage, he gave lands in a much fertile regions of Bishofitu and Adama.[922] Kaufler emphasizes that "conquests provided many Abyssinians with the opportunity to acquire riches and improve their status. Many Amhara originat-ing from poor peasant families became landlords in the conquered territories."[923] Distributions of lands were often commensurate with the ranks and status of the recipients.

> Ordinary soldiers…received…from one to three gasha (…
> One gasha may comprise 40 to 80 hectares). Higher military
> officials received correspondingly larger grants, respective
> to their position in the hierarchy. Usually a part of these
> grants was given as permanent possession, the rest as tem-
> porary usufruct and quasi-salary (maderia).[924]

Doling out lands in the cities and "a larger area in…the provinces conquered by Menelik" continued through the 1960s. As Greenfield noted, it became a means of amassing wealth and power for personal enrichment. The "recipients normally build houses on the areas within the city and often let them to foreign residents" and obtained a "very considerable profit,"[925] Of course, among the "grantees and the emerging "colonial" ruling stratum in the south there were also many northern Galla (especially from Shoa) and many non-Shoa Abyssinians,"[926] mainly from Begemeder, Gojjam.and also from Tigray. While the socio-economic status of recipients of the lands improved for better; the statuses of peasants in conquered lands were worsened as they were now turned into *gabbars* (tenant-serfs) for settler-soldiers, absentee landlords, the church, local and provincial officials.

The tradition of giving *maderia* lands "became wide spread after World War II when Haile Selassie attempted to consolidate his hold over the south."[927] According to Professor Lapiso G. Delebo, from 1941-1974 the southern lands expropriated and owned by ruling classes and religious institutions amounted to 4,828,560 hectares.[928] In post-liberation era, expropriation of lands by the nobility and various powerful men reached to a higher level. For example, *ras* Mesfin Sileshi who was a governor of Illubabor from 1942-46 and Kaffa from 1946-55 was estimated to have owned 50,000 gashas (2, 0000,000 hectares); and another powerful man acquired up to 5000 gashas (200,000 hectares).[929]

Chapter 14

Shewa-Amhara Dominance on Ethiopian Literature & Writing

M enelik deserved credit for embracing the concept of modernization and modern education in the face of "strong opposition from the Church." In 1905 he started school in the palace grounds, and in 1908 *Menelik II School* was opened in Addis Ababa, which was run by an Egyptian named Hanna Salib and "a number of other Copts" were assigned as a compromise between Menelik and Abune Mattewos, himself an Egyptian. Besides Addis Ababa, Copts (Egyptian Christians) were also based in Ankobar, Harar and Dessie. Menelik II School was "open to anyone who could speak and write Amharic" and it had "about a hundred children of the best families."[930] In 1894 Menelik sent three students to study in Switzerland. Later, two students (Tesema Eshete and Astatke Wolde Tsadik) were sent to Germany, several others sent to Burma with Dr. Martin, and seven students were sent to Russia[931] among them was Tekle Hawariat Tekle Mariam who was sent with a Russian, Leontiev.[932] Tekle Hawariyat wrote at length in his autobiography, *Ye Heywote Tarik*, his relations to *ras* Makonnen, how the *ras* arranged his travel to Russia after he asked and got permission from Menelik.

Access to modern education then was "one of the privileges of the traditional elites" and, until the mid-1930s, it was "reserved for the nobility,"[933] at the center of government. Most of the students of "best families" were children and relatives of Shewa nobility, who, in the ensuing years and decades, would dominate government offices and the field of literature in Ethiopia.

At least based on the modern Ethiopian historical experience, one may deduce that political (government and administration) and economic (land & labor) dominance may correlate with cultural dominance of the same class. A Shewa-Amhara's undisputable dominance in the fields of literature & writing can be cited as a case in point. As Kaufeler noted through the 1950s other groups were not represented as much.

> The overwhelming majority of the emerging middle-class was of Abyssinian origin. This is not very surprising, as the educational system was based on Amharinya at the primary level and on English at the higher levels. The non-Amhara thus had to learn two foreign languages in order to receive modern higher education. In the late 1950s, 55 percent of those entering university identified themselves as Amhara and 25 percent as Tigreans, while these two groups comprised not more than 40 per cent of the total population.[934]

Not surprisingly, as Table 7 below depicted, some of the prominent Ethiopians in the fields of literature and writing were Shewans and/or people with Shewa roots.[935]

Table 6: Backgrounds of Famous Ethiopians in Literature and Writing

No	Name	Origin/ethnic background
1	Abe Gobegna	**Gojjam**, Bahr Dar
2	Abera Lemma	**Shewa**, Fiche, Selale. Mother from Merihabete, Grandfather: Menz
3	Abera Moltot Tale	**Shewa,** Menz
4	Afework Gebre Yesus	**Gojjam**, Bahr Dar.
5	Afeworq Tekle	**Shewa**, Ankobar
5	Alemayehu Moges	**Gojjam**
6	Amare Mammo	**Sidamo**, Gedeo. Mother Sefef-Yelesh G. Mikael: **Shewa**, Menze. Father: Godana Amiro: Sodo Mammo Debela —godfather
7	Asefa Gebre Mariam of	**Hararge**, Chercher. Father: **Shewa**, Menz. Brother.of Negash G. M.
8	Assefa G. Mariam Tessema	Father: **Wollo.**Mother: Jirru, **Shewa**
9	Atsme Giorgis	**Shewa**, Ankobar (Harramba**).**
10	Be-alu Girma	**Illubabor**, Supe. Father: India, Gujrat-Babu
11	Beimnet G. Amlak	**Eritrea**, Hamsen
12	Berhane Guchalawork Wolde Hana.	**Shewa**, Tegulat na Bulga
13	Birhanu Zarihun	**Begamedir**, Gondar
14	Dagnachew Worku	**Shewa.** Yifat**,** Agem Berr
15	Dereje Wube Dagne	**Shewa**, Yifat
16	Desta Tekle Wolde	**Shewa,** Tegulate na Bulga
17	Gebre Hanna Gebre Mariam (*Aleqa*)	**Begamedir**, Fogera (Debre Tabor)
18	Gebre Hiwot Bikedagn 1	**Tigray**, Adowa
19	Girma Demenu Bejetoal	**Shewa,** Debre Zeit

20	Girma Tekle Wolde	**Shewa**, Tagulet na Bulga
21	Girma Tsion Mebratu (*Meri Geta*)	**Eritrea**, Seraye Awraja "Compiler of the largest Tigrigna dictionary"
22	Girmachew Tekle Mariam:	**Shewa. Menz.** Brother: Tekle Hawariyat
23	Girmachew Tekle Hawariyat (*Dejazmach*)	**Hararghe**, Hirna. Son of *fit.* Tekle Hawariyat Tekle Mariam
24	Haddis Alemayehu	**Gojjam.** Debre Markos
25	Hiruy (Gebremeskal) Wolde Sellasie, (*Blaten Geta*). Son: Sirak	**Shewa. Menz,** Father: Merabete. "Father of Amharic literature
26	Imru Haile Silassie (*Ras*)	**Shewa, Menz** (born in Gursum Hararghe).
27	Kebede Desta G. Mariam	**Shewa**
28	Kebede Mikael	**Shewa**, Ankober/Debre Birhan
29	Kidane Wolde Kifle (*Aleqa*)	**Shewa, Yifaft na Timuga**
30	Mahtema Silassie Wolde Meskel (*Belaten*)	**Addis Ababa.** Father: t*sehafe tizaz* Wolde Mesk**al: Shewa,** Tegultna Bulga
31	Mammo Wudineh	**Wollo**, Wag
32	Mekonen Endalkachew (*ras*)	**Shewa, Tegulat.**
33	Mekonnen Zewude Gogena	**Wollo.**
	Melaku Ashagre	**Addis Ababa,** Parents: **Shewa,** Jiru,
34	Mengistu Lemma	**Shewa, Addis Ababa,** Father: Lasta
35	Mersehe Hazen Wolde Kirkos (Bilata)	**Shewa,** Jiru
37	Mulatu Astatike	**Addis Ababa**
38	Negash G. Mariam. Brother of Assefa G, Mariam	**Hararge**, Chercher. Father: **Shewa, Menz**.
39	Sahle Sillasie Birhne Mariam	**Shewa,** -Cheha

40	Sibhat G. Egzabiher	**Tigray**, Adwa
41	Sirak Hiruy Wolde Selassie- Son of Hiruy Wolde Selassie	**Shewa,** Menz.
41	Taye Gebre Mariam	**Begemder**
42	Tadese Liben	**Wollega**. Father: **Wollo**,
43	Teddela G. Hiywot	**Shewa**, Welisso. Father: Gamo–Gofa, a son of a settler. "some Tigrean blood in the family further back"
44	Tekle Hawariyat Tekle Mariam.	**Shewa**. Menz, Sidber Brother of Girmachew Tekle Mariam. Father of Girmachew Tekle Hawariy
45	Tekle Tsadik Mekuria	**Shewa,** Tegulat na Bulga
46	Tesfaye Abebe Damte.	**Shewa,** Addis Ababa
47	Tessema Eshete	**Shewa,** Minjar
47	Tessema Hable Michael	**Shewa,** Selale, Goha Tsion
48	Tsegaye Gebre Madhin (Laurete).	**Shewa**, Jibatna Mech**a**. Mother: **Shewa** Ankober. Father: Roba Qawessa
49	Wolde Giorgis Wolde Yohannes	**Shewa**. Minjar "Father of Ethiopian Journalism"
50	Yilma Habteyes	**Shewa, Merhabete**
51	Yoftahe Nigussie	**Gojjam**, Debre Elias

Source: Reidulf K. Molvaer, *Black Lions: The Creative Lives of Modern Ethiopia's Literary Giants & Pioneers*. The Red Sea press, Inc. Asmara 1997. *National Bibliography of Ethiopia 2005-2006,* Ethiopian National Archives and Library Agency. Vol. 24, No.2, 2005-2006. David H. Shinn & Thomas P. Ofcansky, *Historical Dictionary of Ethiopia*, Historical Dictionaries of Africa, No. 91, The Scarecrow Press, Inc. Lanham, Maryland 2004. Emmanuel K. Akyeampmg & Henry Louis Gates, Jr. *Dictionary of African Biography*, Vol. 1-6 Oxford University Press 2012. Fantahun Engeda, *Tarikawi Mezgeb-Seb 2nd. edition. Vol. 1 &2*

Chapter 15

Shewa-Amhara Rulers During Menelik Era: Brief Biography

15.1. *Ras* Darge Sahle Selassie

R *as* Darge was one of the many sons of King Sahle Selassie of Shewa. He was Menelik's uncle and one of Shewa captives in Meqdela. He remained prisoner until he was freed by the British after Tewodros committed suicide in 1868. Darge, together with Girmame and Nadew, was instrumental in helping the young Menelik learn how to govern his subjects and consolidate power as the latter was an inexperienced young man when he first became Shewa *negus*. In 1877 when Menelik's wife, Bafana, organized a coup against her husband; it was Darge who helped to quell the plot. He was loyal to the young king. Shortly after he became a Shewa king, Menelik rewarded him with the highest title of *ras*. He was rewarded with large land grants in Salale, Addis Ababa, Arsi, and elsewhere. He governed Salale, which became private fiefdom for his descendants, which became a dynasty by their own right. Most notable of them was *leul* Asrate Kassa. Menelik appointed Darge as governor of the newly conquered Arsi, where his son, Tessema Darge and their descendants and followers remained immensely powerful for decades. According to Zewde Gabre-Selassie (2014), *ras* Darge was instrumental in mediating between Emperor Yohannes and Menelik whenever there was tension between them; and that emperor had respect for Darge.

Ras Darge's death in March 1900 was a huge loss for Menelik because he lost a fatherly figure and close family advisor. "By his three known wives, Ras Darge had had"five sons and three daughters."[936] His eldest son died in 1882 and Desta Darge died in 1893. Asfaw and Tessema had led expeditions of conquest in various southern territories such as Arsi, Bale, Kambata, Hadiya, Wolayta, Gurage regions. They owned agricultural lands in Salale and other regions. But Asfaw was arrested in suspicion of plotting against the emperor and died in prison. Tessema 'never won Menelik's trust' and he died at home. The fifth son, Gugsa, was sent abroad for education but he defected and joined the Italians shortly before the Battle of Adwa. Italians intended to make him their puppet emperor had they won the Battle of Adwa. Ras Darge disowned him for his betrayal. Ras Darge's daughter, Tisseme, married Haylu, a brother of Tekle Giorgis of Semein. Hailu's son, Kassa became a prominent official during the Haile Selassie era. His son, Asrate Kassa, inherited higher offices and leadership of the Addisge clan of Shewa nobility in Salale. His second daughter Askale's children -Abebe and Desta -from her second husband, Fitawurari Damtew became prominent officials. Darge's third daughter, Tsehaye Worq did not marry but became *balemual* of Menelik and Taytu.[937]

15.2. *Ras* Mekonnen Wolde Mikael

Ras Mekonnen was Menelik's cousin and son of Sahle Selassi's daughter, Woizero Tenagneworq. His father, Wolde Michael, was a *balabat* of Doba, Shewa. As a close family member, he was brought to Menelik's court when he was a young boy of 14 years old.[938] He grew up serving the king. Soon the king allowed him to organize his own army. In January1887 Menelik appointed the young *balambaras*. He was made a dejazmatch and appointed as ruler of the newly conquered Harar. He was nominated for governorship by *dejazmatch* Girmame "Mekonnen was always conscious of his debt to *dejazmach* Girmame and sent him rich presents obtained from the coast and from Europe – indeed in this way Girmame first tasted champagne."[939]

His son, Teferi Mekonnen (later Haile Selassie I), was born on July 23, 1892. Teferi's mother, Yeshiemebet, was the "third wife" of *ras* Mekonnen who had eight still births. She died during childbirth two years after Teferi's birth.[940] *Ras* Mekonen also "...had other children," including his older son, Yilma, "by consorts or concubines or slaves."[941] He expanded his domain and incorporated various Oromo and Somali groups. He became one of the richest men in the country, not the least because he exported chat to the Arab countries "at a fat profit."[942] As one of the emperor's top trusted and loyal blood relatives, he emerged as one of the most powerful people in the empire. Menelik was dependent on him for international relations, especially for his dealings with Italy. After signing the Wuchale Treaty in May 1889 Menelik sent him to Rome to ratify the treaty. While in Rome he signed another agreement with Italian government which Italy used as a justification to occupy more territories in Eritrea. When *ras* Mangesha Yohannes attempted to rebel in late 1890s, Menelik sent *ras* Mekonnen with his large army to Tigray. The former was removed from his father's domain. *Ras* Mekonnen was appointed as a ruler, while still holding the governorship of Harar. Mekonnen also led a conquest against Ben Shangul in 1897/8 and drove back hundreds of conquered natives to the interior for servitude; some of whom were conscripted into the army and were in parade when Italian administrator of Eritrea, Martini, visited Addis Ababa in 1906 (See chapter 4:4).

In January 1901 under the influence of Taytu the 50 years old Mekonnen married a ten-year-old Mentewab Wole, Taytu's niece. On January 31st, three days after he married Taytu's niece, his illegitimate son, Yilma Mekonnen, also married another niece of Taytu, Aselefech Wolde Hanna. Before Yilma's married Aselefech, though, Taytu compelled Mekonnen to recognize Yilma as his son. Mekonnen recognized and Yilma married. The marriage of *ras* Mekonnen and Mentewab Wole, however, did not last long because he divorced her in May 1902. In March 1903 Taytu married Mentewab to Kebede Mengesha Atikem, but the little girl died in 1907,[943] reportedly of childbirth.

Mekonnen was widely seen as an apparent heir to Menelik. But he fell ill on January 12, 1906 while he was heading to Addis Ababa and died in n Qullubi, Hararghe, on March 21, 1906. He was buried at Qdus Michael church in Harar and was mourned for forty days.[944] Menelik was reported to have been incredibly sad about the death of his loyal cousin. He appointed Mekonnen's illegitimate son, Yilma, as ruler of Harar and brought the younger son, Teferi, to his palace where he would be groomed for what lays ahead of him.

15.3. *Ras* Wolde Giorgis Aboye

Wolde Giorgis Aboye was Menelik's *cousin* and grandson of the king Sahle Selassie. His mother, Woizero Ayahlush, was Sahle Selassie's daughter. His father was *merdazmatch* Aboye, prominent Shewan. Wolde Giorgis, besides his blood relation with the emperor, also has another family relation. His father, *merdazmach* Aboye, was one of the husbands of Menelik's ex-wife, Woizero Bafana. He also married Empress Taytu's cousin.[945]

As a blood relative, eleven years old Wolde Giorgis was brought to the king's court. He grew up as an *elfign ashker* (page). He and Mekonnen knew each other from their youth while in the court. Both were later appointed at key positions and both were promoted to the rank of *ras*. By the early 1870s the king allowed Wolde Giorgis to form his own army, promoted him as a chief *agafari* and then as a *dejazmach*. In 1887, *dejazmatch* Wolde Giorgis was governing of the lands between Jimmy and Illubabor, the former Gibe State of Limu-Enarya. In early and mid-1890s he led the conquest of the south-western kingdoms of Kaffa, Kullo, Konta, Gofa and others.[946]

Wolde Giorgis, among others, was married to Yeshiemebet with whom he had two daughters. He also has two other daughters from his first marriages. His wife, Yeshiembebet, also had two daughters from her first husband.[947] He ruled Kaffa and southwestern region for several years. He amassed wealth and established a large army which made him one of the powerful men in the country. When Menelik named Lij Eyasu as an heir, he expected himself to be a regent. He found out that Menelik named *ras* Tessema as an heir. Wolde Giorgis "was offended by the choice of Ras Tessema as regent instead of himself."[948] In Keffa, he acted and lived as a mini king. Following Menelik's incapacitation, "Wolde Giorgis obeyed no orders, had distributed arms to his own men, conferred appointments without informing the central government and was ready to proclaim himself independent king of Keffa."[949] He became one of the many strong men who began displaying themselves and their power to the center, which was weakened by the emperor's poor health, growing regionalism, and sectarian disputes. In 1910, he was transferred to the north.

Events which followed his transfer registered one of the saddest moments for southwestern peoples because Wolde Giorgis, his deputies, and their soldiers forcefully drove thousands of southerners, especially natives of Majji, as slaves to the north, plundered and looted their former subjects and drove everything with them (see chapter 7 and 8). To satisfy his powerful ego he was given a title of *negus* of Begemder and overseer of Tigre. His transfer served multiple purposes for the government in Addis Ababa: it moved him further away from his southwestern stronghold and neutralized potential threat to the center, placed Taytu's base in the north at safer hand at a time when she was calculating her next move, and enabled to watch and check Tigre nobility closely. His *negus* title, however, was nominal. He did not have any ground to become a *negus*, but it happened because the center was weakened by the emperor's illness and by internal power struggle. According to the American Consulate General No. 53 memo sent from Addis Ababa on April 12, 1911, *ras* Wolde Giorgis was in Tigre when regent *ras* Tessema died. He "has refused for some time to come to the capital unless assured by the Government here and by the Abune...that he will be made Regent" and that he will not be imprisoned upon arrival.[950]

15.4. *Ras* Tessema Nadew

Tessema was a son of Nadew Abba Baher and Woizero Qonjit Debneh. His father, Nadew, was a tutor and caretaker of the young Sahle Mariam, Menelik's given name. After Shewa's defeat by Tewodros in late 1855, Nadew accompanied Sahle Mariam when he was taken to Meqdela as a captive. Ato Nadew returned from Meqdela when Menelik and other Shewans escaped. He was made *dejazmach* by Menelik. He served as a commander in Menelik's army in 1870s and continued serving the young king as a trusted counselor until his death in 1886.[951]

Tessema grew up at the king's court where his father was an insider. Menelik rewarded Nadew's service by appointing his son to a highest rank. "Because of his father's position, Tessema was eased into a favored position at Menelik court"[952] Tessema was made *dejazmach* and promoted to *ras* and then *bitwoded*. He 'became advisor and close friend of Menelik.' Menelik appointed Tessema as governor of Illubabaor and the kingdom of Guma. While he was the governor, Etege Taytu arranged marriage with Beleteshachew Aba Jobir. The Empress became a 'god-mother' to the bride. Beletshachew (her native name unknown) was a daughter of the king of Guma, who was conquered in 1880's.

Like *ras* Darge, *ras* Mekonnen, *ras* Wolde Giorgis; ras Tessema also became one of the most powerful Shewans in the country. Menelik appointed Tessema as regent for Lij Eyasu on October 28, 1909. Together with *ras* Hapte Giorgis and Abune Mathewos he led strong opposition against Taytu and forced her into retirement. "He was said to be about 58 years old"[953] when he died on April 10, 1911 of syphilis.[954] Tessema reportedly called himself "a simple soldier with poor head for political matters" and "others agreed" that he "treats his servants worse than slaves, has ruined his province [Ilubabor), is ungenerous with his soldiers...unsure of himself he can never make up his mind."[955] His horse name was *Abba Qemaw*.

Like other powerful Shewans, Tessema's descendants also continued to hold higher positions in the country. His son, Kebede Tessema, was made to inherit his father's post as governor of Illubabor. The birth name of Tessema's "son by a servant of a house" was Wolde Rufael but he was renamed Kebede after Tessema "was obliged...to acknowledge" him in 1907.[956]

One of the several powerful relatives of Ras Tessema was his nephew, Mekonnen Endalkachew. Ras Tessema introduced Mekonnen to Emperor Menelik who sent him to Menelik II School. Mekonnen Endalkachew married Taytu's great niece. He also married Haile Selassies's niece, Princess Yeshasheworq Yilma. During the Italian invasion he a governor of Illubabor, where ras Tessema and his son had been governors. After the liberation, he was appointed as a Minister of Interior and then Prime Minister (1943-1957). Haile Selassie appointed Mekonnen's son, Endalkachew Mekonnen, as Ethiopia's ambassador to Britain, then to the United Nations, and then a Prime Minster of Ethiopia[957] *Dejazmatch*, later *ras*, Luel Seged was also *ras* Tessema's close relative. Harold G. Marcus (1995:248, 255), described him as a "brother" of Tessema.

15.5. *Dejazmatch* Haile Mariam Wolde Michael

Haile Mariam was the older brother of *ras* Makonen Wolde Michael. He was King Sahle Silassie's grandson and a *cousin* of Menelik. Bulatovich described Haile Mariam as his "friend" and "the former type of feudal lord" whose domain is "very great." *Dejazmatch* Haile Mariam along with *ras* Darge and *dejazmach* Wube was a loyalist for whom Menelik liked entrusting the protection of the capital when he went on *zemechas*. Haile Mariam Wolde Mikael died in March 1899.[958]

15.6. *Dejazmatch* Germame Wolde Hawaryat.

Girmame was one of the top Shewans who influenced Menelik in a variety of ways. He accompanied the young Sahle Mariam to his captivity in Meqdela. *Atse* Tewodros married him to Quatero Merso, who was a relative of Taytu Bitul and Tewdros's second wife,

Woizero Tirunesh. It was Girmame who engineered Menelik's escape from Meqdela in conjunction with Tewodros's own son, Meshesha Tewodros, who "had long been out of favor with his father" and who left the gates of Meqdela fortress unguarded for Shewans to escape.[959]

On the day they escaped, Girmame left his wife, *Woizero* Quatero in Meqdela just like Menelik left his first wife, Altash Tewodros, in Meqdela. After Menelik became the *negus* of Shewa Girmame became very influential in Menelik's court. After Gurageland was conquered Menelik gave it to Girmame, but the latter refused it. Menelik then gave him lands in more fertile areas of Bishoftu and Adama.[960] He also owned lands in Addis Ababa, and in other parts of Shewa.

After the defeat of *emir* Abdulahi of Harar, it was Germame who advised Menelik to appoint *balambaras* Mekonnen as a ruler of Harar, for which Mekonnen returned favor by sending him gifts, including Champagne. His descendants remained dominant in the country's socio - political life well into Haile Selassie's era. His descendants, General Mengistu Neway and Girmame Neway, held higher ranks and offices. They also orchestrated a *coup d'état* against Haile Selassie in 1960.[961] As Harold Marcus, in the *History of Ethiopia,* stated both Germame and Mengitu Neway grew up in the emperor's court.

15.7. *Dejazmatch* Demissie Nessibu.

Demissie, aka, Demissew, was a Shewan who grew up in Menelik's court because he was a son of *afe-negus* (mouth of the king) Nessibu. Afe-negus Nessibu, who died in July 1908, "had great influence on the emperor." Demissie was appointed as ruler of Wollega, after the former governor and a Shewan, *fitawurari Tekle*, was killed during the Battle of Adwa. Demissie served as an overlord of territories ruled by both Kumsa Moroda and JoteTullu of Wollega. He was then promoted from *fitawurari* to *dejazmatch.* Prior to Wollega governorship, he ruled the former Gibe states of Guma and Gera.[962] For several years he served as Governor of Wollega and three small districts, and held the positions until he was demoted by Taytu in March 1908 and appointed to "two smaller areas."[963] He was married to Aselefech

Wolde Hanna, Empress Taytu's relative. Aselefech was also married to Yilma Mekonnen, and Seyoum Tekle Haymanot. In line with the tradition of most of the Shewa rulers, Demissies's son, Mekonnen, inherited his father's post as a governor in Wollega.

15.8. Ras Leulseged Atnafe Seged

Dejazmatch, later ras, Leulseged Atnafe Seged was a prominent member of the Shewa-Amhara Addisge clan; and a "close relative" of ras Tessema Nadew. He was one of the successful officials of Menelik during the process of *agar maqnat.* He was a son of *dejazmatch* Afnafe Seged, Menelik's court insider and his brother, Wube Atnafe Seged, was one of the husbands of Zewditu Menelik. Luel Seged was a husband of Etege Menen, who later became Haile Selassie's wife, after *Lij* Eyasu, ordered her divorce from Luelseged (Menen was Eyasu's niece and ras Mikael's granddaughter). Luel Seged led expeditions of conquests successfully against the Sidaama, Gedeo, Gujji, Konso, Gidole and Bale. He was a governor of Bale, Kambaata, and Kaffa. He was killed in 1916 at the Battle of Sagale while fighting with the Wollo army of *ras* Mikael.

Chapter 16

Dejaz. Balcha Safo & *Ras* Habte Giorgis Denegde

16.1. Background and Service

It is not uncommon to hear some Ethiopian elites mentioning Menelik's appointment of Balcha and Habte Giorgis to a higher office as an example of the Emperor's fairness, kindness, and sharing political power with all Ethiopian nationalities. Others use it as evidence for their argument that Menelik's regime was not dominated by any single group in Ethiopia. They argue to make a case of how merit, not blood or birth, mattered most in Ethiopian state for promotion and inclusion. Based on this premise, some even inferred that the Ethiopian system was "super-tribal."[964] In show of support, others boldly declared that both Menelik and Haile Selassie practiced "ethnic-blind system of recruitment."[965] An author of *YeHaile Selassie Tarik* (*A History of Haile Selassie*) went even further to elaborate Menelik's "kindness" to other people.

> Menelik raised *fitawurari* Habte Giorgis Denegde, became his godfather and made him a war minister. And Ras Mekonnen became Balcha's godfather. ...They grew up in the palace and held higher positions. Many others were awarded territories and titles.[966] *My translation*

What was missing from such historians' assertions was *how* and *why* Menelik "raised" and "awarded" them. Such scholars often fall short of explaining the *exceptional circumstances* in which Balcha and Habte Giorgis found themselves at Menelik's hand in the first place. Looking at their exceptional background would be helpful to understand the *raison d'être* of their *exceptional nature* of promotions rather than rushing into a generalized "super-tribal" or "ethnic-blind system" conclusions.

Balcha Safo (1862? – 1936) and Habte Giorgis Denegde (1851? – 1926) were "prisoners of war and slaves."[967] Balcha "had been wounded, captured, and castrated;"[968] as emasculation "at the time was the usual fate of defeated soldiers."[969] Thus he was a eunuch.[970]

Although full account of their early childhood was unclear, it was obvious from historical records that they were captured while fighting against the Shewa army during one of Menelik's *zemecha* in the south. Their ethnic background was not clear. Some assumed both were captured in Gurageland and hence Gurages; and that both came from Chebo Medir in Gurage region. Others say Habte Giorgis belonged to an Oromo ethnic group. Balcha's Gurage origin is un-doubtful. Regarding Habte Giorgis's background, more research, that is not tainted with ownership of history, needs to be done.

Writing about Balcha's background, Paul Henze in *Layers of Time: A History of Ethiopia*, described it as follows: "Born humbly in about 1862 and found castrated on a battlefield in Gurageland, he came to Menelik's notice. He took pity on him, brought him to Addis Ababa..."[971] The American Consulate diplomatic memo no. 72 of January 27, 1910 noted that Balcha's "history is a sad one," and it recounted his background story.

> Of Gurage origin, he was taken prisoner, when a boy, by the Abyssinians who conquered the province of that name. According to the prevailing custom, even up till today, the Balcha was made a slave after having been horribly muti-lated by his captors. Owing to his integrity and devotion to the interests of King Menelik, in whose service he was, he

received his freedom, and was gradually raised to his present important position.[972]

After they were brought to Shewa, as prisoners of war/slaves, Haile Girogis was sent to Menelik's estate in Ankobar. Balcha was given to *ras* Mekonnen's household in Harar. They grew up performing duties of a war captive (slave) in their 'godfathers' households. But they soon distinguished themselves from their fellow captives, demonstrated bravery and rose to prominence, especially after the Battle of Adwa. Balcha's exceptional heroic acts against fascist forces made him a household name.

In addition to their absolute loyalty to the emperor, they became distinguished warriors. The former captives became prime captors of the emperor's enemies during battles of conquests, and slave owners.

Habte Giorgis conquered, among other places, Borena and Chaha Guragelands and provided reinforcement for other generals, quelling rebellion in different regions. He was appointed as governor on the lands and peoples he conquered such as Borana and Gurage. After *ras* Abate Bawyalew was removed, in a move related to power struggle in the center, Habte Giorgis was appointed as a governor-general of Kambaata-Hadiya region in addition to his other possessions (Prouty 1986:337, Marcus 1995:257). He was appointed as 'Minister of War' in Menelik's first cabinet, which he held and served until his death in 1926. In addition to his great military skills, he was also known for his wisdom and wit which earned him a nickname, *Abba Malla*, father of ideas/solutions.

Balcha was made governor of Sidamo, the Sidama-Gedeo and neighboring regions shortly after the region was conquered. After the death of Yilma Mekonnen, Menelik "sent his loyal lieutenant, Dejazmach Balcha Safo"[973] as governor of Harar. Then he was appointed for the second time as governor of Sidamo. After Lij Eyasu seized power, he recalled Balcha from Sidamo. After Eyasu was deposed, Balcha was sent back as a governor, a position he held until Haile Selassie forcefully removed him several years later in 1928. In Sidamo he founded garrison towns and was credited for starting land measurement. "Land measurement which was started by Dejazmatch Balcha was continued by Ras Desta who introduced a consolidated tax assessed at a flat rate of 28 dollars a gasha."[974]

16.2. Balcha: Ethiopian Nationalist or Xenophobic?

Pro-Haile Selassie historian, Ethiopians and Europeans alike, "characterized" Balcha "often as reactionary, xenophobic" in the same way they characterized Empress Taytu as "reactionary" and "xenophobic."[975] Some stated that Balcha was oppressive [as if all the beneficiaries of *gabbar* system and functionaries of imperial government (emperors, nobilities, landlords, rulers, etc.) were fair and just to the people they governed]. They ignored the fact that he "was a pious Orthodox Christian" and "an excellent administrator and soldier."[976] Mockler in *Haile Selassie's War,* summarized Balcha's life as follows:

> As a boy he had lain in his first battlefield castrated by the conquering Amhara; as a young man he had fought under the Empress Taitu at Adowa and seen the Eritreans of Albertone's brigade waver and break under his guns. He had led the armies of Shoa against Lij Eyasu at Harar and the armies of Sidamo against Ras Teferi in Addis Ababa.[977]

The American Consulate diplomatic memo No. 72 of 1910 praised Balcha "as one of the strongest and most capable of all the Abyssinian notables;"[978] the view shared by historian Paul Henze:

> Balcha ranks as one of the most unusual figures among the hundreds of extraordinary personalities in recent Ethiopian history.... Balcha showed talent as soldier, fought with distinction in Wolamo (Wolayta) and at Adwa and became one of Menelik's most reliable officers.[979]

Balcha's critics misrepresented his actions and motivation in at least three areas.

First, they forgot that Balcha was "an Ethiopian nationalist who at his heart felt his opponent (Teferi Mekonnen) was selling the country for foreigners,"[980] when he saw that the young Teferi was giving concessions, making deals and treaties with foreigners and foreign nations, including Italy. In this case, Balcha's fear of Teferi's 'selling the country for foreigners' was akin to Taytu's strong opposition against foreigners' attempt to manipulate Menelik, and her opposition against Italy & Italian agents in Addis Ababa. If we believe the report of an Italian doctor who served Menelik, Taytu accused her husband, Emperor Menelik, and said "you...want to sell your country,"[981] when she found out how Italy benefited from the Wuchale Treaty. Because of Taytu's vigilance against foreigners' activities, she was labelled as 'xenophobic' mainly by Italian representatives and their spies in Addis Ababa. Given Balcha's strong religious background, his knowledge of how Italy ignored its 'friendship' with Menelik and waged war in 1896, and how Italians and other foreigners surrounded the young Teferi; his suspicion of foreigners reflected his genuine fear and nationalism. Balcha fought courageously in Adwa, the memory of which must have been fresh at that time.

Secondly, many historians viewed his antagonism against Teferi in a binary lens. In other words, they thought Balcha's antagonism was because Teferi was a "modernizer" and Balcha was "reactionary." That is too simplistic and superficial interpretation. There were at least two deep rooted reasons for their antagonism.

First, it was a personality clash. Both men knew each other more than anyone else. As a prisoner of war Balcha was officially a slave (*Fitha Negest* clearly stated it as such). He was captured in the battlefield, castrated, and was brought to Shewa and given to ras Mekonnen (Teferi's father), whom Balcha served as *ashker*.[982] It was also due to this 'family' connection that Menelik appointed Balcha as a governor of Harar, after Yilma, Teferi's stepbrother and governor of Harar, died in 1907. Menelik kept Teferi in the palace. Now, when Teferi became a regent he saw that his father's house-servant had become so powerful in Sidamo, monopolized the coffee market, amassed personal armies, and disobeyed his orders.

The second deep-rooted issue between them "involved control over vital, new resources" of Sidamo/Gedeo, mainly coffee.[983] Like their personality clash, the fight over coffee monopoly was also something both Balcha and Teferi knew more than anyone else. After Menelik became bedridden, Balcha was removed from Harar governorship in December 29, 1909, and arrived to Addis Ababa in January 10, 1910.[984] Teferi was "appointed as governor of Harar despite strong protest by Balcha."[985] In Hararghe, just like his father and brother before him, Teferi controlled exclusively rich resources, including *chat*, coffee, taxes, custom centers, and trade route to the sea. The young Teferi had also served as administrator of coffee producing Darassa/Gedeo district for about two years, without physically going there, during which time he accumulated wealth. Since then Sidama-Gedeo fertile lands and lucrative coffee trade were controlled by Balcha. Balcha was "tightfisted" to share the wealth with Teferi, and "as the coffee business and revenues had boomed, the old dejazmach grew to detest the regent's rules and regulations."[986] "Balcha was... defying the Regent's authority...an obstacle to Tafari's control of [a] rich province."[987] Teferi was determined to extend his control over those resources. The fact that his father's *ashker* disregarded their past *ashkerna geta* (servant-master) relationship and openly disobeying him was an insult Teferi had to deal with sooner than later. If Teferi had to succeed and consolidate his power, he must remove Balcha and put him at his right place

This brings us to the third and equally important point. Critics of Balcha often missed his absolute and lifetime loyalty for everything Menelik. Balcha was staunch supporter of Empress Zewditu Menelik. His complete allegiance was to his lord's daughter (his loyalty to her was a loyalty to Menelik). After Taytu was removed from the palace, "as a protégé of Menelik," Balcha's "prime loyalty was to the empress, Menelik's daughter Zewuditu,"[988] rather than to Teferi. Balcha perceived that Teferi was working behind the scene to remove Menelik's daughter. He was "agitated to redress this perceived insult to the Empress and to the dignity of the crown."[989] However, he did not have the power weight behind him like the one Teferi had: the

Shewa's nobility and the Church. Balcha was also outsmarted by Teferi's shrewd maneuvers and growing political power. "His frequent clashes with Ras Teferi…eventually caused his dismissal."[990] He "capitulated" on February 19, 1928 and "was subsequently sent as a prisoner to Gurage country."[991] His Sidamo governorship was given to Teferi's loyalist, Desta Birru. Balcha was "imprisoned for two years, but then having signed an admission of the error of his ways he was permitted by Teferi to retire to a monastery from which he only emerged eight years later to die bravely as a patriot fighting the Italian Fascist invaders."[992]

16.3. "super-tribal" or "ideal instruments?"

Teshale's (1995) description of the Ethiopian emperors' preferences for service is relevant to our discussion about Balcha's and Habte Giorgis rise to power. He wrote that emperors preferred those "without royal connection" and who "were less likely to have aspiration of ascending to the throne, and would therefore, serve more loyally than those with imperial blood."[993] This was exactly why the two ex-war captives were trusted for higher offices.

In the former times, eunuchs had long been given high offices in various royal households in Ethiopia. As sociologist *Lewis A. Coser* explained, appointing eunuchs to higher positions was a widespread practice in Persia, China, and Byzantine; and it has one important reason.

.... many of the high-ranking positions in the classical Eastern empires were held by eunuchs. In Ming China whole departments of eunuchs conducted the emperor's business; in Byzantium, parents castrated their sons to ensure them successful careers as statesmen, diplomats, or generals; in Persia, eunuchs filled virtually all the chief offices of the state. The eunuch system, Coser argued, was so widespread because it satisfied the… demand for absolute loyalty from political officials. Since eunuchs cannot have descendants and typically had little connection to their families, they made ideal instruments for the emperor's will. Without close ties to the community, without roots or kin, eunuchs owed allegiance only to their rulers.[994]

Balcha's and Hapte Giorgis's profile fits Coser's sociological explanation. Menelik's wisdom enabled him to surround himself with persons "without close ties to the community; without roots or kin" because it eliminated fear of conspiracies, plots, or revolts from within. It also ensured continuity of the monarch's authority and power; making them "ideal instruments for the emperor's will."

Habte Giorgis's and Balcha's rise to power had to be noted as an *exception*, rather than a norm. It must be understood from their *exceptional background* and their *unwavering loyalty* to the king. As a matter of fact, their promotion to the higher offices and ranks had *nothing* to do with power sharing or fairness or their southern backgrounds (inclusiveness). It also had *nothing* to do with the so-called "super-tribal" or "ethnic-blind system" (I am not even sure if we ever had such as a system anywhere in the world, let alone in Ethiopia. The phrases themselves need to be defined clearly). Menelik's trust in them had to do *more* with their extraordinary *condition and background* which uniquely positioned them to *fulfil two vital requirements*: *absolute loyalty and not having a* powerbase (past, present & future) to cause trouble against imperial authority. The last one is especially important. It was the main reason why Habte Giorgis was made *ras* and minister of war. During his first cabinet appointment ceremony Menelik gave a gold crown only to Habte Giorgis.

Although Habte Giogis was southerner by birth, he was one of most oppressive and exploitative rulers against southerners. He was also one of the greatest slave owners who always opposed efforts to abolish slavery and slave trade in Ethiopia (see chapters 7 &8). He considered himself as a Shewa *meqwanint* and had viewed Ethiopians into two categories: Conquerors and conquered where the former should maintain its dominance over the latter by a use of force. He expressed it as follows:

Lij Iyyasu is the designated and recognized inheritor of the Ethiopian throne. The Wellos and the Amhara have agreed to conform to the desire of the king, to accept and support Iyassu. The pact between the mekwannint is sufficient to maintain the present dynasty on the throne; as for the people, there no need to worry about them; they will follow. The Gojjamis, men of Kafa, Tigreans, inhabitants of Jimma, the Arussi, the people of Sidamo, Borena, Harar and Gondar, in a word, those [in the] conquered regions are not to be feared. If they arouse themselves, which is likely, we, the true Ethiopians…will be strong enough to reduce them to silence and to restore them to our domination…if it takes ten years for that, we will take ten years; but at the moment we are assured that the real Abyssinians would never recognize any master other than the one designated by the Emperor; we do not doubt final success.[995]

16.4. Men "without of roots or kin"

Balcha and Hapte Giorgis served Menelik, Lij Eyasu, Zewuditu and Teferi Mekonnen. They attained glorious accomplishments. They owned vast fertile lands. They accumulated great wealth. They organized huge armies under their command. They owned hundreds of southerners as slaves (irony of life). For instance, "Ras Habta Giyorgis was a poor man with only 500"[996] slaves when compared to other slave owning Ethiopian officials (see chapter 8). They were pious Orthodox Christians. When it came to power, wealth, and privilege, they had it all just like other top officials of the Menelik era, if not more. But that was until they died.

Unlike other Shewa-Amhara top officials, however, they *did not have a community base or descendants of their own to inherit their offices, their wealth, and to carry on their legacies.* Thus, their legacy ended with their death.

Balcha died in 1936 as a patriot while fighting Italy's fascist occupation. In his final years Habte Giorgis was crippled with rheumatoid arthritis and died in December 1926, to the relief of Regent Teferi Mekonnen. Both patriots were assumed to have been in their 70s.

Balcha's retainers and lands went to Haile Selassie. After Habte Giorgis's death, "the *ras* (Teferi) quickly let it be known that Habte Giorgis's holdings would be divided among cooperative partisans, whom he would directly oversee."[997] Teferi "immediately recruited the *fitawarari's* personal force of fifteen thousand well-armed men and then assumed Habte Giorgis's governmental responsibilities." But he was unable to find a "man in the country that can be *trusted completely...without using his power for his own ends;*" and therefore he "decided to divide *fitawrari's* functions" and created three "new positions."[998] Italics added.

When Habte Giorgis finally crushed the *Chaha* Gurage people's rebellion toward the end of 1880s, Menelik appointed him as a governor of Guragelands."*Chaha Woudema*, over two-thirds of the most fertile land of the *Chaha* tribe" was confiscated and given to Habte Goirgis as his "private property." After he died, Haile Selassie gave the *Cheha Woudem* lands to his own son, Crown Prince Asfa Wossen Haile Selassie.[999] Haile Selassie "took over" Habte Girogis's "15, 000 retainers as well as the lands supporting them, thereby increasing at a stroke his military power and his economic wealth."[1000]

As Richard Greenfield noted that "Teferi has never allowed a monument to be erected to the old warrior Fitwrary Habte Giorgis but there a hospital named after dejazmatch Balcha in Addis Ababa built from money raised from his property, and opened in 1948, it has since been enlarged."[1001] Teferi "transferred Dej. Balacha's property to loyalists, among them, his son-in-law, Fit. Desta Demtu" (Damte).[1002]

Chapter 17

Ras Goban Dache: The "formidable Oromo Warlord"

*"This formidable Oromo warlord brought southern Oromo...
under the Amhara in five years, a mission that Amhara kings
and warlords tried and failed in 400 years."* Getahun Delebo /
Lapiso G. Delebo, (1974:81), quoted by Mohammed Hassen
(1994:199)

*"...blow after blow struck by Ras Gobana... broke the resistance of
the brave tribe...All the best fighting elements of Showa thronged
under his banners. Where Ras Gobana was, there too were success and plunder."* Alexander Bulatovich, *With the Armies of
Menelik I (1900)*, in *Ethiopia through Russian Eyes Country in
Transition 1896-1898*, 2000:184

*"Ras Gobena, supported by numerous Galla nobles and soldiers,
in fact carried out much of the work of conquering Galla tribes for
Menelik."* Donald N. Levine, *Greater Ethiopia: The Evolution
of a Multiethnic Society*, 2000:85

17.1. Early Life and Family Connections

An exact date of birth of Gobana Daachu (also known as
Dachuu, Dachi, Dache, Dacche) was unknown. 1821 was

regarded by many as his year of birth. Mohammed (1994) stated that he "was born in 1821 in Shewa to a princely Christian Oromo family."[1003] Greenfield (1965) stated that "Gobena was deprived son of the great Galla leader Danci of Tulama..."[1004] Alliance between Gobana and Menelik dated back to the early years of Menelik's rule in Shewa. Gobana submitted to Menelik after the latter escaped from his captivity in Meqdela and entered Shewa. Menelik reciprocated Balcha's submission by rewarding him with promotions.[1005]

According to Rosenfeld (1976), Gobana was an "Oromo prince of Fella" and Menelik made him d*ejazmach* in November 1865,[1006] barely four months after he became *negus*. By the time Menelik returned to Shewa he was 21 years old, whereas Gobana was an experienced warrior of about 44 years of age. Greenfield (1965) wrote that Gobana's association to the Shewan ruling family dated back to his youth and therefore, it predated Menelik's return to Shewa. He wrote that Gobana "had lived at court as a youth and who grew to be a great soldier."[1007] Bulatovich stated that Gobana came from mixed -Oromo & Amhara- family background. He wrote that "Ras Gobana is by birth a Shoan. His father was a Galla, (Oromo) and his mother was an Abyssinian"[1008] (Amhara). Others also wrote that his mother was an Amhara.[1009]

Gobana's wife, Ayelech Abarasa, was an accomplished woman by her own right. Greenfield wrote that she "was the daughter, some. say sister, of the leader of Selale Galla, Biru Nagawo, who was later killed fighting with the Chabo group."[1010] Prouty (1968), citing Zewude Gabre Selassie, stated that Ayelech "was related to Menelik's mother"[1011], Ejigayehu. Besides such family relationships, Gobana and Ayelech became in-laws with Menelik. This was because Menelik's illegitimate daughter, Shewarega:

> was first married to Wadijo (Wodajo, aka, Waju) Gobana by whom she had a son in 1884, and she (Shewarega) and her mother had lived under the protection of Ayeletch Abarasa, Shewa Regga's mother-in-law in effect.[1012]

Ayelech did not stop in providing protection to Menelik's illegitimate daughter and her mother. She went a step further to convince Menelik to claim Shewarega as his daughter. "It was Ayeletch who convinced Menilek that he should claim Shewa Regga...Menilke claimed her as such."[1013]

Ayelech had eleven children, of which seven of them had died. She was a pious woman who was actively involved with Father Massaia's mission station. The mission station was established with Menelik's permission. Ayelech, together with her husband, not only provided protection for Massaia's mission; but she also became a friend and protector of Massaia from 1866 to 1879.[1014] Bulatovich in his book, *From Entoto to River Baro*, listed the "Family of the Emperor." Under that list he wrote that Shewarega "had a son by Dajazmatch Waju, son of Ras Gobana. Her son, Balambaras Ayale, is now [1896-7] ten years old. He is very lively, intelligent child, the very image of Menelik."[1015] Prouty wrote that Shewarega also had a son, named Wosen Seged by Wadju Gobana, who has dwarfism condition.[1016] Regardless, their marriage ended when Wodajo divorced her, which angered Taytu.[1017] Menelik's daughter, Shewarega, was later given[1018] to Ras Mikael of Wollo, the union of which produced several children, including Lij Eyasu, heir of Menelik.[1019]

17.2. Legacy & Controversies

> *"Gobana was an excellent horseman, a brave warrior, an able strategist, and an accomplished expert in the knowledge of Oromo warfare and psychology. He was Menelik's ablest general and the greatest empire-builder. However, for the Oromo, Gobana was a traitor."* -Mohammed Hassen, *The Oromo of Ethiopia, History 1500 – 1860.* 1994:198

It may not be an exaggeration to state that the success of Menelik's expansionary ventures, particularly in the early years, had largely depended upon Gobana's leadership, his infamous cavalry and his carrot and stick tactics; which enabled to neutralize various groups in Shewa and Wollo within less than a decade. Their neutralization gave more breathing space to organize, and, above all, to rally around their young king which, coupled with access to new resources, paved a way for further expansion.

Gobana devised a Shewa Oromo Confederation.[1020] which was also exported to other regions as an effective tool to bring the people of those regions under Menelik's rule. The Oromo groups which refused or resisted to join the Confederation were given the ultimatum of facing destruction by Gobana's punitive raids against noncompliant and "unsubmissive" leaders.

> He usually invited the Galla (Oromo) to submit, threatening to destroy them if they did not. Gobana send such admonitions to all the neighboring tribes, but few of them submitted voluntarily. Then Gobana launched raids on the unsubmissive. He didn't take caravans of transport carts with him – these were raids of ten-thousand-man detachments. No one knew when the Ras would set out, where he would go, or when he would return. At night, the order was given to set out, and by morning all communications between the detachment that had moved into the field and the base was severed. Finally, after a long wait, those who stayed at home would see a column of dust on the horizon and say that Gobana was returning.[1021]

Bulatovich further explained the tactics of Gobana's raids. "Approaching the domain of an unsubmissive tribe, the Ras surrounded the border by night. At dawn, his huge horde was already flying like the wind in the all directions, destroying everything that fell in its path...The Ras was situated with the reserves, somewhere on a high central hill, from which a view of the horizon opened up. At the decisive moment, he set his reserves in Motion."[1022] Bulatovich wrote:

> My guide, a participant in the expedition of Ras Gobana, showed me the place from which the Ras unleashed his

detachment in one of the many raids. This was at the foot of Mount Wochech. Many from the Ras's detachment reached the Chabo Mountains that day and managed to return to the rallying point by evening. Fighting and seizing plunder, they covered 53 - 66 miles in a single day."[1023]

The expansion ventures, however, were not without sacrifice to both sides. Both sides had adopted tactics and war games which served them well. Regarding the Oromo tactics, Bulatovich wrote:

> They retreated and escaped from the onslaught of the Abyssinians. But when the Shoans returned to the rallying point, burdened with plunder, tire, and on exhausted horses, entire cavalry detachments of Galla (Oromo), who had hidden in the rough terrain or in empty cattle pens, unexpectedly darted our of ambush...they attacked the Abyssinians, retaking the plunder from them. Many Abyssinian and Galla (Oromo) bones lie in this valley."[1024]

Utilizing Shewa Oromo Confederation as a platform of expansion, Gobana subdued Menelik's uneasy neighbors, who for the last several decades, if not centuries, had given serious headaches for Shewa ruling families, including Menelik's grand-father, Sahle Selassie, and his father, Haile Melekot. During Haile Melekot's reign the very seat of Shewa fell under threat when Abichu Oromo "attempted to retake Tagulat and marched on Ankobar."[1025] Now thanks to Gobana's strong cavalry and his skillful political maneuverings; the threat was eliminated for good. In addition to Menelik's domains, Gobana brought an army which the new king used to subdue other territories, especially the Wollo Oromos to the north. "These forces were used first to subdue the several Galla (Oromo) groups in Wollo in the north, whose settlements had... tended to isolate Shewa from the ancient center of Amhara and Tigre."[1026] After subduing Wollo, Menelik built a palace for himself in Werellu, in southern Wollo Oromo country.

Controlling Wollo was particularly important for him at least for two major reasons. First, it neutralized possible threats to Shewa from Wollo Oromos and enabled him to expand his political and military power base. Secondly, it created a buffer zone between his Shewan kingdom and that of his most powerful foe in Tigray, Atse Yohannes. Incorporating Wollo provided solid ground to further the mission of subduing remaining Shewa and Mecha groups. Confident with his growing modern arm power, Menelik was determined to further expand the Shewa territorial horizon even further. As Greenfield (1965) noted Gobana carried out the expansion further into the adjacent territories.

> After returning from Wello, the Shewan armies turned their attention to the south. Many Galla (Oromo) leaders, through the influence of Gobena, had thrown their lot with Menelik and indeed their followers found the basis for the expansion of Shewa which Menelik and Gobena planned...One of the first to join was Biratu Gole, a leader of Meta Galla (Oromo) from beyond Wachecha,...He had been decorated by Gobena...The Tufamuna, the Galla (Oromo) leader from Gulale,..,refused to join the Shewan Galla (Oromo) Confederation....Tufamuna was killed in the battle and the confederation was then strong enough to take on and defeat the Abu Galla (Oromo) of Mount Zikwala region and the Jille Galla (Oromo) of near Lake Ziway,...the leader of Ambo Galla (Oromo) was killed in battle.[1027]

Submissions of various Shewa and Wollo Oromo groups paved a way for Menelik to easily advance toward the territories and kingdoms in the south and south-west. In the ensuing years, Wollega in the west, Jimma in the south-west, and Guragelands in the south-central would become vulnerable targets of Gobana.

Ever since Gobana submitted, as Henze noted, Menelik "grew to depend upon Gobena."[1028] Realizing his valuable services and his excellent mission executions, *negus* Menelik promoted him from lowest rank to the highest. In the words of Mohammed Hassen, Menelik "intoxicated" Gobana to pursue the king's expansionist policy even further.

> In return Menelik invested Gobana with the title of *Abagaz*, chief of the palace guard. This was the beginning of Gobana's spectacular rise in power. Menelik, perceiving Gobana's talent, prompted him to the rank of *dajazmatch*, commander of the armed forces. By 1878 Gobana was made *ras* (literally head). He was probably the first Christianized Amharized Shawan Oromo to receive this highest title. Intoxicated by his promotion to the title of *ras*, and probably elated at the prospect of a more illustrious title of *negus* (king), Gobana took upon himself the conquest of his own people.[1029]

Menelik made a smart, but shrewd political move regarding Gobana. Recognizing Gobana's brilliance as a cavalryman and the crucial role he had played so far in breaking down resistances; he appointed him as a Governor of the Gibe States and as a King of Jimma before Jimma was brought into the imperial domain.[1030]

Gobana approached Wollega and proposed to Leqa Neqemt and Leqa-Qellam rulers to join the Confederation. The latter agreed to peacefully submit.[1031] In the agreement the land ownership would remain the same, Kumsa would give tribute in gold to Menelik, and no one would be appointed over Kumsa in Wollega.[1032] Wollega became a *maed bet*, emperor's kitchen, whereby tributes were paid directly to Menelik. Gobana followed the same approach of carrot and stick to bring Jimma's Abba Jifar II, under Menelik's control. Czeslow, in *The Ethiopian Paradox (1963)* wrote:

> Ras Gobana made an agreement with Aba Jiffar II, the last king/sultan of Jimma, a Moslem state in the west of considerable antiquity. Through the agreement the passage of Shewan troops was to be allowed, tribute was to be paid to Menelik, military cooperation against the Kingdom of Kaffa

was agreed upon, and in return Menelik undertook neither to invade nor to build Christian churches in Jimma. To this day the descendants of the sultan live in Jiren, in the hills above the modern town of Jimma.[1033]

Gobana's appointment as the King of Jimma or Governor of Gibe States was never materialized and remained in name only. When Jimma Abba Jifar II submitted, Jimma became *ma'ed bet.* Some scholars wrote that Menelik had arranged political marriage between Gobana's son, Wodajo/Waju, and his daughter, Shewarega Menelik.[1034] While Shewarega's marriage to Wodajo was true, it appeared that Menelik did not arrange it.[1035] According to Tekle Tsadik Mekuria (1982 E.C.), some of the Oromo groups and regions subdued by Gobana consisted of Dake, Dara, Borana, Gulale, Selale, Abote, Jarso and Mecha and reached Enariya, Limu.[1036] The list of territories and peoples conquered by Gobana in the western parts of country included: "Chebo, Woliso, Amaya, Nono, Leka, Lekemt, Soyo & Wollega"[1037] Bulatovich, based on reports and oral history he gathered from participants with Gobana, summed up Gobana's role and bravery up as follows:

> Ras Gobana is now a legendary personality in Abyssinia. He was a Galla, a remarkable cavalryman, an outstanding athlete and courageous man. He conquered for Menelik all the Galla lands to the west from Entoto to Beni-Shangul and in the southwest to the river Baro, to the east and south together with the Emperor he conquered …Arussi, Guragye.[1038]

Gabana played critical role at the Battle of Embobo in saving Menelik's own life and in turning the tide of the battle against Gojameis.[1039] However, some of the places mentioned by Tekle Tsadik and Bulatovich such as Borana, Ben-Shangul, Arsi, Gurage were not won by Gobana. He marched to subdue Ben-Shangul together with ras Mekonnen Wolde Mikael, rulers of Nekemte and Qellam. He led zemechas in Guragelands but Habte Giorgis completed it. Gobana also led expeditionary conquests in some of the Hadiya and Halaaba territories. Ras Habte Giorgis subdued Borana. Arsi was defeated by the armies of Shewa led by ras Darge Sahle Selassie, and Menelik himself.

Toward the end of his life, on October 14, 1888 Gobana fought Mahdist forces which occupied the Assosa-Benshangul region up to Najjo area and defeated them at the Battle of Gute Dili;[1040] thus, he eliminated foreign threat which posed serious threat to Ethiopia at a time when Emperor Yohannes faced Italian and Mahdist incursions in the north and west simultaneously. Had it not been for Gobana's action, Mahdi forces had easily advanced and occupied more territories in that region. In 1888, he also dealt final blow to the forces of Hassan Enjamo of Qabeena who organized one of the fiercest resistances against Menelik's expansion in Hadiya-Gurage regions.[1041]

Menelik reportedly liked and respected Gobana. However, the latter was not always seen by others as such. At times he was treated suspiciously, especially by Shewa nobilities who might also have influenced the emperor to put reins on his general. The suspicion against him grew even much bigger during his old age. In late the1880's Gobana faced arguably his biggest problem when he was falsely accused of plotting to overthrow Menelik. This happened after Menelik returned to Shewa in March 1887 after his victory over the Emir of Harar. "Gobana was accused unjustly by certain chiefs of planning a coup...Menelik refused to dishonor him saying it had taken him 30 years to 'make him.'"[1042] For the aged Gobana this was devastating. Before Menelik granted a pardon, Gobana had to beg for mercy in tears and pleaded his innocence.[1043]

> Menelik was also concerned that Ras Gobana, much his elder and an Oromo himself, might have designs on the region as an independent power base. No serious tension arose, however, and Ras Gobana was kept busy defending western Wollega against Mahdist incursions from Sudan in the last part of the 1880s.[1044]

He died in July 1889 and the cause of death was associated with an injury he had sustained after he fell off the horse.

Gobana's legacy has been a mixed one. He served Menelik faithfully. Often betting on his own life, he advanced the king's cause for 24 years, from the time Menelik became a Shewa *negus* until he became a *neguse negest*. He was one of the most, if not the only one, accomplished generals of Menelik. His contribution in the process of modern Ethiopian state formation was immense. Because of his bravery and accomplished military service he was celebrated by many during his lifetime as well as after his death. The small Shewa kingdom's fast rise to the national stage and Menelik's incredible success in conquering and incorporating vast swaths of lands in a relatively short period of time was unthinkable without Gobana's military and successful domestic diplomacy. Such success rightly earned him glory and heroism, which many celebrate today.

On the other hand, Oromo nationalist groups and intelligentsia portrayed Gobana as a "traitor," "sell out" and "collaborator" who "betrayed his people" and who subjected them to a subservient status. The term 'neo-Gobana' or the new Gobana (*Addisu Gobana*) was coined to label and denounce Oromos who co-opt with Ethiopian government and who does not propagate ethno–nationalist agendas.[1045] "Gobana…was ridiculed in different Oromo folk and gebbar songs and nationalist discourses"[1046]

Regardless of such diametrically opposed views of Gobana's legacy, there is one fact all sides would agree. It was summed up by Getahun Delebo (aka Dr. Lapiso G. Delebo): "This formidable Oromo warlord brought southern Oromo…under the Amhara in five years, a mission that Amhara kings and warlords tried and failed in 400 years."[1047]

Glossary

Abune -Patriarch. Head of the Ethiopian Orthodox Church.

Afe negus- literal, mouth of the king. Chief Justice of the king/emperor

Amoyta – Title of the Afar leader, Sultan

Balemberas- low level commander. Literally head of the amba, fort

Bitwoded – king's favorite, close counselor

Dejazmatch – military title below *ras*. Commander or general

Etege -Empress.

Fitawurari – forward commander. Vanguard.

Gabbar – In southern Ethiopian a gabbar was peasant-serf, sharecropper. Required to pay tributes and to provide corvee labor in the farms and households of his master.

Garaad – A Hadiya leader, ruler (Also called adil, amano)

Gult- land from which tribute could be collected. Right to collect tribute.

Gultegna- person entitled with right to collect tribute

Grazmatch – Left vanguard. Commander of the left.

Lij- literally, a child. Used as a prefix as a title for boys of royalties and nobilities.

Liqamqwas- king's double, used to trick the enemy during the battle

Kati –Title of Dawuro kings

Kaate – Title of Malo kings

Kawo – king. Title of Wolayta kings. Also used for Gamo community leaders.

Kegnazmatch – Right vanguard. Commander of the right.

Kefu qen. Rinderpest related Great Hunger (1888-1892) in Ethiopia

Negus – King

Neguse negest – King of kings, Emperor.

Moti – king (usually of Oromo leaders in Gibe States and Wollega)

Rist – hereditary land ownership

Zemecha – Expedition of conquest and/or armed raid against targeted communities.

Tato – King. Title of Kaffa kings.

Woma- King. Title of Kambaata kings.

Appendix I: Post-Conquest Governors in the South until Italian Occupation

Arsi

Arsi was eventually subdued in 1886 after series of *zemechas* were conducted mainly by a Shewa core army led by, *dejaz*. Wolde Gabriel, *ras* Darge and by *negus* Menelik himself (see chapter 4.2.5). Arsi was ruled by Darge and other Shewans. A "head of Shoan Mojo Clan and first cousin of Empress Menen", *dejaz*. Amde Mikael, was the governor of Arsi during an Italian invasion.

Bale

The Bale conquest was led by *ras* Ras Darge, *dejaz*. Wolde Gabriel *Abba Seytan*, and *dejaz*. Tessema Darge. Governors of Bale included: *dejaz*. Asfaw Darge (1891-1894). *Dejazmatch*, later *fitawurari*, Wolde Gabriel (governor of Ginnir in 1894), *ras* Nadew Abba Wollo (1909-16); *ligaba* Beyene Abba Sebseb (1916-18); *fitawurari* Wolde Gabriel (1918-1920); dejaz. Haile Selassie (1920-32), *dejaz*. Nessibu (1932-1933), d*ejaz*. Beyene Merid (1933-36)

Bako

Long time governor of Bako district was *dejazmatch* Merid Habte Mariam (1911 -1930). He was a father of Beyene Merid, who was a governor of Bale during Italian invasion.

Harrar-Hararghe

Conquest against Harar was led by *negus* Menelik himself. Conquest against Ittu/Cherche was done mainly by *dejaz*. Wolde Gabriel. Ras Mekonnen's army incorporated Ogaden region. Governors of Harar/Haraghe were *ras* Mekonnen (1887-March 1906); *dejaz*. Yilma Mekonnen, ras Mekonnen's illegitimate son, (1906-1907); *dejaz*. Balcha Safo (1907- 1909?), Teferi Mekonnen (while regent). D*ejaz*. Nassibu Emmanuel was a governor of Harar during Italian invasion

Hadiya

Various Hadiya groups Qabeena, Leemo, Sooro, Shashogo were subdued by campaigns led by *ras* Gobana, *dejaz*. Wolde Ashagre, and *dejaz*. Wodajo Gobana. [Because of the way the Kambata Province was set up after the conquest, the Kambata governors listed below were also the governors of Hadiya and Halaaba regions]

Gamo Gofa

Dejazmatch Abebe Demetew, brother of Desta Demtew, was a governor of Gamu Gofa during Italian invasion.

Gurage

The Guragelands *zemecha*s were led by *negus* Menelik, *dejaz*. Wolde Ashagre, *ras* Gobana Dache, and his son, *deja*. Wodajo Gobana. After the conquest, Gurage region was governed by *dejaz*. Wolde Ashagre, *dejaz*. Wodajo, *fita*. Habte Giorgis.

Jimma

Jimma was ruled by Abba Jifar II from the time he submitted to Menelik in the early 1880s until his grandson assumed power in 1930. Haile Selassie took advantage of Abba Jifar's age related senility and removed Jimma's internal autonomy status and appointed his son–in-law, ras Desta Damtew, as a governor of Jimma. After Abba Jifar died in 1932, his grandson, Aba Jobir replaced him as a *balabat*. Italians reinstated Abba Jobir as a ruler of Jimma during occupation. In their bid to promote Islam against the Ethiopian Orthodox Church, they had Aba Jobi visit Mecca and Rome.

Kaffa

Kaffa was conquered by *ras* Wolde Giorgis Aboye, *ras* Tessema Nadew, *dejaz*. Demissie. Governors of Kaffa were *ras* Wolde Giorgis (1897-1910), Birru Habte Mariam (1910-1911), Dejazmatch Leuel Seged (1911-), Desta Birru, son of Biru Habte Mariam.

Kambaata

Dejazmatch Wolde Ashagre, who was headquartered at Gurageland in Woliso, assumed the governorship of Kambaata (1886-1891) together with Gurage and Hadiya lands; even though Kambaata proper. was not conquered yet. Final conquest against Kambaata was led by *dejaz*. Tessema Darge, and *dejaz*. Bashah Aboye, which was also reinforced by *ras* Mengesha Atikim while he was in the region for his failed conquest march against Wolayta. Governors of the Kambaata Province were *ras* Tessema Darge, (1895/96), *dejaz*. Wodajo Gobana, (1891-1894), *dejaz*. Bashah Aboye (1894-1895), *ras* Abate Boyalew (1896-1909) and *dejaz*. Ayelew Birru (1909-19910); *Ras* Abate Boyalew for the 2nd time (1910-1911), *dejaz*. Leulseged Atnafe Seged (1911-1914), *dejaz*. Wolde Gabriel Bashah (1914-16) – son of Bashah Aboye? *ras* Getachew Abate – son of *ras* Abate Boyalew – (1917-26); *dejaz*. Meshasha Wolde – son of dejaz. Wolde Ashagre – (1926-35). Ras Getachew Abate collaborated with Italians and they entrusted him with Kambaata Province governorship during occupation. After liberation he was detained for a short time but was released and returned to Kambata-Hadiya. Ras Adefresew Nadew in 1941. He was succeeded by dejaz Damtew Meshesha Wolde (1942-56), a son of dej. Meshesha Wolde and grandson of dej. Wolde Ashagre.

Majji

Conquered by *ras* Wolde Giorgis. Governors of Majji included *ras* Wolde Giorgis (together with Kaffa) 1897-1910; Birru Habte Mariam (married *Lij* Eyasu's sister Sihn), 1910-1911; *dejaz*. Leuel Seged

(1911-). Desta Birru, son of Biru Habte Mariam and Birru's soldiers and settlers remained the dominant powers in Majji for many years.

Sidaama

Conquest against Sidaama, Gedeo, Gujji was led *by dejaz*.Leul Seged and it lasted from early 1890s to 1897. Governors of Sidamo Province included: *dejaz*. Balcha Safo (1900-1907), *Lij* Teferi Mekonnen, Balcha again (1910-1928), Birru Wolde Gabriel (1928-31), and *ras* Desta Damtew (1932-35).

Wollega

Wollega retained limited internal autonomy after its leaders Moroda Bakare and Jote Tullu submitted without fight. Hence, Moroda & his son, Kumsa, ruled Leqa Nekemt and Jote Tullu ruled Leqa Qellam. The central government representative governors of Wollega were *fit.* Tekle (died in Adwa), *dejaz*. Demisse Nessibu, and his son, *dejaz*. Mekennen Demissie; and Mengesha Wube, a son of *dejaz*. Wube Atnafe Seged. The last two were governors during Italian invasion.

Wolayta

Before the final conquest, several attempts were made to subdue Wolayta, among others, by *dejaz*. later *ras*, Mengesha Atkim, *dejaz*. Wodajo Gobana, and *dejaz*. Tessema Darge. The final conquest was led by Emperor Menelik himself, who marshalled almost all armies under his disposal against Walyata (See chapter 4.5). After Wolayta's defeat *kawo* Tona was taken to Addis Ababa, Christened, and sent back to his domain shortly before the Battle of Adwa. *Dejazmatch* Mekonnen Wossene was the governor of Wolayta during Italian Occupation.

Please note that, despite my best effort, the above list is not exhaustive. Due to general lack of records on conquests it was extremely difficult to find accurate information for all territories and principalities, which I hope will be more exhaustive as we continue gathering information.

Appendix II: Emperor Menelik, His Commanders, and Governors

Emperor Menelik II, Emperor

Menelik was an adherent of strict hierarchical structure his grandfather, *negus* Sahle Selassie, was known for. Such hierarchical structure ensured an implementation and enforcement of the king's policies and decrees from top to bottom, a failure of which had resulted in a severe penalty. Putting in place such a system was instrumental for his success as a *negus* of Shewa (August 1865-March 1889); a *neguse negest* of Ethiopia (March 1889-1913), and, above all, as a supreme commander-in-chief during his expansionary conquests. He was a hands-on leader who was engaged in planning, directing, and coordinating the *zamechas,* and, sometimes, leading and fighting.

Menelik, whose birth name was Sahle Mariam, had passed through several challenges in his life. Beginning from his birth he was "an illegitimate child" (Levine (2000:158) whose father, Haile Melekot, "at first denied everything (Marcus 1995:16) about his relationship with the child's mother. His mother, Ejigayehu, was a house servant of his grandmother. His grandfather, *negus* Sahle Selassie died when his was only three years old; and his father died when he was only 11 years old. So, he did not have a chance to learn from them. When was 11 years old *Atse* Tewodros conquered Shewa and took him and several Shewa nobilities to Meqdela. Tewodros reportedly liked and treated him equally with his own son, Meshesha. Tewodros also married his own daughter, Altash, who became Menelik's first wife. Menelik's and most of the Shewa captives escaped from Meqdela. He left behind his wife -Altash – in Meqdela. He entered Shewa, overcame opposing forces, and became *negus* of Shewa.

Shortly after he became *negus,* he fell in the trap of a much-experienced woman – Bafana – and married her against the advices of his counselors and his mother, Ejigayehu. Bafana was twice his age and had 8 children from various husbands. She placed her children in high positions and orchestrated *coup d'état* against her husband. Menelik survived her plot and eventually banished her. He was known to have had several consorts and concubines until he finally married Taytu Bitul, who had already been married to four husbands. Like Bafana, Taytu was strong willed, divorcee, had multiple previous marriages, and was committed in placing her families and relatives in high positions of the government. Unlike Bafana, she did not overtly plot to overthrow him.

Menelik's policies and *modus operandi* (for war or peace) were devoid of perfunctory, and were based on pragmatism, building alliance, and buying time on one hand, and resolute, forceful, and destructive on the other hand. Unlike Tewodros and Yohannes he was not fanatic Orthodox, and, to some extent, he tried to accommodate Muslims and missionaries. This seems to me was an important lesson he had learned from the rise and fall of Tewodros II during his captivity days. Combination of these approaches coupled with his extreme love of firearms had served him very well for his eventual realization of his great ambition of becoming a *neguse negest.*

He demonstrated pragmatism and calculated approach of engagement with Tewodros after he escaped from Meqdela,[1048] with Emperor Yohannes as a "reluctant vassal," with Italians as a source for weapons and allies in domestic politics power play, and with European powers as a friendly ally. On the contrary, he utilized second approach during conquest wars. He waged all out wars and used scorched-earth tactics during *agar maqnat zemecha*s, abolished socio-cultural bases of subjugated societies, and implemented unequal system of governance. "In the southern provinces" he instituted "the administrative pattern" which "was different from the very beginning after their occupation" than the northern regions.[1049] Such system got worse during the interim period of Lij Eyasu and Haile Selassie regime because government officials in the south were given a free hand to act without oversight and to consider it their right to rule southerners at any way they desired. Provincial and district governors – as seen in Arsi, Illubabor, Sidaama, Kambaata-Hadiya, Bale, Wollega, Kaffa, Majii, etc. – inherited the land and the people they governed to their children or close family relatives. When they were transferred, particularly in the southwest, they forcefully removed subject people and took them to the north or interior as slaves (see chapters 8-10). Instead of engaging in impartial academic pursuit most Ethiopian historians chose to reproduce the versions of palace history and to discredit anyone who attempted to discuss topics sidelined by them. Thanks to such writers and historians of a sanitized history, Ethiopians (including southerners) were insulated from the facts of their common national heritage.

Notwithstanding his conquest legacies, Menelik grew from inexperienced young ruler of Shewa to a matured, able, and charismatic leader who was credited for the formation the present-day Ethiopian state. His success could be attributed to several factors. Among them, his beginning from established government base in Shewa kingdom and his devotion to modern firearms could be cited as the main factors. Equally important was surrounding himself with most loyal commanders on one hand, and dedicated Europeans who served as his agents abroad and as military and diplomatic advisors at home.

Below, I presented a brief biography of some of Menelik's prominent Ethiopian officials who had contributed greatly for the success of the *agar maqnat* project.

Abate Boyalew, *ras*: He was *liqamakuas* of Menelik. Abate was a veteran of the Battle of Adwa. He was appointed governor in the north. After the Battle of Adwa (1896-1909) he was made a governor of Kambaata Hadiya Province during which time he moved his headquarters from Angacha to Wachaamo, present day Hossana. After he was transferred from Kambaata, he was sent back for the second time (1910-1911). Using his large army, he attempted to seize power from Eyasu. But Eyasu's father, ras Mikael arrested and sent him to Maqdela prison. He was freed after ras Mikael himself of arrested by Teferi Makonnen.

Asfaw Darge, *dejazmaatch:* He was one of sons of *ras* Darge Sahle Selassie. In 1892, his father appointed him as a governor of Bale (1892-1896).. He led conquests in Bale, Arsi, and south-central regions. Together with his brother Tessema, he owned extensive lands in Salale, Bale, Arsi, among others. He died in prison. (See 15.1)

Bashah Aboye, *dejazmatch:* He was a cousin of Menelik and a brother of ras Wolde Giorgis. He led conquests in the former Gibe regions, was governor of Kambaata Province, and participant of the conquest against Wolayta in 1894. Bashah Aboye believed to have relocated garrison headquarter from Anna in Leemo, Hadiya, to Mt. Hambaricho in Kambaata

Balcha Safo, *dejazmatch:* Balcha's story and life is like that of Habte Giorigis Denagde. He was captured in the battlefield while fighting against the conquest in Gurage region. Unlike Habte Giorgis, he was castrated before being taken to Addis Ababa as a slave. He was christened, placed as an *ashke*r under the service of *ras* Makonnen, Haile Selassie's father. He distinguished himself as a devoted pious and brave soldier. He became a national hero during the Battle of Adwa. After that he was made *dejazmtach* and appointed as a governor of Sidamo (Sidama-Gedeo region) three times. He also governed Harar and Ogaden briefly. When Lij Eyasu was overthrown by a coup orchestrated by the Shewa nobility and the Church; Balcha was given a mission to engage Lij Eyasu who was at Harar at the time. Balcha attacked him, but Eyasu escaped. In 1928 he was removed from Sidaamo for insubordination and jailed by Teferi Mekonnen and then sent to monastery. During occupation, he fought against Italians and was killed in Gurageland in 1936. He was also known by his horse name, *Aba Nafso.* (See more in chapter 16).

Damissie Nassibu, *dejazmatch:* He was a son of *afe negus* Nassibu, a prominent Shewan and one of Menelik's officials. Damissie grew up in the court and was made governor of Guma and Gera, former

Gibe states. He was then made *dejazmatch and* governor of Wollega. His son, Mekonnen, inherited governorship of Wollega (See 15.7)

Darge Sahle Selassie, *ras:* He was Menelik's *uncle and* confidant who was made *ras* early on and was reportedly respected by him. Darge played a big role during Arsi-Bale *zamecha*s. He governor of Arsi, and Salale; which remained at the hands of his families for decades. (See 15.1).

Getachew Abate*, ras:* He was a son of *ras* Abate Boyalew and he grew up in the palace. Getachew inherited governorship of Kambata-Hadiya province. During occupation he collaborated with Italians and was appointed by them. After the liberation he was detained for a short time but was released and returned to Kambata-Hadiya. He confiscated vast lands, especially in Hadiya areas, while he was governor (See Kambaata in Appendix I).

Gobana Dache, ras: Gobana served Menelik with diligence, bravery, and loyalty from 1865 until his death in 1889. He was in-strumental in bringing vast expanses of lands and diverse groups of peoples into Menelik's domain. His contribution for the success of the entire *agar maqnat* process was second to Menelik himself only. Menelik rewarded him with promotions and ranks (from *abagaz* to *ras)*. Gobana's legacy, however, is mixed. He was viewed as a national hero by some and as a 'traitor' and villain by others. Gobana left tre-mendous footprint in Ethiopian empire building process, the legacy of which is not fully studied or understood yet (see chapter 19 for more discussion on his life and legacy)

Gugsa Wole, *ras:* Son of Wole Bitul and nephew of Taytu. He was governor of Gishe, and later Begemder. With the backing of his father and Taytu he became an important figure in the north. In her plan of bringing her families closer to the power center, Taytu arranged for him to marry Menelik's daughter, Zewditu. When Zewditu became Empress of Ethiopia, however, Teferi Makonnen and the Shewan nobility forced Zewditu to divorce him. Ras Gugsa was killed in the battle. On the second day of his death, his ex-wife and Empress Zewditu Menelik died of unexplained condition; and then Teferi Mekonnen crowned himself as Emperor Haile Selassie I.

Habte Giorgis Denegde, *ras:* Habte Giorgis was a prisoner who was captured while fighting against the conquest during one of ras Gobana's *zamacha* in Guragelands and taken to Ankobar as a slave, where he was christened and grew up. He distinguished himself with his diligent services, his piousness, and wit which brought him to the king's attention. He became a loyal soldier and participated in several *zamachas* in the south including in Borana, Qabeena, and Chaha-Gurage. He also marched as a reinforcement to other commanders. He governed the regions he helped to conquer. Following his successful conquest against Borana he established Mega as a garrison town. He was promoted through ranks and was made Minister of War. He led successful campaign which dislodged Eyasu from Meqdela fortress and led 120,000 fighters (mainly peasant army from south) during the Battle of Sagale and returned to Addis Ababa victoriously with *ras* Mikael as a prisoner of war. He died in 1926. In a twist of irony, he was also one of biggest slave owners in the country who subjected southerners, especially, Chaha Gurage, into systematic and direct subjugation. Ras Habte Giorgis considered himself as a *Shewa mequwanint.* He categorized himself and the *mequant* as "we true Ethiopians" and the rest of Ethiopia people as power less masses who could be reduced to silence (See chapter 16 about his service and legacy).

Haile Mariam Wolde Mikael, *Dejazmatch:* He was Menelik's *cousin,* and an older brother of *ras* Makonnen (uncle of Haile Selassie). He was a governor of several districts and was also entrusted several key duties by Menelik (see 15.5).

Hailu Tekle Haymanot, ras: He was a son of negus Tekle Haymanot and was one of the longest ruling governors of Gojjam (1909-1932). He was also one of the few richest people in the country. Haile Selassie mistrusted him. In 1924 he took with him to Europe. Even when he fled the country during Italian occupation, Haile Selassie took ras Hailu with him up to Dire Dawa but he changed his mind and let him go. *Ras* Hailu joined Italians and become one of the high-ranking collaborators. After liberation, Haile Selassie put him in house arrest in Addis Ababa where he died in 1951 (see chapter 12:2)

Leul Seged Atnafe Seged, dejazmtach: He was a son of prominent Shewa-Amhara Adisge clan and official in Menelik's court, dejaz-match Atnafe Seged. Leul Seged led several successful expeditions of conquests in the south and south-eastern parts of the country and was a governor of Bale, Kambaata, and Kaffa. He was killed by ras Mikael army. (see 15.8).

Makonnen Wolde Mikael, ras: Menelik's cousin, who grew up in the court. Balambaras Makonnen came to prominence when he was appointed as a governor of Harar and promoted to dejazamatch and later to ras. He was Menelik's confidant in matters of national and international affairs. With his large armies he was always at hand to carry out critical mission such as the one which forced ras Mengesha Yohannes of Tigre to surrender. He was one of the prime sources of Menelik's revenue as well. This was because he was a governor of a province rich in livestock and agriculture. He also controlled custom posts, sea trade route, and export commodities such as chat, coffee, and ivory which made him "richer than Menelik" himself. Although he was regarded by many as an heir of Menelik, he died in 1906. Yet, his son, Teferi, inherited Menelik's throne and was crowned as Qedamawi Haile Selassie. (See 15.2).

Mengesha Atkim, ras. Mengesha was Gojjamie by birth. However, he was a longtime insider of the Shewa ruling family and a friend of Menelik from the days of Meqdela captivity. Hence, exceptionally higher posts and a bitwoded status. Mengesha was a "son of a minor official of Takle Haymanot" who "had also known Menelik while he was detained by Tewodros."[1050] He joined court soon after Menelik became a negus of Shewa. By early 1880s he was appointed to Wollo as a regent (Marcus 1995:73) to Areaya Yohannes, Menelik's son-in-law. Menegesha participated in the pacification of Kambaata after its conquest and led unsuccessful conquest against Wolayta. Edward Gleichen, who visited Shewa in 1897 wrote that "Ras Mangasha Tekkem [Atkem]...is head of all the Rases...He is a man of much sagacity, and his counsels are much in request."[1051] After negus Tekle Haymanot died, Menelik made him a governor of Damot and Agewmeder. He fell out of Taytu's favor and in March

1908 she demoted him and "took his fief and gave it to Seyoum Tekle Haymanot, who had just married the famous Aselefech" Wolde Hanna. Although he "appealed his demotion to Menelik, the emperor was "too weak to overrule the empress" due to his deteriorating health. Taytu, being shrewd politician, promoted his sons, Kebede Mangesha and Merid Mangesha; and she arranged marriage of Mentewab Wole to Kebede.[1052] Richard Caulk wrote: "Before his death in 1910 Mangasha Atikim became ras Bitwoded, an honor bestowed on a notable out of affection and intimacy rather than any need to reward."[1053]

Mengesha Yohannes. *Ras:* He was a natural son of Emperor Yohannes who, at his deathbed, made him his heir. He ruled all of Tigray until he was removed from suspected of power-struggle and insubordination. The province was divided among three natives of Tigray: d*ejazmatch* Gebre Selassie Baria, Governor of Adwa; *dejazmtach* Abrha Areaya, Governor of Endeerta; and *dejazmtach* Siyoum Managsha, Governor of Tambein. Later Seyoum Mengesha would become governor of all Tigray (See more in chapter 4.4.6).

Mikael Ali, ras. He was born from prominent Yejju Oromo ruling family and was a ruler of Wollo for many years. His first name of Mohammed Ali Aba Bula was later changed to Mikael when he was converted following an edict issued by Emperor Yohannes. He was shrewd and able politician who successfully maneuvered between Yohannes and Menelik. After the former's death, he joined Menelik, married his daughter, Shewarega; who become one of his seven wives. From that marriage, Eyasu and Zenebeworq were born. Eyasu became Menelik's heir and soon after he crowed his father with a title of *negus* Mikael. Mikael determined to take fight to Shewa when his son was deposed. At the Battle of Sagale, however, he was captured and taken to Addis Ababa and sent to prison in Dandi, Chabo country, *ras* Habte Giorgis's fiefdom. He was later transferred to a Holata prison and died there.

Tekle Haymanot Tessema, negus. He was the first *negus* of Gojjam. He hailed from ruling families of Gojjam (ras Hailu, the Great, dejaz. Goshu, and dejaz. Tessema). His given name was Adal

Tessema, which was changed to Tekle Haymanot when he was crown as a negus by Emperor Yohannes in January1881. He ruled Gojjam for many years and died in 1901. He was Menelik's rival until he was defeated in 1882 at the Battle of Embobo. Following Emperor Yohannes's death in March 1889, he submitted to Menelik II and was allowed to retain his *negus* title. After his death, his sons Bezabih, Belew and Hailu ruled Gojjam province.

Tessema Darge, *dejazmatch*: Son of *ras* Darge Sahle Selassie. Tessema was active during conquests in the south. He led zemecha against the Kambaata-Hadiya-Wolayta. He ruled Kambata Province briefly; lived at Hambaricho garrison, and relocated it into a new garrison in Angacha, Kambaata.

Tessema Nadew, R*as:* Tessama was a son of Menelik's tutor and caretaker, Nadew. He was an insider of the Shewa monarch and grew up in the king's court. Menelik returned favor to his father's service with promotions and ranks - *dejazmatch, ras* and *bitwoded* – and with appointments to higher offices: a governor of Illubabor and other territories in that region and a regent for Lij Eyasu. He did in 1911. His son replaced him as governor of Illubabor and his relatives dominated high positions in both Menelik's and Haile Selassie's regime (See 15.4)

Wolde Ashagre, *dejazmatch*, later *ras.:* According to Caulk (2002:46) he was "from Efrata in old Shewa." He was one of the trusted Shewans and foremost leaders of conquest in south-central against Gurage, Hadiya and partly to Halaaba and Kambaata. He was garrisoned at his headquarters in Woliso, which was used primarily to subdue the Gurageland and Soddo. He was a governor of Kambata-Hadiya region (1886-1889); where his son and grand -son became governors. Later he was made ras and governor of Illubabor.

Wolde Gabriel, *dejazmatch*. He was also known by his horse's name, *Abba Seytan*, father of Satan. He was one of Shewa officials who led several *zemecha*s into Ittu, Harar, and Bale. His son, ras Birru Wolde Gabriel, became one of powerful men during the reign of Haile Selassie. Birru was appointed as the governor of Sidamo, of Konta, Wollega, and Kaffa. Birru was rumored to have been a son

Menelik. Menelik reportedly slept with the wife of Wolde Gabriel when the latter was sent out to *zemecha* and Birru was born of that secret affair. Birru grew up in Menelik's palace and the emperor was his 'god father.' In the words of McClellan (2002:186-7) Birru was "a Menelik devotee."

Wolde Giorgis Aboye, r*as*. He was Menelik's *cousin* who grew up in the king's court. He was appointed in the former Gibe State region. He led conquests of Kaffa and adjoining territories; and ruled these regions with iron fist for over a decade. He became one of the most powerful and wealthy officials in the country. When he was transferred to the north in 1910, he took with him indigenous people as slaves to the north and plundered his former domains. He was made *negus* of Begameder (See 15.3).

Wole Bitul, *ras*: Brother of Empress Taytu Bitul. Governor of Yejju and Begemder. Governorship of Begemder was passed onto his son, Gugsa (see Gugsa above).

Wodajo Gobana, *dejzamatch*: He was *ras* Gobana's son and a former husband of Menelik's daughter Shewarega before she was married to *ras* Mikael. Wodajo led several *zamecha*'s in the west and south-central Ethiopian: campaigns of conquests in Hadiya, Halaba, Kambata and Wolayta lands. He governed Gurage, Kambata-Hadiya regions; and ruled from his garrisons in Balbula, Damaalla and Ana in Hadiya region (Braukmaper 2012).

Sources for Appendix I & II: Prouty (1986), Braukamper (2012), Fantahun Engeda Vol. 1 & 2 (2003 E.C), Girma Zewude Anjulo (2010 E.C), Marcus (1995), Mockler (2003)

Notes

Chapter 1: Introduction

1. Wagshum Gobaze married Dinqnesh Marcha, a sister of Kassa Mercha (later Yohannes IV). In 1871 Kassa defeated Tekle Giorgis and took him a prisoner; and crowned himself *neguse negest* the next year

2. Menelik was a "reluctant vassal" who overtly submitted but who was running his domestic and foreign affairs independently of Yohannes, often in ways that undermined his northern lord's interests. Yohannes at no time passed southward from Gojjam and northern Shewa. It was unchartered territory for him to venture especially when he was preoccupied in managing constant threats of foreign and domestic forces in the north. By the time of his death some of the southern regions (from Kambatta-Sidama -Borana, to Wolayta-Gamo-Kaffa) were not even under Menelik's rule. Other parts from Bale to Hadiya- Gurage were still unstable.

3. Zemecha is a general word used to describe military expeditions of conquests, or armed raids, and/or national deployment of armies or civilians for specific mission. In this book it denotes expeditions of conquest and armed raids against targeted communities.

4. Some of the earliest governors and representatives of central government of Wollega were *ras* Gobana Dache, *fitawurari* Tekle, *dejazmach* Demissie Nessibu, and Demissie's son, Mekonnen Demissie.

5. R.H. Kofi Darkwah, *Shewa, Menelik and the Ethiopian Empire 1813-1889.* (New York: Holmes & Meier Pubi8shers, Inc. 1975), 158. Alessandro Triulzi, *Nekemte and Addis Ababa: dilemma of provincial rule* in *The Southern Marches of Imperial Ethiopia (Addis Ababa:* Addis Ababa University Press 2002), 59.

6. Chris Prouty, *Empress Taitu and Menelik II: Ethiopia1883-1910.* (New Jersey: The Red Sea Press, Trenton, 1986), 299-300.

7. Triulzi, *Nekemte and Addis Ababa,* 59-61.

8. Emanuel K. Akyeampong and Henry Louis Gates, Jr, ed. Dictionary of African Biography, Volume 1. (London: Oxford University Press 2012), 8.

9. Heinz Kaufeler, *Modernization, Legitimacy and Social Movement: A Study of Socio-Cultural Dynamics and Revolution in Iran and Ethiopia* (Zurich: Ethnologisches Seminar Der Universitat Zurick, 1988), 96. "Some groups in the south were fortunate in that the crops they produced were less attractive to the Abyssinians than the cereals which they could get elsewhere. *Ensete* ("false banana"), the staple crop of the Gurage and many other groups in the south central Ethiopia, is disliked by the Amhara, and so these people escaped the severe exploitation which fell upon agriculturalists and were generally less affected by the Abyssinian imperial expansion." Shack, (1966:24-2) wrote: "The staple food of the Gurage, *ensete*, has always been unpalatable to the highland peoples…at no time were they able to exploit the utmost the yield of Gurage lands. But human resources were exploited. Ethiopian soldiery from highlands were often dissatisfied when sent to garrisons in Gurageland; they were never able to adjust themselves to the Gurage diet, and whenever possible remained only for a short time. It is perhaps for these reasons that few permanently settled in Gurageland as they did in other tribal areas…To the Gurage, the *ensete* plant is a symbolic monument signifying the role it played in securing their lands."

10. For Gilkes (1975:273*) gabbar* is "historically a serf in the southern provinces; also term given to land that is held in freehold and which pays the land tax.". For Teshale (1994:4) "gabbars" are "tribute providers." James C. McCann (1995:269) in *People of the Plow: An Agricultural History of Ethiopia, 1800-1990,* defined that *gabbar* is "a tribute paying farmer, typically in a non-Amhara region.".

11. Braukamper, Ulrich. *"Indigenous Views on the Italian Occupation in Southern Ethiopia: A Post-Colonial Approach." Aethiopica* 14 (2011), International Journal of Ethiopian and Eritrean Studies),165.

12. William Shack, *The Gurage, A People of the Ensete Culture* (London: Oxford University Press 1966), 22

13. Teshale, 1995:45-6. "The *naftagna/gabbar* system was based on the establishment of the Pax Menelika. The settler "colonies," called *katamma* (from the root word *maktam*, which means to camp), were initially garrison posts that included warriors, administrators, and clergy. They were the locale for "maintaining law and order" and for smooth flow of tribute to the imperial treasury at Addis Ababa."

14. *Ketemas* were garrisons or military outposts established at conquered areas as military administrative centers/colony. They later evolved into towns. *Ketema* (singular) means a town or a city. Some of the earliest *katamas*/garrison towns in the south were *Yirga Alem, Soddo, Angacha, Hossana, Ticho, Chencha, Gobba, Bonga,* Mega, Woliso, etc.

15. Darkwah, 114. Shack 18-19.

16. Balabats were local gentry and co-opted leaders in conquered lands mainly charged with collecting taxes and tributes and implementing orders from top-down. They functioned as accessories of indirect rule.

17. Messay Kebede, *Survival and Modernization: Ethiopia's Enigmatic Present: A Philosophical Discourse*, (New Jersey: The Red Sea press 1999), 261.

18. Data De'a, *Clans, Kingdoms, and "Cultural Diversity" in Southern Ethiopia: The Case of Omotic Speakers. Northeast African Studies.* (Vol. 7, Number 3 (New Series) 2000), 179.

19. Donald Donham, *"The Making of an Imperial State: Old Abyssinia and the new Ethiopian empire: themes in social history" in The Southern Marches of Imperial Ethiopia.* (Addis Ababa: Addis Ababa University 2002), 39.

20. T. O. Beidelman, *The Culture of Colonialism: The Cultural Subjection of Ukanguru.* (Bloomington & Indianapolis: Indiana Univ. Press, 2012

21. Messay, *Survival and Modernization*, 52

22. Edmond J. Keller, *Revolutionary Ethiopia From Empire to People's Republic.* (Bloomington and Indianapolis: Indiana State University, 1988), 18. James C McCann, *The People of the Plow: An Agricultural History of Ethiopia, 1800-1990 (Wisconsin: The University of Wisconsin 1995), 42.* Shack, *The Gurage,* 18-19

23. Michael Parenti, *History as Mystery,* (San Francisco, City Lights Books, 1999), 9.

24. Tesfaye Habisso, *A Short History of the Kambata People of South-Western Ethiopia.* Unpublished.

25. Teshale Tibebu, *The Making of Ethiopian History 1896-1974,* (Lawrenceville, NJ: The Red Sea Press, 1995), xxiii

26. Ibid., 13.

27. Keller, 18.

28. Teshale, 14.

29. Years of conquests in Tables 2, which I compiled from various sources, I believe, represent actual or near actual timeline of conquests. Yet, it may not be complete or accurate. If you find error or seemingly erroneous record, please know that it emanated from general lack of accurate documentation.

30. Harold G. Marcus, *A History of Ethiopia* Updated Edition. (Berkeley, Los Angeles, London: University of California Press, 2002), 76

31. Shack, 23.

32. Teshale, 43. Shack, 42

33. See Table 1 for the titles of the rulers/leaders of southern kingdoms and territories.

34. Harold G. Marcus *The Life and Times of Menelik II: Ethiopia 1844-1913* (Lawrenceville, NJ: 1995), 89

35. Alexander Bulatovich, *Ethiopia Through Russian Eyes: Country in Transition 1896-1898,* Trans. and Ed.by Richard Seltzer. (NJ: The Red Sea Press, 2000), vi.

36. Teshale, 41.

37. Messay, 261.

38. Teshale, 44.

39. Messay, 277.

40. Keller, 63.

41. Messay, 41.

42. Ibid., 18, 60.

43. Ibid., 38.

44. Ibid., 40.

45. Kassahun Woldemariam, *Myths and Realities in the Distribution of Socioeconomic and Resources and Political Power in Ethiopia*, (New York, University Press of America, 2006), 150

46. Messay, 47.

47. Teshale, *The Making*, xxii. Though I never met Dr. Teshale in person, I knew him during my student years at Addis Ababa University *Sidist Kilo Campus* in the early 1980s when he was a young lecturer at the *Political Science and International Relations* Department. He was regarded by many students as a brilliant lecturer and his lecture room were usually full of students. He exhibited that brilliance in his book (1995) save the epilogue.

48. Ibid., 40.

49. Ibid.

50. Professor Haile Larebo is one of those historians who dismisses any notion of 'conquest.' For him anyone who writes about Menelik's conquest is a 'clueless,' 'ideologue of the 1960s' student movement and/or a 'leftists.' He also dismisses subjugation of southern as nothing more than regular tribute payment "ግብር በመጣሉ፣ እንደገና ተቄጥሮ በመተቸት" for which southern were not accustomed to. ["*Menelikn bitwqsu manenetachihun tresu*" blog 1-47. My Facebook chat with the professor on June 15, 2020].

51. Some years ago, I read an article in one of the main Ethiopian news web sites which stated that Empress Taytu had married three husbands before she married Emperor Menelik. Those who felt and believed *wrongly* that Taytu only married Menelik and vice versa, responded swiftly against the writer of the article and labeled him as a traitor, and, worse yet, *tarik mebelez* (diluting or undermining the history). They did not take time to investigate the fact that Menelik was the *fifth* husband for Taytu; and Menelik also had at least *six* known consorts and wives prior to their grand marriage officiated by Patriarch of Shewa, Abuna Mattewos. In 2019 one of my Facebook friends (not historian) read a piece I posted and praised it. And then he commented that it would have been great if I used *mesfafat* (expansion) instead of *worera* (invasion).

52. Robert Aldrich, ed. *The Ages of Empires*. (London: Thames & Hudson Ltd, 2007), 9.

53. Ulrich, Indigenous Views, 180

54. Teshale, 40.

55. Ibid.

56. Aldrich, 258

57. Caroline Elkins, *Imperial Reckoning: The Untold story of Britain's Gulag in Kenya.* (New York: Henry Holt and Company, 2005), 9-14.

58. Ibid.

59. The Gedeo grievances against their land expropriation and alienations in the 1920s, 1930s and 1960s; and the Bale peasants' resistance against oppressive system were crushed using heavy-handed tactics (see McClellan (2002), Gebru (1994), and Bahru (1991).

60. Richard Pankhurst, *Economic History of Ethiopia 1800-1935.* (Addis Ababa: Haile Selassie I University Press, 1968), 155-156. Keller, *Revolutionary Ethiopia*, 61.

61. Donham, 39.

62. Thomas Pakenham, *The Scramble for Africa: The white Man's Conquest of the Dark Continent from 1876-1972 (New York: Random House, 1991)*, 486.

63. I. G. Edmonds, *Ethiopia Land of the Conquering Lion of Judah.* (New York: Hold, Rinehart and Winston, 1975), 120.

64. Keller, 63.

65. Prouty, 115.

66. Teshale, 44

Chapter 2: Loose Definition of 'South' & 'Shewa'

67. In this context South refers to the people and lands in Ethiopian region as discussed in this chapter, but not to a cardinal direction

68. Bahru, *yeEthiopia Tarik*, 15.

69. Marcus, *The Life and Times*, 55.

70. The historical Shewa kingdom became the center of the enlarged Shewa province before Menelik became emperor. After he became the emperor it became the center of the Ethiopian state. This author believes that Shewa's historical evolution, including it modern-day expansions and contractions, should be considered by historians and need to be described specifically in order to avoid ambiguity and distortions.

71. Lapiso G. Delabo, *Ye-Ethiopiawinet Tarikawi Meseretoch na mesariawoch.* (Addis Ababa: Neged Matemia Bet 1999), 218

72. Ibid.

73. Staffan Grenstedt, *Ambarcho and Shonkolla, From Local Independent Church to the Evangelical Mainstream in Ethiopia. The Origins of the Mekane Yesus Church in Kambata Hadiya.* (Stockholm, The Faculty of Theology, Uppsala University 2000), 50-61.

74. Lapiso, 218.

75. Arnold J. Toynbee, *Between Niger and Nile.* (London: Oxford University Press, 1965), 45.

76. Lapiso, 218.

77. Bahru Zewde, *A History of Modern Ethiopia 1855-1974.* (Addis Ababa University Press, 1991), 13.

78. Donham, *The Making,* 3

79. Martin Meredith, *The Fate of Africa, A History of Fifty Years of Independence.* (New York: BBS PublicAffairs, 2005), 208

80. *Donham, 3.*

81. Teshale, 176.

82. Steffanson & Starrett, *Documents on Ethiopian Politics,* Vol. I,. 214 No. 268. American Consulate. Aden, Arabia, April 23, 1919.

83. Teshale, 145.

Chapter 3: Southern Societies Before Menelik's Expansion

84. Berihun Kebede, *Ye Haile Selassie Tariq.* (Addis Ababa: Artistic Printing Press, Meskerem 2, 1993 E.C),* 808. [Berihun also distorted and falsified history in his book by repeatedly claiming that the only Ethiopians fought against foreign aggressions and invasions were the "Amhara, Tigre and Agew'" and "not a single Oromo" or other Ethiopians shed their blood]. p. 808, 812, 822.

85. According to eulogy posted on ethiomedia.com on 2 July 2014, Mr. Berihun "had served his country for 31 years in various capacities as a parliamentarian, High Court Judge, Chief of the Office of the Imperial Court (Zufan Chilot) and President of the High Court until he was forcefully retired by the Military Government (Derg) at the age of 53 in July 1976."

86. Teshale, 12-18

87. Jurgen Osterhammel, *The Transformation of the World: A Global History of the Nineteenth Century,* Trans. by Patrick Camiller. (Princeton and Oxford: Princeton University Press 2014), 327.

88. Richard Greenfield, *Ethiopia A New Political History* (New York: Frederick A- Praeger, Publishers 1965), 58.

89. Ibid. 58.

90. Admasu Abebe, *The Origin, Significance and Physical Condition of the Great Medieval Defensive Dry Stone Walls of Dawuro/Kati Halala Keela, Southwest Ethiopia.* ERJSSH 1 (1), September–October 2014, 19

91. Teshale, xvii.

92. Ibid., 41.

93. G. Mokhtar ed., *UNESCO General History of Africa. II Ancient Civilizations of Africa,* (Nairobi: General Printers Ltd, Home Bay Road, 1994 reprinted), 203.

94. Greenfield, 17

95. *Nature* vol. 466 N. 7308 (12 august 2010): 857–860 http://www.nature.com/nature/journal/v466/n7308/full/nature09248.html. (accessed 05/03/2016).

96. Jamie Shreeve "The Evolutionary Road," *National Geographic*, Vol. 218 No. 1 (July 2010): 36.

97. "Omo River", http://emueum.mnsu.edu/archaelogy/sites/Africa/omoriver.html (accessed 5/21/2013).

98. Reader, *Africa: A Biography of the Continent*, (New York: Vintage Books, September 1999), *75*.

99. Ibid. 75-76.

100. Notes from my visit to the Kenya National Museum in Nairobi on January 3, 2000 from 11:00 AM – 4:00 PM.

101. Encyclopaedia Britannica. Omo: Anthropological and Archaeological Site, Ethiopia. https://www.britannica.com/place/omo. Accessed 04/19/20.

102. *Clark, J. Desmond, "African Beginnings," in The Horizon History of Africa*. Editor, Alvin M. Josephy Jr. (American Heritage Publishing Co, Inc. 1971), 23

103. Science, 09 Aug 2019: vol. 365, Issue 6453, pp. 583-587

104. Ethiopian Academy of Sciences https://www.eas-et.org/node/459 accessed on 05/05/2020

105. John Reader, 209

106. Frederick J. Simoons *Some Questions on the Economic Prehistory of Ethiopia,* in *Papers in African Prehistory (1970, reprinted 1974*. Edited by J. D. Fage & R. A. Oliver. (London: Cambridge University Press, 1970, reprinted 1974*), 117

107. Ibid., 128

108. Ibid.

109. Ibid., 129

110. Greenfield, *Ethiopia*, 58.

111. George Clovis Savard, *The Peoples of Ethiopia* (Reprinted from Ethiopian Observer, Vol. V, No. 3, 1961). in *Life History of Sultan Alimirah*. (Bloomington, IN: authorHouse, 20130, 7.

112. Ibid. 7.

113. Wikipedia defines Wiltonian culture as "an archaeological culture which was common in parts of south and east Africa around six thousand years ago, during the Stone Age, The culture is characterized by a greater number of tool types, distinguishing it from its predecessors." Accessed 04/12/2020. https://en.wikipedia.org/wiki/Wilton_culture

114. Ibid. 6.

115. Ibid.

116. *Lapiso, Yeethiopiawinet,* 96-97.

117. Rick Gore, "The Dawn of Humans, Expanding Worlds," *National Geographic* Vol. 191 No. 5., 94.

118. Clark, *African Beginnings*, 23

119. Basil Davidson, *The Lost Cities of Africa*, (Boston, Toronto: Little, brown and company, 1959), 221.

120. Ibid.

121. Donald N. Levine, *Greater Ethiopia, The Evolution of Multiethnic Society*, (Chicago and London: The University of Chicago Press Second Edition, 1974): 81

122. Bulatovich, *Ethiopia through Russian Eyes*, 380

123. Richard Pankhurst, *The Ethiopian Borderlands: Essays in the Regional History: From Ancient Times to the End of the 18th Century*, (NJ: The Red Sea Press 1997), 90. See also Bahru (1991).

124. G. W. B. Huntingford, *The Galla of Ethiopia, The Kingdoms of Kafa and Janjero* (Ethnographic Survey of Africa, North-Eastern Africa Part II). Edited by Daryll Forde. International African Institute, 1969), 104

125. Bulatovich, *Ethiopia through Russian*, 210-211

126. Ibid., 211

127. Ibid.

128. Huntingford ,(Edited by) Forde, *The Galla of Ethiopia*, 116

129. Bahru, *A History*, 8

130. Bultovich, 211

131. Bahru, *A History*, 8

132. Bulatovich, 214

133. Forde (ed), 111

134. Bahru, 8

135. Mohammed Hassan, *The Oromo of Ethiopia: A History 1570 – 1860* (NJ: The Red Sea Press, 1994), 140

136. Bulatovich, 217

137. Mohammed, *The Oromo*, 141

138. Ibid., 136

139. Bulatovich, 215

140. Ibid., 212

141. Forde (ed), 112

142. Bulatovich, 212

143. Bahru, 8

144. Bulatovich, 216-217

145. Forde (ed), 137

146. Greenfield, 55

147. Bahru, *A history*, (2nd. ed.), 18.

148. Ibid.18

149. 149"*Ethiopia: Konso People Celebrate UNESCO World Heritage Support*" By Editor Aug 2012. The Christensen Fund https://www.christensenfund.org - Accessed 09/12/2019

150. Davidson, *The Lost Cities*, 220

151. Ibid. *The Lost Cities*, 220

152. Gore, *The Dawn of Humans*, 94.

153. Christopher Hellpike, *The Konso of Ethiopia: A Study of Values of an East Cushitic People* (UK: authorhouse, Revised Ed. Feb 2008), 3

154. Ibid.

155. Seyoum Hameso, *"The Sidama Nation: An Introduction." Arrested Development in Ethiopia: Essays on Underdevelopment, Democracy and Self-Determination.* Edited by Seyoum Hameso and Mohammed Hassen (NJ: The Red Sea Press, Inc. 2006), 58

156. Edward Ullendorff, *The Ethiopians An Introduction to Country and People*, (London: Oxford University Press, 1960), 43

157. Davidson, 221.

158. Ibid., 217.

159. Seyoum, 60.

160. Ullendorff, 44.

161. Shack, 5-6. Ullendorff, *The Ethiopians,* 43.

162. Paul Henze, *Layers of Time: A History of Ethiopia.* (New York: palgrave mcmillan 2000), 116; Forde, (ed.), 19.

163. Huntingford. *The Galla*, Edited by Daryll Forde., 20.

164. Henze, 116.

165. McCann, 53, 54.

166. Huntington, Edited by Forde, 19.

167. Levine, *Greater Ethiopia*, 80.

168. Mohammed, *The Oromo*, 61.

169. Seyoum, 58 The "term is no more than a geographic dispensation given to a southern region that included Sidama, Boorana, Gedeo, Burji and Wolayita nations. Such misrepresentation is undertaken to suppress Sidama identity and to dissolve the collective identity of the people. The misrepresentation of reality and the problems of nomenclature are related to the history of the conquest of Sidama nation."

170. Bahru, *A History*, 7.

171. Greenfield, *Ethiopia*, 104

172. Mohammed, The Oromo, 141.

173. Wellby, 142

174. Wolf Leslau, *The Arabic Loan Words in Gurage* (Southern Ethiopia, Arabica, Brill Academic Publishers, September 1954), 266-284. Accessed 03/23/2020 https://www.jstor.org/stable/4054954

175. *Encyclopaedia Britannica,* "Gurage People," accessed 03/23/2020 https://www.britannica.com/topic/Gurage

176. Engdawork Nimane, Yajoka: *Council of Sabat-bet Clan Chiefs and Notables*, (LAP LAMBERT Academic Publishing, 2013), 30.

177. Pankhurst, *Ethiopian Borderlands*, 130

178. Ibid. 140.
179. UNESCO World Heritage Centre accessed 04/15/2017. www.whc.unesco. org/en/list/12.
180. Levine, *Wax and Gold,* 281
181. Richard F. Burton, *First Footsteps in East Africa, or an Exploration of Harar* (New York: Dover Publications Inc. 1987), 1.
182. Ibid.
183. Henze, 72
184. Braukamper, 81-85
185. David H. Shinn and Thomas P. Ofcansky, *Historical Dictionary of Ethiopia,* Historical Dictionaries of Africa No. 91 (Lanham, Maryland: The Scarecrow Press, Inc. 2004), 192
186. Henze, 72, 84.
187. Ibid., 84
188. Ibid.
189. Ibid., 86-88.
190. Shinn and Ofcansky, 192
191. Ibid.
192. W. H. Jani, *Seven House Fortress Sun: Myths and Legends of Kambata Society,* Ethiopia (USA: CPSIA), 12, 13. "The prominent gods of Fandan Hadiya, such as Fujeta of Tarachmanna and Aba Sifos of Mochia and many other Fandanic and Megananic gods are associated with elaborated fire ceremony performed in relation to the worship of the sun."
193. Abdisalem Melesse Sugamo, *Ethno-archaeological Study of Megalithic Tradition in Southern Ethiopia: Muslim Megalithic Builders of Hadiya* (LAP Lambert Academic publishing Feb 2013). 112
194. Mohammed Hassen, 137, 141
195. Shinn and Ofcansky, 192
196. Ibid., 235
197. Gideon P. E. Cohen, *"Language and Ethnic Boundaries: Perceptions of Identity Expressed through Attitudes towards the Use of Language Education in Southern Ethiopia." Northeast African Studies* (Vol. 7 No 3 (New Series) 2000), 196.
198. Ernesta Cerulli, *Peoples of South-West Ethiopia and its Borderland,* (International African Institute, 1956), 86, 118
199. Ulrich Braukàmper, *Die Kambata* (English Summary), (*Geschichte und Gesellschaft eines Südäthiopischen Bauernvolkes,* 1983), 298.
200. Abba was "regarded as regarded as the god of Kambata...national god where members of all tribes participated in the nationally required events of the god...the leader of the gods governed the pantheon...The leadership was based on peaceful governance of various belief systems rather than enforcement of one religion. While each tribal god...independently furnished principles of religion to the tribe, certain spiritual based aspects not resolved by

the tribal god were directed to the leader of the gods. The tribal god might permit ordinary tribal members to consult the national god for higher-level spiritual based treatment. The pantheon was, therefore, a unique organization of tribal gods where on one hand each tribal god the god's own set of religious principles and on the other, all the tribal gods were governed by the leader of the pantheon." W. H. Jani p.2.

201. W. H. Jani, *Seven House Fortress Sun: Myths and legends of Kambata society, Ethiopia* (USA: CPSIA, 2015), 41.

202. Girma Zewude Anjulo, *Asham Kokata: Yetarik Yebahilna Yeemnet Dasesa*, (Addis Ababa: 2010 E.C), 140.

203. Jani, *Seven House*, 171.

204. Braukamper, A History, 112

205. Pankhurst, *Borderlands*, 211.

206. Braumkamper, *Die Kambata*, 219.

207. Ibid., 296.

208. Girma Zewude, *Asham Kokata*, 98.

209. For further lists of the Kambata state administrative institutions see *Kambata: ye astedader akababina ye behareseb tariq be Ethiopia*, (vol. 1 number 2, Hidar 1985), by Tesfaye Habiso and Haile Magicho. I read this important but unpublished work on July 27, 2018 at the Institute of Ethiopian Studies, Addis Ababa

210. Ibid., 100. Braumkamper, *Die Kambata*, 297.

211. Girma Zewude, 168. Braukamper (2012), 177,228.

212. Braukamper, 119-120.

213. Jani, 171.

214. Mohammed, *The Oromo*, 137, 141

215. Yacob Arsano, *"Seera: A Traditional Institution of Kambata" in Ethiopia." The Challenge of Democracy from Below.* Edited by Bahru and Pausewang. (Stockholm: Elanders Gotab, 2002), 48.

216. Ibid., 45-57. See also *Kambata: Yeastedader Akababina Yebehareseb Tarik Beethiopia*, (vol. 1 Number 2, Hidar 1985), by Tesfaye Habiso and Haile Magicho. I read this important but unpublished work on July 27, 2018 at the Institute of Ethiopian Studies, Addis Ababa.

217. Belachew Gebrewold, *"An Introduction to the social and Political philosophy of Kambata." Proceedings of the XVth International Conference of Ethiopian Studies*, Hamburg: July 23-25, 2003. Ed. by,Seigburt Uhilg. (Harassowitz Verlag, 2006).), 33

218. Yacob, 55

219. Christopher P. Sloan, *"Origin of Childhood." National Geographic* Vol. 210 No. 5. (November 2006), 148-159. Shreeve, *Evolutionary Road*, 36

220. Virginia Morell, *"Africa's Danakil Desert Cruelest Place of Earth." National Geographic* Vol. 208, No.4. (October 2005), 46

221. Pankhurst, *Borderlands,* 16-17
222. Ibid., 93.
223. Kadafo Hanfare, *Life History of Sultan Alimirah,* (Bloomington, IN: author-House, 2013), 15. "Sultan Alimirah demonstrated the Afar people's unwavering conviction about Ethiopian unity during the July 1991 Conference which was called by EPDRF after the fall of Derg regime. Sultan Alimirah told the participants: "In my opinion, this conference was not to dismantle Ethiopia but to unite Ethiopia...The Ethiopian people expect us to come out of this conference with a new government and democracy, not two different nations. If Eritreans are allowed a referendum for their future so that Ethiopians are allowed to decide, the voices of the Afar people should have particular significance, as a part of Afar land was part of the Eritrean province. Isaias Afeworki, then leader of the Eritrean People's Liberation Front, stormed out of the room in anger."
224. Marcus, *Life and Times,* 40
225. Kadafo, *Life History,* 13.
226. Tsegaye Tadesse Baredi, in *Threats to Heritage Properties in Ethiopia:The Case of Tangible and Intangible Heritage of the Gede'o, Southern Ethiopia* described that, Baalle is a cultural and administrative system which provides equal participation for "all Gedeo nationalities" or the seven clans, namely, Darashsha, Gorgorsha, Hanuma, Doobbe'a, Hemba'a, Logoda and Bakarro
227. Tsegaye Tadesse Baredi *Threats to Heritage Properties in Ethiopia: The Case of Tangible and Intangible Heritage of the Gede'o, Southern Ethiopia,*.3
228. Wikipedia, https://en.wikipedia.org/wiki/Gedeo_people (accessed 02/25/2020).
229. Tsegaye, 11-23. See Tsegaye's work for a complete list, locations, and number of Gedeo's immovable properties.
230. Mohammed, *The Oromo,* 113
231. Ibid., 99
232. Ibid.
233. Ibid., 133
234. Herbert S. Lewis, *A Galla Monarchy Abba Jifar, Ethiopia 1830-1932* (Madison and Milwaukee: The University of Wisconsin Press, 1965), 24.
235. Ibid., 35
236. Mohammed, The Oromo, 111-112. Lewis, 41.
237. Ibid., The Oromo, 112
238. Lewis, 57.
239. Mohammed, 136
240. Ibid., 136-137
241. Ibid., 131
242. Ibid., 132 Accessed 04/26/2020

243. Admasu Abebe, *The Origin, Significance and Physical Condition of the Great Medieval Defensive Dry Stone Walls of Dawuro/Kati Halala Keela, Southwest Ethiopia. (ERJSSH 1 (1),* September-October 2014), 19

244. Hailu Zeleke, *Some Notes on the Great Walls of Wolayta and Dawro. Annales d'Ethiopie,* 2007-2008, vol. XXIII, 399-412), 410

245. Abebe, The Origin, 29

246. Ibid., 30

247. Ibid., 30-32.

248. Hailu, Some Note, 406-409

249. Asafa Chabo, 86-90.

250. Dena Freeman, *Who are the Gamo? And who are the D'ache? Confusions of Ethnicity in Ethiopia's Southern Highlands.* In Uhling, Siebert (Ed). *Proceedings of the 15th International Conference of Ethiopian Studies.* (Wiesbaden: Harrassowitz Verlag 2006), 1-2.

251. Getaneh Mehari and Getent Tadele, *Sexual Violence and Justice in the Context of Legal Pluralism: Lessons from the Gamo Cultural Setting.* PhD dissertation submitted to the School of Social Work, Addis Ababa University, 2014. (EJOSSAH Vol, XI, No. 2 December 2015), 116.

252. Ibid.

253. Ibid., 119.

254. Ashley Tindall, *Gamo Highlands.* Accessed 04/26/2020. https://sacredland.org/gamo-highlands-ethiopia.

255. Takeshi Fujimoto, "*Social Stratification and its Relevance to Ethno-History: A Case in Malo, Southwestern Ethiopia.*" *Proceedings of the XVth International Conference of Ethiopia.* HamburJuly 20-25, 2003. Ed. by, Seigburt Uhilg. (Harassowitz Verlag, 2006), 99

256. Ibid,

257. Ibid.

258. Ibid, 100

Chapter 4: The Process of *Agar Maqnat*

259. Teshale, *The Making,* 40.

260. Bahru, 64-6.

261. Teshale, 176

262. Braukamper, *A History,* 266.

263. Menelik's first wife was the daughter of Atse Tewdros, Altash Tewdros. He married her while he was in captivity and left her behind when he escaped from Meqdela in 1865.

264. Zewde, Gabre-Sellassie, *Yohannes IV of Ethiopia: A Political Biography* (NJ: The Red Sea Press, 2014 Revised and updated), 163

265. Ulrich Braukamper, A History of the Hadiyya in Southern Ethiopia, Translated by Geraldine Kraus. (Harrassowitx Verlag – Wiesbaden 2012), 254

266. Henze, *Layers,* 132

267. McCann, *People of the Plow*, 198

268. Gobana, an Oromo, was one of the great empire builders of Menelik era. Gobana's life and his distinguished military career and controversies associated with his legacies are discussed at length in chapter 17.

269. Darkwah, *Shewa*, 133, 134

270. Rosenfeld, 79.

271. Greenfield, *Ethiopia,* 97–98

272. The Yeju Oromo dynasty, which controlled imperial power in Gondar during *Zemene Mesafint* era, originated from Wollo. In post *Zemene Mesafint era* issues pertaining to power & religion made Wollo a prime target of the Amhara-Tigre contenders: Tewodros II, Yohannes IV, & Menelik II.

273. Rosenfeld, 50

274. Ibid. 50–51.

275. Ibid., 56–57

276. Ibid., 69

277. Paulos Gnogno, 49–50

278. Rosenfeld, 73–74.

279. By the time of Tewodros's death in 1868 Worqit and Mestewat were rival Wollo Oromo power contenders. After burning it down, General Napier handed over Meqdela fortress to Mestewat.

280. Bahru, *A History*, 48. "...the intolerance, verging on fanaticism, that Yohannes showed toward Islam...There was no room for Islam in his ideological world. The thrust of his repression was directed against Wallo, the same province which had earlier been the main target of Tewodros's fury."

281. Bahru, *A History*, 48–49 "The Muslims of Wallo were told to renounce their faith and embrace Christianity or face confiscation of their land and property. The reactios were varied. The political leaders generally acquiesced...Others conformed outwardly, praying to the Christian God in the daytime and to the Muslim Allah at night - thereby reinforcing the unique juxtaposition of Islam and Christianity that we find to this day in Wallo. Still others preferred exile supporting or spreading Islam in such faraway places as Gurageland and Arsi, respectively south-west and south-east of central Shawa. But a large number of the inhabitants resisted, led by such sheikhs as Talha of Argobba. The repressive rule of Yohannes's son Araya-Sellase... helped to fan the flames of rebellion. The rebellion was finally suppressed by the intervention of both Yohannes and Menilek, and after a campaign characterized by devastation and massacre."

282. Mestewat and her son led Wollo armies, joined Menelik and fought against Tekle Haymanot of Gojjam in 1882. After that battle Yohannes confiscated

Wollo from Menelik and gave it to his son, Araya-Selassie, which deprived Menelik and his Wollo allies, Mestawot and her son, who just returned from Wollega after playing crucial role for Menelik's victory in the battle. Some part of Wollo was given to Yohannes's ally, *ras* Mikael Ali.

283. One of *ras* Mikael wives was Menelik's stepdaughter & Woizero Bafana's, daughter. R*as* Mikael Ali also married Menelik's own daughter, Shewarega, the union of which produced the future heir of throne, *Lij* Eyasu Mikael.

284. Keller, *Revolutionary Ethiopia*, 36

285. Jesman Czeslow, *The Ethiopian Paradox* (London: Oxford Univ. Press 1963), 99

286. Darkwah, 102. (See also Shack, 42).

287. Ibid.

288. *Brian L.* Fragher, *The Origins of the New Church Movement in Southern Ethiopia 1924-1944*, (1996), 39

289. Marcus, *A History of Ethiopia*, 76

290. Ibid., 49

291. Braukamper, A history of Hadiyya, 255. Cited from Atsme Giyorgis (Bahru Tafla) 1987:653.

292. Rosenfeld, 68.

293. Braukamper, 169, 255.

294. Sahle Selassie came to call himself a 'king of Gurage.' Shewa, however, did not penetrated to other parts of Gurage at the time.

295. Greenfield, *Ethiopia,* 102.

296. Bahru, *A History*, 2nd ed., 61 (See also Teshale, 42).

297. Ibid.

298. Engdawork, *Yajoka,* 30

299. Braukamper, 255

300. Shack, *The Gurage*, 19, (See also Bahru, 61).

301. Bahru, *A History*, 61

302. Ibid.

303. Shack, 23.

304. Teshale, 43. Bahru, 2nd ed., 61

305. Shack, 23.

306. Ibid., *41*

307. Ibid., 23.

308. Marcus, *A History of Ethiopia,* 79

309. Zewude, *Yohannes I,* 165

310. Tekle Tsadik Mekuria, *Atse Yohannesna Yeethiopia, Andinet*, (Addis Ababa: Kuraz Asatami Derjit, 1982 EC), 209

311. Zewude, *Yohannes*, 165

312. Truilizi, 53.

313. Following conversion edict issued to Moslems, Yimam Ahmed was given baptismal name, Haile Mariam, the power of Mary. He was aka, Abba Watawu.

314. Tekle Tsadik, *Atse Yohannes,* 210

315. Bulatovich, *Ethiopia,* 232

316. Paulos Gnogno, *Ate Menelik,* (Addis Ababa: Bole Printing Press, Feb. 1984 E.C), 70

317. Tekle Tsadik, 213, 220

318. Teshale, *The Making,* 39

319. In 1878 Abba Jifar became king of Jimma; the same years Menelik became a vassal for Emperor Yohannes.

320. Lewis, *The Galla Monarchy,* 44

321. Ibid., 45.

322. Ibid.

323. Triulzi, *Nekemte,* 53

324. Ibid., 53-54.

325. Ibid., 56.

326. Ibid., 59

327. Ibid., 60

328. Ibid., 59

329. Ibid., 61

330. Braukamper, *A History of Hadiya,* 255

331. Umar Baksa "succeeded as political leader of the tribe and religious leader... who himself was not a Qabeena but who had descended from the Mogumanna clan living among the Chaha-Gurage." Braukamper, p. 168

332. Ibid.

333. "Hassan a son of an influential follower of the imam Umar, was anyway the designated candidate for the succession and earned great respect as a successful war commander...Like his predecessor, Hassan Enjamo was not a Qabeena from descent and originated from the Dulaa tribe, a widespread Hadiyaa-Oromo mixed group in Gurageland who were famous for their military capability." Braukamper, p.171.

334. Ibid. 171.

335. Ibid, 256

336. Shack, *The Gurage,* 19, (See also Bahru, 61).

337. Ibid., 256

338. Ibid., 257

339. Bahru, *A History,* 61

340. Braukamper, 256.

341. Ibid., 257.

342. Ibid.

343. Girma, *Asham Kokata,* 199

344. Ibid., 199-201

345. Bahru, A History, 61.

346. Braukamper, 257-259

347. Ibid., 257

348. Ibid.

349. Ibid., 259.

350. Ibid., 258

351. As told to me by Ato Kibru Kifle. 06/30/2018. Addis Ababa.

352. Braukamper, *A History of Hadiyya*, 261

353. Marcus, *A History*, 78

354. Abbas Gnamo, *Conquests and Resistance in the Ethiopian Empire 1800-1974: The Case of the Aris Oromo* (Brill Academic Pub 2014), 147

355. Braukamper, *A History of Hadiyya*, 262.

356. Ibid.

357. Bahru, *A History,* 2[nd ed.,] 62

358. Zewude, *Yohannes IV of Ethiopia,* 265. According to Harold Marcus (1995:89) Menelik appointed Ras Darge in April 1886.

359. *Abbas*, 149-151

360. Zewde, *Yohannes IV*, 265

361. Marcus, *The Life and Times*, 89.

362. Zewde, *Yohannes IV*, 265

363. Bahru, *A History*, 2nd ed., 62

364. Fargher. *The Origins*,.39

365. Shack, *The Gurage*, 19

366. Braukamper, 264.

367. Pankhurst, *Economic History*, 155

368. Ibid., 155-156

369. Shin & Ofcansky, *Historical,* 49

370. Menelik remained a nominal vassal to the emperor. But, in reality, he needed no permission. He did not ask permission when he signed treaties with Italy and Egypt several years before Harar invasion. Yohannes was busy fighting foreign forces and his domains in the north were depleted in terms of resources. On the other hand, revenues from conquered lands and exportable commodities made Menelik wealthier than his northern master. His armies had also made qualitative changes in terms of manpower and modern weapons, although Yohannes still remained powerful.

371. Leonard Mosley, *Haile Selassie: The Conquering Lion* (Englewood Cliffs, New Jersey: Prentice-Hall, Inc, 1964), 19

372. Zewde, *Yohannes IV*, 267

373. Mosley, 19

374. Pankhurst, *Fire Arms*,155

375. Mosely, *Haile Selassie*, 19

376. Pankhurst, *Fire-Arms in Ethiopian History (1800-1935)*. *Ethiopian Observer* 6(2) (1962), 155
377. Zewde, *Yohannes IV*, 266
378. Ibid., 267
379. Pankhurst, *Fire-Arms*, 155
380. Greenfield, *Ethiopia*, 99
381. Prior to this appointment, there was no record of Mekonnen holding any important office. The primary requirement to pick someone who can manage a key city, its trade to the sea & communication with outside world seemed to be putting a most trusted and loyal person. Who better fulfil that requirement than a cousin who grew up in king's own court? He was nominated by a powerful Shewan, Girmame, whom Mekonnen later showered with luxurious gift (See chapter mentioned in ch. 15.2.
382. Zewde, *Yohannes IV*, 267
383. Mosely, 20.
384. David Abner Talbot, *Contemporary Ethiopia*, (New York: Philosophical Library, 1952), 98-99
385. Braukamper, 266
386. Ibid., 267
387. Ibid.
388. Ibid.
389. Ibid.
390. Ibid., 268
391. Ibid., 269.
392. Ibid.
393. Ibid., 270
394. Ibid.
395. Ibid.
396. Ibid.
397. The Battle of Gallabat/Metemma was fought on March 9-10, 1889. Emperor Yohannes died on March 11. Upon hearing his death, Menelik declared himself Emperor. He signed the Wuchale Treaty few weeks later in Wuchale camp in Wollo with an Italian representative the Contre Pietro Antonelli, who prepared a draft of treaty while Menelik was a Shewa *negus*.
398. Prouty, *Taytu*, 115
399. Pankhurst, *Economic*, 223
400. Braukamper, 264
401. Ibid.
402. Abbas, 161
403. Braukamper 265
404. Ibid.
405. Abbas, 162

406. Caul., 289
407. Forde (ed.) 137
408. Caulk., 289-90
409. Forde., 137
410. Braukamper, 271
411. Ibid.
412. Girma Zewude, *Asham Kokata*, 105-6.
413. Yacob, *Seera,* 54
414. Braukamper, A History, 271
415. Girma Zewude, 106
416. Ibid., 112.
417. Pankhurst, *Economic,* 24.
418. Girma Zewude, 106
419. Bulatovich, "With the Armies of Menelik II," *Ethiopia,* 380
420. Zerihun Doda, *Ethnohistory & Culture of Tambaro of Southwest Ethiopia,* 80-81
421. Bulatovich, 380.
422. Kambaata and Baadawaacho had established & maintained common military alliance against their common enemies for a long time. The demise of Dilbato deprived them of their reliable ally. Braumkamper described their alliances as follows: [P. 234. "In the second half of the 19th century, during Dilbato's rule, the Kambata were bound to a fixed alliance with the Baadawwaachcho, and the contingent of the Oyeta clan under the command of a gaaxanna was always at the ready to march south." P.235. "friendly relations existed between the Baadawwaachcho and the Kambaata and Arsi-Oromo during the whole of the 19th century."]
423. Ibid, 271.
424. Ibid., 280
425. Ibid., 283
426. Ibid.
427. Ibid.
428. Ibid., 283-285.
429. Richard Caulk, *Between the Jaws of Hyenas: A Diplomatic History of Ethiopia 1876-1896*. Edited by Bahru Zewde. (Harrassowitz Verlag-Wiensbaden, 2000), 290.
430. Grenstedt, *Ambarcho and Shonkolla,* 49
431. Caulk, 290.
432. Rosenfeld, *A Chronology,* 146.
433. Ibid.
434. Braukamper, *A History,* 282
435. Caulk, 290.
436. Braukamper, 282
437. Bahru, *A History,* 2nd ed., 64

438. Prouty, *Taytu,* 115
439. Braukamper, 282
440. Bahru, *Yeethiopia Tarik*, 72. Translation from Amharic by me. See also Bahru, 64-65)
441. Rosenfeld, 167.
442. Braukamper, 283
443. Darkwah, *Shewa*, 177
444. John Illife *Africans, A History of the Continent*, (London: Cambridge University Press, 2007), 171
445. Braukmper, 282-3.
446. Rosenfeld, 167.
447. Braukamper, 283-4.
448. Greenfield, *Ethiopia*, 103
449. Wellby, 141
450. This story was told to me by Anbese, a Wolayta native and a freshman student at Addis Ababa University Social Science Faculty at Sidist Kilo campus in the early 1980s.
451. Bahru, *Yeethiopia Tarik*, 72. Translation from Amharic by me.
452. Assefa Chabo, *Yetizita Feleg*, (Addis Ababa: Nabadan Media, April 2016)130. See also Braukamper 2012:284
453. Prouty, *Taytu,* 115
454. Marcus, *The Life and Times*, 156
455. Ibid., 67-8
456. Prouty, 115-117
457. Bahru, *Yeethiopia Tarik*, 72. Translation from Amharic by me.
458. Rosenfeld, 169.
459. Prouty, 116.
460. Ibid.
461. Chris Prouty Rosenfeld, *A Chronology of Menelik II of Ethiopia 1844-1913, (Lansing, Michigan: Michigan State University 1976)*, 214
462. Braukamper, A History, 266
463. Ibid.
464. Shinn & Ofcansky, Historical, 357
465. Balcha was a Gurage boy who was captured in the battlefield, castrated and taken to Addis Ababa as a slave. He was freed and proved his fierce loyalty to the emperor, later rose to a national prominence and provided remarkable service to the king (Discussed in chapter 16).
466. Pankhurst, *Economic History*, 156
467. Talbot, *Contemporary*, 98
468. Fargher, *The Origins*, 40.

469. Donald Donham, *"From Ritual kings to Ethiopian landlords in Maale."* The *Southern Marches of Imperial Ethiopia*, (Addis Ababa: Addis Ababa University, 2002 2nd ed.), 84
470. Bahru, *A History*, 2nd ed., 65
471. Bulatovich, *Ethiopia through Russian*, 217
472. Greenfield, *Ethiopia*, 104
473. Ibid.
474. Bulatovich, 210
475. Ibid., 215
476. Greenfield, *Ethiopia*, 104, Bahru, *A History*, 2nd ed., 65.
477. Bahru, *A History*, 65
478. Bulatovich, 220
479. Greenfield, 104
480. Bulatovich, 210
481. Greenfied, 104. See also Bahru (1991).
482. Paulos, 35.
483. Bahru, *A History*, 66
484. Bulatovich, 206.
485. Ibid.
486. Ibid., 206–207
487. Ibid., 225
488. Ibid., 212
489. Greenfield, 104
490. Prouty, *Taytu*, 199
491. Ibid. 311
492. Greenfield, 104
493. Ibid. 104
494. Bulatovich, 253
495. Ibid.
496. Ibid., 72
497. Bahru, *Yeethiopia Tarik*, 101, Pankhurst, *Economic History*, 111
498. Prouty, 206
499. Pankhurst, *Economic History,* 252
500. Kebede's birth name was Wolde Rufael and his mother was "a servant of a house." He was renamed Kebede after Tessema "was obliged...to acknowledge" him in 1907. Prouty (1986:233).
501. Bahru, *A History*, 66
502. Resenfeld, *A Chronology of Menelik II,* 186
503. Ibid.
504. Triulzi, *Nekemte*, 58
505. Prouty, 285
506. Triulzi, 63

507. Ibid.
508. Ibid., 65
509. Mckelburg, *Slavery*, 35
510. Bahru, *A History*, 2nd ed., 66-68
511. Hallpike, *The Konso,of Ethiopia* 6
512. Ibid.
513. Ibid.
514. Shinn and Ofcansky, *Historical*, 242
515. Ibid.
516. Pakenham, *The Scramble*, 486
517. Rosenfeld, A Chronology, 152.
518. Ibid., 155
519. Ibid., 157
520. Ibid., 165

Chapter 5: Tactics and Rationale

521. Marcus, The life and Times, 65-66
522. Ibid. "An ad hoc group of fighters, *fanno*, lived off the land and by their wits. Armed with lances, swords, and shields, they preceded the main force, provided intelligence reports, and kept the enemy off balance with supervise attacks."
523. Ibid., 66-7
524. Ibid.67
525. Ibid.
526. Ibid.
527. Darkwah, *Shewa*, 194
528. Ibid., 195
529. Bulatovich, 184-85
530. Prouty, 206
531. Pakenham, Scramble, 528
532. Pankhurst, *Economic History*, 577
533. Ibid.
534. Bulatovich, 220
535. Ibid., 206
536. Bahru, *A History*, 2nd ed., 65. (See also Greenfield, 104)
537. Ibid., 64-65
538. Darkwah, *Shewa*, 192
539. Ibid., 192-3
540. Osterhammel, *A Transformation*, 327
541. Teshale, *The Making*, 40

Chapter 6: Major Factors Contributed for Menelik's Victories

542. Darkwah, *Shewa,* 11

543. Ibid., 12

544. John Illiffe, *Africans: The History of a Continent* (London: Cambridge, 2007), 171

545. Darkwah, 182.

546. Pankhurst, Fire-Arms, 136

547. Ibid., 149

548. Triulzi (*2002:.59-61*) described that Menelik's troops stationed in the western Ethiopia, particularly those in Wollega, were referred to as the *"gondere"* including in official correspondences with Addis Ababa. The whole army was referred as 'gondare' through the early decades of the twentieth century.

549. Pankhurst, *Fire Arms,* 149.

550. Ibid., 149-150.

551. Darkwah, 58

552. Marcus, *The Life and Times,* 44

553. Seyoum Hameso, *"Myths and Realities of the Ethiopian State.,"* Arrested Develoment in Ethiopia: Essays on Underdevelopment, Democracy and Self-Determination. Editors. Seyuom Hameso and Mohammed Hassen, (Lawerencevill, NJ: The Red Sea Press Inc 2006), 100-101

554. Pankhurst, *Fire Arms,* 155

555. Darkwah, 177

556. Iliffe, *Africans,* 171.

557. Ibid., 199

558. Mohammed, *The Oromo,* 197

559. Ibid., 197-8

560. Montagu Sinclair Wellby, *Twixt Sider and Menelik: An Account of a year's expedition from Zeila to Cairo through unknown Abyssinia,* (1901), 189

561. Uri Almagor, *"Institutionalizing a fringe periphery: Dassanetch-Amhara relations."* The Southern Marches of Imperial Ethiopia, ed. by Donald Donham & Wendy James, (Addis Ababa: Addis Ababa University Press 2002), 114

562. Ibid.

563. Ibid.

564. Donald L. Donham, *Work and Power in Maale, Ethiopia, Studies in Cultural Anthropology,* (Ann Arbor, Michigan: UMI Research Press 1985),.58

565. Alexander Meckelburg, *"Slavery, Emancipation, and Memory: Exploratory Notes on Western Ethiopia."* International Journal of African Historical Studies Vol. 48 No.2 (2015), 346

566. Naty, Alexander, *The thief searching (leba shay) institution in Aariland, Southwest Ethiopia, 1890s-1930s.* Page.

567. Levine, *Greater Ethiopia*, 85

568. Mohammed, *The Oromo*, 199. Cited from Getahun Delibo, 1974:81

569. Levine, *Greater Ethiopia*, 78

570. Bahru, *A History*, 2nd ed. 62

571. Lewis, 45

572. Richard Pankhurst, *The Ethiopians, A History, (Blackwell Publishing, 2001)*, 179

573. Marcus, *The Life and Times*, 73

574. Lewis, 99

575. Messay, 277

576. Marcus, *The Life and Times*, 140

577. Martin Meredith, *The Fortunes of Africa: A 5000-Year History of Wealth, Greed and Endeavor* (New York: PublicAffairs, 2014),.428

578. Pankhurst, *Economic History*, 400. Professor Richard Pankhurst compiled it from the British consular report, and I adopted it from Pankhurst's book.

579. Mosley, *Haile Selassie*, 23

580. Pankhurst, *Fire-Arms*, 149

581. Darkwah, 58

582. Keller, *Revolutionary* 37.

583. Darkwah, 58–59

584. Rosenfeld, *Chronology of Menelik II*, 187

585. Alfred Ilg, among other things, served as Minster of Public Works and Chief Advisor on foreign affair. His son was born in Addis Ababa and was named "Menelik." Emperor Menelik became a godfather for his son and granted the title of Lij." Bulatovich, *Ethiopia through Russian Eyes*, 122, 202, 203

586. Robert Peet Skinner, *Abyssinia of to-day: An Account of the fist mission sent by the American government to the court of the King of Kings (1903-1904)* (New York: Longmans, Green & Co. 1906), 73

587. Tekle Hawaryat Tekle Mariam wrote in his autobiography, *Yehiwote Tarik* that *ras* Mekonnen asked Emperor Menelik for permission to send him to Russia for education and the emperor granted it. Then ras Mekonnen introduced him to the two Russian military advisors, Babichev and Leontievn; facilitated his travel to Russian for study. See *Black Lions* 1997:50.

588. Skinner, 77, 78

589. Bulatovich, 122

590. Henze, *Layers of Time*, 175

591. Henze, 174

592. Prouty, *Taytu*, 262–264.

593. Bahru, *A History*, 191.

594. Peter P. Garretson, *"Vicious Cycles: ivory, slaves, and arms on the new Maji frontier"* in *The Southern Marches of Imperial Ethiopia*, (Addis Ababa: Addis Ababa University Press, 2002), 199

595. Bahru, A History, 93

Chapter 7: Subjugation and Pillage

596. Braukamper, A History, 293
597. Levine, *Wax and Gold*, 4
598. Ibid.
599. Caulk, 291
600. Ibid.
601. Bahru, *A History*, 87
602. Garretson, 199
603. Prouty, *Taytu*, 243
604. Ibid.
605. Ibid., 244
606. Wilfred was born in Addis Ababa in 1910, where his father was a British Minister. In 1930 the young Wilfred and his family were personally invited to attend coronation ceremony by Regent Teferi Mekonnen, who was crowned as Haile Selassie I. Wilfred remained as Haile Selassie's friend and had been to the country several times
607. Thesiger, *The Life of My Choice*, 1987:45.
608. Braukamper, A History, 302.
609. Garretson, 202
610. Ibid. 203
611. Braukamper, A History, 302-3.
612. Bulatovich, 374
613. Bahru, *Yeethiopia Tarik*, 101. Translation from Amharic is by me.
614. Prouty, 206
615. Wellby, *Twixt Sider and Menelik*, 31
616. Ibid., 183
617. Ibid., *184*
618. Ibid., 185
619. Ibid., 189
620. Wellby often referred anyone who was not 'Amhara' or 'Habesha,' as 'Galla' or 'Shangkallas.' He used the same expression when he was passing through Kambata, Wolayta, Gamo lands, and the lower Omo Valley.
621. Ibid.,169
622. Pakenham, *The Scramble*, 528
623. Ibid.
624. Ibid.
625. Ibid.,531
626. Reidulf K. Molvaer, *Black Lions: The Creative Lives of Modern Ethiopia's Literary Giants & Pioneers* (Asmara: The Red Sea press, Inc. 1997), 50.
627. Prouty, 263

628. David Mathew, *Ethiopia, The study of a polity 1540-1935*. (London: Eyre and Spottiswoode, 1974), 239.

629. Prouty, *Empress Taytu*. 263

630. Ibid., 264

631. Garretson, 202

632. Thesiger, *The Life of My Choice*, 47

633. Wendy James, *"Lifelines: exchange marriage among the Gumuz"* in *The Southern Marches of Imperial Ethiopia*, (Addis Ababa: Addis Ababa University Press 2002), 121

634. Ibid. 120.

635. Ibid., 121

636. Ibid., 120.

637. Walter Chichele Plowden in 1848 observed and wrote in his book, *Travels in Abyssinia and the Galla Country, With an account of a Mission to Ras Ali in 1848*: "The entire circumference of the lake is surrounded by the hamlets of the Wytos, the hunters of the hippopotami, that abound here. All these countries, however, though productive and beautiful, are unhealthy, and fevers at certain seasons are prevalent." P.215.

638. Gabru Tareke, *Ethiopia: Power & Protest Peasant Revolts in the Twentieth Century* (Lawerenceville, NJ: The Red Sea Press 1996), 71

639. Bulatovich, 204-205

640. Wellby., 182

641. Ibid. 173

Chapter 8: The New Slavery

642. *Fiteha Negest* means the Justice/ Law of the Kings. It was believed to have been written in 13th century in Arabic by an Egyptian and translated into Geez and introduced in Ethiopia in fifteenth century. It served as 'supreme law' of the country until the 1st modern constitution was introduced in 1930.

643. Teshale, 57. Martin Meredith (2014:96) wrote that in the 15th century West Africa enslavement "was frequently the result of wars of expansion or civil wars."

644. Kevin Shillington, *History of Africa*, (Palgrave Macmillan; 2012 3rd ed) ,171-172

645. Nathan Nunn, *"The Long-Term Effects of African's Slave Trades"* in The Quarterly Journal of Economics, (February 2008), 151.

646. Ibid., 152

647. Teshale, 65.

648. Richard Pankhurst, *A Social History of Ethiopia: The Northern and Central Highlands from Early Medieval Times to the Rise of Emperor Tewodros II, (Lawrenceville, NJ: The Red Sea Press, 1992), 241*

649. Anthony Mockler, *Haile Selassie's War* (New York: Olive Branch Press 2003), 154. "Within the traditionally large market demand for Ethiopian slaves, particularly prized were the Oromo...This by no means exclusively because of their light complexity, since they came in varying...shades to the darkest. They were sought for their commonly slim shape, regular features, celebrated gazelle-like eyes, and long, straight, or slightly curled hair. Market convention ascribed peculiar beauty to Oromo girls and peculiar intelligence to Oromo boys. By 19th century, Oromo slaves predominated among those exported from the markets at Gondar and Gallabat in northwest Ethiopia. They were favored prey of Egyptian raiders from Sudan and were supplied to Muslim dealers by Oromo chiefs in their own western areas."

650. Ibid.

651. Ibid.

652. Marcus, *A history of Ethiopia,* 81. Mockler, 154. Menelik's biographer, Harold Marcus (1995:73) wrote that Menelik used Muslim agents for the transaction of slaves, remained supplier of slaves, and received slaves as tribute from the south-western regions. See also Pankhurst (1968), Meckelburg (2015).

653. Donham, *Work and Power in Maale,* 58. See also Mecklburg (2015).

654. Meckelburg, 347

655. Marcus, *A History,* 81. Marcus, *The Life and Times,* 73. Also see Meckelburg (2015:315).

656. Marcus, *The Life and Times,* 73; Meckelburg, *Slavery,* 351 See also Marcus, 2002: 81

657. Meckelburg, *Slavery, Emancipation, and Memory,* 351

658. Marcus, *The Life and Times,* 73. See also Marcus, *A History of Ethiopia* 81

659. Mockler, 154-155

660. Marcus, *The Life and Times,* 73. en.wikipedia.org cited from *Stokes, Jamie, Gorman, editor; Anthony; consultant, Andrew Newman, historical (2008). Encyclopedia of the peoples of Africa and the Middle East. New York: Facts On File. P.516.*

661. Pankhurst, *Economic History,* 75

662. James, *Lifeline,* 122

663. Ibid., 122

664. Mockler, 155

665. Steffanson and Starrett, *Documents on Ethiopian Politics,* Vol. I No. 266, 183

666. Ibid.

667. Ibid., 181

668. Marcus, *A History of Ethiopia,* 81, Teshale, *The Making,* 57

669. Assefa Chabo, 130.

670. *Oscar Neumann, From the Somali Coast through Southern Ethiopia to the Sudan,* The Royal Geographical Society (with the Institute of British Geographers. *The Geographical Journal* Vol. 20, No. 4 (Oct. 1902), 388.

671. Ibid., 391.

672. Ibid., 392

673. Pankhurst, *Economic History*, 105

674. Pankhurst, *The Ethiopian History*, 179

675. Garretson, 196

676. Pankhurst, *Economic History*, 107. Bahru, *A History*, 101.

677. Achame Shana, "*The Shekacho People: Untold Stories.*" *Arrested Development in Ethiopia: Essays on Underdevelopment, Democracy and Self-Determination.* Ed. Seyoum Hameso and Mohammed Hassen, (Lawrenceville, NJ: The Red Sea Press, Inc. 2006), 86

678. Pankhurst, *Economic History*, 107; Bahru, *A History*, 101

679. Bahru, 101

680. Pankhurst, *Economic History*, 107.

681. Ibid., 75.

682. William Cornwallis Harris *The Highlands of Aethiopia*, vol. 3, 198

683. Mohammed, *The Oromo*, 124. In Gibe States slaves "were exchanged for horses, mules, guns, beautiful clothes, paid as prices for medicine, and given as gifts."

684. Bahru, *Yeethiopia Tarik*,.101

685. Pankhurst, *Economic History*, 75

686. Lapiso G. Delebo, *ye-ethiopia yegebbar sereat na jemer capitalism 1900-1966. (Addis Ababa:* Neged Matemia bet), 124. Dr. Lapiso wrote that forty-five years later (since 1908) the total population of Addis Ababa city in 1953 was 268 000. Out of this, the house-servants (*ye bet ashker*) constituted 33,722 (12.6%).

687. Pankhurst, *Economic History*, 75

688. Garretson, 204

689. Ibid., 117.

690. Atse Tewodros reportedly gave anti-slavery decrees, but "he himself reportedly informed slave caravans of the safest routes for transport." Mockler, *Haile Selassie's War*, 154

691. The edict of October 2, 1909 reminded me of the Fugitive Act of 1850 in the United States which obligated states to return escaped slaves to their masters.

692. Rosenfeld, 248

693. Pankhurst, *Economic History*, 107

694. Meckelburg, *Slavery,* 351

695. Ibid., .346

696. Donham, "*From Ritual Kings to Ethiopian Landlords,*" 81-82

697. Ibid., 81

698. Donham, *Work and Power,* 58

699. Ibid., 58-59

700. Donham, *From Ritual Kings*, 81

701. Naty, Alexander. *"The Thief-Searching (Leba Shay) Institution in Aariland, Southwest Ethiopia, 1890s-1930s." Ethnology* 33, no. 3 (1994): 261-72. Accessed January 30, 2015. doi:10.2307/3774010
702. Ibid.
703. Shinn & Ofcansky, *Historical Dictionary*, 360

Chapter 9: Depopulation

704. Bulatovich, *Ethiopia through Russian*, 206
705. Ibid., 220
706. Ibid., 226
707. Ibid., 212
708. Achame Shana, *The Shekacho People*, 86
709. Pankhurst, *The Ethiopians*, 179
710. Pankurst, *Economic History*, 111
711. Steffanson and Starrett, *Documents on Ethiopian Politics Vol. I*, 183
712. Pankurst, *Economic History*, 111
713. Ibid.
714. Ibid.
715. Forde (ed.), 105
716. Pankhurst, Ibid., 106
717. Forde (ed.), 105
718. Garretson, *Vicious Cycles*, 202
719. Ibid, 202-205
720. Ibid.
721. Ibid.
722. Ibid.,202
723. Bahru, A History, 93.
724. Ibid.
725. Meredith, *The Fortunes of Africa*, 96

Chapter 10: Resistances, Rebellions and Counteractions

726. Hallett Robin *Africa to 1875. A Modern History*. (Ann Arbor: University of Michigan Press), 57
727. Ibid.
728. Mosely, *Haile Selassie*, 19
729. Marcus, *The Life*, 89. Zewde, *Yohannes IV*, 265
730. Bahru, *A History*, 62
731. Zewde, *Yohannes IV*, .265
732. Shack, 19
733. Marcus, *A History of Ethiopia*, 76
734. Marcus, *The Life*, 49

735. Shack, 19, Bahru, *A History*, 61
736. Girma, *Asham Kokata*, 199
737. Ibid., 199-201
738. Bahru, *A History*, 61
739. Girma, *Asham Kokata*, 226-7
740. Yacob, *Seera,* 54
741. Bahru, *A History*, 2nd ed., 64-65
742. Ibid., 65
743. Bulatovich, *Ethiopia through Russian*, 217
744. Ibid, 229
745. James, *Lifelines,* 120
746. Donham, *Old Abyssinia, 42.*
747. Ibid., 45
748. Garretson, *Vicious Cycles,* 202-205. In 1910 Ras Wolde Giorgis and his deputy Dejazmach Damte and their soldiers raided Maji., plundered and took natives as slaves to the north. The governors who came after them (Dejazmach Birru Haile Mariam, his son, Degezmach Desta Birru, Dejazmach Meshesha, and Degazmach Mekuriya and his wife woizero Aselefech raided Maji and took locals as slaves.
749. Garretson, *Vicious Cycles,* 202-203.
750. Ibid, 206.
751. Charles W. McClellan, *"Coffee in centre-periphery relations: Gedeo in the early twentieth century." The Southern Marches of Imperial Ethiopia* (Addis Ababa: Addis Ababa University Press 2002), 190.
752. Charles W. McClellan, *Coffee in centre-periphery relations*, 189.

Chapter 11: "Lands of the Cross"

753. Harris, *The Highlands of Aethiopia,* 202
754. Pankhurst, *Economic History,* 142
755. Menelik's liberal attitude toward protestant missionaries and Europeans at his court and his friendship with Italian Catholic bishop, Abba Massaja had caused rumors and gossip among Church circles of him being secretly converted.
756. Harris, Ibid., Vol. II, 28
757. Greenfield, *Ethiopia*, 39
758. Ibid. 26
759. Levine, *Wax and Gold*, 174
760. Teshale, 81.
761. Levine, Wax and Gold, 174
762. Keller, *Revolutionary, 55*
763. Ibid.

764. Kaufler, *Modernization, Legitimacy and Social Movement: A Study of Socio-Cultural Dynamics and Revolution in Iran and Ethiopia* (Zurich: 1988), 97

765. Shack, 18-19

766. Kaufler, 97

767. Darkwah, 114

768. Mohammed Ali, *Ethnicity, Politics, and Societies in Northeast Africa, Conflict and Social Change* (Lanham, New York, London: University Press of America, Inc. 1996), 66

769. Greenfield, *Ethiopia*, 26

770. Keller, 1991, 54

771. Levine, *Wax and Gold*, 175

772. Shack, 18-19

773. Kaufeler, 97

774. Lapiso, *Yeethiopia Yegebar,*102. Cited from V. Vtitz, *Foundation of Churches* 1975.

775. Patrick Gilkes, *The Dying Lion: Feudalism and modernization in Ethiopia,* (London: Julian Friedmann Publishers, LTD, 1975), 55

776. Prouty, Empress Taytu, 246

777. Ibid.

778. Keller, 18

779. Ibid.

780. McCann, 42

781. John W. Herbeson, *The Ethiopian Transformation: The Quest for the Post-Imperial State* (Boulder and London: Westview Press, 1988), 69

782. Prouty, 115

783. Ibid., 115-116

784. Bahru, 2nd. ed. 48

785. As a condition of peaceful submission arranged by Gobana and approved by Menelik, Abba Jifar II could keep his faith and his name. On the other hand, those rulers who resisted such as Gaki Sherocho of Kaffa languished in state prison for many years and died in miserable conditions.

786. Fargher, 24. Teshale, 17

787. Abas, *Conquest,* 164.

788. Ibid., 183.

789. Teshale, 17

790. Ibid., 49

791. Bahru, 2nd ed., 48

792. As told to me by a Sidaama native, D. Rikie.

793. Darkwah, 108

794. Guidi, Pierre, *Wolaita Memories of Garmame Neway Governorship (1958-1959): Radical Reforms and Political Consciousness* (Michigan State University: Northeast African Studies, Vol 13, No. 2, 2013), 16

Chapter 12: "Dual Society"

795. Harbeson, *The Ethiopian Transformation*. 35.
796. Ibid.
797. Bahru, *"Hayla Sellase,"* 48
798. Kaufeler, 96
799. Marcus, *The Life and Times*, 192
800. Ibid.
801. Ibid. 156. Keller, *Revolutionary Ethiopia*, 61
802. Shack, 22
803. Bahru, *A History*, 93
804. Pankhurst, *Economic History*, 107. Bahru, *A History*, 93
805. Ibid. 75, Wikipedia, The Free Encyclopedia, "Menelik II," https://en.wikipedia.org/wiki/Menelik_II (accessed April 22, 2018).
806. Marcus, *The Life,*,73.
807. Donham, *From Ritual Kings,* 81–82; Meckelburg, *Slavery*, 346,
808. Bahru, *A History*, 101
809. Meckelburg, 351.
810. Pankhurst. *A History*, 107
811. Teshale, 44
812. Gebru Tareke, *Ethiopia: Power & Protest Peasant Revolt in the Twentieth Century*, Lawreneville, NJ: The Red Sea Press Inc. 1996), 71
813. Braukamper, A History, 358
814. Ibid., 346
815. Ibid., 347
816. Ibid., 348
817. Ibid.
818. Ibid.
819. Ibid. 358.
820. Gabru, 64, 68
821. Teferra Haile Selassie *The Ethiopian Revolution 1974-1991 From Monarchical Autocracy to Military Oligarchy* (London–New York: Kegan Paul International 1997), 59
822. Ibid.
823. Teshale (1995), Bahru (1991) and others regarded Shewa as Northern provinces belonging to the 'core.' From the time Shewa Kingdom began its expansion beyond its tradition domain, it was comprised of other territories and peoples. Until the fall of Derg regime in 1991, the Shewa province, in addition to Shewa-Amhara, it consisted of several southern regions and peoples such as Gurage, Oromo, Silte, Kambata, Halaba, Hadya, Tambaro, Alaba in which tenancy predominated.
824. Teshale, 147-148

825. Gilkes, 120
826. Teshale, 149. Cited from Schwab 1972:71
827. Lapiso Delebo, 238
828. Teferra, 45
829. Marcus, *The Life and Times*, 191
830. Ibid.,139
831. Ibid.,139–40
832. Messay, 52
833. Ibid.
834. Gilkes, 39
835. Ibid.,43
836. Ibid.
837. Ibid.,49
838. Mengesha Yohannes of Tigre sought the title of *negus* but Menelik's mistrusted to bestow such title on him. The former holding grudge vacillated between loyalty and rebellion. As a result, he was forcefully removed from his domain and exiled to Ankobar prison, where he died in 1906.
839. Gebru, 164
840. Ibid,.202–206
841. Gilkes, 33
842. Ibid.
843. Ibid.
844. Mockler, 78.
845. Ibid., 110
846. Imru, 266–78.
847. Mockler, 391
848. Ibid., 86
849. Ibid., 152–3
850. Gebru, 164
851. Mockler, 392
852. Ibid., 399
853. Henze, 225.
854. Mockler, 154
855. Gilkes., 181
856. Bahru, *A History*, 217
857. Ibid., 217
858. Achame Shana, in "*The Shekacho People: Untold Stories*" (2006) recounted one "cruel incident" of Tsehayu Inqu Selassie's oppression against the Kaffa natives: "An Amhara regional governor called Inqu Selassie toured the Shekacho area using his private car. The entire population of the area were press-ganged to build an 18 km. road for his convenience. However, the car soon got bogged down in mud. Shekacho men were forced to carry the car

on their shoulders for the rest of the journey using two heavy logs, while the governor sat in the car. Shekacho women were forced to clap and shout in praise of the governor as they watched their men begging to be released from their torment. About eight people died from injuries sustained during this cruel incident and many others were crippled." Achame, 87.

859. Gebru, 166
860. Gebru, *167. He quoted it from the "Petition to emperor, signed by forty people and received on 10 January 10, 1950 (2 Tir 1942) MIA-G29/42/2."*
861. As told to me by Assefa Tarekegn on December 22, 1999 in Nairobi, Kenya
862. Gebru, 167
863. Gilkes, 181.
864. Ibid.
865. Ibid.
866. Gebru, 167
867. Gilkes, 181
868. Ibid., 182.
869. Gebru, 167.
870. Bahru, *A History*, 216.
871. Gabru, 156
872. Ibid.
873. Ibid., 157
874. Bahru, *A History*, 217
875. Gabru, 149
876. Bahru, *History*, 216
877. Ibid.
878. Ibid.
879. Ibid., 218
880. Ibid.
881. Ibid., 217-8.
882. Gabru, 178
883. Bahru, 216-7.
884. Kassahun, 117
885. McClellan, 194

Chapter 13: Dominance of Shewa-Amhara Ruling Class

886. Bulatovich came to Ethiopia as a member of the Russian Red Cross mission in 1896. Soon he earned favor from Menelik and began conducting expeditions in the country, often embedded with regional rulers and their armies. He wrote, *From Entoto to River Baro (1897)* and *With the Armies of Menelik II* (1900). Both books were translated from Russian by Richard Seltzer and published in 2000.

887. Bulatovich, 123-124

888. The non-Shewa-Amhara officials such as ras Gobana, ras Habte Giorgis, and dejazmatch Balcha, although they were ultra conservative pious, and known loyalists, they were not members of Mahber ZeMariam

889. Bulatovich, 123-124

890. Bulatovich, *Ethiopia through Russian*, *123*.Bulatovich stated that "people who have permission to enter chambers without previous announcement are called balamuals."

891. The British envoy, William Cornwallis Harris, wrote in *The Highlands of Aethiopia*, (199-202) that Finfine was conquered by King Sahle Selassie, Menelik's grand-father army in the early 1840s and described the scene as "carnages" and "devastating irruption." See also Harold Marcus, *History of Ethiopia Updated Edition* 2002, 65

892. Kaufeler, 86.

893. Darkwah, 140

894. Gilkes, 49

895. Henze, 194

896. Gilkes, 278

897. Henze,, 195.

898. Gebru, 50

899. Messay, 64

900. Levine, *Wax and Gold*, 47

901. Henze, 195

902. Donald Rothchild, *Managing Ethnic Conflict in Africa: Pressure and Incentives for Cooperation*, (Washington D.C: Brookings Institution Press, 1997), 77.

903. Gilkes, 73-74. Bahru, 204.

904. Bahru, 204.

905. http://en.wikipedia.org/wiki/Mkonnen_Endelkachew accessed on 12/09/2016. Bahru, 204.

906. Gilkes, 74. Bahru 204-5.

907. Gunther, *Inside Africa*, (New York Harper & Brothers, 1955), 272

908. Kayetuna Kemastawusew, Ras Imiru's memoir. Addis Ababa University Press, 2002 E.C. https://en.m.wikipedia.org/Imru-Haileselassie accessed on 10/16/2017.

909. https://en.wikipedia.org/wiki/Mikael_Imru (accessed on 12/12/2017). Fantahun Engeda, *Mezgebe-Seb.216-218*.

910. Ryszard Kapuscinski, *The Emperor: Downfall of an Autocrat* (New York: Vintage International, 1983), 31. "Listen here...not only did the Emperor decided on all promotion, but he also communicated each one personally. He alone. He filled the posts at the summit of the hierarchy, and also its lower and middle levels. He appointed the postmasters, headmasters of schools, police constables, all the most ordinary office employees, estate managers,

brewery directors, managers of hospitals and hotels–and, let me say it again, he chose them personally."

911. Donham, *Old Abyssinia,* 27

912. Gilkes, 247.

913. Ibid., 248

914. Among Amhara scholars who ardently dismissed the Shewa-Amhara ruling class dominance in Ethiopia is Kasahun Woldemariam. In his book, *Myths and realities in the distribution of socioeconomic resources and political power in Ethiopia* ((2006). Kasahum falsely wrote about " marginalization of the majority of Shoan Amhara by the ruling class" (p.6), "by political necessity, President Mengistu, Emperor Haile Selassie, or any of the previous rulers may have surrounded themselves with a few Amhara nobles," (p.7). He also claims Haile Selassie "was more Oromo than Amhara" (p.5) and was "partly Gurage" (p.153).

915. Bahru, A History, 203

916. Gilkes, 49

917. Ibid., 49

918. Pankhurst, *Economic History.* 102

919. Keller, 54.

920. Messay, 52

921. Greenfield, 102

922. Ibid., 103

923. Kaufler, 102

924. Ibid., 96

925. Greenfield, 102

926. Kaufeler, 86

927. Keller, 54

928. Lapiso G. Delebo *Ye Ethiopiawinet tarikawi meseretoch na mesariyawoch,* 238

929. Gilkes, 51

Chapter 14: Shewa-Amhara's Dominance in Literature and Writing

930. Pankhurst, *Economic History,* .676.

931. Ibid., 674

932. Molvaer, *Black Lion,* PAGE

933. Kaufeler, 105

934. Ibid. 106

935. Note that some of them were born in predominantly non-Amhara parts of Ethiopia. For example, Ras Imru Haile Selasiie was born in Gursum, Hararge; Tedela Gebre Hiwot was born in Gamo Gofa; Amare Mamo was born in Feseha Genet, in Gedeo region. This was because they were the

children of peasant settlers-soldiers, commonly known as *neftegna*, or of those in government services.

Chapter 15: Shewa-Amhara Rulers: Brief Biography

936. Prouty, *Empres Taytu*, 221.
937. Ibid. 221-222.
938. Greenfield, 100
939. Ibid.
940. Mosely, 16; Keller, 128.
941. Ibid.
942. Ibid., 20. Gilkes, (1975:278) wrote that ras Mekonnen was "richer than Menilek. Makonnen was able to take a share out of the Harar customs receipts that amounted to about 80,000 or more MT dollars."
943. Prouty, 219-220. Rosenfeld, 201
944. Asfa-Wossen Asserate, *King of Kings: The Truimph and Tragedy of Emperor Haile Selassie I of Ethiopia*. Translated by Peter Lewis. (Spain: Haus Publishing Ltd, 2015), 10.
945. Prouty, 12,
946. Bulatovich, 219, 220, 238
947. Ibid., 248
948. Prouty, 325
949. Ibid., 326
950. B. G. Steffason & R. K. Starrett (ed.) *"Death of Ras Tessamma." Documents on Ethiopian Politics* Volume I, American Consulate General No. 53, April 12, 1911
951. Akyeampmg & Gates, Jr. *Dictionary of African Biography*, Vol. 5, 3.
952. Ibid.
953. Steffason & Starrett (ed.), *Vol.* I, No. 53, April 12, 1911
954. Prouty, 229
955. Ibid., 322
956. Ibid., 323
957. Prouty, *Empress Taytu*, 38. Mockler, *Haile Selassie's War*, 394. www.en.wikipedia.org/ wiki/ Mekonnen_Endalkachew; en.wikipedia.org/wiki/ Endalkachew_Mekonnen accessed 12/9/16,
958. Bulatovich, 6, 199, 122, Rosenfeld, 194
959. Prouty, 6
960. Greenfield, 102
961. Greenfield (1975, Prouty, (1986), Mosely, (1964)
962. Bulatovich, 10
963. Prouty, 318

Chapter 16: *Dejaz.* Balcha Safo & *Ras* Habte Giorgis Denegde

964. Messay, 257
965. Teshale, 171-172
966. Berihun, *808-809*
967. Messay, 38, 162. See also Pankhurst (1968).
968. Shinn and Ofcansky, 57. www.en.wikipedia.org/ wiki/ hapte_giorgis_denagde *accessed on 12/11/16.*
969. www.en.wikipedia.org/wiki/Balcha_Safo 12/08/2016
970. Mockler, 166. Thesiger, *24;* www.en.wikipedia.org/ wiki/ hapte_giorgis_denagde *accessed on 12/11/16.*
971. Henze, 190
972. Steffason &Starrett (ed.) *Documents on Ethiopian Politics* Volume I, *"The Decline of Menelik II to the Emergence of Ras Tafar, later known as Haile Selassie 1910-1919."* American Consulate General, Addis Ababa. No. 72, January 17, 1910. Documentary Publications Salisbury, N. C. U.S.A. 1976 p. 7
973. Henze, 190.
974. Talbot, 98.
975. McClellan, 178
976. Ibid.
977. Mockler, 166
978. Steffason & Starrett, 5
979. Henze, 190
980. McClellan, 178.
981. Prouty, 76-77. Dr. Traversi, who served as Menelik's physician for "six years" was "treated like a dog" by Empress Taytu when she learned that Italy was using Wachale Treaty to claim Ethiopia at its protectorate. She learnt about it in July 1890 from Queen Victoria's letter. And then she "mocked Menilek and said, 'How is it that Emperor Yohannes never gave up a handful of our soil, fought the Italians and Egyptians for it, even died for it, and you, with him for an example, want to sell your country! What will history say of you?"
982. Shinn and Ofcansky, 57. See also Pankhurst (1968).
983. McClellan, 178
984. Rosenfeld, 251, 252
985. Harold G. Marcus, *Haile Sellassie I The Formative Years 1892-1936 (*Berkeley: University of California Press, 1987), 88
986. Rosenfeld, 253
987. Marcus, *Haile Sellassie I,* 88
988. McClellan, 178
989. www.en.wikipedia.org/wiki/Gugsa_Welle. Accessed on 01/11/2017
990. Shinn and Thomas, 58

991. Marcus, *Haile Sellassie I,* 89
992. Greenfield, 160
993. Teshale, 172. Teshale described Ethiopian rulers' preference for people of humble origin and slaves to make a case that Ethiopian emperors had adopted "ethnic-blind system of recruitment." He furthermore wrote that Haile Selassie's "appointment to high offices hardly showed any ethnic preference." P. 171. This was factually untrue as Haile Selassie's government was heavily dominated and even monopolized by Shewa-Amharas. Messay Kebede described it as "the Shewan tribalism of Haile Selassie" (1999:64). According to Donald Donham: *"In the years from 1941 to 1966, for example, the portions of Shewans appointed to the rank of vice-minister or above was a remarkable 62 percent. (P. 27).*
994. Lewis A. Coser, Steven L. Nock, Patricia A. Steffan, Daphine Spain. General Editorship by Robert K. Merton, *Introduction to Sociology* Third Edition (New York: HBJ Harcourt Bruce Jovanovich Publishers), 15
995. Marcus, The Life and Times, 237. Marcus cited from Brice to Minister, Addis Ababa, 25 March,, 1909, French Archives, *Politique, II.*
996. Pankhurst, Economic History, 75.
997. Marcus, *Haile Selassie I,* 79
998. Ibid.
999. Shack, 23.
1000. Bahru, A History, 132.
1001. Greenfield, 160
1002. Marcus, *Haile Selaassie I,* 90

Chapter 17: *Ras* Gobana Dache: The "formidable Oromo warlord"

1003. Mohammed, *The Oromo,* 198
1004. Greenfield, 97
1005. Mohammed, 198
1006. Rosenfeld, 32
1007. Greenfield, 97
1008. Bulatovich, 184
1009. Fantahun Engeda, Tarikawi Mezgeb-Seb Ketint Eskezare, 2003 E.C:524) wrote (without reference0 that Gobana's mother's name was *woizero Goradit.* I doubt it was her real name because *Goradit* is often a nickname given to girls and women whose nose bridge is flat & less pointed.
1010. Greenfield, 97.
1011. Prouty, 13
1012. Ibid., 105
1013. Ibid.

1014. Ibid., 13, 52

1015. Bulatovich," *From Entoto to River Baro." Ethiopia through Russian Eyes, 119*

1016. Prouty, 219

1017. Ibid. 105

1018. Ibid. 102-3. Menelik reportedly attempted to refuse marrying his daughter to Ras Mikael. He reasoned that he cannot marry his "two children" to each other, namely, his daughter Shewarega and his 'god son' the former Mohammed Ali, who was baptized years ago as Mikael).But Taytu was determined to reward *ras* Mikael for taking her brother's archenemy out of the political scene. Hence, Shewaraga was married to *ras* Mikael "under the influence of Taytu as a reward for capturing Ras Zewde of Begameder, who posed threat to her brother Ras Wole." [Ras Mikael's first 'godfather' was Emperor Yohannes, who ordered forceful conversion of Wollo Moslems].

1019. Prouty, 219. This marriage produced several children who were placed under Taytu's care in the palace after Shewarega's death, including the future heir to Menelik's throne, Eyasu, and, Zenebe Work Mikael, who was married briefly to Bezabih Tekle Haymanot of Gojam.

1020. Czeslow, 102, Greenfield, 97'

1021. Bulatovich, 184

1022. Ibid., 184-85

1023. Ibid., 185

1024. Ibid.

1025. Henze, 132

1026. Greenfield, 97

1027. Ibid., 97-98

1028. Henze, 151

1029. Mohammed, 198

1030. Ibid.,199, Asafa Jalata, The *Invention of Ethiopia*, 53.

1031. As a matter of fact, their options were limited because by early 1880s Gobana had built massive army and formidable cavalry, which would have overrun them easily. His army was so powerful that it compelled the army of Gojam led by *ras* Darso to leave south-west, which eventually precipitated the Battle of Embobo.

1032. *Czeslow*, 102; Henze, 151

1033. Ibid.

1034. Asafa, 53; Blatovich, 118

1035. Shewarega was an illegitimate child who was recognized by Menelik later in life. Seemingly, their marriage did not appear to have been arranged by Menelik. Prouty (1986) wrote that Shewarega was legitimized by Menelik after her mother-in-law and Gobana's wife, Ayeletch Abarasa acted as an intermediary. Had Shewaraga's marriage to Wodajo been arranged by Menelik, Ayeletch would, more likely, not have intervened.

1036. Tekle Tsadik Mekuria, *Atse Yohnnes na YeEthiopia Andinet*, (Addis Ababa: Kuraz Asatami Derijet, 1982 E.C), 203-4.

1037. Tekle Tsadik, *Keatse Tewodros Eske Qedamawi Haile Selassie*, (Addis Ababa, Berhanena Selam Printing Press, 1935 E.C. 9th ed), 59-61

1038. Bulatovich, 99

1039. Tekle Tsadik, *Atse Yohannes*, 213, 204, 233

1040. Bahru, *A History*, 59

1041. Ibid., 61

1042. Prouty, 56

1043. Ibid.

1044. Henze, 151

1045. Asafa Jalata, "*The Oromo Struggle: Knowledge and Oromo Agency in the Age of Globalization*" in JOS (Vol 25, No. 1& 2. 2018), 34. See also Asafa (1993). Mohammed, *The Oromo of Ethiopia,* 198.

1046. Abbas, 149, Mohammed, 198.

1047. Getahun Delibo, (1974:81), Quoted by Mohammed, 199

Appendix I & II

1048. Philp Marsden, The Barefoot Emperor: An Ethiopian Tragedy 2007:241-4 Two years after he escaped from Meqdela, Menelik appeared to have confidence and military power to punish Tewdros. He mobilized about 30,000 men and reached to the vicinity of Meqdela. However, he reassessed possibilities of defeat and changed course and "wheeled back" to Shewa without fighting.

1049. Braukmaper, *A History*, 287.

1050. Caulk, 2002, 46

1051. Edward Gleichen, Lord, *With the Mission to Menelik, 1897 (London, 1898)*, 153

1052. Prouty, 31

1053. Caulk, 46

Bibiliography

Abdisalem Melesse Sugamo. *Ethno-archaeological Study of Megalithic Tradition in Southern Ethiopia: Muslim Megalithic Builders of Hadiy*a. LAP Lambert Academic publishing Feb 2013.

Achame Shana. "The Shekacho People: Untold Stories." In *Arrested Development in Ethiopia: Essays on Underdevelopment, Democracy and Self-Determination*. Edited by Seyoum Hameso and Mohammed Hassen. Trenton, NJ: The Red Sea Press, Inc. 2006.

Admasu Abebe, *The Origin, Significance and Physical Condition of the Great Medieval Defensive Dry Stone Walls of Dawuro/Kati Halala Keela, Southwest Ethiopia*. ERJSSH 1 (1), September–October 2014, 19

Akyeampong, Emanuel K and Henry Louis Gates, Jr, ed. *Dictionary of African Biography*, Vol. 1. & Vol. 5. London: Oxford Univ. Press 2012.

Aldrich, Robert ed. *The Ages of Empires*. (London: Thames & Hudson Ltd, 2007),

Ali, Mohammed. *Ethnicity, Politics, and Societies in Northeast Africa, Conflict and Social Change*. New York: Univ. Press of America, Inc. 1996.

Almagor. Uri. "Institutionalizing a fringe periphery: Dassanetch-Amhara relations." in *The Southern Marches of Imperial Ethiopia*, edited. by Donald Donham & Wendy James. Addis Ababa Univ. Press 2002.

Assefa Chabo, Yetizita Feleg, memoir. Addis Ababa: Nabadan Media, April 2016.

Asafa Jalata. *Oromia & Ethiopia: State Formation & Ethnonational Conflict, 1868-1992*. US: Lynne Rienner Publishers Inc, 1993.

_____. "*The Oromo Struggle: Knowledge and Oromo Agency in the Age of Globalization*" in JOS (Vol 25, No. 1& 2. 2018.

Asfa-Wossen Asserate. *King of Kings: The Truimph and Tragedy of Emperor Haile Selassie I of Ethiopia*. Translated by Peter Lewis. Haus Publishing Ltd. 2015.

Bahru Zewde. *A History of Modern Ethiopia 1855-1974*. Addis Ababa: Addis Ababa Univ. Press, 1991

_____. *Ye Ethiopia Tarik ke 1847 – 1981*. Addis Ababa Univ. Press 2003

Beidelman, T. O. *The Culture of Colonialism: The Cultural Subjection of Ukanguru*. Bloomington & Indianapolis: Indiana Univ. Press, 2012.

Belachew Gebrewold, "*An Introduction to the social and Political philosophy of Kambata*" in Proceedings of the XVth International Conference of Ethiopian Studies, Vol. 65 Hamburg. July 20-25, 2003. Ed. By Seigburt Uhilg. (Harassowitz Verlag, 2006).

Berihun Kebede. *Ye Haile Selassie Tarik*. Addis Ababa: Artistic Printing Press, 1993 E.C.

Braukàmper, Ulrich, A History of the Hadiyya in Southern Ethiopia: Translated from German by Geraldine Krause (Harrassowitx Verlag – Wiesbaden 2012)

_____ *Die Kambata*, English Summary. *Geschichte und Gesellschaft eines Südäthiopischen Bauernvolkes,* 1983.

_____. "*Indigenous Views on the Italian Occupation in Southern Ethiopia: A Post-Colonial Approach.*" Aethiopica 14 (2011), International Journal of Ethiopian and Eritrean Studies),165

_____ Islamic History and Culture in Southern Ethiopia: Collected Essays (, Gottinger Studien Zur Ethnologie Lit Verlag), 2004

Bulatovich, Alexander. *Ethiopia Through Russian Eyes: Country in Transition 1896-1898*, Translated & Edited.by Richard Seltzer. Lawrenceville: The Red Sea Press, 2000.

Burton, Richard F. *First Footsteps in East Africa, or an Exploration of Harar.* New York: Dover Publications Inc. 1987.

Cerulli, Ernesta. *Peoples of South-West Ethiopia and its Borderland,* International African Institute, 1956.

Caulk, Richard. *Between the Jaws of Hyenas: A Diplomatic History of Ethiopia 1876-1896.* Edited by Bahru Zewde. Harrassowitz Verlag-Wiensbaden, 2000.

Clark, J. Desmond, "African Beginnings," in The Horizon History of Africa. Editor, Alvin M. Josephy Jr. American Heritage Publishing Co, Inc. 1971.

Cohen, Gideon P. E. *Language and Ethnic Boundaries: Perceptions of Identity Expressed through Attitudes towards the Use of Language Education in Southern Ethiopia,* in Northeast African Studies, Vol. 7 No 3 (New Series) 2000. 189-206.

Coser, Lewis A., Nock, Steven L., Steffan, Patricia A., & Spain, Daphine General Editorship by Robert K. Merton, *Introduction to Sociology* Third Edition (New York: HBJ Harcourt Bruce Jovanovich Publishers),

Czeslow, Jesman. *The Ethiopian Paradox.* London: Oxford Univ. Press 1963.

Darkwah, R.H. Kofi. *Shewa, Menelik and the Ethiopian Empire 1813-1889.* New York: Holmes & Meier Pubi8shers, Inc. 1975.

Data De'a, *Clans, Kingdoms, and "Cultural Diversity" in Southern Ethiopia: The Case of Omotic Speakers.* Northeast African Studies, Vol. 7, Number 3 (New Series) 2000. 163-188.

Davidson, Basil. *The Lost Cities of Africa,* Boston: Little, brown and company, 1959.

Donham, Donald "The Making of an Imperial State: Old Abyssinia and the new Ethiopian empire: themes in social history, *The Southern Marches of Imperial Ethiopia.* Edited by Donald Donham and Wendy James. Addis Ababa: Addis Ababa University 2002

_____ "From Ritual kings to Ethiopian landlords in Maale" *in, The Southern Marches of Imperial Ethiopia*. Addis Ababa Univ. 2002.

_____ *Work and Power in Maale, Ethiopia, Studies in Cultural Anthropology*. Ann Arbor, Michigan: UMI Research Press 1985.

Edmonds, I.G. *Ethiopia Land of the Conquering Lion of Judah*. New York: *Hold*, Rinehart and Winston, 1975.

Elkins, Caroline. *Imperial Reckoning: The Untold story of Britain's Gulag in Kenya*. New York: Henry Holt and Company, 2005.

Encyclopaedia Britannica, Gurage People.

Engdawork Nimane, *Yajoka: Council of Sabat-bet Clan Chiefs and Notables*. LAP LAMBERT Academic Publishing, 2013.

Fragher, Brian L. The Origins of the New Church Movement in Southern Ethiopia 1924-1944, 1996

Freeman, Dena. *Who are the Gamo? And who are the D'ache? Confusions of Ethnicity in Ethiopia's Southern Highlands*. In Uhling, Siebert (Ed). *Proceedings of the 15th International Conference of Ethiopian Studies*. (Wiesbaden: Harrassowitz Verlag 2006), 1-2.

Forde, Daryll (ed.), *The Galla of Ethiopia, The Kingdoms of Kafa and Janjero* (Ethnographic Survey of Africa, North-Eastern Africa Part II), International African Institute, 1969

Fujimoto, Takeshi "Social Stratification and its Relevance to Ethno-History: A Case in Malo, Southwestern Ethiopia" in Proceedings of the XVth International Conference of Ethiopia. Hamburg July 20-25, 2003. Ed. By Seigburt Uhilg. (Harassowitz Verlag, 2006).

Garretson, Peter P. *"Vicious Cycles: ivory, slaves, and arms on the new Maji frontier"* in *The Southern Marches of Imperial Ethiopia*. Addis Ababa Univ. Press, 2002.

Gebru Tareke. *Ethiopia: Power & Protest Peasant Revolt in the Twentieth Century*. Lawrenceville: The Red Sea Press Inc. 1996.

Getaneh Mehari and Getent Tadele, *Sexual Violence and Justice in the Context of Legal Pluralism: Lessons from the Gamo Cultural Setting.* PhD dissertation submitted to the School of Social Work, Addis Ababa University, 2014. (EJOSSAH Vol, XI, No. 2 December 2015).

Gleichen, Lord Edward. *With the Mission to Menelik, 1897.* London, 1898.

Gilkes, Patrick. *The Dying Lion: Feudalism and modernization in Ethiopia.* London: Julian Friedmann Publishers, LTD, 1975.

Girma Zewude Anjulo. *Asham Kokata: Yetarik Yebahilna Yeemnet Dasesa.* Addis Ababa: 2010 E.C.

Greenfield, Richard. *Ethiopia: A New Political History.* New York: Frederick A- Praeger, Publishers 1965.

Grenstedt, Staffan. *Ambarcho and Shonkolla, From Local Independent Church to the Evangelical Mainstream in Ethiopia. The Origins of the Mekane Yesus Church in Kambata Hadiya.* Stockholm: Uppsala University 2000.

Gore, Rick. "*The Dawn of Humans, Expanding Worlds.*" In *National Geographic* Vol. 191 No. 5 May 1997.

Guidi, Pierre. *Wolaita Memories of Garmame Neway Governorship (1958-1959): Radical Reforms and Political Consciousness in* Northeast African Studies. Michigan State Univ. Vol 13, No. 2, 2013.

Gunther, John *Inside Africa.* Harper & Brothers, New York, 1955.

Hailu Zeleke*, Some Notes on the Great Walls of Wolayta and Dawro. Annales d'Ethiopie,* 2007-2008, vol. XXIII, 399-412

Hallpike, Christopher. *The Konso of Ethiopia: A Study of Values of an East Cushitic People.* UK: authorhouse, Revised Ed. Feb 2008

Harris, William Cornwallis *The Highlands of Aethiopia*, vol. 3, 198

Herbeson, John W. T*he Ethiopian Transformation: The Quest for the Post-Imperial State.* Boulder: Westview Press, 1988

Henze, Paul *Layers of Time: A History of Ethiopia.* New York: palgrave mcmillan 2000

Howard, Michael & Louis, Roger. Ed. *The Oxford History of the Twentieth Century.* Oxford Univ. Press 1998.

Illife John *Africans, A History of the Continent.* London: Cambridge University Press, 2007.

Imru Haile Selassie. *Kayehut Kemastawusewu,* Addis Ababa University Press 2002 E.C

James, Wendy. "Lifelines: exchange marriage among the Gumuz" in *The Southern Marches of Imperial Ethiopia.* Addis Ababa University Press 2002.

Jani, W. H. *Seven House Fortress Sun: Myths and legends of Kambata society, Ethiopia.* USA: CPSIA, 2015.

Kadafo Hanfare. *Life History of Sultan Alimirah.* Bloomington, IN: authorHouse, 2013

Kassahun Woldemariam. *Myths and Realities in the Distribution of Socioeconomic and Resources and Political Power in Ethiopia.* New York: University Press of America, 2006.

Kaufeler, Heinz *Modernization, Legitimacy and Social Movement: A Study of Socio-Cultural Dynamics and Revolution in Iran and Ethiopia.* Zurich:1988

Kapuscinski, Ryszard. *The Emperor: Downfall of an Autocrat.* New York: Vintage International, 1983.

Keller, Edmond J. *Revolutionary Ethiopia From Empire to People's Republic.* Bloomington: Indiana State Univ. 1988

Lapiso G. Delebo. *Ye-Ethiopia yegebbar sereat na jemer capitalism 1900-1966. Addis Ababa:* Neged matemia bet.

_____ *Ye-Ethiopiawinet Tarikawi Meseretoch na Mesariyawoch: Ye Ethiopia na ye-ethiopiawuyan yemenesha na yemanenet genezabe aretegna metsaf.* Addis Ababa: *1999.*

Leslau, Wolf. The Arabic Loan Words in Gurage (Southern Ethiopia, Arabica, Brill Academic Publishers, September 1954), 266-284.

Levine, Donald N. *Greater Ethiopia, The Evolution of Multiethnic Society.* Chicago and London: The University of Chicago Press, 1974.

_____ *Wax and Gold. Tradition and Innovation in Ethiopia Culture. Chicago and London: The University of Chicago Press, 1967.*

Lewis, Herbert S. *A Galla Monarchy Abba Jifar, Ethiopia 1830-1932.* Madison and Milwaukee: The University of Wisconsin Press, 1965.

Marcus, Harold G. *A History of Ethiopia* Updated Edition. Berkeley: University of California Press, 2002.

_____. *The Life and Times of Menelik II: Ethiopia 1844-1913.* Lawrenceville: The Red Sea Press 1995

_____. *Haile Sellassie I The Formative Years 1892-1936.* Berkeley: University of California Press, 1987.

Mathew, David *Ethiopia, The study of a polity 1540-1935.* London: Eyre and Spottiswoode, 1974.

McCann, James C. *The People of the Plow: An Agricultural History of Ethiopia, 1800-1990. Wisconsin: The University of Wisconsin 1995.*

McClellan, Charles W. "Coffee in centre-periphery relations: Gedeo in the early twentieth century." In *The Southern Marches of Imperial Ethiopia.* Addis Ababa Univ. Press 2002.

Meckelburg, Alexander "Slavery, Emancipation, and Memory: Exploratory Notes on Western Ethiopia." In *International Journal of African Historical Studies* Vol. 48 No.2 (2015). 345-362

Meredith, Martin. *The Fate of Africa, A History of Fifty Years of Independence.* New York: PublicAffairs, 2005.

_____. *The Fortunes of Africa: A 5000-Year History of Wealth, Greed and Endeavor.* New York: PublicAffairs, 2014.

Messay Kebede. *Survival and Modernization: Ethiopia's Enigmatic Present: A Philosophical Discourse.* New Jersey: The Red Sea press 1999

Mockler, Anthony. *Haile Selassie's War.* New York: Olive Branch Press 2003.

Mohammed Hassan. *The Oromo of Ethiopia: A History 1570 – 1860.* Trenton, NJ: The Red Sea Press, 1994.

Mokhtar, G. ed. *UNESCO General History of Africa. II Ancient Civilizations of Africa.* Nairobi: General Printers Ltd. 1994.

Molvaer, Reidulf K. *Black Lions: The Creative Lives of Modern Ethiopia's Literary Giants & Pioneers.* Asmara: The Red Sea press, Inc. 1997.

Morell, Virginia. "Africa's Danakil Desert Cruelest Place of Earth." In *National Geographic* Vol. 208, No.4. October 2005.

Mosley, Leonard. *Haile Selassie: The Conquering Lion.* Englewood Cliffs, New Jersey: Prentice-Hall, Inc, 1964.

Naty, Alexander. *"The Thief-Searching (Leba Shay) Institution in Aariland, Southwest Ethiopia, 1890s-1930s." Ethnology* 33, no. 3 (1994): 261-72

Neumann, Oscar, *From the Somali Coast through Southern Ethiopia to the Sudan.* The Royal Geographical Society (with the Institute of British Geographers. *The Geographical Journal* Vol. 20, No. 4 (Oct.,1902), 373-398.

Nunn, Nathan. *"The Long-Term Effects of African's Slave Trades." The Quarterly Journal of Economics,* February 2008.139-176.

Nature vol. 466 N. 7308 (12 august 2010): 857-860.

Osterhammel, Jurgen. *The Transformation of the World: A Global History of the Nineteenth Century.* Translated by Patrick Camiller. Princeton and Oxford: Princeton University Press 2014.

Pankhurst, Richard. *A Social History of Ethiopia: The Northern and Central Highlands from Early Medieval Times to the Rise of Emperor Tewodros II. Lawrenceville, NJ: The Red Sea Press, 1992*

_____. *Economic History of Ethiopia 1800-1935.* Addis Ababa: Haile Selassie I University Press, 1968.

_____. Fire-Arms in Ethiopian History (1800-1935) in *Ethiopian Observer* 6(2) (1962

_____. *The Ethiopian Borderlands: Essays in the Regional History: From Ancient Times to the End of the 18ᵗʰ Century.* NJ: The Red Sea Press 1997.

_____. *The Ethiopians, A History. Blackwell Publishing, 2001.*

Pakenham, Thomas. *The Scramble for Africa: The white Man's Conquest of the Dark Continent from 1876-1972. New York: Random House, 1991.*

Parenti, Michael. *History as Mystery. San Francisco: City Lights Books,* 1999

Paulos Gnogno. *Atse Menelik.* Addis Ababa: Bole Printing Press, Feb. z1984 E.C.

Prouty, Chris. *Empress Taytu and Menelik II: Ethiopia1883-1910.* Trenton NJ: The Red Sea Press, 1986.

Reader, John. *Africa: A Biography of the Continent.* New York: Vintage Books, September 1999.

Robin, Hallett. *Africa to 1875. A Modern History.* Ann Arbor: Univ. of Michigan Press

Rosenfeld, Chris Prouty. *A Chronology of Menelik II of Ethiopia 1844-1913.* Lansing, Michigan: Michigan State Univ. 1976),

Rothchild, Donald. *Managing Ethnic Conflict in Africa: Pressure and Incentives for Cooperation.* Washington D.C: Brookings Institution Press, 1997

Rubenson, Sven. *The Survival of Ethiopian Independence.* Addis Ababa Univ. Press, 1976.

Science, 09 Aug 2019: vol. 365, Issue 6453, pp. 583-587

Seyoum Hameso, *"Myths and Realities of the Ethiopian State."* In *Arrested Development in Ethiopia: Essays on Underdevelopment, Democracy and Self-Determination.* Edited by. Seyuom Hameso and Mohammed Hassen. Lawrenceville, NJ: The Red Sea Press Inc 2006. 97-107.

_____. "The Sidama Nation: An Introduction." In *Arrested Development in Ethiopia: Essays on Underdevelopment, Democracy and Self-Determination.* Edited by Seyoum Hameso and Mohammed Hassen (Lawrenceville, NJ: The Red Sea Press, Inc. 2006.

Shack, William. *The Gurage, A People of the Ensete Cultur. London: Oxford University Press 1966.*

Shillington, Kevin. *History of Africa.* Palgrave Macmillan; 2012 3rd ed.

Shinn, David H. and Thomas P. Ofcansky. *Historical Dictionary of Ethiopia*, Historical Dictionaries of Africa No. 91. Lanham, Maryland: The Scarecrow Press, Inc. 2004.

Shreeve, Jamie. "The Evolutionary Road." In *National Geographic*, Vol. 218 No. 1 July 2010.

Simoons, Frederick J. *Some Questions on the Economic Prehistory of Ethiopia,* in *Papers in African Prehistory (1970, reprinted 1974.* Edited by J. D. Fage & R. A. Oliver. (London: Cambridge University Press, 1970, reprinted 1974*),* 117

Skinner, Robert Peet. *Abyssinia of to-day: An Account of the fist mission sent by the American government to the court of the King of Kings (1903-1904).* New York: Longmans, Green & Co. 1906.

Sloan, Christopher P. "Origin of Childhood." In *National Geographic* Vol. 210 No. 5. November 2006.

Steffason, B. G. & R. K. Starrett (ed.). *Documents on Ethiopian Politics* Volume I, *The Decline of Menelik II to the Emergence of Ras Tafar, later known as Haile Selassie 1910-1919.* American Consulate General, Addis Ababa. No. 72, January 17, 1910. Documentary Publications Salisbury, N. C. U.S.A. 1976

_____. *Documents on Ethiopian Politics,* Vol. I No. 266.

_____. "*Death of Ras Tessamma," Documents on Ethiopian Politics* Volume I, No. 53, April 12, 1911.

_____. "Suggestions as to Possible Methods of Reforming Abyssinian Affairs." *Documents on Ethiopian Politics,* Vol. I P. 214 No. 268. April 23, 1919

Talbot, David Abner. *Contemporary Ethiopia.* New York: Philosophical Library, 1952.

Teferra Haile Selassie. *The Ethiopian Revolution 1974-1991 From Monarchical Autocracy to Military Oligarchy.* London–New York: Kegan Paul International 1997.

Tekle Tsadik Mekuria, *Atse Yohnnes na YeEthiopia Andinet. Addis Ababa:* Kuraz Asatami Derijet, 1982 E.C.

_____. *Ke Atse Tewodros Eske Qedamawi Haile Selassie.* Addis Ababa, Berhanena Selam Printing Press, 1935 E.C.

Tesfaye Habisso, *A Short History of the Kambata People of South-Western Ethiopia.* Unpublished.

Teshale Tibebu. *The Making of Ethiopian History 1896-1974. Lawrenceville, NJ:* The Red Sea Press, 1995.

Tindall, Ashley. *Gamo Highlands.* Accessed 04/26/2020. https://sacredland.org/gamo-highlands-ethiopia.

Toynbee, Arnold J. *Between Niger and Nile*. London: Oxford University Press, 1965.

Triulzi, Alessandro. *"Nekemte and Addis Ababa: dilemma of provincial rule." The Southern Marches of Imperial Ethiopia.Edited by Donald Donham & Wendy James. Addis Ababa* University Press 2002.

Tsegaye Tadesse Baredi *Threats to Heritage Properties in Ethiopia: The Case of Tangible and Intangible Heritage of the Gede'o, Southern Ethiopia,.3.*

Ullendorff, Edward. *The Ethiopians An Introduction to Country and People*. London: Oxford University Press, 1960.,

Wellby, Montagu Sinclair. *Twixt Sider and Menelik: An Account of a year's expedition from Zeila to Cairo through unknown Abyssinia*, 1901.

Yacob Arsano, "Seera: A Traditional Institution of Kambata." In *Ethiopia: The Challenge of Democracy from Below*. Edited by Bahru Zewude and Seigfried Pausewang. Stockholm: Elanders Gotab, 2002. 45-58.

Zerihun Doda, *Ethnohistory & Culture of Tambaro of Southwest Ethiopia*,

Zewude Gabre-Sellassie, *Yohannes IV of Ethiopia: A Political Biography*. NJ: The Red Sea Press, 2014.

Index

D

Daato Mountain 110
Damaalla 104, 298
Damot, Damoota 33, 40, 50, 111, 295
Damte dejazmatch 162, 163, 192, 251, 272, 328
Dar Agar 18, 73
Darge Sahle Selassie, ras 244, 253, 281, 292, 293, 297
Darkwah, R. H. Kofi 79, 136, 138, 140, 181, 208, 214, 238, 299, 300, 312, 313, 318, 320, 321, 322, 329, 333, 343
Darso, Ras 86, 88, 149, 338
Data De'a 7, 301, 343
Davidson, Basil 42, 48, 49, 306, 307, 343
Dawro 70, 311, 345
Debre Markos 18, 227, 250
Demissie Nessibu 260, 299
Depopulation 125, 158, 174, 183, 189, 190, 191, 192, 193, 200, 219, 327
Deres 68
Desta Birru 64, 163, 192, 269, 287, 288, 328
Dilbato Degoye, woma 12, 60, 93, 108, 109, 130, 198
Donham, Donald 7, 22, 29, 30, 118, 201, 242, 301, 303, 304, 319, 321, 325, 326, 328, 330, 334, 337, 341, 343, 351
Dorma 52, 53
Double jeopardy 74
Dual Society 7, 217, 330
Dubusha 68, 69

E

Edmonds, I.G 22, 303, 344
Egiziabher, dejaz 227
Ejigayehu 274, 289, 290
Eleni 56, 57
Elkins, Caroline 303, 344
Enaqor 93, 198

Enarya 33, 40, 52, 57, 61, 64, 65, 84, 130, 152, 256
Endalkachew Mekonnen 242, 259
Engdawork Nimane 53, 307, 344
Ensete 50, 51, 300, 349
Ethiopianization 8, 10, 14, 151, 224
Ethiopian Orthodox Church, EOC 206, 207, 208, 209, 210, 227, 283, 287
Eunuch 264, 269
European colonialism 14, 21
Expansionary conquest 15, 101

F

Fagiisso Goddee 111
Famous Ethiopians 249
Fandano 57
Fantahun Engeda 251, 298, 333, 337
Fatansa Illu 129
Fernandez, Antonio 47
Fincha Habera 39
Firearms 143, 144
Forde, Daryll 306, 307, 317, 327, 344
Fragher, Brian L 313, 344
Freeman, Dena 68, 311, 344
French Somaliland 184
Fujimoto, Takeshi 311, 344

G

Gaarad 56
Gabbar system 6, 8, 21, 64, 96, 118, 161, 171, 200, 201, 202, 203, 218, 219, 220, 221, 223, 233, 266, 300. *See also* serfs of state
Gabra 169, 192, 200
Gaki Sherocho, Tato 44, 122, 130, 140, 199, 329
Gamo 66, 68, 69, 70, 105, 116, 129, 145, 165, 180, 186, 199, 209, 251, 283, 286, 299, 311, 323, 334, 344, 345, 350
Gardula 41, 48
Garretson, Peter P 161, 177, 192, 322, 323, 324, 326, 327, 328, 344

Garrison towns 74, 75, 83, 91, 106,
      108, 112, 117, 128, 151, 162,
      227, 244, 265, 292, 294, 297, 300
Gatiso Balango 96, 111, 129
Gebru Tareke 195, 330, 344
Gedeo 35, 50, 52, 63, 64, 105, 116, 117,
      130, 145, 202, 203, 231, 232,
      233, 234, 249, 261, 265, 268,
      288, 292, 303, 307, 310, 328,
      334, 347
Geedo Bashiro 103, 130
Gelawudwos, Atse 57
Germame Wolde Hawaryat 259
Gessesse Belew, dejaz 226, 227
Gessess Wolde Hana 133
Getachew Abate, ras 287, 293
Getaneh Mehari 311, 345
Gibe States 46, 70, 84, 183, 279, 280,
      284, 326
Gidole 127, 129, 261
Gilkes, Patrick 209, 224, 226, 230, 237,
      238, 243, 300, 329, 331, 332,
      333, 334, 335, 345
Gimira 50, 66, 124, 125, 129, 147, 163,
      169, 180, 182, 193, 201, 202, 219
Girma Zewude Anjulo 60, 298, 309,
      345
Gleichen, Lord Edward 295, 339, 345
Gobana Dache 15, 78, 286, 293, 299,
      337
  Neo-Gobana 282
Gobaze Tekle Giorgis 3, 77, 154, 254,
      299
Gobba 106, 300
Gofa 49, 50, 68, 70, 105, 109, 116, 129,
      145, 186, 199, 209, 222, 241,
      251, 256, 286, 334
Gojjam xv, 3, 6, 7, 16, 18, 28, 50, 51,
      52, 57, 77, 84, 85, 86, 87, 88, 89,
      92, 120, 132, 133, 149, 160, 178,
      180, 199, 209, 212, 221, 222,
      224, 225, 226, 227, 228, 229,
      230, 231, 232, 233, 234, 242,
      246, 249, 250, 251, 294, 296,
      297, 299, 312

Gonfamo 93, 198
Governors of the Kambaata 287
Gragn Ahmed, ibn Ibrahim al-Ghazi
      144, 196
Greenfield, Richard xi, 5, 33, 34, 36,
      40, 47, 53, 82, 120, 123, 246,
      272, 274, 278, 304, 305, 306,
      307, 312, 313, 316, 318, 319,
      320, 328, 329, 334, 335, 337,
      338, 345
Grenstedt, Staffan 303, 317, 345
Gubba 177, 179
Gugsa Wole, ras 7, 293
Guidi, Pierre 214, 329, 345
Gumuz 70, 163, 170, 171, 200, 324,
      346
Gunther, John 242, 333, 345
Gurage 6, 12, 26, 27, 28, 38, 46, 51, 52,
      53, 54, 57, 60, 65, 74, 78, 80, 81,
      82, 83, 84, 85, 86, 91, 92, 93, 94,
      96, 97, 101, 104, 107, 108, 113,
      129, 145, 148, 183, 184, 197,
      201, 245, 254, 264, 265, 269,
      272, 280, 281, 286, 287, 292,
      294, 297, 298, 299, 300, 301,
      307, 313, 314, 315, 318, 330,
      334, 344, 346, 349
Gurage Mountains 38, 101

H

Habte Giorgis Denegde, ras 163, 263,
      264, 294, 336
Habte Mariam Gabre 227
Hadiya xiii, 12, 27, 28, 35, 46, 50, 52,
      55, 56, 57, 60, 63, 66, 70, 74, 76,
      78, 82, 83, 85, 91, 93, 101, 103,
      108, 110, 111, 145, 148, 197,
      198, 201, 254, 265, 281, 283,
      286, 287, 291, 292, 293, 297,
      298, 299, 303, 308, 314, 341, 345
Haile Mariam Wolde Mikael 259, 294
Haile Melekot 26, 77, 78, 206, 277, 289
Haile Selassie 5, 7, 8, 10, 25, 26, 27,
      31, 34, 52, 64, 84, 117, 118, 126,

www.ingramcontent.com/pod-product-compliance
Lightning Source LLC
Chambersburg PA
CBHW062147080426
42734CB00010B/1590